Manfred Fuchs

From Legislators to the End-User

VS RESEARCH

Manfred Fuchs

From Legislators to the End-User

Practical Difficulties of Implementing European Directives

VS RESEARCH

Bibliographic information published by the Deutsche Nationalbibliothek
The Deutsche Nationalbibliothek lists this publication in the Deutsche Nationalbibliografie; detailed bibliographic data are available in the Internet at http://dnb.d-nb.de.

1st Edition 2011

Editorial Office: Verena Metzger | Dr. Tatjana Rollnik-Manke

VS Verlag für Sozialwissenschaften is a brand of Springer Fachmedien.
Springer Fachmedien is part of Springer Science+Business Media.
www.vs-verlag.de

Cover design: KünkelLopka Medienentwicklung, Heidelberg
Printed on acid-free paper
Printed in Germany

ISBN 978-3-531-17787-8

Contents

Abbreviations

ACE	Architect's Council of Europe
BMVBS	Bundesministerium für Verkehr, Bau und Stadtplanung (Federal Ministry for Transport, Building and Urban Affairs) (DE)
BMWA	Bundesministerium für Wirtschaft und Arbeit (Federal Ministry of Economics and Labour) (AT)
BRE	British Research Establishment (UK)
BSI	British Standardisation Insitute (UK)
CE marking	mark on a product or its accompanying documents symbolising the compliance of the product with European technical specifications (CPD)
CEN	European Committee for Standardisation (Comité Européen de Normalisation)
CEPMC	Council of European Producers of Materials for Construction
COREPER	Committee of Permanent Representatives (Comités des représentents permanents) consisting of heads of MS delegations (COREPER II) or deputy heads of delegation (COREPER I)
CPD	Construction Products Directive
CPR	Construction Products Regulation
CUAP	Common Understanding of Assessment Procedure (for European Technical Approvals without ETAG)
DIBt	Deutsches Institut für Bautechnik (DE)
EN	European standard
ENV	European pre-standard
EOTA	European Organisation for Technical Approvals
ETA	European Technical Approval
ETAG	European Technical Approval Guideline
EUOJ	Official Journal of the European Union
FIEC	European Construction Industry Federation (Fédération de l'Industrie Européenne de la Construction)

GNB	Group of Notified Bodies
hEN	harmonised European standard (developed under the CPD)
ITB	Instytut Techniki Budowlanej (Building Research Institute) (PL)
NB	Notified Body
OIB	Österreichisches Institut für Bautechnik (AT)
ON	Österreichisches Normungsinstitut (Austrian Standards Institute)
TC	Technical Committee in CEN

1 Introduction: The "insider's" view

> Sir Humphrey: If people (...) start talking about it (...), in the end they will start thinking about it. They will come to realise the problems, the flaws in the reasoning. The nation will get worried. Agitation, questions, criticism ... CHANGE!
>
> Bernard (shocked): CHANGE?
>
> (Yes Prime Minister: The Ministerial Broadcast)

Having been working for the European Commission for about one decade and in the field of construction since mid-2000, producing a specific study on the practical implementation of a European Directive and the Construction Products Directive (CPD) might look like an easy task. Being (theoretically) in the "centre" of the network that discusses and defines the finer points of a Directive and being in contact with so many stakeholders should give a perfect overview on how the system is working at European and national levels. It would also seem logical that a study would focus on the political intentions of the Commission and Member States, the creation of the legal and administrative framework and the implementation by Member States – choosing either a neutral or friendly way of describing an international system or highlighting mistakes in the system and distributing blame.

However, taking a few steps back from my current position as a European civil servant and imagining that I would still be an engineer in the private sector, I would ask myself what I would know about the Construction Products Directive – and even more important: what would I know about the role and practical use of CE marking on construction products in my day-to-day work? The answer would be rather sobering, at least from the point of view of a Commission civil servant: most likely I would not be aware of it. Or, less exaggeratedly, I might have got wrong ideas about what this would mean for my work. In contact with friends and former colleagues who are still civil engineers in the private sector in different Member States in the EU, I became aware that the quantity and quality of the information available to civil engineers might differ, but in general CE marking was either of minor importance or simply a "non-issue".

This would not necessarily indicate that there is a problem in efficiently implementing a directive. First of all, my previous asking around can hardly be considered as a statistically valid sample. Neither does this indicate that all these civil engineers are missing an important piece of information.[1] National systems – formal or informal ones – might deal with all relevant points before they reach designers and engineers on the construction sites and therefore relieving them from any problems or additional efforts to cope with European requirements. One should also not forget that the CPD is an instrument to support the Internal Market and is therefore more relevant for *manufacturers* of construction products than their final users.

Coming back to the European level, this optimistic assumption would not (completely) bear close scrutiny. In fact, in some cases even for issues like assessing the performance of construction products, the Commission, Member State authorities and other interested parties are still struggling with interpretations of the Directive. Sometimes these problems – in particular when the use of CE marked products are questioned even by national authorities, or several actors get confused about the role of CE marking vs. national marks – have even initiated legal steps from several parties. In 1996 the Commission itself published a report highlighting several problems which have prevented the CPD from being implemented – in particular the fact that not a single standard had been adopted by then.[2] Finally, the Commission decided the CPD should become an even stronger instrument by changing it from a *Directive* to a *Regulation*, which would leave less room for interpretation by Member States. This was more than just an editorial change and indicates that there were problems that could not be solved within the existing framework of the CPD and the instruments the Commission and other interested parties have at their disposal.[3] All in

1 The more scientific approach in this study unfortunately does not completely neutralise the problem (shared by any other study on the CPD so far) that the sample is relatively small. However, this more structured approach should have provided a reasonably representative picture of roles, perceptions and activities of several professional groups across the construction sector and Member States.

2 Commission Report on the Construction Products Directive COM(96) 202final.

3 However, this study is intentionally focusing on the Construction Products *Directive* and not making any references to the draft text of the Construction Products *Regulation*. (NB It could be useful to mention this as a stand-alone disclaimer at the beginning of the report!)While the Regulation is still only a concept, *aiming* at improving the system for actors on different levels of the "chain of implementation", even the final text of the law, not to mention its actual impact, is unknown. The CPD on the other hand provides experience of nearly two decades

all, while publicly supported by all actors at EU and national levels (at least the ones who have heard about the CPD and CE marked construction products), the implementation of the Directive in some cases seems to face serious problems at different levels and with different actors involved.

Moving form one level to another – also changing my role from "insider" to "outsider" and back – it became more and more obvious that different perceptions and interpretations by different interested parties at all levels have significantly influenced the information flow from the Commission to the final "end users": designers, architects and civil engineers in the public and private sectors on a construction site. The "gap" between the intentions on the European level (placing a product on the market in each Member State of the EU) and the needs on the "end-user" level (actually being able to *use* them in their practical work), in particular lack of information and communication provided by public or private bodies in the information chain can "neutralise" any goal defined on the European level.

This study is not searching for flaws in a system as such or is trying to put the blame on one or the other actor. (In fact, despite the problems that will be highlighted in the study, the common approach under the CPD has produced a number of well accepted standards now in use all over Europe and no one can question that over all these years all actors have learned to communicate and cooperate more effectively.) I was more interested in what perceptions and priorities the different interested parties (starting with the Commission) had – and still have – when working with the CPD and its national implementations, and how they were trying to achieve their goals. There were of course specific interests for each party that have affected their cooperation. But keeping in mind that their reactions depended on what information they received and how, as well as their own available resources, one should not too easily jump to conclusions when judging the behaviour of different actors.

Therefore, while not ignoring specific economic or political priorities of each party involved (since they *do* influence their interaction with others), the

from the original aim (the stage of the CPR) to the practical implementation. Therefore, this study is not *comparing* both laws or even indicating that all problems highlighted by interviewees will be solved in the new CPR. The new CPR might inspire hope for improvements in actors on EU and national level (and might make them more critical in their assessment of the "old" CPD) but since the aim of this study is the evaluation of an *existing* implementation circle, future developments are excluded in this study (in the theoretical part as well as in the summary of the comments provided by different actors on EU and national level).

main focus is on the *information network* that should provide information up and downstream and the organisations and individuals creating and maintaining it. Did they have the resources to follow and participate sufficiently in the ongoing work? How were they selecting information that they intend to distribute and what were their communication tools to do it? And last not least: Did any party (at European, national, regional or "construction site" levels) know about the quantity and quality of data that was needed one level above or below in the information chain – and do they sufficiently *reach* other actors?

The aim of the study is to provide a better picture of a system created to ensure compliance with a European Directive by installing and using several means of producing and distributing information between authorities, industry, standardisation bodies, test laboratories and other interested parties. It should help to understand how and why one party is acting in a certain way. Only when the different actors are aware of practical and political limits and/or potentials of the others they can facilitate their work in the information chain.

Of course, communication is not a goal in itself. The target of the CPD is to use CE marking to get (if needed by customers) more products on national, regional and local markets and have them used in construction works. Therefore, communication should have resulted in a general but also sufficient awareness about the role and use of CE marking by all downstream actors. CE marking should be used as significant – or at least as useful – information when buying (distributing) and using construction products – which would be one parameter to evaluate the effectiveness of the communication flow. On the other hand, efficient communication could not guarantee acceptance and use of CE marking if other practical needs and considerations of end users were considered as more important. While not foreseen as major issues in the study at the beginning, it became clear that these practical considerations at the level of construction works were significant factors for the assumptions and actions of downstream actors. The differences in perception between actors on different levels were playing an important role when passing information to other levels. What seemed of importance at EU level might not have caused any worries on the "construction site" and *vice versa*. Reactions based on these different assumptions could change (and actually *have* changed) the role and use of CE marking from the EU level to the "construction site" level – partly reported back to other levels, partly "lost in translation". While the Directive and its supporting documents were written at EU level, it would be dangerous to focus only on a "top-down" approach by assuming that everything thought up at EU level is automatically beneficial for downstream actors. Considering the needs and expectations of downstream actors as equally relevant, any research on communication includes how much their needs have been mentioned by themselves and how much they have been taken into consideration in upstream levels. As will be shown in this study the information flow upstream (e.g. raising issues, providing feedback) was generally seen as only partly successful.

In my work in the Commission and with interested parties I have encountered several stereotypes about the political or economic goals of different actors – stereotypes, which have (most likely) influenced the interaction on several levels right from the beginning. Getting to know the other side better provides a better understanding *why* these goals have been selected and how much flexibility specific actors actually *have* to move closer to a common position. There are no "good guys" or "bad guys" but a lot of different aims and ways to communicate and cooperate.

For students of political, administrative and social sciences this view on the practical implementation might also provide some interesting insights. Different theories of (actor-centered) interaction are trying to explain how different constellations of positions, options and assumed gains could influence the final result – starting from the famous "prisoner's dilemma" to more complex schemes. While being correct on the abstract level that these theories have chosen, their assumed level of abstraction could give the impression that in general, actors have (at least in theory) a certain freedom to define their goals before the interaction with other actors. Looking at the example of the Construction Products Directive and its different actors involved, the focus will change from *actors trying to achieve specific goals* to *actors who are more concerned about their means* before even reaching the level of *setting their goals*. In practice the availability or the lack of resources might be the most decisive factor for actions and reactions of actors, or even worse: their lack of control of developments inside and outside their sphere of influence. Studying the implementation network around the CPD will show that the *potential* "power" of a few individuals interacting on EU and national level as "decision-makers" does only partly result in *real* power of actually influencing the behaviour of downstream actors. These downstream actors have a strong role as providers of information for the "decision-making level". Without them, upstream actors have little information and might even be forced to "guess" potential interests, needs and expectations of downstream users – which might significantly reduce their abilities to influence downstream actors to act in an intended way. Therefore, the question of how "powerful" EU or national actors are, is only partly relevant in this context – the quality and quantity of information actors could get from upstream and downstream users on the other hand plays a significant role *if* and *who* is finally able to influence actors at different levels.

Closely linked to the availability of data is the availability and participation of all relevant actors. Keeping in mind the wide range of construction products covered by the CPD and their potential use, one could ask if representatives of all relevant parties *were* actually participating in the information flow – or if some parties were missing – how realistic could the assumptions by these representatives be? How have the ones participating today been selected? How can one motivate other relevant parties to join and to keep them interested enough to make them stay in the system? Defining the impact of a Directive, selecting all relevant interested parties and keeping the whole network intact is a responsibility of all information providers (with different importance) on each level of the information flow. Highlighting the complexity of this task and the limits of actors to comply with it will be another aim of this study.

Assessing an existing system and talking to several parties involved, I got a lot of different views about the positive and negative parts of the system. But it also provided me with several of ideas and comments on potential improvements based on specific needs. This has helped to come closer to achieve the third aim of this study (NB first and second aims could be made clearer!): to provide an indicative list of potential improvements in the information flow. The emphasis lies on "improvements", not on "perfect solutions", because as the following pages will show, the different actors have not always chosen a specific approach because they considered it as the *optimal* solution, but because it fitted best with their existing resources, potential support by other parties or because it would avoid deadlocks within the EU or their national system. If "politics is the art of the possible", "political" solutions were one of the trademarks of implementing the CPD.

Last but not least, this study should not only be seen as an assessment of the practical implementation of *EU* legislation. As we will see, there are *in general* only few links between different levels – not only between the regulators on EU level and national actors, but also between different levels within a national system. When looking at the implementation of the CPD, national actors could also ask themselves if the same problems would not – and did not – occur when implementing national laws. Is communication easier – and does it happen – in the same intensity when dealing with national provisions? Is the check on the actual "usefulness" of a national law (clearly defined target; empirical evidence of the achievements of the laws) possible and has it been done? Or more precise for our specific field of construction products: How has it been ensured in the past that only "good" products have been used in buildings? How is it done today? New concepts introduced via "the EU" can also initiate a critical assessment of existing national schemes – and using the chance for improvement.

As mentioned before, the CPD will most likely be replaced by the Construction Products Regulation in the next years. One could ask if it is not a little bit too late to assess a Directive that will soon become history anyway. If this study would have been an attempt to influence the content of the new Regulation, it would now indeed be close to "archeological" work. However, there are several arguments justifying my decision of looking only at the Construction Products *Directive*: Firstly, the new Regulation might change some positions and approaches of the Commission vis-à-vis Member State authorities, but it does not change the need for an efficient information flow in both directions. The new text and its status as Regulation might clarify some issues which have been serious problems in the past, but the need for interpretation of the legal text by all interested parties and its impact on the day-to-day work will still remain. Therefore, the study will not change anything in the *text* of the new Regulation, but it might provide some positive contribution as to its practical implementation.

Secondly, the CPD was selected for pragmatic reasons – I knew it better than other Directives and I had more contacts in this field to discuss expectations, needs and limits with most of the interested parties involved. In addition, the CPD is not an absolutely *unique* piece of legislation (even if this argument is used quiet often to explain the difficult implementation of it). In fact, the question of what happens after a Directive has "passed" the European Parliament and the Council, and after it has been implemented by national laws, is also relevant for many other regulatory initiatives of the Commission. It is on purpose that not the "power game" between *European* and *national* institutions are studied in the following pages, but the practical use of European initiatives for the "end user" and how different interested parties can influence (positively and negatively) the outcome – far away from the framework that has been created by a Directive or a national law. A Directive like the CPD that has already passed the "power game" on the political level should be more "stable" against *political* pressure which makes the scheme for the practical implementation more relevant and should facilitate the identification of its practical results.

Third, since the CPD has been in place for more than one and a half decade, most actors should be familiar with it. In particular on the EU-national level the phase of "guessing" and interpreting the text of the Directive has passed long ago and has made many individuals "experts" in this field. On the other hand, 15 new Member States have joined since the adoption of the CPD which provides a good opportunity to compare the "pioneers" of the Directive with a legal text only and "newcomers" with less "guesswork" and already harmonised technical specifications in place to use it in practical work.

Another question that was raised during the interviews was "Why have you selected a Directive with so many problems on so many different levels?" Besides the arguments mentioned above, the complex history of the CPD and the large number of interested parties involved or affected by the Directive provides good examples of the difficulties and risks of ambitious scopes – but it also provides better examples of how different actors have managed to overcome these difficulties. A less controversial Directive might cover its problems and misunderstandings in a way that a study like this would not been able to detect – or the interested parties involved might not even have noticed them themselves. Problems – upstream or downstream – on the other hand are forcing actors to be more sensitive about the actions and reactions of other actors than in a more or less "unproblematic" environment. Last not least (even if it is a little bit cynical): if everybody agrees that there *are* problems, nobody has to "sell" the system as a perfect solution and therefore – intentionally or un-intentionally – hiding the weak points of it.

Bottom line: a Directive as the CPD brings the worst and the best out of the actors involved.

***

Since this study should provide information and suggestions for different actors within the information flow, I will try to keep it as informative as possible for the practical use. Therefore, *a few hints for readers under time pressure*:

The study consists of three parts: the first ("Stayin' alive, stayin' alive – Interaction, problem solving and 'European' actors") is providing the theoretical scientific background on communication and the roles of EU and national actors, largely based on existing theories and empirical research work in the field of political and administrative sciences. *The second part ("The practical implementation of the CPD") consists of the empirical work*: describing the construction sector in general and the actors involved on EU, national and "construction-site" levels, their instruments to provide information and their perceptions and a first summary conclusion for each level (based on data obtained by interviews, publications, questionnaires and personal observations in different meetings on EU and national level). In the *last part ("Conclusion") the findings will be summarised and recommendations* for actors (mostly at EU level) will close this study.

The first part of the study will cover more general and theoretical issues about communication and the interaction between European institutions and organisations and their national counterparts. This might seem a little bit too theoretical for any practical use – and actors in the construction sector are free to skip that part – but nevertheless, it provides information on why and how actors – in particular the ones dealing with the CPD – have to choose specific positions or ways of interaction. In addition, it covers the legal and political framework of European Directives, the "New Approach" and *Comitology* Committees. Here I am slightly contradicting myself that the CPD is not unique. Developed earlier than the general concept of the "New Approach" (NB New Approach should be explained, perhaps in a footnote!) the Construction Products Directive includes many aspects that became later the basic principles of the "New Approach". However, the strong regulatory aspect of the CPD and (from the Commission's point of view) obligatory nature of CE marking for products covered by harmonised European standards (while CE marking under European Technical Approvals became *voluntary* at a later stage – see: "Similarities and differences to the New Approach) still confuses parties that are not closely linked to the CPD. The "pet monster"[4] of the New Approach *does* have more confusing points than many other Directives.

The second part takes us to the implementation of the CPD and the structure of the empirical research of this study. Since the Commission is the starting point of the information flow, this part of the study gives an overview on the position and work of the Commission and the role of the instruments available, in particular the Standing Committee on Construction (SCC) – already with a strong focus

4 This expression was used for the CPD by a senior official dealing with EU regulations for the Single Market;

on how information is produced and distributed via the official networks of the Commission and the SCC. More important, this part looks at the first of three levels: the EU level, the parties involved on it and actors linking the EU level with the national ones.

First group of actors *receiving* (but also influencing) information are authorities of all Member States in the EU. Four Member States have been selected: two of the "pioneers" – Germany and the UK, working with the CPD right from the beginning – and two countries of two later accessions to the EU in 1995 (Austria) and 2005 (Poland).

Also involved at this stage are private organisations on EU level. It is difficult to define a purely *European* actor, a definition that might only cover European institutions like the European Commission. All other actors – European federations, CEN, EOTA and the Group of Notified Bodies – are clearly rooted in the European level, but depend heavily on resources, support and cooperation from national bodies and members. In particular, federations might delegate specific tasks of collecting information and assessing it to some of their members, who could themselves be European federations (for a specific sector), national federations, or big international or national companies with strong interests in specific issues – and enough resources to follow them closely. In other cases some actors might bypass established routes of communication and address specific issues directly to European bodies. These different roles, potentials and limits do influence quantity and quality of data received, interpreted and distributed down the information flow.

Already this mix of roles and responsibilities indicates that a clear cut between European and national actors is sometimes a matter of interpretation. Member State authorities are more transparent in their role as interface, interpreter and provider of information between the European and the national levels. But even here, the "different hats" that some of these institutions and organisations have to wear (and have to change several times during a meeting at EU or national levels) can put additional burden on individuals representing more than one interest (group) and also affects the information flow in both directions.

The second level – the national one – covers sometimes the same organisations and even the same individuals, but puts a stronger emphasis on national priorities and also includes now some purely national actors, in particular companies of manufacturers and contractors who are operating only on national level. The number of individuals involved is significantly increasing. They are closer to the "receiving end" of the data flow, but being farther away from the "source" and having more actors involved, the risk of misinterpretation is increasing on this level, which might actually affect the outcome of anything that has been discussed and decided on the European and European-national levels. But actors on national level are not only "receivers". Depending on quality and quantity of information provided by actors on EU level, they also play a major role as the ones describing (their) national scheme to the "upstream" actor, and therefore shaping their assumptions and positions at EU level. While their role as "interpreters" is acknowledged by everybody within the communication system, their importance as "coauthors" is often underestimated. This includes not only authorities and certification bodies (assessing products) but also federations of manufacturers and individual manufacturers. As the ones who have to interpret and use European technical specifications, they play an important role within the standardisation process and as customers of standards and European Technical Approvals, defining to a large extent quality and quantity of the information provided to the "end users" in this implementation chain.

Last but not least this study will reach the level of designers, architects and civil engineers in the public and private sectors who are planning, constructing and controlling construction works (which I called the "construction-site level"). While the other levels are providing more networking for individuals, the civil engineer on the "construction-site level" is in many cases "left alone" to collect and interpret information that might be relevant for his or her practical work. Having reached the last level of the information flow, the focus here is on how much this group *wants* to know (or considers as relevant to know), what they *need* to know, and if all levels above them are aware of it and provide the necessary quality and quantity of data. Manufacturers (and distributors) are playing a role on this level too, as providers of products linked to designers, architects and civil engineers by contracts defining relevant performance parameters and expected product quality.

For each level (EU/EU-national, national and "construction site" (NB One assumes this means three levels. However, if EU is separate from EU-national, they should be written separately, not with a slash, which usually infers and alternative choice)) this study will first describe the actors in place, their (officially) defined roles and their instruments to receive and provide information, based on qualitative interviews with representatives from the different bodies as well as some practical research on the information publicly available (i.e. websites, documents). In a next step the perceptions and experience of these individuals addressed in the interviews as well as received from quantitative questionnaires that have been sent out to a wider group of civil servants, federation representatives, specification writers and certification bodies should bridge the gap between the formalised network and the individual experience of upstream and downstream users.

The final part will be the analysis of the system. First, by analysing the findings of each level, and at the end of this study by combining these findings to make the information flow transparent. Assessing the complexity of the task of implementing a Directive on the practical (construction-site) level and comparing the resources, perceptions and initiatives should provide a better understanding of all parties involved, while suggestions for changes should provide some "food for thought". I am explicitly not using the word "improvement" because – like all proposals – they can never include all aspects and might therefore have their own practical limits. I have tried to keep my suggestions as practical as possible. Some might claim that this did not go far enough. Others might find them being already too optimistic. In general, the ones writing studies are in the lucky position that they do not have to follow their own advice (or they are in the *unlucky* position if they seriously want to change something). In my case, I have to combine my task of giving advice with the responsibility to initiate change at least in my own line of work – and changing something is much harder than writing a study about it!

***

This part of the introduction – my thanks to all the people who have helped to make this work a reasonably realistic picture of the construction sector dealing with construction products (I will never claim that it *is* a realistic picture, but only a glimpse at reality) – is one that I usually skip in other books, asking myself "Who on Earth is reading this part? – Except the ones who want to check if their contributions were appreciated enough". But after having got so much feed-back and help, and in particular getting open answers (to a Commission official who is often enough "on the other side") made me realise that this *is* an important part of any introduction – even if it is a more "private" one for everybody who has contributed to this study. In addition, following the information flow to so many different parts of the construction sector in four countries, without the help of several individuals providing me with contacts to federations, companies and individual engineers, this work would have been a very theoretic assessment of this complex sector.

Since practically everybody contacted and interviewed, as well as the information received in the questionnaires to CEN, EOTA and Notified Bodies, has been extremely helpful and informative, I would like to thank here everybody who has spent quiet some time (sometimes even hours!) patiently answering my questions and providing additional information during the interviews.

But there was also a number of experts on different levels and in different professions who have been contacted but had to reply that in their specific field interest in or knowledge about CE marking was rather low or non-existent. Despite that these were (polite but nevertheless) negative answers, these comments were as useful as the more detailed comments of others. Highlighting where CE marking has reached its "final frontier" – or where there is no demand for it – was also important feedback. Therefore, I would like to give my thanks also to this small group.

I hope that my interviews as well as this study is providing a reasonably neutral assessment of the situation around the CPD and that it even includes some (additional) information that even the veterans in this field could use. I also hope that my research work has not changed the willingness and interest of all these individuals to participate in future research from other students. Without your participation the combination between science and practical work would hardly be possible.

2 “Stayin’ alive, stayin’ alive” – Interaction, problem solving concepts and “European” actors

I am thoroughly convinced that political societies are not what laws make them but what, in advance, they are prepared to be by the sentiments, beliefs, ideas, and habits of heart and mind of the men who compose them, as nature and education have made them.
(Alexis de Tocqueville)

2.1 Organisations, institutions and individual actors

This study aims at different administrative and technical levels. Organisations, individuals and relevant technical and legal requirements might change, but the basic principles of interaction and problem solving mechanisms remain the same. As will be shown, actors at all levels try to reduce the complexity of information, create reliable instruments to receive this information and finally, to *trust* this information (to a certain extent). Therefore, the following general overview on interaction – while often referring to the EU level (where most research has been done in the past) – also applies to all other levels.

This study will use the term “actor” when referring to an individual or a group that has been accepted as representative of one of the groups of interested parties involved in the discussion and decision finding process. These actors could play slightly different roles, depending if one favours an *actor*-centered or an *institution/organisation*-centered approach. The first is considering individuals and their resources, goals and methods for achieving them as more influential than the organisation they represent. The latter is putting more emphasis on the environment, norms, goals and resources provided by institutions or organisations as affecting the behaviour of their representatives. In this study a combination of an actor-centered and an institution/organisation-centered approach has been chosen, with a strong emphasis on individual actors. But to avoid confusion, one has to get a clearer definition of the different types of "actors" that will be encountered:

In the discussion about the influence of the European Union on national systems ("Europeanisation"), mostly European institutions and national governments (and their administrations) have appeared as actors on transnational level. However, no European Directive is only addressing EU and national *institutions*. Industry sectors, specific professions, workers, consumers as well as individual citizens (as the ones who should finally profit from this interaction) are directly or indirectly affected. Federations, unions and NGOs have taken over the part of representing specific interests or groups, being mostly complementary to representatives of national governments and their administrations, but sometimes also in competition or confrontation with them. All of them could have either a very broad and horizontal agenda or being interested only in very few specific issues. Depending on the size of their organisation, their membership and their available sources, they have chosen different approaches in how to introduce their positions and goals into a discussion process.

No matter which interested party is selected, one has to distinguish between institutions/organisations and individuals.[5] In this study, I will refer to private federations or NGOs as "organisations" and will keep the term "institution" for public authorities (i.e. the European Commission and its administration and national administrations or bodies empowered by regulators to fulfil tasks of public bodies) In general, discussions at EU level are mostly between very few individuals, but they represent at least one institution or organisation. Being embedded in an organization the individual will use what is in general referred to as the "common position" or "common knowledge" of *this specific organisation*: Each organisation perceives reality in a specific way and has specific assumptions about causes and effects of specific actions ("social construction of reality")[6]. Based on that, it will develop a set of normative convictions about the appropriateness and rightfulness of specific actions and a set of social norms and institutional rules that will become a more or less binding reference for all its

5 See: Hooghe/Marks: Multi-Level Governance and European Integration 2001 p. 70; Börzel: States and Regions in the European Union 2002 p. 23ff.; Parsons: Aktor, Situation und normative Muster 1994; Parsons: On institutions and social evolution 1982.

6 Berger/Luckmann: The Social Construction of Reality 1991.

individual members.[7] In the institution/organisation-centered[8] view the individual practically disappears as *independent* actor, depending practically completely on the guidance and feedback of the organisation, and therefore being a reflection of its preferences, which are now as a "collective actor".[9]

The difficulty with the second concept is the lack of control over individuals representing an organisation. A set of common values and assumptions does not guarantee a perfect match in each situation. The situation might have changed to an extent that no longer allows direct reference to existing norms created by the organisation. Also guidance from the organisation to an individual rarely prescribes one *and only one* course of action. When moving to more practical and technical/scientific issues, "collective actors", representing only the positions of organisations without the risk of interference of individual preferences and actions, would face difficulties in actively participating in the discussion process, because they would need more and more feedback and guidance from their organisation, depending on how detailed the discussion will become. In reality, the chances of having all information and guidance available every time are very slim, always leaving an asymmetry between the knowledge needed and the resources available to provide it. Therefore, if the organisation wants to influence the discussion, it has to give a certain freedom for individual choices to be able to react *in time*.

A more flexible approach gives individuals more freedom for their own interpretation and actions. The "corporate actor"[10] enjoys this autonomy because the ultimate beneficiaries (the members of the organisation) consider the individual still closely enough attached to the cognitive orientation of the organisa-

7 Scharpf: Games Real Actors Play, 1997 p.19ff.; Berglund et al: Mass production of law 2006 p. 699.

8 Organisation and institution are both defining system boundaries like values, interests and specific mechanisms for its internal function and external interaction. However, organisations could be only temporary creations (i.e. created for very specific tasks or interests) while institutions are embedded in a "social structure", giving it more stability and more reliability vis-à-vis other actors. Organisations established and maintained under (international) treaties or other legal frameworks are the most prominent (but not exclusively) bodies that can be considered as institutions. (see also: Parsons: Aktor, Situation und normative Muster 1994 p. 218ff.).

9 Scharpf: Games Real Actors Play, 1997 p. 54.

10 Scharpf: Games Real Actors Play, 1997 p. 54; Berger/Luckmann: The Social Construction of Reality 1991 p. 70ff.; Schimank: Teilsystemische Autonomie ..., 2006 p. 153f.

tion and its preferences[11] that significant deviations from its interests will not *intentionally* occur. This more actor-centered approach still keeps the assumption that an individual is acting in the interests and the perspective of larger units than themselves[12] but shifts the focus back on the individual as a partly independent actor.

At first glance, institutions and authorities would be good candidates for providing "corporate actors". Since they are perceived as relatively stable bodies, and their members will remain in this environment for a relatively long period, the individual should have time enough to internalise the group identity, its norms, interests and interaction orientations – and its very specific role within the system ("habitualise" his or her actions within the system). Being firmly embedded in the institution should reduce deviant behaviour to an acceptable minimum. However, considering the size and complexity of administrative bodies or big companies, internalising a general "corporate identity" might not be enough to avoid inconsistencies when individuals are facing complex situations. Trying to find solutions on a transnational level might lead to the creation of an *additional* role as part of a transnational group (and therefore an additional *esprit de corps*) to the one of representing a national position – which might be complementary or could lead to a role conflict. Having acquired very specific experience (at EU level) individuals get an exceptional role, even vis-à-vis their own institution. Also, representing several national actors might influence the actual role and behaviour of individuals. By doing that, individuals and groups of individuals still operate in the context of these institutions, but they might (intentionally or unintentionally) try to change them[13].

However, *the* classical "corporate actors" are representatives from industry federations and (to a certain extent) NGOs and technical bodies. But this is not so much based on a preference of private organisations and industry for a more flexible approach, but on the fact that practically all private actors lack the manpower to compete with EU or national administrations in the discussion process. As we will see, the obligatory forum for discussions on the implementation of European law (*comitology* committees) have been created for administrations,

11 Based on a membership that includes the internalisation of its identity (interests, norms) or based on a contract that binds the individual to the organization.

12 Scharpf: Games Real Actors Play, 1997 p. 12.

13 Hogghe/Marks: Multi-Level Governance and European Integration, 2001 p. 70.

with other actors *added*, but not considered as main actors. Therefore, non-public actors have to make their own choice when and if they want to participate – a decision that is even harder to make if the scope of their work and its potential outcome are not clear.

In addition, industry actors (federations and individual companies) are not *political* actors *per se*, but *market actors,* being active in production, distribution and construction. Participating in the discussion process initiated and dominated by public administration forces industry to withdraw manpower from the "production process" to the "discussion process". Industry and NGOs alike can often not afford the creation of a strong monitoring and guiding system for their representatives in different committees. Since these organisations/enterprises cannot in most cases afford to use a large number of experts, each individual is covering more than one specific policy or technical field, and has to select priorities and hence his or her use of resources individually. In addition, these individuals have in many cases been seconded from national members (NGOs, federations) and in case of (national) industry federations from individual companies. These individuals are clearly working with several backgrounds, roles and role expectations: from their company, additional/complementary/competing positions from national federations and preferences and interaction orientations of the EU umbrella federation. Providing autonomy is therefore the least cost-intensive way for them to remain in the system.

In reality both types – the "collective" and the "corporate actor" – are often mixed. In the end, the actual involvement of an individual actor depends on how much relevance both the institutions/organisations and the individual actors give to the issues under discussion for the good of the collective unit – the institution/organization or even more horizontal: the economy or the environment. But no matter if an individual can be considered as "corporate" or "collective actor", both types have in common:

- (at least) one reference unit – the institution or organization,
- specific perceptions (perceptions of reality, perception of interaction modes, normative role orientation), and
- specific preferences (interests, norms, identities, interaction orientations),
- specific capabilities (collective or individual action resources – existing or newly created for this specific field of interest),

- a basic self-interest (self preservation, autonomy, growth).[14]

In this study, the focus is on the importance of the individual working in a field that often requires technical expertise. As mentioned before, there are only a few individuals active at EU level in a specific field. Having only few close links to other (national or regional) actors and therefore being in a unique position of collecting, interpreting and providing information to other actors, the individual as "expert" becomes (at least partly) his or her own "interpreter" to the national level, decreasing the influence of institutions/organisations and increasing his or her autonomy. On the other hand, the price for this autonomy as "individual" actor is the "burden of decision" forcing the individual more and more to make assumptions on his or her own while keeping a certain balance between available knowledge and "acceptable ignorance".

As will be shown later, this delegation of decision making power and the lack of control are not necessarily seen as disadvantageous by the institutions or organisations behind the individual and sometimes are even actively encouraged. Within institutions/organisations delegating to one individual or just a small number of individuals (i.e. an administrative unit) also means to "isolate" a problem, and therefore freeing the rest of the body from the responsibility of following each development at EU level on their own ("that's what we have created this post/this unit/this organisation for in the first place"), and should even help to focus resources (specific experts or data) of executive, legislative, economic and social actors in specific issue networks to develop and implement specific (political or technical) approaches.[15] However, the concept of "isolation" of specific issues for pragmatic reasons could create problems if it is taken too literally. Individual actors might find themselves without an *efficient* supporting network and a lack of necessary feedback because other actors within their national or organisational system are considering their involvement and cooperation as no longer necessary ("now we have somebody to deal with these issues").

---

14 See Schrapf: Games Real Actors Play 1997 p. 43 & p. 60ff.; Jordan sites Guy Peters elements of organizational culture: The Europeanization of National Government and Policy 2003 p. 270f.; Schimank: Teilsystemische Autonomie ..., 2006 p. 147.

15 Lesmeister: Informelle politische Kommunikationskultur 2008 p. 33.

2.2 Organising and stabilising interaction

Looking at interaction where different actors want to preserve their interests, and starting with the assumption that all of them have – at least in theory – no system-specific limitations of making these interests known, the first question would be *how* these actors want to interact with others. How important do they see their own goals and how strongly would they defend or "upload" them on others? Two "classic" positions are defined under the terms of the *homo economicus*[16] and the *homo sociologicus*[17]:

The economic approach highlights the need for maximising gains that have been defined by the actor himself/herself. Only his/her own priorities and goals are taken into consideration, and should be achieved with the absolute minimum of efforts from his/her side. Therefore, the *homo economicus* is only cooperating if this is necessary or helpful to reach his/her goals. In international relations, this behaviour is linked to an *enforcement approach*: While nations in particular but also other actors have an interest in rules and compliance, and are therefore willing to contribute to establish and maintain structures that would facilitate and enforce common rules, temptation always exists to profit as a free-rider from the efforts of others. To identify, discourage or punish deviant behavior, mechanisms to sanction it have to be developed to make compliance more profitable even for potential free-riders.[18] Therefore, other actors have to develop strong monitoring and sanctioning mechanisms to keep the *homo economicus* (no matter if one looks at nation states, organisations or individuals – even within states and organisations) from deviating from agreed procedures and commitments

The *homo sociologicus* could be seen as the other end of the spectrum of human behaviour – also trying in general to achieve one's own goals, but the individual is more bound to accept social norms and expectations, which are influencing and restricting its options. Contrary to *homo economicus,* who accepts norms only to maximise his own profits and does not follow norms that are not supported by sanctions, *homo sociologicus* uses them for decisions, whether sanctions are protecting these norms or not. At international level this

16 Diekmann/Eichner/Schmidt/Voss et al: Rational Choice 2008.

17 Dahrendorf: Homo sociologicus 1977.

18 See: Börzel/Hofmann/Sprungk: Einhaltung von Recht jenseits des Nationalstaats; in: Zeitschrift für Internationale Beziehungen 2/2003 p. 249f. und: Gehring: Die Europäische Union als komplexe internationale Organisation 2002 p. 47ff.

behaviour is defined as a *management approach* which indicates that parties are in general more willing to cooperate, even if this would increase their overall costs. Here too, non-compliance is possible, but is not based on intention by one or more parties but caused by inefficient communication or unclear defined goals and expectations which could affect the quality of the implementation of an agreement. Also lack of resources or lack of (legal or political) competence of even one of the agreeing parties could affect the implementation or the cooperation process.[19]

Reality of course is rarely showing one of these two extremes in its pure form. On the contrary, neither the behaviour of one or nor of the other is very predictable. Even very profit-oriented players might choose a less profitable communication and coordination system if it could positively influence the information flow and the interaction process in future. On the other hand, co-operative players facing significant deficits in information might fall back to well defined (national) positions, rather than using highly "insecure" cooperation instruments.

In this study too, both *homo economicus* as well as *homo sociologicus* will appear – sometimes even complementarily in the actions of one individual or organisation. Nevertheless, the focus will be on the *homo sociologicus* as the main behaviour pattern for most actors for several reasons:

- all actors have *officially* indicated their interest in *dialogue*, if not in *co-operation*. This already forces them to acknowledge certain rules of interaction, and also to expect that other actors are in general not intentionally deviating from them;
- as will be shown in this study, most positions in the interaction and bargaining process are filled with very few individuals. In most cases, they have only limited resources or possibilities to monitor the behaviour of other actors on this level (who are in an equally weak position), and are therefore dependent on the norm-compliance of others. While this would be a perfect opportunity for deviance of individual actors, being embedded in a very special environment (the still "exotic" EU level) supporting the creation of a certain *esprit des corps*, which might not go very far, but guarantees a

19 See: Börzel/Hofmann/Sprungk: Einhaltung von Recht jenseits des Nationalstaats; in: Zeitschrift für Internationale Beziehungen 2/2003 p. 249f. und: Gehring: Die Europäische Union als komplexe internationale Organisation 2002 p. 47ff.

certain minimum of cooperation even if deviant behaviour could not easily be detected or sanctioned;

- the unique position of these individuals theoretically gives them more power when setting goals as well as interpreting and distributing information to downstream actors. On the other hand, the power of these individuals diminishes the more complex or detailed a specific issue becomes – and therefore other (expert) opinion is needed from additional actors. In this situation they too have to depend on supporting actors who are "playing fair" in providing (correct) information on time or who are cooperating in the implementation of agreements made at upstream levels;
- also downstream actors have only limited experience or resources to control their representatives in upstream levels. They are *de facto* in the same position as the upstream actors, depending on their *intentional* compliance with norms and expectations instead of being able to force compliance;
- last but not least: while the construction sector might not have the most untarnished reputation, it consists to a large extent of *professionals who are interacting with each other*. I would argue that "professional pride" is a factor that one has to take into consideration when making assumptions about the behaviour of individuals or groups in this sector, in particular the more one moves from a "political" level to the "construction-site" level. As one of the "oldest" sectors, training and achieving specific positions are still based on traditions and/or long training which separate these professionals from the "outside world" (i.e. do-it-yourself enthusiasts). Being efficient and able to solve technical problems is part of their external – but also *internal* – role expectations – which would make them even more committed to the behaviour of *homo sociologicus* than the monitoring and sanctioning of public bodies.

On the other hand, one cannot exclude behaviour closer to *homo economicus*:

- the general problem of getting sufficient data on the positions, needs, abilities and limits of upstream and downstream actors (the cognitive lack of transparency of different institutions and organisations for each other[20]) makes it easier to deviate from any agreement without a high risk of detection;

---

20 Schimank: Teilsystemische Autonomie 2006 p. 255.

- considering another basic problem for all actors of monitoring activities outside their sphere of influence (mostly along national or regional borders or between national and EU level), the temptation for *free-riding* is relatively high. Information could be presented in a way more profitable for specific actors. Ignoring agreements at upstream levels would be an option that could serve *homo economicus* if monitoring and sanctions are not seriously expected;
- the above-mentioned lack of resources for monitoring and sanctioning even between national actors (i.e. on different implementation levels) provides actors with significant room for maximising their (individual) gains;
- the still-competing environments of "the EU" (the "Eurocrats") and a national one ("we XXXians") facilitate the development of a "national solution", because the chances that within this overall environment national actors would protect each other is higher than in the more complex and fragile transnational environment.

Both approaches –*homo economicus* and *homo sociologicus* – have in common that the actors (organisations or individuals) define their goals and options on their own. Their "environment" is formed by established social, economic and administrative expectations, working structures and implementation instruments. Planning and implementation patterns are based on social and cultural backgrounds of each political or social group or profession involved in the international interaction process ("obligational trust"[21]). "Experience" or "expertise" of an individual or a group is not necessarily the same as access to and use of empirical data. It could also be based or at least be affected by social conditioning of individuals by their peer group or its own social environment which defines (partly based on past experience but also on assumptions and stereotypes) how far trust and cooperation (or withholding it) could be used when interacting with other groups[22].

Despite different priorities and means, both approaches reduce the risk of wrong first assumptions and wrong reactions resulting from them, if all parties exchange their views and agree on a common description of the current situation.

---

21 Lane: Theories and issues in the Study of Trust; in: Lane/Bachmann (eds): Trust within and between Organizations 1998 p. 9.

22 Knorr Cetina: Sozialität mit Objekten & Schimank: Rationalitätsfiktionen in der Entscheidungsgesellschaft; both in: Tänzler/Knoblauch/Soeffner (Hrsg.): Zur Kritik der Wissensgesellschaft 2006 p. 71 & p. 110ff.; Schimank: Teilsystemische Autonomie ..., 2006 p. 128ff.

Even if the first step does not necessarily lead to a *common* definition, the discussion which highlighted all different positions has reduced the complexity of the situation for all parties, because by presenting them, all positions not mentioned can be considered as less important and negligible for the time being (now being obviously less likely to succeed than they seemed before without any knowledge about the positions of the others). This gives everybody a better chance to predict the next steps of interaction of the other actors, and also limits the number of options for oneself, but at the same time reduces the risk of misinterpretation by the other interaction partners. No matter how low the chance might be for predicting the actions of *all* actors when facing new challenges, it is generally accepted that any system that is providing at least some information on the (bargaining) positions and options of other parties is preferable to a situation with higher insecurity and higher bargaining costs.[23] The more the different actors have tried to find common definitions for specific situations and the more these attempts have been successful, the more complex and complete is the pool of common experiences which could and will be used by all interested parties for the next interaction.

One problem embedded in this scheme is its exclusiveness when defining problems and goals. To solve a complex problem one has to define as precisely as possible the relevant aspects of the problem. Only aspects that are mentioned in the definition of a problem will be treated within the system. If the system boundaries are too rigid, useful options might not be accessible within the established framework. On the other hand, a lack of clear definitions might reduce the ability of the system to act efficiently – or a lot of time would be lost at a later stage of creating additional specific definitions before the work on practical solutions could even begin. While the system is not completely closed to a wider environment, the costs of adding additional aspects in a specific definition might be too high for some parties to even try to add them at a later stage.[24] Therefore, each party is interested in having all aspects that are considered as relevant from its point of view included right from the beginning, or at least during the first definition phase. This partly explains the emphasis on specific issues and the vehemence of all parties at this important stage, but also the complexity of some definitions and approaches developed at European level.

23 Gehring: Die Europäische Union als komplexe internationale Organisation 2002 p. 61ff.
24 Ditto p. 89ff.

While this phase is one of the most crucial for the following communication and cooperation, it is also the one where most actors have only limited information on what their own priorities might be. The definition of the problem is still vague and open for changes which might also affect national positions. Most representatives are using positions and priorities defined on national or organisational level, but they might lose their usefulness during the discussion at European level when the definition of the problem moves (too far) away from the assumptions of the national/organisational actors. The (national) representatives might very soon be reaching a point where they are "interpreters" of the positions of their counterparts on European level to their own national system and *vice versa*. But while they will most likely make accurate assumptions about national expectations and reactions, interpreting positions based on different (national) social-cultural, economic or administrative frameworks bears a higher risk of misinterpretation. National interested parties could try to compensate this potential lack of accurate information by taking a more flexible position, giving their representatives only general guidelines and allowing them to use more their expertise and experience. Others might fear that their priorities might get "lost" in favour of other issues and fall back to clear but inflexible positions and increase control and guidance of their representatives. Lack of guidance might even force representatives to make their own assumptions or excluding them as an active party in the discussion process.[25] The former might facilitate coming to an agreement, but might increase the risk that the national implementation is less efficient or even facing strong resistance from national actors. The latter keeps national approaches generally intact and reduces adaptation costs for national actors, but risks a blockage in the discussion at higher level.

As a next step to facilitate communication, special conventions might be introduced. They are the (normative or non-normative) collective expectations on how each party will interact. One of the major advantages of this approach – in addition to reducing the level of complexity of a system – is providing a framework which allows comparing and judging the behaviour of one party in relation to these conventions. Important for the acceptance and use of such a system is the usefulness of data that it is providing. Additionally, this system does not only provide channels for sending and receiving information but it is also creating a type of "informative lens" focusing on specific issues and thereby reducing the costs for all actors to present not only the most relevant interests and positions

25 Beyers/Trondal: How Nation-States "Hit", 2003 p. 7ff.

within their own national system but also to identify what the priorities of other actors might be.

A solution often used in practice is a system of mutual adjustment, which allows the first party that becomes active in a system (i.e. "agenda setting", providing specific input) to define certain criteria which would provide the best outcome for this party. This step should not discriminate any other party to an extent that would no longer allow its willingness or ability to cooperate within the system. The next party will also try to get a positive outcome for itself, but has to do this already within the system boundaries that the first actor has set. All following parties are more and more restricted in their options, but they are still allowed to actively participate in the system.[26] Nevertheless, this approach depends on the self-restraint of its members not to harm any other member by any action. The best example within the European Union is the accession of new Member States. On the one hand, the pressure to adapt to the existing rules is very high[27] and the "room for manoevre" is very limited. On the other hand, the costs for reducing the complexity of a system of different positions are much lower, because they have been "paid" by the "old" members in the past.

The implementing actors are now facing the problem of balancing on national/organisational level:

- the resource needs for the new activity,
- the resources and priorities of existing activities (obligatory or voluntary),
- the resources and demands of interested actors who should be involved in the implementation of the new activity (while supporting other projects too),
- the political and practical pressure from these actors.

Being forced to make their own compromises with all relevant actors at national level, the possibilities of national actors at EU level to provide enough support and resources might vary significantly from the expectation at international level. This could put them in a difficult position if the implementation is hampered outside their own sphere of influence while they are still the ones who have to explain and justify the results at EU level – in particular if they have put a lot of efforts in convincing (national) actors to cooperate. "Misfits" could force other

26 Schimank: Teilsystemische Autonomie ..., 2006 p. 205.

27 *acquis communautaire*: http://ec.europa.eu/enlargement/archives/enlargement_process/future_prospects/negotiations/eu10_bulgaria_romania/chapters/index_en.htm.

national/organisational actors to rethink the previous national/organisational compromise – deciding either to block any changes or to reopen the discussion by adding additional demands as the price for changing the agreement. But on the other hand, this split of responsibilities could also be an opportunity for national actors at EU level to "correct" decisions that they have not fully supported. But changing (voluntarily or involuntarily) a position taken at EU level vis-à-vis other actors could also put more pressure on national actors, because they might now face the criticism and also legal action from the Commission services. While in general, all actors try to solve the discrepancies more in a cooperative than a confrontational way ("compliance bargaining"),[28] national actors who have found solutions at EU level might have to face official complaints and infringement procedures and have to defend national positions that were developed outside their own sphere of influence.

But nation states and international actors have added an additional approach to avoid being too much dependent on an efficient communication, monitoring and sanctioning system. To avoid conflicts – in particular in the implementation phase – most actors are trying to keep the adjustment requirements in general as low as possible. Therefore, many agreements tend to codify *existing* behaviour (i.e. culturally ingrained national preferences) rather than introducing new, far-reaching or complex requirements on each actor. By avoiding conflicts at international and also national levels as much as possible, nation states and other international actors have in general few incentives to defect from a common agreement.[29]

28 Tallberg/Jönsson: Compliance bargaining 2005 p. 79ff & p. 86.

29 Tallberg: Paths to Compliance 2002 p. 612; see also: Scharpf: What Have We Learned? 2001 p. 20f.

2.3 European and national actors

2.3.1 The EU level and the European Commission as a communication and bargaining system

One could now simply – and quite reasonably – argue that most of the nation states in Europe do not have the choice to decide if they want to create an international organisation to facilitate communication and coordination or not. With the creation of an international cooperation which became today's European Union, all member states have reached a new level of complexity far away from voluntary or even only temporary structures. While bilateral bargaining systems or ones with only a small number of states involved often keep a level of low complexity and the (administrative) costs remain transparent and affordable for all parties, the system complexity increases with each additional nation state or other actors joining the process. New actors very often introduce new requirements and priorities based on their political, administrative and economic structures. For a single member state the costs of getting information on the (bargaining) positions of each other member state, of interpreting them and acting accordingly are continuously increasing. In particular, smaller member states and their administrations do not have enough resources at their disposal to guarantee effective and sufficient communication with all other actors on European level. But even larger member states very often depend right from the beginning on a communication process based on the instruments provided by the Commission to distribute information about a specific problem, its role as coordination point for sending replies and as interpreter of each national reaction. For national actors the European Commission fulfils specific functions in the communication and bargaining system which is not done in this form by national administrations:

- it provides all actors involved a "landmark", by providing data and by using established social norms, thus providing a commonly used framework for interaction between different national and international actors;
- it provides a system for interaction based on communication between different actors;
- it splits institutional discussion and decision-finding processes into sub-processes, which increases the decision-finding capability of the system;

- it provides a forum for learning from other experiences (and therefore reducing one's own research and learning costs) which could lead to a dynamic collective learning process[30];

The most basic function of the Commission is to organise and provide a framework which allows communication between all Member States of the EU. This includes in most cases its function for selecting which topics are *within* and *without* the discussion as well as deciding on the right of specific actors of participation in the discussion process.

Within this framework all actors are interacting by bargaining and arguing. They are therefore restricted to using essential and factual arguments to convince the other parties of joining their position or proposal[31]. For this the Commission not only provides linguistic interpretation but sometimes also a social-cultural and political-administrative interpretation of national positions for each party involved. Therefore, the Commission plays a major role in defining the specific institutional problem to be discussed, and its success and acceptance of its role by all actors depends on the Commission's ability to identify *relevant* and *reliable* information and to provide it to all actors.

2.3.2 *The Commission as an actor in its own role*

The previous section described the role of the European Commission as a (relatively) neutral organisation as "host" and "interpreter" in international negotiations. These functions are reflected in the concept of *inter-governmentalists* who consider the Commission only as an *agent of the interests of national governments*, providing the platform for a consensus-finding process, but only *reacting* to national interests and developments, not being an actor on its own.[32] This view is supported by the fact that the Commission has no strong administrative body and means to enforce its laws, neither is it able to use a public discourse which

30 For all three points see: Gehring: Die Europäische Union als komplexe internationale Organisation 2002 p. 16ff.; sowie: Gehring: Die Bedeutung spezialisierter Entscheidungsprozesse … und Grande: Multi-Level Governance, beide in: Grande/Jachtenfuchs (Hrsg): Wie problemlösungsfähig ist die EU? 2000 p. 89f. &. p. 16ff.; Nugent: The European Commission 2001; Peterson: „Policy Networks“ 2003: Ackermann: Pfadabhängigkeit, ... 2001 p. 70.

31 Gehring: Die Europäische Union als komplexe internationale Organisation 2002 p. 103ff.

32 Bulmer/Lequesne: The EU and its Member States: An Overview; in: Bulmer/Lesquesne (eds): The Member States of the European Union 2005 p.6ff.

might strengthen public acceptance of a specific European law or its interpretation by the Commission. More than any national administration, the Commission depends on the cooperation of other actors, which includes their contribution to a well developed and efficient system of communication.[33] While the supportive nature of several tasks and activities of the Commission is not denied, the view of the Commission as a passive instrument is contested as not providing the whole picture of its role and real function in the discussion process.[34]

While the Commission focuses on communication and mediation functions and is therefore significantly different from national administrations who have (thanks to several monopolistic powers at national level) a wide range of instruments at their disposal to "enforce" implementation of national (or international) laws, this limitation has been partly turned into an advantage by the Commission "against" the EU Member States. Since the Commission could focus on its communicative expertise and resources ("network governance"[35]) it has gained a lead within the EU compared with national administrations and other interested parties. This becomes even more obvious with each accession and the increase of additional Member States in the EU.

The Commission could become even more important in the system the better it could develop commonly accepted and binding rules for treating several problems. Avoiding time-consuming and expensive discussions and negotiations with each Member States is an advantage for most national actors which makes in many cases even the "loss" of their bargaining power (rules are reducing the number of options for each actor) acceptable. Using its role as the developer and provider of rules for discussions and negotiations, the Commission very often dominates the coordination and definition process right from the phase when a problem has been identified. Member States are of course in many cases the ones

33 Therefore, the Commission services are using a "fire brigade" approach, putting less resources on constant monitoring ("police patrol" approach) but reacting to complaints by international or national actors about breaches of EU legislation and treaties. But even then they often use "name and shame" instruments (i.e. statistics on national compliance or non-compliance with EU law being publicly available to everybody) than taking the complaint to the European Court of Justice (however, in these cases the Commission services have been careful in choosing cases where the Court would most likely support the position of the Commission – which is visible in the "success rate" of the Commission of about 90% of the infringement cases having been won by the Commission (Tallberg p. 671ff.).

34 Bauer/Voelzkow (Hrsg.): Die Europäische Union – Marionette oder Regisseur? 2004.

35 Kohler-Koch: European Networks and Ideas 2002 p. 4; Scharpf: What Have We Learned? 2001 p. 7f.

identifying a problem, but after that, they only become involved in an active role after the Commission has provided the framework for dealing with it ("agenda setting")[36]. Member States could change the framework even at a later stage, but because they have to convince so many different other Member States and other actors to do so, they would be facing a much more difficult task than the Commission who has been working on the framework for a long time which gave it more opportunity to get to know the positions of other actors and to take them into considerations than other (national) actors.

Another option for the Commission (or any other international organisation) to reduce the influence of national actors is to include selectively non-governmental organisations in the discussion process. Depending on the issue, there are always federations, companies or NGOs who have an interest in introducing their position and solutions into the discussion. Taking other actors on board has several advantages for the Commission: it opens new sources of information and data, therefore increasing the professional competence of the Commission *and* gaining new allies to promote its own position.[37] Acceptance of the results of the negotiations by these newly included actors increases the general acceptance and also increases the position of all actors within their own organisational environment.[38]

But one should not overestimate the Commission's role. The Commission can only get and hold this position if it is fulfilling its role as collector, interpreter and provider of information in a way that assures national actors that their

36 Nugent: The European Commission 2001 p.17ff.; Pollack: The Engines of European Integration 2003 p. 52ff.; Pollack: The Commission as an Agent, & Matláry: The Role of the Commission, both in: Nugent (ed): At the Heart of the Union 2000 p.124f. & p.279f.; Peters: Agenda-setting in the European Community, in: Nugent (ed): The European Union Vo. 2, 1997.

37 See also: Richardson: Policy-making in the EU, in: Richardson (ed): European Union 2006 p. 18f.; Gehring: Die Europäische Union als komplexe internationale Organisation 2002 p. 232f., 274 & 280ff.; Bauer/Voelzkow (Hrsg.): Die Europäische Union – Marionette oder Regisseur? 2004; Matláry: The Role of the Commission, in: Nugent (ed): At the Heart of the Union 2000 p.276; van Schendelen: Machiavelli in Brussels 2005 p. 32 & 39; Demortain: La légitimation par les norms; 2008; Friedrich: Partizipatives Regieren in der EU 2008 p. 220f.

38 This approach is not something specific for the Commission. National administrations are using the same instruments and are achieving similar results. Apart from gains of one's status within a specific system is it very difficult to assess the real influence and success of NGOs in this process. (see: Roose: Die Europäisierung von Umweltorganisationen 2003 p. 195ff.; und Grande: Multi-Level Governance, in: Grande/Jachtenfuchs (Hrsg): Wie problemlösungsfähig ist die EU? 2000 p. 21).

interests have been acknowledged and have been properly taken into consideration.[39] Both sides are therefore highly dependent on each other and one-sided advantages are bought with heavy costs in the future communication process.

One additional aspect highlights the dependency of the Commission on support from national actors: the Commission might be in a unique position in the bargaining process and the information flow, but it lacks in general technical experts. Already its predecessor, the High Authority, aimed at being an organisation "all-rounder", coordinating different national interests rather than experts in a specific field. With the agenda of the Commission growing and the complexity of issues increasing, a system of temporary agents[40] – seconded national experts (*Expert National Détaché* – END) – with a specific technical or scientific background seconded by national authorities or other interested parties was introduced. This gives the Commission the possibility to increase its abilities to coordinate actors even in more technical or scientific fields, but this ability depends on the availability of experts at national level (at least theoretically favouring larger Member States with potentially more manpower to "second" a number of individuals to EU institutions), as well as the willingness of Member States to provide these individuals. What seems like a win-win scenario for the Commission (services) and Member State (authorities) – having additional technical expertise for the one; having "our man in Brussels" for the others – is more complicated for the individual who finds himself/herself in this position. On the one hand, they have to use a vaguely defined "European perspective" when working on specific issues, on the other hand, they are expected to go back to their previous *national* jobs. Lacking the support of an established background (not really a European official and no longer a "pure protagonist" of national interests) demands more individual competence of balancing different interests than either Commission officials or national officials have to show.

39 Siehe auch: Gehring: Die Europäische Union als komplexe internationale Organisation 2002 p. 214ff.; Bauer/Voelzkow (Hrsg.): Die Europäische Union – Marionette oder Regisseur? 2004

40 Their secondment is limited to three years with one additional year possible; (see also: Scholz: Lobbyismus aus der Sicht der Europäischen Kommission, in: Dagger/Kambeck (hrsg): Politikberatung und Lobbying in Brüssel 2007 p. 68ff., Egeberg: The Organisational Dimension of Integration in the EU 2000 p. 13); Suvarierol/van den Berg: Bridge Builders or Bridgheads in Brussels? In: Geuijen/'THart/Princen/Yesilkagit: The New Eurocrats 2008 p.103ff.

2.3.3 Member State authorities – the national/transnational actors

2.3.3.1 Member States "in Brussels"

Most Member States have developed specific approaches on how to link their national systems with the activities at EU level. This starts already with monitoring developments, discussions and first drafts of documents and legislations written by European institutions – in the case of legislation: solely the European Commission, and informing the relevant interested parties at national level. The next step is to react and – if relevant for this specific Member State – to influence these activities as described above. Next to Member States governments, their administrations are the main representatives of national positions. Compared with federations, individual (multinational) companies and NGOs, they are the ones strongest embedded in a national environment. Companies could have crossed national borders and have different nationalities in their staff. Political alliances or recruiting experts could also allow NGOs a more multinational combination of individuals working for them. National authorities on the other hand are in general still recruiting their own citizens for their permanent staff (although immigration has indirectly brought some heterogeneity into the system of national administration). However, one should not overestimate the heterogeneity of non-governmental groups. The potential flexibility does not necessarily lead to a stronger multinational working structure in these organisations, or the ability to cooperate with other actors more easily. Nevertheless, their chances to discuss an issue from several cultural and national perspectives at an early stage remain higher.

National authorities are more likely to present a homogenous "national identity" since they are also the instrument of the national state to provide services and protection in a clearly defined national territory,[41] allowing consistent focus on national positions. But on the other hand they might be hampered when they want or have to take other positions into consideration. The national background might also help to create an image as being given the task of defending national positions rather than finding common positions with actors of other nations. This image is even strengthened by existing theoretical concepts and assessments on how Member States *react* when being confronted with multi-

41 See: Goetz: The Development and Current Features of the German Civil Service System, in: Bekke/van der Meer (eds): Civil Service Systems in Western Europe 2000 p. 67 & Stehr: Die Zerbrechlichkeit moderner Gesellschaften 2000 p. 28ff.

national activities. The emphasis on *reaction* indicates that European institutions (which paradoxically include the Council – consisting of the heads of Member States, national ministers and national ambassadors) are mostly *initiating* actors, which leaves for national actors only the role of supporting or opposing these initiatives. This image is less convincing when looking at the low number of political and administrative proposals that really originated from the Commission and its services[42]. Nevertheless, the theoretical monopoly of the European Commission to introduce European legislation has certainly influenced how the administrations of Member States are interacting with other actors "in Brussels", focusing on assessments as to how the Permanent Representations in the EU, ambassadors and civil servants of these Member States are working in high-level bodies like the Council and COREPER I and II[43].

Next to these political bodies on EU level, the Permanent Representations in the EU are official bodies that have been created as parallel structures to national embassies, focusing solely on EU issues and representing their countries vis-à-vis European institutions. Depending on their national administrative structure, they could have more of a monitoring role, being the "early-warning" system for national administrations to react on time, or more active interlocutors between specific national interests and European institutions. In Member States where regions play a significant political role, additional representations have been established to lobby for regional policies, interests of specific actors and competing with other regions for investors. (See below)

While these representations are more interested in *new* developments, national ministries or agencies have established their own networks when it

42 In 1998 only about five to 10 percent of the Commission's legislative proposals originated from the Commission services. The majority was adapting to existing obligations laid down in EU laws and treaties (35-40%), international obligations (35%) and about 20% were initiated by demands of national governments or interest groups (NB This fact would be better in the text!) (see: Hooghe/Marks: Multi-Level Governance and European Integration 2001 p. 13; slightly different but overall very similar figures are provided by Strohmeier: Die Europäische Kommission im Gefüge von Politikberatung und Lobbying, in: Dagger/Kambeck (hrsg): Politikberatung und Lobbying in Brüssel 2007 p. 62).

43 Kassim/Menon/Peters (eds): The National Co-ordination of EU Policy 2004; Kassim/Menon/Peters (eds): The National Co-ordination of EU Policy – The domestic level 2003; Bekke/van der Meer (eds): Civil Service Systems in Western Europe 2000; Egeberg: Transcending Intergovernmentalism? 1999; Trondal: Beyond the EU membership-non-membership dichotomy? 2002; Trondal/Veggeland: Access, Voice and loyalty 2003; Beyers/Trondale: How Nation-States "Hit" Europe 2003; John: Europeanization in a Centralized State; in: Jeffery (eds): The Regional Dimension of the European Union 1997.

comes to the implementation of existing European Directives and Regulations. Mostly representing their countries in specific *comitology* committees (see below) on specialised issues, they are in contact with specific services or units of the Commission.[44] For these national bodies, two lines of communication are open: official ones (i.e. receiving and responding to official contacts and documents – in many cases via their Permanent Representation) and unofficial ones, discussion of specific problems or details directly with their counterparts in the Commission services. Depending on the time that a national official has been working in a specific field, they can create their own personal networks for exchanging information and discussing issues informally. In some cases, national civil servants could even be more knowledgeable than their counterpart in the Commission services because of the relative mobility of officials within the Commission. This could give them a certain advantage by playing the role of the more experienced actor ("your predecessor said ...", "it was decided in the past ...") or by allowing for finding a better solution with a new official. But it could also become a problem, if a common understanding between them and the previous European officials on specific points is modified or ignored by the successor.

2.3.3.2 Four selected Member States in a multi-level network

Comparing the four Member States selected in this study (Germany, The United Kingdom, Austria and Poland), Poland has a unique position. Not so much because it is one of the newest EU Member States, but because of its more recent changes in its political, social and economic systems, moving from a "state-led society" to a society which will include several elements that can be found in the "old" Member States but also developing its own specific characteristics. These transition phases makes it more difficult for researchers but also for the public within and outside Poland to identify which changes are more influenced by a general move to "catch up" with the more economy-based systems of Western European countries, which are more strongly related to changes required by EU laws and the famous *"Acquis communautaire"*. Closer links to specific European

44 Geuijen et al have highlighted this change in "foreign" policy from one line of information (via the ministries of foreign affairs) to a more de-centralised approach of specialised authorities or agencies dealing directly with their counterparts in the Commission and other Member States ("direct-dial diplomacy") (Geuijen/'THart/Princen/Yesilkagit: The New Eurocrats 2008 p. 15ff.)

policy fields or implementation systems might have also been developed by small "enclaves" of individuals or small groups[45]. In addition, both the economic and the administrative sectors have different external incentives for cooperating or change: Companies were in many cases bought by Western competitors which were introducing their own technologies, manufacturing processes and administrative and financial structures. Compared to the economic sector where combining political and economic interests was a new concept that still needed strong efforts by national actors to adapt, public administrations had a stronger and more independent role vis-à-vis external interests. The post-communist system could rely on an organised administration that – while also in transition – was stable enough to defend its position vis-à-vis other international or EU actors.

The other three Member States (for reasons of simplification *Western* Germany is used here as a reference for the implementation of the CPD) could look back at relatively stable and "uneventful" evolution over the last 50 years. This is reflected in the position of their civil services as providing a stable administration (which is not so different from the situation in Poland), and even a balancing factor "vis-à-vis the political forces that shape the life of the state".[46] Nevertheless, all four administrations have in common that, over the last decades pressure was increasing (either initiated by the public or by their own governments) to improve their efficiency or to outsource some of their tasks to (assumed) more efficient and effective private actors. This has forced administrations to abandon some of their monopoly positions (i.e. shifting the responsibility of building control to private actors), but with the loss of them, they were also motivated to shift their approaches more and more from being "authoritative institutions" (i.e. setting rules, monitoring and enforcing them) to "mediating institutions"[47] (leaving some of these tasks or parts of it to actors outside the public administration). Communication, coordination and convincing actors have set new requirements on existing systems.

45 See: Goetz: Making sense of post-communist central administration 2001.

46 Goetz: The Development and Current Features of the German Civil Service System, in: Bekke/van der Meer (eds): Civil Service Systems in Western Europe 2000 p. 66 citing the German Federal Court of Constitution; see also: Fry: The British Civil Service System; in: Bekke/van der Meer (eds): Civil Service Systems in Western Europe 2000.

47 Bekke, Hans A.G.M./van der Meer, Frits: Civil Service Systems in Western Europe: An Introduction; in: Bekke/van der Meer (eds): Civil Service Systems in Western Europe 2000 p. 3.

The United Kingdom[48] seems to be the administration that is the least affected by becoming a mediator because this role was already a strong part of its function in the national system. At national level, authorities are intervening or monitoring less on a regular basis (the so-called "police patrol" approach) but remain more reactive in case of irregularities and illegal practices (the "fire brigade" approach). The lack of active monitoring and administrative interventions have been compensated by a stronger emphasis on commonly shared social values (the "society-led state" model) and providing information to all interested parties and citizens, and therefore allowing *them* to react and inform the authorities. However, when interacting with EU institutions and other Member States at EU level, the system introduced is in fact the "police patrol" approach. Being one of the more sceptical countries when it comes to European activities, the UK´s Permanent Representation (UKREP) aims at monitoring *all* activities and reporting back to all relevant national ministries which coordinate their positions on national level between the different departments, but also with industry and other interested parties, as soon as possible to be able to act on their behalf at a very early stage of the decision finding process on EU level. This ("corporate actor") approach also supports an early discussion at national level and reduces the risk of contradictory positions by different UK officials all representing their country in Brussels ("singing from the same hymn sheet"). This high level of coordination within the national administration and therefore the strong consistency in positions of UK representatives was also practically not affected by changes from Euro-sceptic to Europhile ministers or *vice versa* in different ministries.

The UK preference and ability to coordinate different public and private actors is also based on a specific development in its civil service: Generally, decision-making positions are filled with generalists, who have accumulated experience rather than with (technical or scientific) experts – as in Germany and

48 See: Kassim: Representing the United Kingdom in Brussels; in: Kassim/Menon/Peters (eds): The National Co-ordination of EU Policy 2004; Kassim: The United Kingdom; in: Kassim/ Menon/Peters (eds): The National Co-ordination of EU Policy – The domestic level 2003, Knill: The Europeanisation of National Administrations 2001; Wallace: Relations between the European Union and the British administration, in: Mény/Muller/Quermonne (eds.): Adjusting to Europe 1996; van Schendelen: Machiavelli in Brussels 2005 p. 135; John: Europeanization in a Centralized State; in: Jeffery (eds): The Regional Dimension of the European Union 1997; Jeffery: Regional Information Offices in Brussels and Multi-Level Governance in the EU; in: Jeffery (eds): The Regional Dimension of the European Union 1997.

Austria. Experts can be found in a separate hierarchy in the UK, supposed to provide technical advice rather than being involved in policy formulation. Germany, Austria and Poland on the other hand have established a system where policy is developed (mostly) by experts (job descriptions already require a specific education and expertise) who might *in addition* require specific expertise. Additionally, German or Austrian civil servants are not expected to change their position regularly (in contrast to UK administrators) and therefore they are accumulating additional expert knowledge in their specific field. The advantage is that administrations have technical or scientific expertise already "in house" (as well as technical or scientific experts from outside). Therefore, the administration can easily communicate with other actors on a common level of expert knowledge. On the other hand, rarely specific requirements have been formulated for coordination and communication abilities, which might make it more difficult for actors *outside* a specific field of expertise to have their position taken into consideration.

The UK administrative system also enjoys a higher level of flexibility compared with its "continental" counterparts. This can be explained by the strong position of the central government in the past (including the lack of coalitions of political parties as governments) when defining (and shifting) administrative competences on or between central and sub-central administrations ("the fastest law in the West"[49]). Its executive leadership can only be challenged by Parliament but otherwise no (legal) veto players could interfere with government decisions (in contrast to institutionalised veto players – i.e. the *Länder* – in Germany and Austria).[50] It is also one of the characteristics of the UK system that bodies are often created on an *ad hoc* basis rather than placing new responsibilities on existing bodies or structures. But while the stability of an administrative structure and the competences allocated to specific bodies is rather low, they have a high degree of autonomy on how to do their work (in particular by clearly separating national and local politics), being less "constrained" by legal or administrative guidance and requirements.

49 See: Knill: The Europeanisation of National Administrations 2001 p. 102 citing Dunleavy.

50 The UK also lacks strong federations which represent a large number of members in an discussion and bargaining process, as well as the fact that these federations are not strongly linked to political parties to allow them a stronger influence on the party level.

Germany and Austria[51] too have established their systems for coordinating different sectoral policies and positions. However, they have chosen the opposite approach: Due to the role of Germany as a more integrating force in the EU, monitoring of EU initiatives is more focused on "deviance" from German interests (the "fire brigade" approach) which needs less resources at the early stage of any development on EU level, but demands clearly more (and late) efforts at a later stage if reactions are needed. Austria is following more or less the same approach, but in this case it might be much more a question of available resources than an intended policy. On national level, authorities are supposed to put more resources in monitoring and controlling (the "police patrol" approach), based on the concept that national authorities have a stronger responsibility than citizens vis-à-vis society (the "state-led society" model) – a responsibility that is laid down in national law and binds the administrations stronger to it (*Gesetzesbindung der Verwaltung*). While the interested parties on national level (the *Länder*, chambers of commerce, associations, unions and NGOs) are in many cases part of any consultation process (aiming at a system of consensual interaction with other actors, but always under the "shadow of the law"[52]) for issues developed at EU level, it is clear that national and regional authorities have a more ambivalent and sceptical position vis-à-vis other interested parties than UK authorities. Therefore, their positions might be influenced by two different (and

---

51 See: Derlien: Germany; in: Kassim/Menon/Peters (eds): The National Co-ordination of EU Policy – The domestic level 2003; Maurer/Wessels: Germany; in: Kassim/Menon/Peters (eds): The National Co-ordination of EU Policy – The domestic level 2003, Müller, Wolfgang C.: Austria; in: Kassim/Menon/Peters (eds): The National Co-ordination of EU Policy – The domestic level 2003; Müller: Ministerial Government at the European level: The Case of Austria; in: Kassim/Menon/Peters (eds): The National Co-ordination of EU Policy 2004; Knill: The Europeanisation of National Administrations 2001; Schmidt: Procedural Democracy in the EU 2006; Falkner, Gerda: The Europeanisation of Austria 2001; Wessels/Rometsch: German administrative interaction and the European Union, in: Mény/Muller/Quermonne (eds.): Adjusting to Europe 1996; van Schendelen: Machiavelli in Brussels 2005 p. 135ff.; Jeffery: Farewell the Third Level? in: Jeffery (eds): The Regional Dimension of the European Union 1997; Jeffery: Regional Information Offices in Brussels and Multi-Level Governance in the EU; in: Jeffery (eds): The Regional Dimension of the European Union 1997; Morass: Austria: The Case of a Federal Newcomer in European Union Politics; in: Jeffery (eds): The Regional Dimension of the European Union 1997.

52 *Van Schendelen* als highlights that the long internal deliberation process of this "collective actor" approach causes actors to arrive late at the EU level to contribute to the discussion. This limits the input often to a more formalistic approach, because the period of less formal interaction has already passed. (van Schendelen: Machiavelli in Brussels 2005 p. 136ff.).

maybe even contradicting) positions of supporting the interests of national actors on the one hand[53] while on the other hand avoiding that their monitoring and controlling potential vis-à-vis these national actors would be reduced in the discussion on EU level.

Sectoral ministries play a stronger role and focus more on their specific policies in both Germany and Austria. Therefore, also monitoring activities at EU level or even cooperation of specific ministries with committees working in Brussels is more specific and based on the interests and activities at national level. Due to the federal structures of Germany and Austria, the regions (*Länder*) are involved in the EU decision-finding process and even keep their own representations in Brussels[54]. These mostly consult or coordinate with the activities of federal ministries vis-à-vis the Commission services, but sometimes they also work as independent actors or even representing the whole nation in specific committees. However, in general, *Länder* representatives and other interested parties do not play a strong *active* role but are mostly observers. The less-intensive coordination and the dual system of national and *Länder* representation might force the responsible ministries and their representatives at EU level to reduce national (i.e. interdepartmental) conflicts by defining and presenting the *lowest common denominator*, which might reduce their flexibility in the negotiation process significantly, or positions presented by different ministries might be (slightly) contradictory. On the other hand, the departmentalisation

53 Both the German and the Austrian systems include a large number of "veto-players" on *Länder* level, which is increasing the stability of the system (changes need more consensus and are more "expensive" in the discussion and bargaining process) but also decreasing its flexibility in regional policy or the European multi-level system ("joint decision trap". (see: Benz: Entflechtung als Folge von Verflechtung, 2000 p. 158f. and Scharpf: The joint-decision trap, 1997 p. 155; Kohler-Koch: European Networks and Ideas 2002 p. 9)

54 Börzel: States and Regions in the European Union 2002; Derlien: Germany; in: Kassim/Menon/Peters (eds): The National Co-ordination of EU Policy – The domestic level 2003; Maurer/Wessels: Germany; in: Kassim/Menon/Peters (eds): The National Co-ordination of EU Policy – The domestic level 2003Müller, Wolfgang C.: Austria; in: Kassim/Menon/Peters (eds): The National Co-ordination of EU Policy – The domestic level 2003; Müller: Ministerial Government at the European level: The Case of Austria; in: Kassim/Menon/Peters (eds): The National Co-ordination of EU Policy 2004; Keating/Hooghe: Bypassing the nation state? in: Richardson (ed): European Union 2006 p. 275f.; Scharpf: Föderale Politikverflechtung 1999; Jeffery: Farewell the Third Level? in: Jeffery (eds): The Regional Dimension of the European Union 1997; Morass, Michael: Austria: The Case of a Federal Newcomer in European Union Politics; in: Jeffery (eds): The Regional Dimension of the European Union 1997.

allows continuing cooperation in other policy fields (which would be less likely in the UK if a common position could not be defined).

Another difference between the two countries is based on the position of Germany as a "founding member" and Austria as "accession country". Joining the EU in 1995, Austria had on the one hand to accept several decisions and legislations developed before the accession, without being able to influence them, on the other hand it had the advantage to learn from past experience of the "older" Member States – in particular from Germany as to which specific systems could even been copied and only slightly adapted – and therefore the chance to adjust its system with lower adaptation costs. However, Austria and in particular the Austrian *Länder* have in many policy and administrative fields less resources available than their German counterparts. This fact either initiated attempts to make their system more efficient or resulted in less participation and input at EU level[55].

In general, nation states and their administrations are both very trusting and very sceptical at the same time. Trusting actors in certain parts of the decision-making process and leaving them practically unobserved, other parts are intensively monitored[56]. It is interesting to note that Member States in general keep their focus on *EU* institutions, despite the fact that "harm" for national interests (in particular economic ones) is less likely to come from EU institutions but more from (economic) competitors operating in other Member States (e.g. blocking entrance of products into a national market or entering other national markets). This could indicate a certain (certainly not complete) trust in the conform

55 Another difference between the two countries is the weaker federal framework in Austria, which leaves on the one hand many competences in the hands of the Federal State ("zentralistischer Bundesstaat"/ "Federation without Federalism"), on the other hand, competences of the *Länder* are therefore strongly defended and could result in different positions about the most efficient implementation of policies and laws. (see: Mayer: Verfassung im Spannungsfeld politischer Interessen 2005; Bussjäger: Homogenität und Differenz 2006; Steger (Hsrg.): Baustelle Bundesstaat 2007) – see also the chapters describing the positions of Austrian actors on EU and national level.

56 My observations (and existing research work) have focused on national actors "fighting" on their own. What would be interesting for further research if, when and how Member States are (intentionally or unintentionally) splitting the work of monitoring the activities on EU level. Now with 27 Member States, it is less and less likely that European institutions could be active without at least *one* Member State noticing it. This does not necessarily indicate an exchange of information between Member States. The fact that one is reacting (in particular in the *comitology* committees) might "appear on the radar" of other Member States and alert them on developments on EU level that they might have missed otherwise.

behaviour of actors in other Member States and the assumption that the Commission services are acting effectively as monitoring and sanctioning mechanism.

2.3.4 Federations[57] *– industry's "early-warning system"*

The moment one crosses the line from authorities or public bodies representing a specific (national) position to private actors, the image of the discussion process changes. By institutionalising the interaction between authorities (based on treaties or laws), it is not only an acceptable and highly formalised way of communication, it becomes nearly "natural". Private actors on the other hand trying to introduce their point of view into this official discussion can only partly refer to a given right, and often even if this right exists the resources are lacking for active participation. Looking for less formalised but potentially more effective ways of interacting with authorities puts non-governmental organisations (NGOs), no matter if they are working on economic, environmental or social issues, into the large group of "lobbyists" – the "grey area" of political intervention.

Working somewhere beneath the radar of the public and journalist's scrutiny, "lobbying" became a synonym for activities that *on purpose* are hidden from the public. If the issue at hand is also more of a technical than a political nature, it is transferred to a specific technical body (i.e. the *comitology* committees) which are often far beyond the technical expertise or interest of most actors (and rarely providing a chance for mobilising the public – "outside lobbying" – outside this specific field of expertise for actions), and therefore leaving the field more or less completely to experts appointed either by national administrations or specialised interest groups. Finding different terms for describing this type of activity (like "*advocacy*" or "*Politikberatung*") unintentionally even increases the suspicion that something *is being* camouflaged ("where there is smoke …") and negative terms like "*lobbycracy*" achieved more popularity than neutral or more descriptive terms. This image is even strengthened by some "lobbying" actors themselves when describing the potentials and working methods of some actors competing with them: while their own group is mostly seen as small but

57 Practically all interested parties involved in the discussion process in the CPD are represented by federations. "Classical" non-government organisations in the environmental and social field are nearly completely missing, but will be dealt with later in this chapter.

dedicated to its task, any competing actor is by definition stronger (in resources) and more ruthless in achieving a goal. In addition, only a few political systems (at EU, national and regional levels) have managed to develop a transparent mechanism for identifying non-state actors' "lobbying", the lines of communication used, or even providing a good definition helping to identify what might still be within and what would be outside "acceptable" lobbying work[58].

Looking a little bit more closely at "lobbying" as form of discussion and intervention, one will find a system that is as complex and demanding to each individual involved as the one that representatives of public bodies have created and are working with. Even the line between public bodies and private actors vanishes, because regional bodies or authorities in different ministries and agencies might also have decided to use more informal routes to get and provide information – in particular if they do not consider their position well represented by the formal representatives. Also very similar to the relationship between European institutions and national ones, lobbying too is seen as a *competition* between different interests, where each side is trying to make the others adopt its own position.

However, research on lobbying has a strong focus on the activities of *lobbyists*, their interests and approaches[59]. Public bodies, parliaments and governments are in this concept either seen as more passive actors, or their own activities to defend and maintain their positions has been of less interest for researchers. This image of very *active private actors* versus *passive institutions* gives the impression that actors outside institutionalised political and administrative structures not only have a strong role when discussing policies or proposals for laws but also play a strong part by *initiating* new proposals. While this

58 In 1993 the Commission published a report indicating that about 3.000 interest groups with about 10.000 employees have been established in Brussels with about 500 of these groups with a European scope and transnational interests. (EC Communication: „An open and structured dialogue between the Commission and interest groups") In the meantime the interest in lobbying seems to have been increased (but also more Member States have joined and brought their „lobbyists" with them: Now about 13.500 men and women are working for about 700 professional associations, 400 interest groups. (Goergen: Lobbying in Brussels 2006 p.22 – see also: EC Register of interest representatives: http://ec.europa.eu/transparency/regrin/)

59 Roose: Die Europäisierung von Umweltorganisationen; 2002; Schendelen: Machiavelli in Brussels 2005; Goergen: Lobbying in Brussels 2006; Desselas: Un lobbying professionnel à visage découvert 2007; Kleinfeld/Zimmer/Willems et. Al: Lobbying 2007; Dagger/Kambeck (hrsg): Politikberatung und Lobbying in Brüssel 2007; Mahoney: Brussels versus the Beltway 2008;

reflects the image of a modern society as a framework for dialogue and as a consensus-finding system, it seems less obvious that private actors are significant "instigators" in particular when it comes to practical implementation: the creation of a law. This is because on the one hand, it is hard to prove that a specific position has *actually* influenced an ongoing discussion (which makes it hard for researchers to identify the actual contribution of any interested party). On the other hand, it is also because political institutions and administrations have in most cases more resources at their disposal to develop their own ideas and legal texts. This fact forces other actors to spend *their* resources more on monitoring political and administrative activities ("constantly fire fighting"[60]) rather than using them for more directly active approaches.

A second argument against the image of institutions as passive "targets" for private interested parties is the interest of institutions in including actors from different levels in the discussion at an early stage[61]. This should not only be seen as an early attempt at "testing the water" but also as the first opportunity of *convincing* other actors of this proposal. In the case of the European Union, the unique position of the European Commission as the only institution legally empowered to make proposals[62], the dependency of all other actors on the willingness of the Commission (services) to allow them access to the discussion process is even stronger. If actors want to form and modify a Commission proposal, alternative routes via the European Parliament and/or the Council might be too late. In any case, depending on national authorities is even adding an additional layer between an actor and the Commission and therefore reducing his or her influence.

Developing this argument further: because of the large number of public, private, political and economic interests that are part of a modern society, there are more actors competing with each other to make their position known rather

60 Mahoney: Brussels versus the Beltway; 2008 p. 33.

61 In the case of the Commission by announcing all legislative initiatives in advance in an annual work programme and by providing a consultation plan when and how interested parties will be consulted. Also Commission Communications, "Green Books" and "White Books" can be considered as first signals of the Commission services' intentions, inviting discussion before work on European legislation per se is started. (see: Kohler-Koch: European Networks and Ideas 2002).

62 The European Council can make recommendations, but it (at least in theory) is up to the Commission to decide if and when it should act on these recommendations. The European Parliament is even more a reactive actor, being officially involved only after the Commission's proposal has been finalised.

than "targets". This gives the latter a very strong position vis-à-vis any lobbying attempt. In addition, even well-organised industry sectors or professions are often not able to agree on one common position but are faced with competing members having different positions[63]. Therefore, actors working as interfaces between "Brussels" and their members (be they federations themselves or individual companies) are forced to take only a very general position vis-à-vis European institutions, and have only limited guidance on where and how they could influence a proposal in the often several and varied interests of their members. The variety of members might also complicate the communication flow to such an extent where information could not be provided fast enough and – even more important – their feedback would not be received in time. Therefore, if federations want to actively influence the decision-making process within the European institutions, they have to depend in quiet a number of cases on their own sector-specific or individual knowledge and their individual expertise on where and how this has to be brought into the discussion.

But just stating a position will in most cases not be enough to ensure that it will not easily replaced by another argument from a competing group. Only actors who can support their arguments with (reliable) data are providing an added value to the discussion and are strengthening their position vis-à-vis the Commission, the Parliament or the Council. Therefore, (non-governmental) actors have a strong interest in being aware of new developments within the Commission so as to inform their members at national and/or regional levels to ensure that feedback and data be available soon enough to be taken into consideration in the starting discussion process. It is their ability to get enough support from their members who provide technical expertise (by either sending experts to conferences or let them evaluate European proposals), which gives them either an important role as useful partners for European institutions or leaves them only with the role as less influential "observers" in the decision-making process.[64]

63 In the construction sector, competition between different materials used for the same construction product could create friction between members of the same federation (or the creation of several – material-specific – federations). Similar, the profession of architects shows a wide range of national interests, in particular the definition of its profession, access to the market and established national monopolies. (Greenwood: Interest Representation in the European Union 2007 p. 73ff.).

64 Interviewees of this study have highlighted that an important aspect of "lobbying" work is to ask questions and to clarify points on an informal level, which provides everybody ("lobbyists" and their "targets") with a more nuanced position than the formal approach (mostly via official "position papers" or complaints) would provide.

Closing that argument that when looking at other "interested parties" (industry federations and other public or private organisations) in the discussion process, the emphasis should shift from pro-active "lobbyists" to more *re*active actors, their position becomes even less "threatening" when considering the number of potential Directorates-General in the Commission, its agencies and units that could develop policies or regulations that might affect specific interests. Compared with the above-mentioned assumption that always "the others" have more resources at hand, most interested parties (no matter whether in the environmental, social or economic fields) have to operate with only a few employees. To cover their interests, but also just to learn how the "system" is working, they have either to specialise in specific issues and abandon issues of lower priority (with a higher risk that they are more likely "by-passed" by their members or strong companies), or to create networks with actors with similar interests, each covering special issues and keeping the others informed. This already requires already a certain amount of trust in each other, such that no relevant fact be ignored but brought to the attention of the federations affected.[65] (On the other hand, due to the rather small community of individuals in this field, free-riders could easily be identified and excluded from this network.) In addition, interested parties who have strong national interest groups, federations or companies as members could also share the burden with national actors, who could also represent the European body in the discussion. In some cases this type of splitting responsibilities is actively pursued by European and national actors, leaving the European actors in general the role as "early-warning system".[66]

However, "lobbying" on issues dealt with at EU level is for interested parties mostly a *multi*-level activity: While the text of a law is written by the Commission services, *Member State representatives* are voting for or against it. Therefore, at least these two levels have to be covered to give any intervention certain likeliness for success. (see also: Mahoney: Brussels versus the Beltway 2008 p.139f.).

65 Another level of trust is displayed on national federation or company level investing in "lobbying" work. In particular when the actual impact is often not visible or cannot be clearly linked to specific activities. Since the final result is a combination of different position, interests and their interpretation by EU institutions, "one cannot always measure the output of "lobbying" – one has to believe in it" (as one interviewee in this study phrased it).

66 *Greenwood* has identified only few industry federations larger than 20 employees on EU level (with only one of them belonging to the construction sector: the federation of the cement manufacturers – CEMBUREAU) which leaves most federations highly dependent on support from their members and only little autonomy from their interests. However, "federations of federations" seem to have established a system of burden-sharing that gives the European one still

Therefore, four main aspects are best describing interested parties and their tasks and activities:

- a strong focus on monitoring and analysing activities at EU level, in particular the Commission services;
- being able to identify the needs of their supporting members at national and/or regional levels and keeping the information flow open in both directions;
- coordinating members and ensure their support and feedback for data and/or experts, so as to allow active participation in the discussion process;
- coordination with similar actors to share the burden of monitoring and reporting;

It is obvious that federations have more or less the same tasks as national authorities. The main differences are that there is no obligation from the Commission services to *actively* provide information to them. Compared with the obligatory lines of communication between the Commission and Member States, federations depend more on the "good will" of the EU services and their own network. Due to the risks of missing information in this non-formalised communication network, private actors are also more likely to be contacting other actors at EU level or in other Member States than would their own national authorities.

National and international federations have no direct role in the decision-making process but they are well aware that political decisions and regulatory provisions developed at the European level could significantly influence their working environment. Being informed even about planned initiatives by the European Commission or the European Parliament, defending the interest of their members and informing their members about specific developments and potential impacts of one or the other activity on European level are the main roles of these federations.

Being in most cases installed as monitoring and lobbying instruments for *market* actors, industry federations could – at least in theory – be *the* most obvious representatives of the *homo economicus*. Being able to focus on few issues they could defend the interest of their members, leaving the coordination work to EU institutions and national authorities. Also the lack of control by national federations gives them enough leeway to decide on tactics – but also

more room for manoeuvre than federations representing companies (Greenwood: Interest Representation in the European Union 2007 p. 53ff.).

how to present the outcome of their activities in a way most favourable for them. However, as shown, they also have to face limitations in manpower and information, making them highly dependent on external input. In particular if the actors they want to influence are professionalising themselves and are demanding higher quality and quantity of data and a more professional presentation and argumentation by "lobbyists". Here a split between two different types of (industry) actors is necessary: federations, which have to cover a wide field of interests (diversity of their members) and depend on external input; and individual companies, which could more easily focus on single issues and bypass the consensus-finding process within federations. The former is strongly driven to accept rules – even if they are not enforced – because similar behaviour would improve their relatively weak position. The latter can act relatively unaffected by these concerns and could *de facto* represent the profit-oriented *homo economicus*.

2.3.5 Technical specification writers – the Men in Black?

The focus on European and national institutions as "agenda-setting" actors working on the legal and administrative framework is a very logical first step when looking into the creation and implementation of pan-European schemes. However, in many fields of European and national economies, the specific issues at hand are far too technical to be sufficiently covered at the administrative level. Here policies, laws and administrative requirements are defining system boundaries in very general terms, leaving more detailed and practical requirements to the discretion of other (technical) bodies. These bodies could be specialised public bodies or private bodies (who are sometimes closely linked to public administrations, or financially supported to fulfil this specific task, or even private bodies independent from the intervention of public administrations).

The best examples for this type of more or less close cooperation are standardisation bodies. In most Member States of the EU these bodies are completely private enterprises, but several of them are receiving financial support from specific national authorities and/or have specific contracts with them. Also in most cases (in particular in all four countries selected in this study) these standardisation organisations have a clearly defined or at least *de facto* monopoly on developing standards used in their countries. The same applies for the European Standardisation Organisation CEN which has officially a monopolistic position in the EU.

It is necessary to look more closely at the position and function of standardisation bodies in Europe, because they play a major role in implementing several national laws and European Directives – including the Construction Products Directive. In many technical fields, technical standards (or in general: *technical specifications*)[67] are *the* instrument for communicating how to design or how to use products in specific sectors. They are the basis for professional training, provide reference for communication between different actors in the same sector (e.g. architects and construction companies), and last but not least, provide very essential (but not the only) references in legal cases.

The increasing use of standards commonly accepted by a large group of actors (compared with locally used standards) and therefore the increasing importance of national standardisation bodies was a process which has been ongoing over the last century, during which several interested parties became involved. Starting with governments and their administrations to guarantee a level of quality in specific fields (i.e. infrastructure and the military), consumer protection and health-related issues introduced several other interested parties (and strengthened the position of the public administration as implementers of national safety laws) in the eighties and nineties of the 20th century. In addition, the complexity of technical systems (i.e. machines, buildings, IT) led to a system of more and more providers of *elements* to the system which had to exchange information on requirements and performance between their business partners. At least equally important became the arrival of foreign competitors on national markets. For different reasons, public and private actors demanded more transparency from and for national industries. A demand that was (at least partly) fulfilled by producing technical standards which – correctly used – would guarantee commonly accepted data quality and comparable product performances. As an additional bonus, national standards could on the one hand provide information to other national actors and business partners, while on the other hand they could also define performance criteria and levels that could easily be fulfilled by existing *national* industries, but which were more difficult to achieve or to prove by foreign competitors.

---

67 Standardisation bodies have a wide range of technical documents of different nature and importance at their disposal to cover different needs of their private or public customers. Technical standards are the most well known, giving in many cases very detailed information on design issues or on the use of specific products. Other means are technical reports which are more focussed on a "state-of-the-art" description in a specific field, or more general guidance in various forms.

While several parties might be interested in the development and use of technical standards, their development lies *de facto* in the hands of the industry sectors manufacturing or using specific products. National standardisation bodies provide the organisational framework and the procedure to guarantee the acceptance of the produced standards, but industry representatives and experts are the ones discussing and selecting technical parameters and technical solutions. Other actors are – in theory – allowed to participate or at least to follow the standardisation work but, due to the huge number of man-hours and technical expertise needed in this work, even within an industry sector only few actors could provide enough resources for a continuous and active participation.[68] Therefore, public administrations and other interested parties still put a strong emphasis on additional instruments to balance their disadvantaged position in the standardisation work. While public authorities could add requirements or introduce additional actors as controlling bodies into the system, other interested parties (in particular NGOs) are more active at the political level, trying to influence the preciseness of a law under discussion or by cooperating with national authorities when adding additional requirements to the finalised standards.

Moving now to the European level, CEN is in the same position as its national members, depending on the expert input and cooperation from industry sectors (even when they are nominated by national standardisation bodies). Compared to national approaches standardisation at EU level is facing some additional challenges, very similar to the ones that national administrations and federations are facing when entering the transnational arena: a larger number of (unknown) actors involved, different (national) approaches, potential language barriers, a more complex interpretation and communication role for national representatives. CEN meetings could also be hosted in different Member States which increases the costs just for participation at a level that might eliminate smaller actors from the discussion process or at least restrict their participation. Also comparable to national standardisation, harmonising does not only facilitate

68 At first, mostly consumer protection organisations and later more and more environmental organisations. Since the Commission cannot *force* one of the European standardisation organisations (CEN, CENELEC and ETSI) to include these interested parties in specific standardisation work, it worked more with financial support to get additional groups involved. For small and medium enterprises a special organsiation – NORMAPME –s generally monitors and contributes to the standardiszation work. (see also: Bücker/Schlacke: Die Entstehung einer "politischen Verwaltung" durch EG-Ausschüsse, in: Joerges/Falke (Hrsg.): Das Ausschusswesen der Europäischen Union 2000 p. 202f.).

entering new markets (within the European Union), it also opens (national and/or previously more "secluded") markets to competitors within and outside the EU.

Member State authorities might see the shift of standardisation work to the EU level as limiting their abilities to "correct" developments in standardisation work via additional administrative requirements (depending on how much room for manoeuvre they had under their national schemes). On the other hand, putting emphasis on specific technical requirements on EU level could be used to influence priorities on national level – and therefore strengthening or weakening positions of (other) national public or private actors.

Accordingly, the harmonisation of technical approaches at EU level is not seen by all interested parties as an advantage *per se*. Moving the process to less-known arenas might decrease the possibilities for several actors to follow developments and might make them feel as if they are losing more and more control of the process. In addition, increasing the costs for participation might reduce the heterogeneity of the parties involved to a small number which might reduce the credibility of the approach. Starting standardisation work at EU level also increases the risk that national compromises between different parties might no longer be valid and the discussion be reopened on EU level – now with some of the (previously involved) national parties missing.

But if European standardisation has these (potentially) severe setbacks – why is it used anyway? Firstly, reopening political discussions at a technical level is not seen by everybody as a disadvantage. Not only national actors who have not been so successful at national level might find this approach appealing, but also new developments that could demand changes in national standards might be achieved faster by doing it already at EU level. Another reason – in particular for smaller or export-oriented countries in the EU – this approach reduces their costs for adaptation to several different national schemes presently in place. European standards might also remove or at least "soften" the dominance of specific national competitors: in general, actors with more resources could adapt more easily to different requirements and could even use the existing *lack* of harmonisation as an advantage against smaller competitors (or even support more additional *national* requirements). Harmonisation at technical level would at least partly reduce this advantage. Last but not least: what is valid for national markets also applies for the European Internal Market: imports from outside the EU indicates either strong competitors (for technically more developed products) or low-price products. In both cases European standards could set additional requirements – based on the experience and expertise of *European* industries.[69]

2.4 "After the dust has settled ..." – the implementation of EU legislation by national actors

The previous chapters have covered several types of interactions between different actors at EU level, defining policies as well as developing and discussing European legislation. Reaching the next level – *transposition*, *implementation* and *enforcement* (TIE) – the actors might be the same by name ("the Commission", "Member States"), but in fact the new tasks have in most cases been shifted to other authorities, organisations or units. Therefore, the complexity of the system has slightly changed because the text of legislation is reducing the options for each actor. On the other hand, with new bodies or individuals entering the system, they are facing to a large extent the same challenges of reducing complexity.

In recent years the transposition and implementation of EU legislation got more and more attention from researchers:[70] It is a phase where willingness and ability to cooperation by Member States "on their own turf" can be assessed. How fast and how complete have Member States implemented EU Regulations and Directives in national law? What could be delaying factors?[71] Do Member

69 It should be mentioned here that CEN is by definition *not* an instrument for excluding technical approaches or expertise from outside the EU. In fact, CEN and the International Standardization Organization (ISO) have an agreement of not duplicating work (the so-called "Vienna Agreement") and several ISO standards have been adopted by CEN as European standards and vice versa. However, complementary standards (being more detailed or more sector-specific) might be developed by each of them, which might give specific actors a chance to re-modify specific requirements.

70 Interests were directed at specific policies – environment, health and social – which allowed first comparisons in these fields, but left industrial and economic Directives mostly still "undiscovered countries".

71 Tallberg: Paths to Compliance 2000; Knill: The Europeanisation of National Administrations 2001; Weber: Umweltpolitische Steuerung in der Europäischen Union, in: Bauer/Voelzkow (Hrsg.): Die Europäische Union – Marionette oder Regisseur? 2004; Kaeding: Lost in Translation or Full Steam Ahead? 2007; Berglund/Gange/van Waarden: Mass production of law 2006; Börzel: Pace-Setting, Foot-Dragging, and Fence-Sitting 2001; Falkner/Hartlapp/Leiber/Treib: Transforming Social Policy in Europe? 2002; Versluis: Explaining Variations in Imple-

States face the same problems of finding consensus and getting support when the number of actors (in particular ones with vetoing power) is increasing? Also important is the reaction of the Commission on delayed transposition or incorrect implementation. How much discretion is given to Member States?[72] What are the driving factors for the Commission to act and start infringement proceedings?[73]

Previous research has shown a certain lack of predictability of national reactions and compliance. How much Member States were following the framework created and agreed at European level or how much different actors were influencing and changing the national implementation depended not only on the political, social, economic and administrative structures of a Member State, but also current priorities of different actors, perceptions of the need for adaptation or change, and developments at transnational level which might influence national systems. Being supportive and compliant in one political and regulatory field does not necessarily indicate that the same cooperation can be expected in another field or vice versa. Even within a political field (as we will see for construction products), positions might change. Therefore, national reactions and implementations of agreements reached at EU level are often shifting between theoretical "worlds" (see table below), making assumptions more difficult, but also leaving the "window of opportunity" for finding new compromises and solutions open for all actors.

mentation of EU Directives 2004; Kaeding: Lost in Translation or Full Steam Ahead 2008; Kohler-Koch: European Networks and Ideas 2002; Mastenbroek, Ellen: The Politics of Compliance 2007; Toshkov: Between Politics and Administration 2009; Steunenberg/Voermans: The transposition of EC directives 2006; Haverland/Romejin: Do Member States make European policies work? 2007.

72 Tallberg: Paths to Compliance 2000; Hartlapp/Falkner: Inkonsistent, inconsequent und intransparent? In: Bauer/Voelzkow (Hrsg.): Die Europäische Union – Marionette oder Regisseur? 2004 ; Peters: The Commission and Implementation in the European Union, in: Nugent (ed): At the Heart of the Union 2000 p.200f.

73 The perception that transposition, implementation and enforcement is a type of interaction purely between political and administrative actors at EU and national levels might partly be responsible for the very few cases where private parties are demanding the implementation of EU legislation by Member States – and even demanding compensation for economic losses. Since research is also focused on political and administrative actors, private actors remain a "blind spot" in the system.

Table 1: Member State compliance,
Source: Falkner et al: Complying with Europe p. 322

	World of law observance	**World of domestic politics**	**World of neglect**
Political importance of compliance with EU law	Highly valued, typically overrides domestic concerns	One ambition among many, domestic concerns frequently prevail	Not an aspiration per se
Transposition is typically ...	... on time and correct (even where conflicting domestic interests coexist)	... on time and correct only if there is no conflict with domestic concerns	... late and/or "pro forma"
Factors facilitating compliance	Culture of good compliance as a self-reinforcing social mechanism	Fit with preferences of government and major interest groups	Accelerating issue linkage with domestic reforms, high profile of particular cases
Conditions of non-compliance	Unawareness; otherwise non-compliance occurs rarely and briefly	Political failure (lack of compromise among conflicting interests or compromise against terms of EU law). If non-compliance occurs, it tends to be rather long-term	Bureaucratic failure (inefficiency, overload, non-attention). Non-compliance is the rule rather than the exception
Predominant logic	Cultural	Pursuit of political interests	Pursuit of interests within the administration
Typical process	Dutiful adaptation	Conflict/compromise	Inertia

However, complying, delaying and defying by Member States was so far studied only at the level of implementing directives – transposing them into national law. The advantage (and temptation) was that the Commission's scoreboard on compliance of Member States[74] allowed a first start with empirical data available.

74 See: Ziller: Europäische Implementierungsforschung 2006.

While there is more and more doubt as to whether undetected or untreated cases might not blur the picture, the empirical evidence shows that transformation and implementation of EU legislation on Member State level is very often only achieved *after* the officially agreed deadline for the transformation phase has already passed.[75] It has also been shown in several cases that this is not so much caused by any resistance of other interested parties, but by different administrative and organisational approaches trying to be the most efficient within a national structure. Rather than merely complying with European requirements, they also show willingness to improve national systems.[76]

In this study, the researched *transformation phase* is no longer relevant, because the CPD has been transposed into national laws several years ago.[77] But this does not make the theoretical concepts and empirical findings of this phase any less interesting when looking into the *implementation phase.* Several aspects and problems identified in *transposition* also apply in *implementation* and *enforcement* and will be used for assessing these "downstream" levels.[78] As we will see, the *implementation* is still ongoing – partly because new Member States have entered the system, partly because new standards are still produced and have to be implemented in all national systems, and partly because the *inter-*

75 Allio/Fandel: Making Europe work: improving the transposition, implementation and enforcement of EU legislation 2006; Berglund/Gange/van Waarden: Mass production of law. 2006; Sverdrup: Compliance and conflict resolution in the European Union 2002; Kaeding: Lost in Translation or Full Steam Ahead, 2008.

76 Berglund/Gange/van Waarden: Mass production of law 2006; Tallberg: Paths to Compliance 2000; Sverdrup: Compliance and conflict resolution in the European Union 2002; Berglund/Gange/van Waarden: Mass production of law. Routinization in the transposition of European directives 2006.

77 However, only one of the 12 Member States already being in the EC when the CPD was adopted – Denmark has transformed it into national law at the deadline of June 1991. The UK followed with only one month's delay, but Germany needed one additional year. Considering that the UK had only to introduce a national law, Germany needed in addition the implementation in the building laws of the *Länder*, which added another year and made the requirements of the CPD only applicable in Germany in July 1993. (Laylock/Graham/Fewings: The effective implementation of the CPD 1995 p. 121ff.).

78 Unfortunately, there is a certain lack of research results on how national approaches correspond or differ from the approaches defined in European legislation. Surprisingly, even in Member States with federal structures, interaction between local, regional and national/federal administrations has rarely been theoretically or empirically researched, and comparisons between the implementation of EU legislation and national/federal legislation are therefore not possible. (see also: Jordan: The Europeanization of National Government and Policy 2003 p.267; Sverdrup p. 12 & Levi-Faur p. 107 in: Graziano/Vink (eds): Europeanization 2008).

pretation of the CPD still keeps several actors busy, which leads directly to the problems of *enforcing* the Directive and *complying* with it.

In addition, compliance is only to a certain extent the task of (national/regional/local) authorities or within their power to enforce it. In several cases private bodies (i.e. standardisation institutes, test laboratories) are playing a significant role. As mentioned before, private bodies – in particular industry federations and/or companies – might use their influence via technical standards to introduce or defend their positions, but these actors too might have to face skepticism, resistance and even communication problems with other actors or even their own members.

Therefore, while using research on the implementation by national *authorities,* the following explanations for delays, deviations or misapplication developed in the debate on *transposing* European directives have been selected for describing different (intentional and unintentional) reactions in the *implementation* and the *enforcement phase by public authorities, as well as by private actors*:

- different cultural or political backgrounds could result in different interpretations and assumptions on correct compliance in different Member States ("policy misfit");[79]
- national administrative or political structures do not "fit" with the requirements of the Regulation/Directive and have to be adapted ("institutional misfit");
- lack of precision of directives leaves room for interpretation by all actors (the Commission, Member States and other interested parties) which has increased the risk of wrong or non-compliance;[80]

79 Allio/Fandel: Making Europe work: improving the transposition, implementation and enforcement of EU legislation 2006; Berglund/Gange/van Waarden: Mass production of law 2006; Versluis: Explaining Variations in Implementation of EU Directives 2004; see also: Hooghe/Marks: Multi-Level Governance and European Integration 2001 p. 76: Tallberg: Paths to Compliance 2000; Börzel/Hofmann/Sprungk: Why Do States not Obey the Law? 2003; Knill: The Europeanisation of National Administrations 2001; Falkner/Treib/Hartlapp/Leiber: Complying with Europe 2005 p. 24ff.; Kaeding: Lost in Translation or Full Steam Ahead 2008; Allio/Fandel: Making Europe work 2006.

80 Börzel/Hofmann/Sprungk: Why Do States not Obey the Law? 2003 p. 21ff; Tallberg: Paths of Compliance 2002 p. 613; Kaeding: Lost in Translation or Full Steam Ahead, 2008 p. 72ff.

- due to changes in the administrative structure or the introduction of new laws the number of actors is increasing, and therefore increasing the risks of deadlocks and delays;[81]
- domestic actors might have different interpretations or goals or oppose the approach defined in the Regulation/Directive which could result in a legislative or administrative "drift" on lower levels in the implementation system.[82]

The first three explanations include high-level actors which are the driving forces behind specific, national approaches. While the bargaining process might have been delegated to a small number of individuals or bodies, the discussion and acceptance at national level might include more actors, in particular ones that have vetoing power in the national discussion. They might be the individuals or bodies that have been involved in creating the EU legislation in the first place, coalition partners in governments, other interested parties closely linked to political parties or national parliaments which have to approve the agreement made at European level. As in this study, the additional actors often have a specific (here: technical) background. These "technical" actors can be seen as "fail-safe points" that should prevent or at least reduce any negative impact on national level. But these "fail-safe points" could also be used as a possibility to reopen discussions on specific points – either in line with the intentions of the "political" actors to "reclaim" ground that was lost during the bargaining process on EU level – or *against* the wishes of the political level.

Already in the second bullet point, additional and influential actors are introduced: Since Parliaments or specific parts of a national government are not involved in the practical implementation of laws they have developed and approved, these tasks have been delegated to public administrations or bodies given implementing powers. Theoretically, these delegated powers are clearly defined and restricted to very specific tasks. However in practice, these definitions could not always be too precise if they cover a wide range of policies. Not all practical implications could be foreseen at that stage and too-restrictive

81 Falkner/Treib/Hartlapp/Leiber: Complying with Europe 2005; Kaeding: Lost in Translation or Full Steam Ahead, 2008; Steunenberg: Turning Swift Policy-making into Deadlock 2006 p. 314; Versluis: Explaining Variations in Implementation of EU Directives 2004.

82 Falkner/Treib/Hartlapp/Leiber: Complying with Europe 2005; Kaeding: Lost in Translation or Full Steam Ahead, 2008; Versluis: Explaining Variations in Implementation of EU Directives 2004.

system boundaries could limit flexibility to a level that could contradict the primary political intentions. Therefore, in many cases national laws (similar to EU directives) remain very general, and leave a wide "room for manoevre" for public or private bodies in defining their own framework, responsibilities and duties.

The second and the fourth points are also linked to the potential problems if existing structures do not allow for implementation without (significant) changes. If the requirements of the Directive are very similar to existing national ones and therefore only few adaptations have to be made on national level, authorities should not have too many problems in introducing them, even if this would mean that several national authorities and bodies are involved. It is more complicated for authorities at Member State level (but also for the Commission) if a European Directive covers issues that were the responsibility of several national bodies in the past, but which were not coordinated to fulfil their previous specific administrative or technical tasks. These additional bodies are not always aware of the demands of their new responsibilities, and even if they are, the new European requirements might shift the balance between the interested parties involved. This would force all (national) actors to discuss and rearrange their roles and influence in the implementation process. Therefore, institutions remain highly resistant to fast adaptations ("historical institutionalism"), which does not mean that they are not adapting at all – but the pace is closer to the previous historical speed rather than to fast reactions. In addition, institutions try to stay as long as possible within a given path, preferring adjustments that are close to existing procedures. This rather conservative and path-dependent approach is only interrupted if an external crisis puts strong pressure on specific actors and bodies[83].

In general, *perceptions* and *goals* of different actors at national and local levels are the main factors for leading to deviation from the original intentions at EU level. Some of these perceptions are rooted in long-existing traditions within a political or administrative system. Changes are affecting established working

83 Jordan: The Europeanization of National Government and Policy 2003 p.267; Berglund et al: Mass production of law 2006 p. 712f.; Knill: The Europeanisation of National Administrations 2001; Kohler-Koch: European Networks and Ideas 2002; Ackermann: Pfadabhängigkeit, Institutionen und Regelreform 2001.

Roose is highlighting a similar risk for environmental NGOs. Experts specialised in a field might resist changes of policies and goals and therefore reducing the adaptability of NGOs. (Roose: Die Europäisierung von Umweltorganisationen 2002 p.245).

arrangements between different actors which will increase the level of uncertainty and might also increase the risks of misinterpretations. This could reduce the credibility of these actors in the eyes of other interested parties, not only in the new field but also in fields already covered. If previous work, interpretations and decisions of an actor have been facing negative reactions in the past, the new uncertainty might be used by other parties to underline the rightfulness of previous criticism. Therefore, actors will try to avoid this interference in established patterns, in particular if they are not convinced that the changes will provide more advantages after the implementation phase. Adaptation might also demand additional resources provided by lower-level actors which are not available or would significantly reduce their efficiency in other fields.

Increasing adaptation costs for downstream actors during the implementation phase or reducing their efficiency are very strong incentives for these actors to search and to use strategies avoiding this additional burden. It is not so important if these burdens *are* significant[84] – it depends on whether these actors *consider* them as significant to create a drift from the original EU goals to the interests of downstream actors. This resisting power of actors at downstream levels has been recognised in several studies and a closer look at the implementation of several EU directives has shown that downstream actors could have a strong influence on how national administrations e comply with EU directives.[85]

What is missing in most of the existing approaches is the influence on the *other* roles and tasks these downstream actors have to fulfil. Keeping in mind that most of them have not been especially established for the implementation of new European legislation but have been selected as the ones most likely to fulfil this task efficiently, they had – and most likely still have – to cover other tasks as well. This would not only relate to the implementation of national and/or regional laws, but also to the implementation of several EU policies and laws. Identify-

---

84 Mostly required in European Directives is the obligation of Member States to monitor or control specific requirements. The manpower used for inspections is mostly delegated to "downstream" authorities and bodies, which could (based on existing practice) opt for a more reactive inspection scheme ("fire brigade") to reduce adaptation costs. Market surveillance is an example where most Member States have chosen a very reactive approach and kept the numbers of inspectors rather low.

85 Versluis: Explaining Variations in Implementation of EU Directives 2004; Steunenberg: Turning Swift Policy-making into Deadlock 2006; European Commission: Thirteenth Annual Report 1996; Berglund/Gange/van Waarden: Mass production of law. Routinization in the transposition of European directives 2006; Kohler-Koch: European Networks and Ideas 2002.

ing priorities or at least the most relevant input from upstream (EU or national) actors might already create a situation of laws and policies "competing" for limited resources of actors at the national, regional and/or local levels. Even more important: these actors work in a specific environment with different interested parties involved. Keeping or even expanding one's influence might not be considered as relevant by the institutional approach, but in research it is often considered as one of the goals of several actors strongly influencing their actions. Therefore, the change of their roles and their coping strategies are not only important at the highest decision-making levels of the EU and national governments and administrations but equally relevant to understanding the reactions of downstream actors when facing the task of implementing European legislation: how have these actors managed to cope with the additional work? Has the efficiency decreased? Or have the actors got prestigious new tasks and roles (or got rid of some less welcomed ones) which would change their preferences? Has their position within the national system improved? Or was it a mixed blessing, leaving the actor with the problem of balancing the pros and cons?

Last but not least: The above-described aspects and "misfits" might be strongly influenced by the *availability of information*[86] and the *interpretation of information*. While it is in most administrations' common practice to get feedback from other interested parties during the development of a European Directive or the transposing national regulation (and therefore, it is very likely, that these administrations have a good idea about what *they* themselves want to know), it is less reasonable to assume that they always know how to address other actors and provide information to them. It partly depends on how used public bodies are to communicating with other actors. A strong "top-down" approach might facilitate the work for the "instigators" by deciding autonomously on the quality and quantity of the information provided but this could increase the problems of interpretation at all subsequent levels. This approach is also less likely to have an effective feedback mechanism ready to react on changes. As we will see, there are two main reasons for authorities to choose this "top-down" approach: lack of manpower – reducing the workload by shifting the communication work to "downstream" levels – and the cultural and historical background of an administration and its embodiment in a "state-led society" or a "society-led state". As the case of the CPD will also show, one has to keep in mind that implementation is a dynamic process, for which the results could change over the

86 See also: Falkner/Treib/Hartlapp/Leiber: Complying with Europe 2005 p. 38f.

years. Political or economic changes might influence the perception and reaction of different actors, causing an "ex-post misfit"[87]. Also, late awareness of new requirements could result in problems for actors, even long after the official implementation of a Directive. As we will see for the CPD and the late publication of European standards, several actors are affected years after the administrative implementation has been finalised at national level.

2.5 Knowledge, lack of knowledge, trust

> I could never join a club that would accept me as a member.
> (Groucho Marx)

It is time to take one step back and to look at what has been identified as important factors in the interaction between EU and national actors so far: A very complex environment, a wide range of potential misunderstandings and few instruments that could reduce the complexity – provided that all actors are more or less willing to play fair. And even if an agreement can be found, would the outcome be what was expected? Following this assumption, that *information* is a reliable and guiding parameter, rational choices should be easily made if only enough data is available. But considering the complexity of the environment, more data is weakening the "taken-for-granted" familiarity which leaves not even for the *homo economicus* – being less focused on a positive outcome for *all* actors than the *homo sociologicus* – the chance to predict sufficiently precisely the outcome of his or her actions – and in particular the reactions of the other actors.[88] In fact, with so many variables and different outcomes, it seems highly unlikely that *any* individual could make a rational decision when interacting with other actors.

One should also keep in mind that "institutionalised" networks of distributing and discussing data – and therefore creating additional knowledge – are only possible if actors have enough resources to maintain these networks. "Softer" networks where individuals or organisations have intensified their communi-

87 Börzel: How the Eruopean Union interacts with its Member States, in: Bulmer/Lesquese (eds): The Member States of the European Union 2005 p. 51.

88 Lane: Theories and Issues in the Study of Trust; in: Lane/Bachmann (eds.): Trust within and between Organizations 1998 p. 10.

cation and could even create flexible "knowledge spaces" for their members[89] are often more frequently available and therefore more important. *Comitology* committees and many of the networks established by public authorities can be considered as "institutionalised" while private actors have to depend more often on "softer" structures. The former provides a certain guarantee that actors who have managed to enter the system will remain in it. The latter provides more possibilities to add – even on an *ad hoc* basis – additional actors (or allowing them to join), but their involvement and commitment remains less obligatory, but also less secure for themselves and also for all other actors. In both cases, the quality and quantity of the actual input of each actor cannot be guaranteed, leaving all actors "at the mercy" of others willing to cooperate within a given system.

To give an existing system any chance of success, another variable has to be introduced that was already indirectly included in all previous observation, but without being specifically mentioned: *trust – lots* of trust. One of the reasons for putting so much emphasis on this specific aspect is the personal experience of the author that *trust* is the main "*social glue*" (or more scientific: a *social resource*) keeping transnational *and* national institutions, communication and decision-finding processes operational. In particular when keeping in mind the increasing dependency of actors on information generated and provided by several sources on different levels of a transnational or national system. Without trust, actions of others could hardly be foreseen and in the worst case actors could or would not want to react at all.[90]

Comparisons between national and transnational/European approaches are often confusing *assumed knowledge* about national systems, based on individual experiences of researchers, journalists, the public or even public and private organisations of *being in possession of empirical data* or at least a thorough assessment of the national system. In fact, being embedded in national systems, individuals and organisations have developed instruments that were providing *familiar* symbols, procedures and actors one has trusted already in the past[91] to

89 Matthiesen: Raum und Wissen, in: Tänzler/Knoblauch/Soeffner (Hrsg.): Zur Kritik der Wissensgesellschaft 2006 p. 166.

90 Luhmann in Hartmann/Offe (Hsrg.): Vertrauen 2001 p. 158.

91 Luhmann: Vertrautheit, Zuversicht, Vertrauen, … (p. 146); Endreß: Vertrauen und Vertrautheit (p. 167ff.) both in: Hartmann/Offe (Hsrg.): Vertrauen, 2001; Kopp-Malek/Koch/Lindenthal: Die Europäische Kommission als lernende Organisation? 2009 p. 29f.; Coleman: Foundations of Social Theory 1994 p. 175ff.

reduce the complexity of the social environment.[92] Compared with this familiar environment, the European system seems more complex and the outcome of any action less predictable. But both, the European and national environments are *social constructs*,[93] were societies, organisations and individuals depend much more on their assumptions that other actors are following commonly accepted values and norms, than having any certainty that this would be the case. Following a more critical view, one could argue that many of these social constructs are “surviving” *because* of the ignorance of individuals and organisations about their actual efficiency (or inefficiency).

Both organisations and individuals have to assume that certain orientations, values, norms and behaviour are commonly accepted and used within the system of the organisation (as organisational *routine*[94]). But the larger the organisation becomes, the more it depends on mutual trust that these norms are respected and “taken for granted” than any form of monitoring and sanctioning the behaviour of its members.[95] It also has to give each member more autonomy (in particular

---

Providing familiar elements is also used to “translate” new or unfamiliar situations and positions of other actors back into familiar routines, norms and typologies. (Endreß: Vertrauen und Vertrautheit; in: Hartmann/Offe (Hsrg.): Vertrauen, 2001 p. 180.

92 As we will see, the development of national standards has in general a long history and provides all actors with enough information how the system works (“*Erfahrungswissen*”), while standardisation work in on EU level can still be described as learning process. Standards are also very good examples of instruments to reduce complexity and insecurity and therefore allows manufacturers, planners and product users to move to higher levels of complexity (including taking higher risks) than they would have done if standards would not have “covered the base” (see also: Strulik, citing Japp in: Nichtwissen und Vertrauen in der Wissensökonomie 2004 p. 57 Hartmann p. 14; in: Hartmann/Offe (Hsrg.): Vertrauen, 2001).

93 This does not make them appear less real to actors within or outside the system, but puts a stronger emphasis on the fact that their orientations, purpose and activities need more *explanation* to actors outside the system/organisation to legitimise these constructs. For example: Specific procedures are part of how an organisation will work (its “memory”), but they are *accepted* and *internalised* because of the given frame, but not because other individuals can refer to their own personal experience. (see: Berger/Luckmann: The Social Construction of Reality 1991 p. 123ff.).

94 Becker/Knudsen: The role of routines … 2003; Lillrank: The Quality of Standard, Routine and Nonroutine Processes 2003; Feldman: Organizational routines … 2002; Pentland/Rueter: Organizational routines … 1994.

95 Offe also refers to the dilemma of simply “trusting” that established mechanisms in organisations could compensate for “trust” since organisations themselves are always “incomplete” and “controversial”. (Offe: Wie können wir unseren Mitbürgern vertrauen? in: Hartmann/Offe (Hsrg.): Vertrauen, 2001 p. 275; Adler, Paul S./Heckscher, Charles: Towards Collaborative Community; in: Heckscher/Adler (eds): The Firm as a Collaborative Community 2007 p. 16ff.

the "corporate actor") assuming – *trusting* – that he or she will still be close enough to its cognitive orientation. But the individuals might also be aware that the organisation cannot be sure of the compliance of each member. Therefore, to secure the binding (and disciplinary) nature of its orientation and norms, the organisation has to ensure that individuals have close contacts (networks and routines) which would (directly or indirectly) monitor each other and strengthen the common position and values.[96] But since these individuals could together develop their own priorities which might deviate from the ones generally applied by the organisation, another approach has to ensure compliance of smaller entities: The organisation has to present the *image* of commonly accepted rules. These *images* are supported by specific symbols, identifying an organisation, its values and the commitment of individuals. Good examples are specific ceremonies, (technical) certificates, (academic) degrees, but also specific procedures of how to handle issues – again via certificates or an administrative structure indicating the position of individuals and the value of specific positions and issues.[97]

Referring to familiar symbols and procedures is in general a successful scheme as long as the organisation is not supposed to be a "problem solver" but an "action-generator", and therefore fulfils (pre-)defined tasks and uses established patterns.[98] Following established paths (and therefore reducing ambiguity and insecurity for individuals) the risks for deviations which avoid conflicts within the organisation and with its outside environment are limited. This also explains the preference of organisations for the *historical institutionalism* of organisations and their reluctance for (fast) adaptations. Resisting changes could also create trust because actors outside the organization do not have to monitor its action all the time and they are not forced to interpret every new action of it.

However, since monitoring and certification systems are in general rather conservative, they include the risk that all incentives of finding and using alternative routes are in general no longer taken into consideration (inflexibility and

& p. 30; Lane: Theories and Issues in the Study of Trust; in: Lane/Bachmann (eds): Trust within and between Organizations 1998 p. 8ff.

96 Feldman: Organizational routines … 2002 p. 315ff.; Pentland/Rueter: Organizational routines … 1994 p. 487.

97 Ortmann: Als ob 2004 p. 100ff.

98 Ortmann: Als ob 2004 p. 96ff.; Adler/Heckscher: Towards Collaborative Community; in: Heckscher/Adler (eds): The Firm as a Collaborative Community 2007 p. 28.

"potential inefficiency")[99]. Even worse, an institutionalised approach could introduce a static scheme of compliance, shifting the emphasis from self-acknowledged obligations and intentions to fulfil them, even without direct control by other actors ("active trust")[100] to a procedural based ritual that lacks capabilities of responding to internally or externally induced changes.[101]

Even more than organisations, individuals are forced to give the "benefit of doubt". Within an organisation, the split of tasks and responsibilities has institutionalised but also "excused" the "ignorance" of the individual.[102] Segmenting an activity into different tasks does not allow for the individual to know all different steps and being sure about the quality of the work of his or her colleagues and how much their work has been in line with the norms and values of the organisation. Specific procedures and the above-mentioned symbols (i.e. the signature under a document, a specific certificate) help the individual (as well as actors outside the organisation) *to assume* that everything has been done within the given framework of compliance ("usable ignorance")[103]. Contacts to and information provided by "external" actors leaves even more room for insecurity. Again, the individual cannot control the quality and quantity of all data received, but has to make "shortcuts" in his or her assessment. Common backgrounds of actors (i.e. same technical training, social backgrounds) or past experience might facilitate the acceptance of the data and might influence how it will be used. The risk for the individual (as well as for organisations using similar "shortcuts") is that an "accident" is caused by or is linked to this flexible approach.

The dependency of individuals vis-à-vis the image of an organisation becomes even more obvious where the positions of an individual and the organisation would significantly differ: if the claimed knowledge of the organisation (the *image*) would be compared with the actual available knowledge of the individual, the *image* will in most cases be used as reference. It shows the power of the *image* that in most cases it will survive with its structure, orientation and instru-

99 Ackermann: Pfadabhängigkeit, Institutionen und Regelreform 2001 p. 20f. & 33ff.

100 Giddens in: Beck/Giddens/Lash: Reflexive Modernisierung 1996 p. 167ff.

101 Lane: Theories and Issues in the Study of Trust; in: Lane/Bachmann (eds): Trust within and between Organizations 1998 p. 19; Ackermann: Pfadabhängigkeit, Institutionen und Regelreform 2001 p. 70f.

102 Ortmann: Als ob 2004 p.96; Lane: Theories and Issues in the Study of Trust; in: Lane/Bachmann (eds): Trust within and between Organizations 1998 p. 14.

103 Wheling: Im Schatten des Wissens? 2006 p. 96ff.; Ackermann: Pfadabhängigkeit, Institutionen und Regelreform 2001 p. 149f & 155f.

ments intact, while the attempts of the individual of trying to work with more "realistic" assumptions and instruments will be seen within and outside the organisation as deviation from "reality".[104] Here the anonymity of the individual provided by the organisation becomes a burden for the individual. Deviating from the image puts him or her outside the system, allowing the organisation to isolate the individual and cutting its links and responsibilities for individual actions and therefore creates "plausible deniability" for the organisation ("if he or she would have done it "by the book" (another symbol) everything would have been fine"). Facing this risk, the individual has to trust in the willingness of the organisation to overlook or deny the existence of deviation, and declaring it as part of the defined and accepted procedure. In exchanges, deviations by other individuals will be judged less harshly (and possibly also ignored as flaw in the system) to protect the *image* of an efficient and reliable system to the outside world.

In the technical field of the CPD, allowing other actors to reduce the complexity – or being allowed to reduce the complexity of one's own data – is a very common approach at different levels within a national or organisational system. Since trust increased the tolerance of insecurities and allows acting even in situations of higher complexity,[105] all actors have a strong tendency of choosing this approach. In particular the technical field has introduced several instruments like technical standards and certificates that are setting pre-conditions are commonly used, without needing new or additional interpretation work by most actors. (NB please check this sentence: All of these steps require mutual trust and, the more complex a given environment becomes, the more stronger actors demand simplifications – but thereby put more trust into the system, the more its elements and actors involved.) However, a changing environment makes knowledge and expertise based on past experience (compared with generating *new* knowledge) less and less useful for predicting and coping with present and future developments, therefore putting pressure on existing systems and challenging their efficiency. Even public administrations are no longer automatically able to guarantee the trust in existing national or transnational systems.

The major challenge of the "trust system" started in the 80s and 90s of the 20th century when the public awareness of potential risks of developed technolo-

104 Ortmann: Als ob 2004 p. 102ff.

105 Strulik: Nichtwissen und Vertauen in der Wissensökonomie 2004 p. 8 & p. 24ff.; Scharpf: Games Real Actors Play 1997 p. 137f.

gies grew and serious accidents (i.e. in nuclear power plants) raised questions about the efficiency of the systems introduced to monitor and to control them. The main problem for the "trust society" vis-à-vis the "risk society"[106] was not so much its ignorance of potential risks or its attempt to avoid responsibility (even though its reluctance to take this responsibility was one of its most damaging reactions), but rather its pretension in possessing data and expertise instead of acknowledging that the system depended so heavily on mutual trust. The fact that discussions were often taking place in closed circles of experts raised even more questions if these relatively closed sub-systems of experts were still taking all relevant aspects into account or if their positions became less reflexive of external data and demands and more self-referential – therefore creating their own circular assured "reality" ("*spezialisierte Sinnprovinzen*")[107]. Also the relevance of existing expert knowledge did not escape new scrutiny: especially the new awareness that "knowledge" is always to some extent linked to assumptions, substituting for the unknown parts of a problem, and is therefore always including risks of wrong assumptions and miscalculations.[108] This did not correspond with the approach of most expert communities (in the field of science and technology) still presenting their expert knowledge as "complete". Keeping the discussion (and doubts) within a closed circle – which also made internal power struggles and discontent less visible and actually strengthened the social relationships between the different actors involved[109] – has turned to a disadvantage because it clearly reduced the transparency and therefore the credibility of the "trust system". In addition, the previously assumed preference of actors in civil administrations or politics for "the common good" as a main goal (at least clearly *presenting* the role as *homo sociologicus*) was increasingly questioned ("problem solving bias"[110]). While the "foreground goals" clearly stressed this preference (even providing the main justification of specific powers of public actors in the national system), the interest of gaining and keeping special positions within the system (and therefore accumulating specific political and

106 Beck: Risikogesellschaft 1986.

107 Schimank: Teilsystemische Autonomie ... 2006 p. 129.

108 Willke defines relevant knowledge as: 1) continuously revised 2) permanently improvable 3) in principle not "the truth" but a resource 4) unavoidably linked with non-knowledge and risks (Willke cited in Strulik: Nichtwissen und Vertrauen in der Wissensökonomie 2004 p. 51).

109 Sverdrup: Compliance and conflict resolution in the European Union 2002 p. 6.

110 Mayntz cited in: Schimank: Teilsystemische Autonomie ... 2006 p. 162.

regulatory power[111] – which could in some cases also include economic interests) was seen as at least a similar motivation of actors ("background goals")[112] for specific actions and reactions – even encouraging stronger moves in the direction of more autonomy and monopolistic positions[113] (which earned even public authorities the image of being at least partly "profit-oriented" actors, close to the *homo economicus*).

However, this new challenge was weakened by its own inert problems of lacking clear definitions to indicate and to analyse assumed and real inefficiency of the existing system. Definitions of "risks" and "hazards" are strongly contested and defended by different actors and leave enough room for actors to introduce or dismiss with ease new issues in a discussion[114]: Should every potential hazard be considered as a threat? Should the discussion focus on hazards instead of risks? And who is deciding which hazard has to be considered as e.g. "high-risk"?

Ironically, several of these "risk" issues were transferred to transnational organisations (e.g. UN, WHO) or institutions (e.g. the European Commission) to achieve more transparency and a more common approach. But at transnational levels, like the European level, collecting, analysing and using data to an extent that would allow well-founded decisions seemed even less realistic, in particular when looking at the small number of individuals (experts, civil servants, or representatives from other interested parties) involved in that work. While trust at EU level is even more needed as "social glue", it is not often transferred to this level. National actors might be tempted to increase trust into their own national systems (or at least silencing critics) by raising doubts about the credibility and

---

111 *Hardy, Phillips* and *Lawrence* are highlighting that trust could also be built on asymmetric dependencies of strong actors who *have* to be trusted because they are *dominating* the interaction between different actors. (Hardy/Phillips/Lawrence: Distinguishing Trust and Power in Interorganizational Relations,;in: Lane/Bachmann (eds): Trust within and between Organizations 1998 p. 67ff.).

112 "Background goals" influence choices of actors in two ways: influencing the ordering of alternatives and influence the salience of the goal-frame (in favour of the "best" solution) (Lindenberg, in: Diekmann/Eichner/Schmidt/Voss (Hrsg.): Rational Choice 2008 p. 67).

113 Schimank: Teilsystemische Autonomie ... 2006 p. 130ff.

114 In the construction sector too, the perception of "acceptable risks" and "potential hazards" remains in the hands of national actors (in the field of regulations and standardisation) trying to strengthen the national system of trust but (due to a lack of common definitions) weakening trust in other (national or European) systems.

trustworthiness of European approaches. In fact, the *risk of trusting*[115] other actors (or in a different system) is often highlighted when looking at *other* systems: risks in the familiar scheme are often ignored, downplayed or favourably compared to other (seemingly less successful) schemes, which keeps the own system relatively intact and resistant against changes. Increasing insecurity about European "input" could result in a stronger demand for the existing national approach, stressing the need for at least some autonomy of these specific national sub-systems of committees or expert groups.[116] Unfortunately, as shown above, organisations are based on routine and created for maintaining established procedures. Their abilities to react on changes in the system and providing solutions on the other hand are rather limited. Therefore, reducing *trust* in one system might not necessarily increase the *efficiency* of another one. As a reaction to a decline of trust in a European approach, the Commission itself might fall back to more stringent rules (less ambiguity) – and therefore also withdraw from a system of mutual trust *within* the system hoping that this will increase the credibility and trust in it by the *outside* world. Both approaches include a high risk of maintaining the *status quo* without trying to find solutions outside established paths.

However, as will be shown, even established national systems are "incomplete" (i.e. lack of market surveillance), therefore working with a certain "usable ignorance" which renders "trust" in a common understanding and cooperation of the actors involved a *non-option* ("trust" *could* be given), but a *necessity* for operating the system (actors *have* to be trusted)[117]. Even authorities have to delegate – but even more: to *depend* on – the competence of actors to organise themselves in a way that they will comply to existing norms, or to develop ones specific for their organisations that are compatible with the ones already used by other actors. Most illustrative for this approach is the nearly complete lack of

---

115 Eisenstadt: Vertrauen, kollektive Identität und Demokratie; in: Hartmann/Offe (Hsrg.): Vertrauen, 2001 p. 334.

116 Insisting on autonomy for specific sectors, sciences or other fields of expertise is not a special behaviour between actors on EU and national level, but also quiet common within national systems or even on the level of organisations. However, while autonomy is often seen as allowing for better results ("leave us alone, and you will get useful results"), proof of the efficiency of this approach are still debatable. It is even argued that actors providing specific data could make their position within a system even less substitutable, which would leave other actors no alternative for getting comparison able data for their decision finding process (Schimank: Teilsystemische Autonomie ... 2006 p. 10f. & p. 126).

117 See: Endreß: Vertrauen und Vertrautheit; in: Hartmann/Offe (Hsrg.): Vertrauen, 2001 p. 200.

empirical data on how actors have actually been complying with norms and expectations at national and/or regional levels.[118]

The weak position of all actors when it comes to complex systems would allow two main assumptions about how actors might operate in the system: one could argue that the lack of monitoring abilities will make defiant behaviour less detectable, and therefore, the "profit-driven" *homo economicus* might have been active all the time, with only few actors being aware of and even fewer being able to *do* anything about it. In fact, the long list of late and incomplete adoption of European law into national systems would justify this argument. On the other hand, the same data shows less *intentional* non-compliance but different interpretations and approaches as to how these transnational laws have to be implemented.

Going one step further: the *homo economicus* could have created much more "damage" to the European system if the strife for own gains would have been so strongly dominating the behaviour of several actors. Therefore, it seems reasonable to assume that actors have followed (at least partly) a more norm-oriented approach. They might not have been able (or willing) to follow it all the time, including wrong perceptions and interpretations by different actors. But in general, accepting rules within a given *European* framework and following them has created a *new* environment for actors in addition and complementary to the ones they are embedded on national and regional level. It defines the positions and roles of the actors involved – mostly the role as *homo sociologicus* – as a fair and trustworthy actor – not only to partners within this system but also to external actors – including those outside the EU – maybe even presenting this competence as a characteristic of *European actors*.

---

118 Most research has been limited to evaluate if actors have fulfilled their legal obligations "on paper" – screening (legal) texts on national, regional or local level. The actual compliance in day-to-day work however remains mostly unknown. (see: "After the dust has settled").

3 The practical implementation of the CPD

3.1 Researching one's own backyard

3.1.1 EU Directives as research topics

European Directives and their implementation are becoming more and more interesting for researchers in the field of political and administrative sciences. Finally resulting in a timely or delayed transformation into national laws,[119] several of them have been used to evaluate the activities of different European and national actors. However, the large number of directives developed over half a century and the specific interests of researchers have created a field of EU laws which have been subjected to several studies, while other directives were not covered at all. In particular "modern" policy fields like environmental or social protection have drawn much attention, while directives setting the framework for the Internal Market seem to have not been as interesting. As a result, existing theories and studies provided very useful background information and references for EU and (partly) national actors in general, but the selection of EU laws – and their restriction of following the implementation in most cases only up to the level of national authorities – left the wide field of the practical transformation and implementation relatively "uncharted". Therefore, going beyond that field to

---

119 See chapter: „After the dust has settled" and also: Tallberg: Paths to Compliance 2000; Knill: The Europeanisation of National Administrations 2001; Weber: Umweltpolitische Steuerung in der Europäischen Union, in: Bauer/Voelzkow (Hrsg.): Die Europäische Union – Marionette oder Regisseur? 2004; Kaeding: Lost in Translation or Full Steam Ahead? 2007; Berglund/Gange/van Waarden: Mass production of law 2006; Börzel: Pace-Setting, Foot-Dragging, and Fence-Sitting 2001; Falkner/Hartlapp/Leiber/Treib: Transforming Social Policy in Europe? 2002; Versluis: Explaining Variations in Implementation of EU Directives 2004; Kaeding: Lost in Translation or Full Steam Ahead 2008; Kohler-Koch: European Networks and Ideas 2002; Mastenbroek, Ellen: The Politics of Compliance 2007; Toshkov: Between Politics and Administration 2009.

the level of the "final users" had to be done with few references – and several assumptions on my side.

Not only the lack of research at regional and practical levels made this study challenging: also the fact that the rather "traditional" Construction Products Directive has never created enough interest for researchers, left only a few studies on the CPD which were (for obvious reasons!) more instruments to identify how the CPD could be more effective in the few areas that it addressed directly, rather than providing a scientific evaluation of the impact of the CPD at all levels of the construction sector.

The construction unit of the European Commission has initiated three studies which were done by external consultants:

- *Effects of Regulation and Technical Harmonisation on the Intra-Community Trade in Construction Products* (WS Atkins international 2000).[120] This study was initiated to assess if and which quantifiable benefits harmonisation could have on testing and certification costs and effects on (national) markets for construction products. The first harmonised European standards were already available and national actors were asked about the benefits experienced or assumed.
- *Study to evaluate the Internal Market and competitiveness effects of the CPD* (PRC 2007):[121] This study evaluated the impact of the CPD and sought to identify options for improvements. Since an amendment of the CPD was already considered as an option by the Commission services, the recommendations of the study were also aiming at changes beyond minor adaptations to reported problems of the current implementation.
- "Stakeholder consultation on the revision of the CPD (2006):[122] The questions developed and published by the Commission focused on specific aspects of the efficiency of the instruments established under the framework of the CPD (i.e. organisations on EU level and their work).[123]

---

120 http://ec.europa.eu/enterprise/construction/internal/atkins/wsatkins.htm.

121 http://ec.europa.eu/enterprise/construction/cpdrevision/study_evaluate_int_market-compet_effects.pdf.

122 http://ec.europa.eu/enterprise/construction/cpdrevision/cpd_cons_en.htm.

123 The response rate differs in Germany, the UK, Austria and Poland, but it also corresponds to the positions of actors in all four countries in the following chapters of this study (see the chapters on actors, their assumptions and conclusions of all three levels): the strong interest in Germany of all parties but also of individual manufacturers and regional authorities; the absence of regional (*Länder*) authorities and other industry actors besides manufacturers in

In all three studies (the last one aiming less at a scientific approach and analysis but more a general feedback on specific questions), the construction unit has set the targets and the framework of the research work already in its specifications for the public call for tender. In each case, a "steering committee" of Commission officials and also actors from Member State authorities, industry and others, followed the work and discussed their intermediate and final results. Despite the wider range of interests covered in these committees, the dominating position of the Commission (the construction unit) could not be challenged and the consultants had to consider the comments and lead of the construction unit as the binding input.

Not directly linked to construction products, but important for the CPD implementation via technical standards, a study initiated by the unit in the Commission responsible for coordinating the contacts of the different Commission services with the European standardisation bodies CEN, CENELEC and ETSI, focused on the possibilities and barriers that different actors might face when trying to get access to standardisation work at EU level.[124] Participation in the standardisation process, as well as in the final voting for big and smaller actors, was highlighted several times and possibilities of improving participation (via IT tools) were presented by different actors.

Furthermore, the European Parliament has been probing into the field of construction products covered by the CPD. In a "Study on Safety and Liability Issues Relating to Construction Products",[125] the perception of users (planners, contractors, general consumers of construction products) was evaluated and in particular the misunderstanding of seeing CPD-CE marking as safety mark was highlighted.

In addition, the German Federal Ministry for Transport, Building and Urban Affairs (BMVBS) has initiated a study to get feedback from a larger group of national actors (federations, manufacturers, planners, contractors and test laboratories) on their experience and expectations of the use of CE marking and which

Austria; the relatively low response rate in the UK (where CE marking is not obligatory); the few replies from Poland as a very "young" Member State having few experiences with CE marking and also still creating representative associations at national and EU levels.

124 http://ec.europa.eu/enterprise/standards_policy/document/access_to_standardisation_1103 2009_en.pdf.

125 European Parliament/Policy Department – Economic and Scientific Policy: Study on Safety and Liability Issues Relating to Construction Products; 2007

aspects should be taken into consideration in a possible new Construction Products Regulation (see: "Construction sector – CPD").[126]

More general in their scope, EFTA has commissioned a study on certification and marks in Europe, evaluating the acceptance and use of CE marking and other European and national marks[127]. The Construction Products Directive was only one of several European Directives chosen in this study, but the difference between the CPD and other "New Approach Directives" and the different nature of CE marking in the CPD as well as some general problems of CPD-CE marking was highlighted.

For this study the following results can be seen as relevant background information:

- the goal of the CPD and the role of CE marking remained to a large extent unclear and confusing (even in 2006). The main goal of the CPD – removing "barriers to trade" – was never challenged in principle, but the definition remained vague. (PCR & BMVBS study) The "performance-based" approach (see chapters on "presumption of actors" at EU and national levels) was a different approach from several past national approaches t and the limited scope of the CPD (only covering product performance but not the performance of buildings or civil engineering works) did not facilitate transformation into national schemes (WS Atkins & PCR & stakeholder consultation & BMVBS study);
- the system was considered by several actors as complicated and burdensome – obviously linked to the problem of setting clear goals and instruments (PCR & stakeholder consultation & BMVBS study);
- this created different perceptions about the nature of CE marking by several actors. It ranged from specific (national) market requirements (in particular the need to link technically information on product performance to the practical use of these products), the involvement of public authorities on different levels of the national administration to other barriers in the field of construction which influenced the general perception of "barriers" and "market protectionism" of several actors (WS Atkins & PCR & BMVBS study);

126 Bundesamt für Bauwesen und Raumordnung: Studie über die Verwendungsregelungen CE gekennzeichneter Bauprodukte in den Mitgliedstaaten der EU als Grundlage für Deutschland für Verhandlungen bei der Revision der Bauproduktenrichtlinie; 2008.

127 EFTA: Certification and Marks in Europe, 2008.

- weak or ineffective market surveillance at national level and its coordination between Member States of the EU (PCR & stakeholder consultation & BMVBS study);
- a general lack of coordination in providing information and guaranteeing cooperation of actors at national level (and vis-à-vis the EU level) (PCR & stakeholder consultation & BMVBS study).

3.1.2 Research on the CPD from the EU level to the "construction-site" level

While the general goal of evaluating *the information flow from the EU level to the "construction-site" level* remained during the whole research work, the comments received during the interviews indicated that the scope of the study might be too narrow to allow for useful conclusions and useful and practicable recommendations.

I started my research work with the assumption that the more I get in contact with actors at *different* levels, the more *new* information I would get, indicating other priorities and interests and highlighting different interpretations and reactions on information and requirements from upstream and downstream actors. This *has* actually happened, which lead me to the conclusion that, not only the information flow and the efficiency of communication[128] has to be evaluated, but also the general approach of the CPD vis-à-vis the specific interests of actors at the "construction-site" level. The lack of information at different levels for all actors and the compensation by using "trust" as a tool to reduce complexity, highlighted relevant aspects to provide a consistent picture of the environments and instruments actors were using to deal with construction products at EU, national and "construction-site" levels. Therefore, the research work was adapted and did not only cover the creation, interpretation and distribution of information, but also the persistent *lack* of information, how actors have compensated for it within national schemes and how they did it (or not) when confronted with a new European approach. Also the issue of *trust* in specific schemes became more and more important, when references were made to schemes that actors felt more realistic, less complex and "safer" to use (which was practically always the system one had to work with). While lacking empiri-

128 As Erving Goffman has said: "Although communication has often been offered as the medicine, it has seldom produced a cure." (quoted in: Hanrieder 2008).

cal data to support the claim that one (EU, national, regional or local) system was actually better than another, the strong believe in the (familiar) system in use was rarely questioned by any interviewee.

Keeping in mind that the Construction Products Directive's aim is to facilitate the use of construction products in the Internal Market by providing common assessment methods and therefore reliable product performance declarations, the focus of this study has been on four main points to evaluate the efficiency and "added value" of the CPD to previous national schemes:

- the assumptions of actors (how and if the CPD can be of advantage for different groups of actors);
- the national, administrative, legal and cultural environment of the actors involved (including the interests of organisations *and* individuals, existing knowledge, lack of it and trust in national schemes and actors);
- the information flow (creation, interpretation, transmission, and receiving information upstream and downstream – and comparing the "CPD/CE marking scheme" with previous experience with national schemes);
- the assumed and experienced impact of CE marking.

Since the information flow was going from a more political?/?administrative level (the EU level – in short: "Brussels") to a very practical, technical and economic level (the "construction-site" level), three different levels have been defined in this research design to indicate differences in the legal framework, perceptions and use of information about the CPD and CE marking:

- the "EU level" (the Commission services, EU organisations – i.e. the European standardisation organisation CEN – official representatives of Member States, European federations of manufacturers, architects and contractors);
- the "national level" (national and regional authorities –e.g. the German and the Austrian *Länder* – national organisations – i.e. national standardisation bodies, technical institutes, certification bodies – and national federations);
- the "construction-site level" (local planning and building control, architects, contractors and individual manufacturers and distributors);

The line between each level was seldom clear-cut because authorities and organisations but also individuals were often active at more than one level.

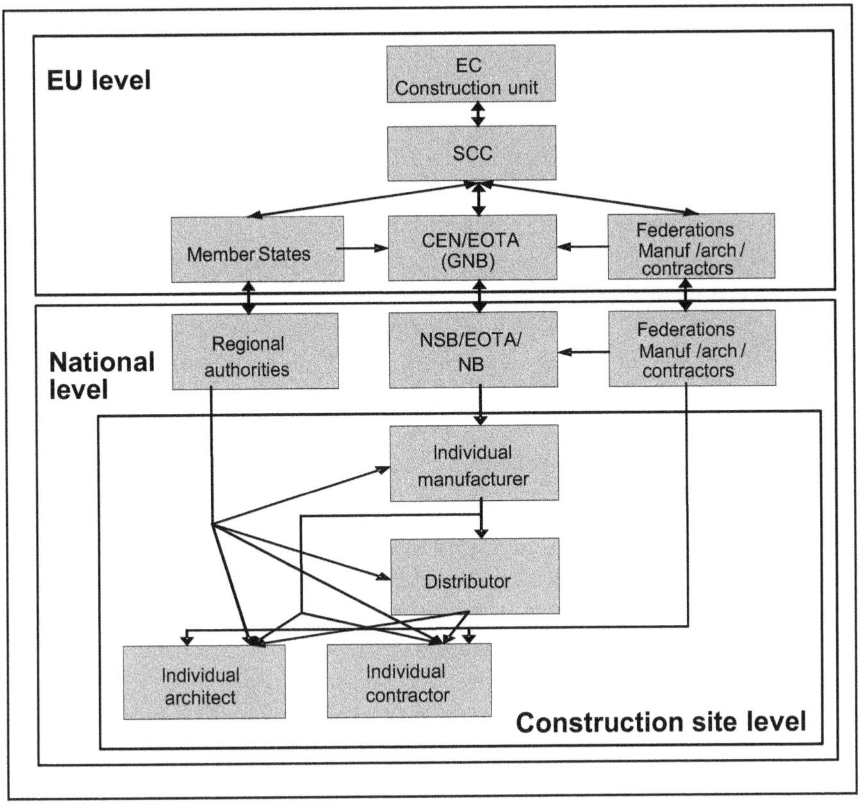

Figure 1: EU, national, construction site levels

The focus was on the actors of four Member States of the EU:

- Germany and the UK have been chosen as the ones who have been involved in the creation and interpretation of the CPD from "day one". However, at first glance their approaches seem to be very opposite to each other. Not only does their perception of the nature of CE marking differ significantly, but also the political, administrative and practical approaches seem to position them at respective ends of the spectrum of Member States of the EU12 implementing the CPD.
- Austria joined in 1995 and missed most of the "interpretation phase" but was still involved in the creation of technical mandates to CEN and got

soon after the accession a set of harmonised standards to be introduced in the national regulatory and technical system. Having a very similar political and administrative structure to that of Germany, a closer look at the performance of the Austrian actors should allow comparing implementation techniques when entering a scheme at a different stage. Did both countries follow the same route or did it matter that both Member States were starting at different phases of the implementation of the CPD?

- Joining the EU in 2004, Poland had even fewer possibilities to participate in the creation of the system surrounding the CPD, but on the other hand, was provided with a larger number of ready-made, harmonised standards. Due to a lot of internal changes in the national political, administrative and economic landscapes, this country was facing different opportunities and limits, and therefore providing this study with another specific national system linking itself with the European one.

However, interviewees from EU organisations and federations were also coming from other Member States. Therefore, I used the opportunity to include their experiences on and their feedback from national actors, so as to compare those with the positions and perceptions from the actors of the four Member States. In some cases, additional information on national approaches was provided outside the framework of this study (and therefore not counted as interviews).[129]

In general, interview partners were those working in different professions or were dealing with very specific product groups. While additional information was not excluded, I have decided to focus on the information flow of three specific construction products: thermal insulation products, ceramic materials (e.g. bricks, tiles) and mortar. All three product groups are generally used in buildings and this fact would allow following the positions and information provided by federations at EU level to the national level and from there to individual manufacturers to the final downstream users, whereas more specialised products might have produced fewer results on the "construction-site" level). The authorities, federations and companies that I have contacted and which have provided feedback (in interviews or by using questionnaires) are described in each chapter of actors on EU, national and "construction-site" level.

129 In particular actors from Ireland, the Netherlands and Romania provided useful and detailed information or confirmation on presumptions made by interviewees in the target countries.

3.1.3 Risks and advantages of researching in one's own field of work

Being a Commission official, I had to face the risk that, already at the beginning, my personal preferences would significantly affect the approach and even more the analysis. Of course, some points of view were formed by my first experience in the Construction Unit and the opinions and discussions about the CPD within the construction unit – and to assume that I could have had a completely unaffected view on the CPD would have been extremely naïve. But having the advantage of being trained as an engineer and as a sociologist has helped me to look at the CPD and the activities it has initiated from more than one angle. Asking a university (of a Member State not even covered in this study) for support was one of several steps to reduce any personal bias on my side. In addition the fact that I was never directly involved in the *interpretation* of the CPD and even in my work only dealing with one specific aspect of it, I have considered my personal involvement with the CPD as not strong enough to be too tempted to defend specific (Commission or Construction Unit) positions and interpretations in this study.

But my position as civil servant in the Commission had even more implications when I reached the stage of interviewing interested parties *at EU level*: practically, in most cases I was talking to the same individuals with whom I interacted in my daily work. While there were nearly no problems for my colleagues within the Commission to reply to my questions (there was even the risk that they would have taken too much information for granted and both sides might have overlooked some important aspects), my interview partners from European organisations, federations and representatives from national administrations faced a dilemma. On the one hand, they should reply as honestly as possible; on the other hand what would have been the chances that "everything you say can and will be used against you" by the interviewer, who was working for the Commission. For me, the risk remained that they would use the interview more as an opportunity to defend their positions (against the Commission) or – more subtly – to expect a more cooperative reaction in future from the Commission official, who right now depends on their cooperation for his study. Bottom line: both sides had to show a great deal of trust in each other to make the interviews more than just a presentation (and repetition) of official positions.

On the other hand, there were also several factors in favour for both sides to reduce these risks: in the past, the contacts between the construction unit and other interested parties have always (even when there was disagreement) been professional and, while one might not accept the position of another party, each side could "at least agree that they disagree" and continue work in other fields, without being completely blocked by a problem in one specific field. Another advantage for both sides was the existing knowledge about the Directive in question and that I was aware of the official position of the organisation, administration and federations of my counterpart. Therefore, one could start the interview already at a point where more detailed information could be provided and the interviewees could describe their experience and expectations in more detail. Both – the professional interaction in the past and the existing knowledge about each other – might have had an influence on the quality of the interviews, since "propaganda statements" would have been easily detectable from both sides and would have been dismissed as relatively useless information.[130] Of course – as with the interviewed Commission officials – this could have created some "gaps" when neither the interviewees nor I were aware of an information deficit on my side.

In fact, I was counting on the good working relationship of the past with practically all interview partners to get as open answers as possible, without harming the interests of the parties they represent. At all levels, I have avoided taping the interviews. Since some of the comments – positive and negative – were linked to specific individuals and some criticism was also raised against the organisational structure or function of the interviewee's own body. Thus, it has seemed only fair to the interviewees to "leave no trail" – not only because they might be traced back (in particular within the rather small "community" in Brussels) but also to give the assurance that I, as a Commission official, would not, but indeed cannot, use any statement against them.

In the end, I was positively surprised *how much* additional and new information I got during the interviews already at EU level. The interviews gave both sides the opportunity to go beyond what we normally need to know and communicate to each other (or the outside world in general). Some aspects of the information flow were well established, therefore taken for granted and one has learned to live with the advantages and learned to deal with the shortcomings. But it might not always have been what "the Commission" had expected. Getting

130 Fortunately, a specific group of actors were in a position to compensate some of these gaps: experts in authorities or federations who were assigned to follow developments at EU level and to distribute this information without being permanently posted in Brussels. Still being informed at a high level, their perception and knowledge differed enough to highlight additional aspects in *their* interviews.

this additional information was facilitated by the approach chosen for these interviews that, in general, I only *started* the interviews with a few questions to indicate the direction. After that, the interviewees had much freedom to choose where and how to select and put emphasis on points that they considered as most important to answer the questions. This left more room for individualistic description of the working structure by the interviewees which should also help to identify information gaps on both sides.

The first analysis of the interviews was used to develop a quantitative questionnaire, focusing on the main aspects that have been identified during the interviews and might also be relevant at the national and also the "construction-site" levels and should be used for statistical comparison. The questionnaires should also compensate to a certain extent the impracticality of doing interviews with all individuals involved – in particular at the national level, where the sample would significantly increase. On the EU-national level, the small number of individuals involved in the CPD did not necessarily demand the use of questionnaires but helped to include more individuals involved even if they are not working in Brussels or the capital cities of the four Member States selected in this study.

The next level – the national level – sometimes included s the same individuals but covering different roles. These were mostly clearly indicated and different actions depending on each role were not only highlighted during the interviews, but they were even stressed as important tasks as "distributors" and "interpreters" of information. Sometimes – surprisingly, national actors I have contacted during my study have been in contact with me on issues related to my work in the Construction unit of the Commission. This facilitated the willingness to cooperate with this study, but here, even more than with previous interviewees, an additional factor influenced the structure of the interview: referring to other issues related to my work as civil servant during the interview and discussing them after the interview. For several actors, the interview also provided an opportunity to get "up to date" on other issues. For example, actors at EU level had more opportunities and were more used to contacting Commission officials directly. This fact has split the interview in the "research part" and some parts in which I either had to refer to a discussion *after* the interview or giving a short answer or explanation to a specific question during the interview. While this has sometimes put me in a more reactive and responsive role, I nevertheless considered this as helpful because it also showed that the interests and concerns of the interview partners were also taken seriously and they were not just "targets" for this study, which in the end (in my opinion) facilitated an open atmosphere and more open replies.

The national level highlighted another problem that all research projects encounter: the individuals replying were aware of CE marking and they were willing to cooperate. In particular, their very *awareness* was the weakest point of this study. As the chapters on the practical implementation and the perceptions of actors will show, downstream actors have different economic and administrative environments to take into consideration than do EU actors. What seemed relevant "in Brussels" might have got a different priority at national level – if indeed it was considered as relevant at all. Actors who were willing and able to follow developments at EU or national levels were also the ones who had enough resources – or have been included in an efficient network for providing information. This limited the number of actors at national, regional and local levels to larger federations (or interested and committed individuals working for them) or larger enterprises who could afford keeping manpower on monitoring developments on EU or national level. Small and medium enterprises – and as will be shown in the study: micro-enterprises like most architects – were rarely able to *follow* the development of new requirements but were just implementing them ("following the letter of the law"). Getting in contact with SMEs was therefore the most difficult part of this research work and hence also only partly successful.

In addition, the lack of awareness changed the original planning of this research work which aimed at decreasing the number of qualitative interviews at downstream levels and putting more emphasis on questionnaires. Already at national level, some interviews were relatively short because some actors were only *generally* aware of CE marking, but did not consider that as of major importance for their work and the interests of their members and provided only limited information to downstream users or did not provide information at all. As will be shown in later chapters, EU issues were often considered as "not touching my *real* work" and therefore considered to be covered by upstream actors (federations or authorities). This partly changed my research strategy: while at EU level and for individuals acting as an interface between the EU and the national level, a first contact by phone or e-mail easily confirmed awareness about the CPD and CE marking, a first contact by phone became more and more relevant at national level, because only with more information and explanation from my side, were several actors able to decide if and how they were involved in this specific topic.

Table 2: Interviews and questionnaires

	EU level	MS level	Construction-site level
European Commission	10	–	–
MS authorities	12	21/1**	4
Manufacturers	6/9**	17	9
Contractors	3	4	5
Architects	1	1/3***	4
CEN*/EOTA	6/18**	13	–
Notified Bodies	3/9**	5	2
House Owners/Distributors	–	5	6/5***
Others (universities)	–	5	–
∑ individual interviewees/ questionnaires/short interviews	**104/37**/8***		

* Interviewees from CEN were in most cases working for manufacturers or their federations

** Second number is referring to questionnaires returned

*** Second number refers to short interviews

In several cases, this also shifted the importance of face-to-face interviews to telephone interviews, because some individuals were only able to provide some background information which was very helpful to get a more complete picture but would not have justified a longer interview – and the associated travel to one of the four Member States.

The following table provides an overview on actors interviewed or have responded to one of the questionnaires distributed for CEN, EOTA, manufacturers and Notified Bodies. Since some of them were active on more than one level, they were counted at each level. The number in the last row indicates the actual number of individuals interviewed.

The low number of face-to-face interviews with architects and contractors, and the number of short interviews already indicates the relatively low interest of these groups in CE marking. Interviewees at national level were well aware of the existence of CE marking, but did not consider it as very relevant for their members and provided only general information to downstream users. In this table, the questionnaires returned were counted at EU level (since most questions were identical, these questions were used for a statistical analysis. See: Assumptions of actors at EU level). However, since some questions were referring more to specific day-to-day practice (for EOTA and CEN members: direct contacts with individual customers), these replies were used in the assessment at national level. (See: Assumptions of actors at national level). Despite the small sample, I am confident that it is broadly representative of the above mentioned groups of actors, their interests, positions, awareness and use of CE marking.

3.2 The EU level

Before looking at the feedback from the "real world" of implementing the Construction Products Directive (see: Assumptions of actors on EU level), a look at the theoretical role of the different parties, as well as their instruments should give an idea how the CPD was supposed to work.[131] Which are the laws that actors at different levels had to take into account and which ones are more important for these actors? How have different actors organised themselves? How are they connected to other (national) authorities and other actors? What type of instruments do they have in place (in general and specifically for the CPD) to provide information and how can "insiders" and "outsiders" (including interested parties from other countries) get it?

The first step is to identify their *positions as actors at EU level* (e.g. members of specific bodies, official representations, observers). Starting with the Commission services – and from this point of the study onwards, practically always the construction unit of the Directorate General for Enterprises and Industry: The construction unit is responsible for the implementation of the CPD and, at this practical level (in theory) uncontested in its position on EU level as the one which *has* to provide guidance and clarification on regulatory and administrative issues. One could rightfully argue that the Standing Committee on Construction is an important instrument of Member State authorities to influence

131 In this overview of actors information publicly available such as documents, guidelines, presentations and – last but not least – websites of these actors have been included to provide a picture of the priorities of these actors and the instruments they have used to distribute information (on CE marking). This data was collected between mid 2008 and mid 2009. Changes might have occurred in the meantime on quantity and quality of these publications.

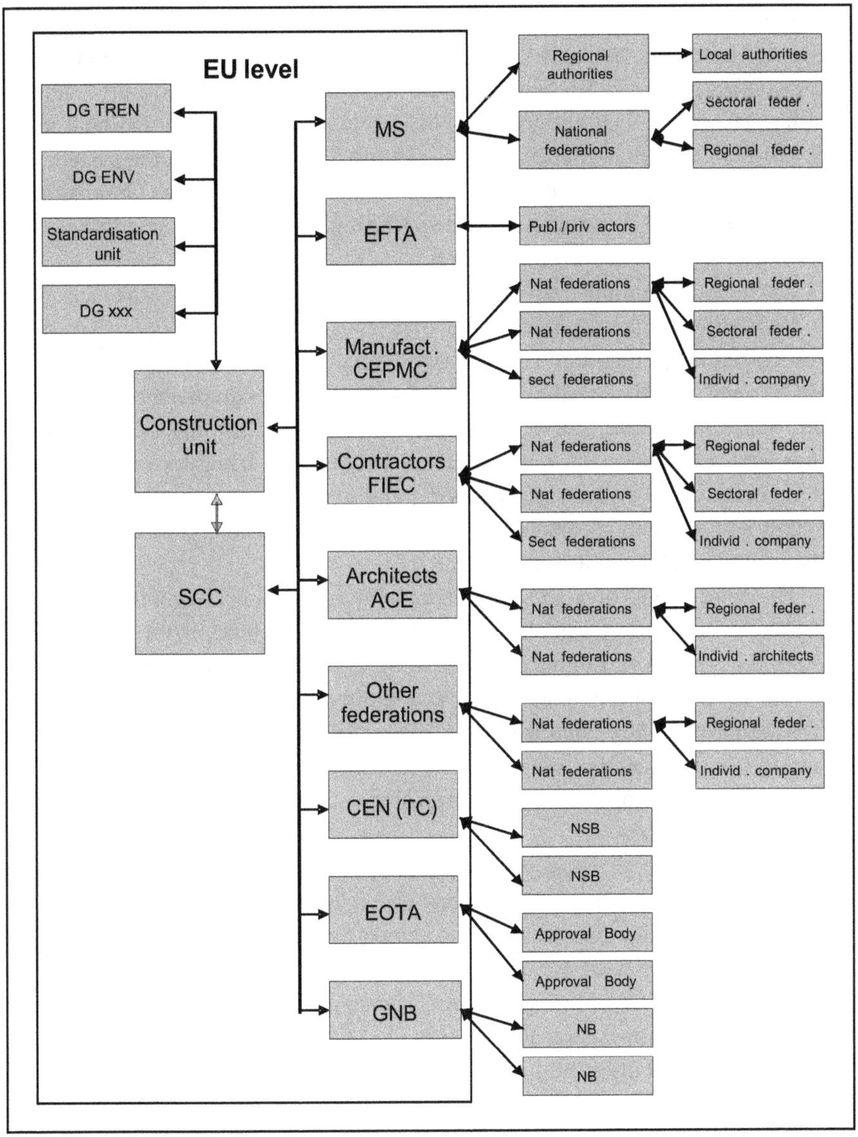

Figure 2: European actors – overview

this work, but these authorities are in the first place representing *national* interests (i.e. protecting national regulatory requirements, defending national economic interests), while finding European solutions might be only their second priority. Therefore, they are not "pure" EU actors but focused on national interests. Other interested parties have no mandatory positions within the system, but since in some Member States authorities have delegated some administrative powers to private (or privatised) bodies, the line between administrations and *other* interested parties becomes blurred.

Outside the administrative structure, specification writers (the European Standardisation Organisation (Or the official name: European Committee for Standardization) (CEN) and the European Organisation for Technical Approvals (EOTA)) and Notified Bodies can be considered as a complementary system, where other actors are active: technical experts from national standardisation bodies and approval bodies, certification bodies, test laboratories and manufacturers. Here too systems for applying and accepting membership exists but they are less stringent[132] than on the regulatory level where private and public bodies *might* be allowed to participate.

The third group of actors, manufacturers and technical professions in the construction sector (in particular architects and constructors), is the least institutionalised at EU level. Being observers in the Standing Committee on Construction (via their European federations) and the most active contributors to standardisation work, they have a more advisory position (which is however very strong in standardisation work) at EU level and cannot take for granted that the Commission or Member State authorities in the SCC will give their position enough consideration.

The second step is to *identify the structures and instruments* put in place *to provide information*. On the regulatory and administrative levels (besides the CPD), supporting documents were developed by the construction unit and the SCC. The channels used for their distribution were to a large extent via the representatives and observers in the SCC, leaving it to them to choose what and how detailed the information will be provided to other (downstream) actors. As we will see, distribution and discussion on "downstream" levels were facing different perceptions and acceptance, depending on the Member State, the organisation and the target group defined at EU level. Direct contact with other

132 Except for EOTA where membership depends on the designation of an organisation by national authorities.

actors, either in groups specifically set up for dealing with CPD/CE marking issues or participating in discussion in other (sometimes more general) networks, was another way of distributing information that was widely used at EU level. This channel was also used by actors to provide feedback and to contribute to the position specific representatives should present and defend at EU level. The third instrument was of a more passive nature, but allowed identifying how much importance different actors gave the CPD and CE marking and how relevant they saw it to provide background information and guidance: the websites and regulatory publications of public authorities, federations, companies and other interested parties (e.g. standardisation bodies). Websites were also giving an indication on what different actors consider as *their* target groups that should be addressed via the internet. Did administrations and organisations want to provide a wide audience with information, or were they targeting very specific actors? How useful was the information for individuals or groups who were not so deeply involved in the discussion on CE marking? Could small and medium-sized enterprises (SMEs) have used this information in their daily work? Were there language barriers for actors who were less accustomed to working with English texts (which is in several cases the only language that documents were written and distributed in at EU level)?

In the third and last step, the possibilities for receiving feedback provided by "downstream" levels should be identified. In most cases the bottom-up information flow is less obvious, because it is less institutionalised and therefore dependent on the willingness and the capability of the providers of information (i.e. the Construction Unit (I do not change this from here. MF must decide the change. My advice is "Construction Unit" in all case, since it is a proper name. But this can be done with the spell-checker), Member State authorities, federations) on how feedback is received and used. In fact, the feedback mechanisms were in many cases identified during the qualitative interviews and the questionnaires used. Therefore, more information on that part of the information flow will be found in the next chapter (Assumptions at EU level) indicating that this is based more on individual perceptions than clearly defined and publicly available procedures.

3.2.1 The European Commission

As a Directive "approximating" national European and national regulations on the performance of construction products, several other European Directives, and therefore several other Commission services than the construction unit of the Directorate General for Enterprises and Industry, are influencing the practical requirements of the Construction Products Directive (CPD). On the other hand, only two units – a horizontal unit covering all general aspects on standardisation, and a sector-specific unit for issues of the construction sector – are specifically relevant for the practical implementation of the CPD. Since the CPD is only in some parts considered as a "true" New Approach Directive, and its obligatory CE marking raises still many questions by interested parties (in particular Industry), the horizontal unit is also contacted in providing interpretations about CE marked products.

However, it is the sector-specific construction unit that provides most of the information and interpretation of the CPD and its implementation instruments. It is also the one dealing with assumed infringements of the Directive. Therefore, European and national interested parties are firstly looking for interpretation and guidance from this unit – or trying to have their positions more efficiently taken into consideration by that unit.

As mentioned earlier, while the general approach was pre-defined by the text of the Directive, each head of unit and each desk officer had to define their own priorities, based on the current situation. In the first period all parties tried to fill the gaps between the requirements of the Directive and the need for more specific information. The Interpretative Documents were the first to be created by the construction unit and the SCC, following previous guidance, which was later summarised in several Guidance Documents. In the meantime, the lack of technical standards forced another change of priorities for the construction unit by reallocating much of its resources to follow the standardisation work in CEN and then pressing the organisation to speed up the process. Nevertheless, the interpretative work remained a major task of the construction unit in all phases (see: The long history of the implementation of the CPD).

Instruments to provide information:

The Commission has several instruments providing information, which could also be partly used as feedback mechanism:

The Construction Products Directive:[133]

Published in the Official Journal and on the Commission website, it was made available for all interested parties. But while the Directive is only providing the *framework* for national implementation, it nevertheless indicates the goals of the Commission and the guiding text used in all Member States. The link to the national regulations (which are the binding laws for all national actors and international ones operating in a Member State) on the other hand is missing from the website.

The Standing Committee on Construction (SCC):

The "Comitology Committee", SCC, is one of the major tools of the Construction Products Directive to ensure that all relevant national requirements are taken into consideration and to guarantee a smooth implementation of the CPD.

The work of the SCC can be split into a "regulatory" and an "advising/ informative" part. The first covers among other things:

- the creation of specific working groups?/ technical committees to develop Interpretative Documents (see below);
- being involved in developing technical mandates for CEN and EOTA (see below);
- selecting the level of Attestation of Conformity (AoC) for products (from a declaration of the manufacturer to a stringent third-party control by technical bodies);
- acceptance of national technical specifications transmitted to the Commission as being considered by the Member State as relevant for fulfilling an essential requirement;
- consultation on Guidelines for European Technical Approvals before their publication.

The "advisory" or "informative" part can be considered as the "feedback mechanism" to the Commission and the SCC:

- the Commission and the SCC shall monitor the development in CEN and EOTA on the progress of technical specifications;

133 http://eur-lex.europa.eu/Notice.do?val=149656:cs&lang=de&list=149656:cs,&pos=1&page=1&nbl=1&pgs=10&hwords=.

- if a Member State or the Commission is considering that a (new) technical specification does not sufficiently cover the essential requirements, the SCC has to discuss this issue and, in severe cases, Member States can invoke the "safeguard clause" of the CPD (its Article 5.1) to avoid that a faulty specification might be obligatorily used, the SCC has to be consulted;
- discussing technical specifications (in force) which a Member State or the Commission might consider as no longer fulfilling the requirements of the CPD.

Member States are officially represented by a civil servant of the national ministry responsible for the implementation of the CPD (e.g. accepting a proposal of the construction unit for a Commission Decision – see below). This representative is also the one who would vote for his or her country. Nevertheless, up to two thirds of the Member States send more than one person to meetings. In some cases, the federal structure of a country gives its regions a strong position (albeit not a voting right) to follow the discussion in the SCC and present their points – in general coordinated with the official representative. In some Member States, more than one ministry is responsible for the implementation of the CPD – which in one case created the curiosity of having two *official* representatives in the SCC (but still only one voting right). Also seen in the SCC is the delegation of the role of official representation to a technical body that is assumed to be in a better position to deal with technical questions. All of this gives the Standing Committee on Construction a wide variety of national representation, expertise and interests.

A major task of the "regulatory" SCC is the discussion and acceptance of proposed Commission Decisions (therefore legally binding on all Member States) on the so-called Attestation of Conformity (AoC), which indicates if the declaration of conformity (with a harmonised European standard or an ETA) can be done by a manufacturer or if more control by an independent third party is required. The higher Member States are considering the relevance of a product in construction works (like structural components or insulation products in specific uses), the more stringent are the controls – including for a certification body (under the CPD called "Notified Body") as an independent, third-party checking of the product and the frequent checking of the production itself (AoC class 1 or 1+). All Member States vote for the Commission proposal and the final Decision will be published in the Official Journal of the European Union and the national Official Journals.

While Member States have regulatory power when voting for or against Commission Decisions, at least half of the time of a SCC meeting is used for questions concerning more technical than regulatory questions. Guidance Papers (see below) or other documents written by the construction unit were discussed and if consensus could be found, provided to other interested parties for guidance and reference. This second (non-regulatory) part is also open to all interested parties that have been invited by the construction unit. Therefore, industry federations, representatives of constructors, standardisation bodies, Approval Bodies and the Group of Notified Bodies (see below) are taking part in this discussion – in several cases because *they* have raised the issue in the first place and requested clarification.

The Preparatory Group of the SCC:

While the CPD has defined the role of the SCC, several issues were of a very technical nature and it seemed necessary to discuss them *before* a SCC meeting where, due to a tight agenda, these points might not be covered to an extent that would allow a well-founded decision in either the advisory or in the regulatory part of the meeting[134]. The Preparatory Group is a technical "offspring" of the SCC (followed later by additional working groups – called "regulator groups" or "expert groups" with very specific technical tasks). While this group is open to other experts than the ones participating in the SCC meeting – and in fact it is expected that representatives from all interested parties with a stronger technical and less political/administrative background will join – the group is as heterogeneous as the SCC. In some cases the same representatives attend both meetings, while other Member States authorities and interested parties send selected experts for very specific items on the agenda (who have to explain their positions later to the representatives in the SCC).

---

134 While the role of today's PG is definitely seen as work-reducing instrument for the SCC, its history was more linked to a struggle between the construction unit and Member States representatives. Personnel changes in the construction unit have also changed its approach about the scope and the content of the Interpretative Documents which faced resistance from some Member States in the SCC. In particular the question about how technical or political the content should be blocked the discussion and acceptance of the ID. Using the PG delegated some questions to another level and avoided a blockage in the SCC (see also: Bücker/Schlacke: Die Entstehung einer "politischen Verwaltung" durch EG-Ausschüsse, in: Joerges/Falke (Hrsg.): Das Ausschusswesen der Europäischen Union 2000 p. 188ff.).

"Regulators Groups" and "Expert Groups":

Even more focused on technical issues were specific working groups that have been set up by the Standing Committee on Construction and/or the construction unit around the year 2000. As the name "Regulator Groups" indicates, these groups consisted of civil servants from national authorities or experts for specific technical issues nominated by the relevant national authorities. Other interested parties were given observer status. These groups had to identify all relevant national laws and administrative provisions to be included in standardisation work. While considered as either focused on regulations or technical issues, the "Regulators Groups" as well as the "Expert Groups" also had a strong political role through providing arguments that were in general accepted by the construction unit in its decisions at technical and administrative levels. Therefore, defending specific national or sectoral interests of national administrations or industry sectors became part of the work of the experts in these groups.

Interpretative Documents (ID):[135]

One of the sometimes confusing points of the CPD for several actors is the link between construction products covered under the CPD and the technical requirements for buildings which are addressed in national or regional regulations and are in fact the basis for any product assessment. The six Essential Requirements of the CPD have identified the main performance criteria of a building, but the link between the planning and construction phases on the one hand and the performance of construction products on the other needed to be described in supporting documents. The Interpretative Documents were meant to provide this link. Each covering one Essential Requirement, the IDs were prepared in the first years of the work of the SCC by special technical committees adopted by the Standing Committee and Member States representatives providing the secretariat for them.[136] However, while technical and political approaches have changed since their first publication (e.g. stronger emphasis on energy

135 http://ec.europa.eu/enterprise/sectors/construction/documents/legislation/interpretative-documents/index_en.htm.

136 TC 1 (mechanical resistance): Germany; TC 2 (fire safety): United Kingdom; TC 3 (Hygiene, health and the environment): the Netherlands; TC 4 (safety in use): Spain; TC 5 (noise protecttion): Italy; TC 6 (energy economy): France; Additionally, the Commission's involvement in this work consisted mostly of the input from national experts (except for ID 3 and 4) because of their technical background.

performance, "sustainability"), they remained largely unchanged and were only partly reflecting developments in this sector which is reducing their use as reference. Also, the construction unit has only published the English version of these documents, but a number of actors in different Member States (i.e. Germany and Poland) have translated these documents.

Guidance Papers (GP):[137]

The Guidance Papers were developed mostly between the mid-nineties and the end of that decade (with the exception of a few GP still written after 2000 – see below) whenever any principal questions were raised by an interested party who needed not only clarification but also a large degree of consensus between the construction unit and Member States authorities, as well as the support of all relevant interested parties. While the construction unit was drafting the documents, all members and observers in the SCC had the right to comment on the text, but the control of the content remained with the Commission.

These papers are, in many aspects technical and very specifically addressing an issue important for one or more of the parties involved in the implementation of the CPD. But on the other hand, they had to be general enough to cover all relevant aspects, without restricting future developments too much. Some of the GPs cover administrative aspects of the CPD (GPs: A, D, I, K and M) others more technical aspects (GPs: B, C, E, F, G and H). In particular, the need to giving additional clarification on the first group shows the wide gap between the text of the CPD and different interpretations by several actors.

Guidance Papers A (Approved Bodies), D (CE marking) and K (Notified Bodies) are the most relevant ones for this study. It is interesting to see how very detailed certain procedures are described, including technical terms, the format of reports or the use of calculation methods versus testing (GP K). On the other hand, the wide range of "intended uses" of products left most of the competence of defining and declaring them to specification writers (GP D). Keeping in mind that these documents are addressed to experts with technical backgrounds, this strong emphasis on being as precise as possible in Guidance Papers suggests at least two different positions by different actors which the construction unit tried to bring together by developing its GP:

137 http://ec.europa.eu/enterprise/sectors/construction/documents/guidance-papers/index_en.htm.

- neither Member State authorities nor the construction unit were absolutely convinced that other actors (in this case in particular manufacturers and Notified Bodies) would agree and follow one common approach. Leaving the interpretation of the CPD and its implementation on technical terms to actors outside the European or national administration also partly defies the concept of the SCC as the control instrument used by national authorities. Therefore, detailed guidance left other parties less room for interpretations and increased the transparency and level of control by these authorities;
- in addition, national public authorities could transfer the official responsibility of the content of these documents to the construction unit ("the Commission"), while still being able to influence the content of these Guidance Papers wherever it seemed appropriate for them.

This concept might have also appealed to the federations of manufacturers and the Notified Bodies. The efforts of finding a common solutions was left to the authorities and reduced the burden of getting a common agreement on a specific approach between the members of a federation, a standardisation body, EOTA and the large number of Notified Bodies in the EU.

The fact that these Guidance Papers *were* in fact instruments of removing uncertainty with the text of the CPD is not only visible from their role of trying to clarify technical and procedural aspects to a very detailed level but also from looking at the dates when they were first issued: Guidance Paper A was approved in the mid 90s, about half a decade after the implementation of the CPD. Guidance Paper D followed in 1998 and GP K was finalised in the year 2000, just before the first harmonised standards became available (The last GP was finalised in 2005).

These documents are not part of the regulatory framework and therefore not legally binding on the different actors. However, they were seen as consensus between the main actors in the field of the administrative and regulatory system providing "state of the art" definitions and procedures within the framework of the CPD which should give these documents a *de facto* binding role.

These documents are only available in English, but national interested parties might have translated them into their own language. (The four Member States selected in this study have found different ways to deal with the lack of translations: The UK had obviously no adaptation costs; Germany translated the GP and they can be purchased from the DIBt; in Poland too, all GP were translated into the national language; Austrian actors are purchasing the DIBt translations where necessary).

Mandates[138] to technical specification writers (CEN and EOTA):[139]

Mandates are specific contracts between the European Committee for Standardisation (CEN) or the European Organisation for Technical Approvals (EOTA) on one hand and the European Commission on the other. They are the technical part of framework contracts between the Commission and these two organisations and should clearly define technical performance criteria that have to be addressed in the harmonised product standards and ETAGs (European Technical Approval Guideline) developed under the specific mandate. These mandates were (and are) prepared by the construction unit in cooperation with Member State authorities and industry (either using special working groups of the SCC or other ad hoc working groups chaired by the construction unit) and presented to the Standing Committee for discussion and approval. During the discussion, Member State authorities have the chance to check if all relevant national regulations have been taken into account or if the specifications in the mandate might make the practical implementation in their MS difficult and could ask for amendments in the mandate. This is also possible after a mandate has n already been given to CEN or EOTA but additional national requirements have been defined in the meantime (or have been considered as specifically relevant when the mandate was discussed for the first time). The mandates are publicly available documents and give specification writers (national standardisation bodies or EOTA members), test laboratories (future Notified Bodies) and industry an indication about the range and detail of the future harmonised standards[140] and ETAGs/ETAs.

---

138 33 product mandates and 3 horizontal mandates (for fire issues, construction products in contact with drinking water, dangerous substances).

139 The text of the CEN mandates, ETAs and European Technical Approval Guidelines (ETAG) can be found in the Commission's NANDO-Database: http://ec.europa.eu/enterprise/newapproach/nando/.

140 However, the contract between the Commission and CEN does include a reply by CEN on how the organisation plans to fulfil a specific mandate (e.g. number and scope of standards envisaged, additional technical documents to be developed) – the *work programme*. Compared with the discussion in the SCC on the content of the mandate, the discussion on the work programmes remained mostly between CEN and the Commission and are not publicly available.

The construction unit's website:[141]

This website provides the full text of the CPD, of all Interpretative Documents and of all Guidance Papers. It also gives some general guidance on how and when to use CE marking as well as a short "Frequently Asked Questions" section (last uploads in 2002). Links to product groups and available standards have been added, but they have not been updated recently. The website also tries to link several issues with the relevant text of the Directive and its supporting documents, but on the other hand links to other relevant European or national bodies do only exist in a few cases.

While used as references by many websites of national administrations and European or national federations, the information provided is only available in English. Also, links to national public or private bodies are missing.

NANDO[142]/NANDO-CPD
(New Approach Notified and Designated Organisations):

?To allow each party to rely on the information provided with CE marking, Member State authorities have to notify those certification bodies for which they are able to declare that they professionally fulfil their tasks.? The Commission services provide a database for the public, including data on construction products covered by harmonised product standards, and the Notified Bodies who are allowed to do it. In the past, the data were sent to the Commission services by the relevant Member State authorities and put into the database by the unit in the Commission responsible for maintaining the database. A new system now allows the national authorities to add the information on their own. The data is only available in English (a multilingual version was envisaged but has not yet been introduced).

The Official Journal of the European Union (EUOJ):

Like most national Official Journals the EUOJ consists of several parts, indicating regulatory announcements and legal texts in one part "L" and supporting issues in part "C". The EUOJ is used for the CPD to publish:

141 http://ec.europa.eu/enterprise/sectors/construction/index_en.htm.
142 http://ec.europa.eu/enterprise/newapproach/nando/.

- Commission Decisions for Attestation of Conformity Classes;
- lists of references (titles) of harmonised European standards for construction products covered under the CPD;
- European Technical Approval Guidelines endorsed by the Commission.

The three bullet points are references to documents that are legally binding (for harmonised standards, only their specific CPD related annex ZA). Therefore, this information is published in all official languages of the EU. The titles of a harmonised European standard are translated by CEN's national members.[143]

CEN Task Group, consultants and specific guidance/feedback:

The large number of documents developed at EU level did not remove the need for more detailed information, in particular when technical experts in CEN, EOTA and the GNB were facing (product-) specific questions in practical implementation. While consultants were used to provide most of the information and therefore were acting as "filter" to the construction unit, even they needed sometimes an "official" position of the construction unit. This need for clarification as well as the increasing need of the construction unit to monitor progress in CEN resulted in partly "institutionalised" exchange of information and guidance (like the CEN Task Group) but also the less formal participation of officials in different working groups, TCs or sector groups of all three EU-based organisations.

3.2.2 Member States authorities

The four Member States in this study have several things in common, like the split into a political administrative body (ministry) being in charge of implementing a national law on construction products (based on the CPD) and a technical body providing more user-oriented input. While the ministries cover national issues and providing access to national regulations on their websites, the techni-

143 If they are provided significantly late after the standard has been officially adopted by CEN and accepted by the construction unit, a gap between the official publication and use of the standard and the publication in the OJ of the EU will occur. Since the publication in the OJ is the official starting date for the coexistence period, delays could create confusion in the market and create problems (and financial losses) for manufacturers who have invested in an early use of CE marking.

cal bodies are (in these four cases) either directly market actors (e.g. as EOTA members) or they have experienced a recent split into a scientific technical organisation and an economic-oriented organisation, providing product assessments and national certificates. But while these arrangements are similar in all four countries, a closer look reveals more differences of the national political and administrative structures but also the practical implementation of their construction products regulations.

3.2.2.1 Germany

The federal structure of Germany has created several levels of regulatory responsibilities, resulting in partly different priorities but also common goals which are dealt with using different instruments by the respective authorities at federal, regional (*Länder*) and local levels. The two most relevant authorities in this study are the *Bundesministerium fur Verkehr, Bau und Stadtplanung* (Federal Ministry for Traffic, Construction and Urban Development – BMVBS) and the *Deutsche Institut für Bautechnik* (DIBt) as coordination body of the German *Länder*. While the additional tasks introduced by the CPD had their impact on the administrative structure by allocating resources to it (like the new task of the DIBt as a "notifying authority" or as an EOTA member), the personnel structure has been very consistent over the years.[144]

The Federal Ministry for Transport, Building and Urban Affairs (Bundesministerium für Verkehr, Bau und Stadtplanung – BMVBS)[145]

Like all German federal ministries, the Federal Ministry for Transport, Building and Urban Affairs covers national policies beyond specific *Länder* competences (such as railways and transport on water, which naturally affects all regions). In its own field, it also provides guidance on regional and urban planning and on public tendering rules for federal authorities (*Vergabe- und Vertragsordnung für Bauleistungen – VOB* – and more specific: general technical requirements in

144 Beside the point that Germany is in general not using a rotation system for its civil servants, it was stressed during the interviews that the national regulatory system was not significantly affected after the adoption of the CPD and therefore also the administrative structure and the use of resources did not need serious changes.

145 http://www.bmvbs.de/.

contracts – *Allgemeine Technische Vertragsbedingungen – ATV*)[146]. It is also responsible for the implementation of the CPD on federal level via the German "*Bauproduktegesetz*" (Federal Law for Construction Products, my translation) and the adaptation of other relevant regulations at Federal level. The BMVBS officially represents Germany in the Standing Committee on Construction (SCC).

There is a split in responsibilities and priorities when it comes to *quality* of construction works. Being responsible for federal construction works (like federal buildings, national highways or waterways owned and maintained by federal bodies), the Federal Ministry is active in planning and construction.[147] The rules of this approach are only obligatory for federal construction works, but they are also considered as guidance that should influence other public and private actors ("filtering down effect"). This approach reflects very well the general position of the ministry (and also in the position presented in the interview): it provides guidance to the German construction market and therefore it is using instruments to promote and convince more than obligatory measures.[148] Nevertheless, for federal construction works, the required use of CE marked construction products also directly affects the federal level in Germany and so is introduced into the technical tendering requirements of Federal actors.

Based on the "principle of subsidiarity", most regulations about the requirements for buildings (e.g. design, safety) are developed and enforced at regional (*Länder*) level. While the Ministry is involved in the development of regional building regulations, defining requirements for buildings (e.g. design, safety) lies within the responsibility of the building authorities of the *Länder,* who have to include all relevant aspects of the *Bauproduktegesetz*, but who still have a wide range of possibilities to define any specific use or limitations for specific uses of construction products if necessary (e.g. specific performance of buildings where higher safety standards are of importance – like hospitals or kindergartens).

146 The VOB refers in annex TS specifically to European technical standards and European Technical Approvals.

147 A position that has been used to develop its own system on "sustainable construction" criteria, but also to evaluate them on Federal buildings.

148 This would correspond to *Scharpf's* assumption that the lack of a federal administrative infrastructure (in construction) and the dependency on administrative support on *Länder* level would make instruments below an obligatory level (like voluntary agreements) more appealing because they could be implemented without trying to get specific requirements trough the structure of the state. (Scharpf: Games Real Actors Play 1997 p. 203)

The German Länder – Bautenministerien der Länder and the Deutsche Institut für Bautechnik (DIBt)[149]

Each of the sixteen German States (the *Bundesländer*) is responsible for defining requirements of buildings in their respective regional building codes, also addressing possible specific climatic or cultural issues that have to be taken into consideration during the planning and the construction process. The ministries of the *Länder* are also in charge of accepting construction products which are not (yet) covered by technical standards for their intended uses in buildings. However, it was not considered practical to develop planning and material?/product requirements in each of the *Länder*. A coordination body for various aspects in construction was considered as a better solution. The German *Länder* agreed on transferring some technical, scientific and administrative tasks to a specific body: the *Deutsche Insitut für Bautechnik* (DIBt) which was set up by law in 1968.

Because of the technical background and expertise of the DIBt, this organisation is also representing the interests of the *Länder* at the European level: on one hand in the field of standardisation, mostly by participating in mirror committees of DIN following and commenting the work in CEN's technical committees (TC), or – in cooperation with the German Federal Ministry for Transport, Building and Urban Affairs – by participating together in the Standing Committee for Construction (SCC) or when addressing issues to the Commission (e.g. in the Preparatory Group of the SCC) either together or at least closely coordinated. Also, in an official administrative function is the DIBt coordination and advisory body for market surveillance for the authorities of the *Länder*.

Being partly a research institute, the DIBt, combines its resources of internal and external experts with its tasks to provide guidance to several design and construction issues, as well as evaluating and certifying the construction products used in the different *Länder*. Keeping in mind that about 2000 certificates (*Ü-Zeichen*) are given to manufacturers every year, this part of the work not only uses a large part of DIBt's resources, but it can also be considered as a relevant source of income for a body that can only partly depend on the authorities of the *Länder* to cover its expenses.

In addition, this organisation has also been nominated by Germany (based on an agreement between the federal and *Länder* levels) as EOTA member of Germany (as federal body) and is therefore active in the work of EOTA on

149 http://www.dibt.de/.

several levels and technical fields as well as assessing products for European Technical Approvals (ETA).

***

Being the official link between Germany and the Commission and representing the Federal Republic in the SCC, the BMVBS has used a special group of representatives from the public side and interested parties ranging from the German *Länder* (represented by the DIBt), the German standardisation organisation DIN, to federations of manufacturers and constructors, called "*Vorbereitender Ausschuss EG-Harmonisierung*" (VAEG – Preparatory Committee EC-Hamonisation, translation MF). This committee meets in advance of the next SCC meeting to discuss the agenda items and documents provided by the Commission. During the meetings, the different interested parties (about 30-50 out of about 100 actively participate in the meeting) can present their own political or technical position[150]. However, they only have an advisory role to the Ministry, leaving it to the discretion of the representative of the FMVBS how and when to include these comments in the discussion in the SCC.

A more technical body has been set up to deal with specific technical issues, in particular the Commission's mandates to CEN. The "*Koordinierungskreis Mandate*" (KKM – Coordination Group Mandates, translation MF) supports the German delegation and providing information before the Preparatory Group meeting of the Commission in Brussels.

In addition, special national committees dealing with technical issues (e.g. *Fachkommission Bauplanung, Fachkommission Bau* at federal level and ARGEBAU conferences and technical committess – *Fachkommission Bautechnik, Gundsatzausschuss* – on *Länder* level) could invite the representatives acting as interface between EU and national activities to coordinate their approaches. However, the most active link exist between the BMVBS and the DIBt as representatives of Federal and *Länder* interests and since both are participating in all SCC meeting.

The CPD is only one of several issues on the agenda of the ministry. References to the CPD and CE marking on the ministry's website can only be found on a link to a conference on the ongoing amendment of the CPD in Berlin in

150 This group has been in place as discussion forum before the CPD came into force and was afterwards maintained and used for CPD specific issues.

May 2007. While here a link to the Commission's EUR-Lex database has been provided where the full text of the CPD can be found, information on the function and use of CE marking are not available on the BMVBS's website. The information on the website is only available in German

The website of the DIBt is focussed on its role as provider of information on technical questions and as provider of certificates (*Ü-Zeichen* and ETAs) for construction products. Therefore, the emphasis is put on information on how certificates could be requested and finally given to a manufacturer. References to CE marking, its nature as well as the quantity and quality of the information provided by a CE marking can only be found in a guidance paper on the national implementation of harmonised standards.[151] Considering that this document seems to be written for authorities and testing or inspecting bodies, manufacturers, civil engineers or other interested parties might not get much information on CE marking.

A little bit more information on CE marking for practical users can be found in the annual report of the DIBt. While the annual report is placing the description on its own *Ü-Zeichen*, references to its membership in UEAtc and information on ETAs *before* the reference to CE marking – it provides a transparent and easily understandable overview on CE marking and more detailed information on the six essential requirements (to be found in the chapter on regulatory requirements for construction products and construction works). But again, because of the logical line of thought from national regulatory requirements to harmonisation in harmonised European standards or Technical Approvals, the link between regulatory requirements and CE marking is not always clear. The website allows choosing between a German and an English version.

3.2.2.2 The United Kingdom

Department for Communities and Local Government[152]

Compared with Germany, the administrative structure, in particular the public body and the unit which were in charge of implementing the administrative and technical aspects of the UK Construction Products Regulation have seen several changes. Another difference is the link between administration and the technical body dealing with CPD issues: while the German Federal Ministry and the DIBt

151 http://www.dibt.de/de/data/hEN_Merkblatt.pdf.

152 http://www.communities.gov.uk/corporate/.

have different origins and tasks, the link between the Department for Communities and Local Government and the British Research Establishment (BRE)[153] is much closer. In fact, the BRE was part of the Department before it was privatised in 1997.

However, the move to the private sector has not affected its specific work and today BRE still fulfils some tasks for the authorities (now on a contractual basis): providing technical input for the department in charge, and also informing and training authorities, industry and interested parties on the requirements of the *Construction Products Regulations* (the national implementation of the CPD) and the use of CE marking. Based on the system used in the UK of rotating civil servants over intervals of about three to four years, the department has seen several individuals working with the CPD, while BRE has been more consistent in keeping the same experts for European issues in general and the CPD in particular. Nevertheless, after the "rush" of the implementation phase was over (and even more important: no harmonised European standards followed which would have required continuous strong involvement from the authorities), both the Department and BRE have seen significant reductions in employees working on these issues.

Similar to the German DIBt, BRE is in general a provider of technical and scientific knowledge to authorities and therefore very much involved in creating and adapting building codes – in the UK for three regions: England and Wales, Scotland and Northern Ireland. Also similar is its role as providing technical expertise for the national delegation in the Standing Committee on Construction (SCC). In fact, BRE is represents the UK in the Preparatory Group of the SCC because of the more technical nature of the issues discussed in these meetings.

While in the past the German DIBt and the Austrian OIB (see below) were holding the presidency of EOTA, BRE has been more involved in the Group of Notified Bodies (GNB) and has provided the secretariat for several years.

***

Compared with Germany, the UK does not consider CE marking as obligatory or the only marking that market surveillance authorities have to take into consideration. However, references to the CPD, CE marking can be found in the relevant (national) regulatory and technical documents.

153 http://www.bre.co.uk/index.jsp.

Building regulations define the general functional requirements of buildings. While the fourteen requirements ("parts" of Schedule I of the Building Regulation) cover all relevant aspects of a building (i.e. structure, fire safety, ventilation, hygiene or access to and use of buildings), they are still very general in setting performance criteria and refer to "reasonable", "adequate" or "appropriate". To guarantee that at the end the building *will* perform "adequately" for common practice, the regulations are supplemented by "Approved Documents" providing more technical definitions, guidance or even practical examples on designing according to common practice and reference to relevant national or European standards (i.e. hENs). Alternative methods to the ones mentioned in the Approved Documents could also be used if compliance with the basic requirements can be proven.

Also the role of CE marking and European Technical Approvals are described in the Approved Documents. Keeping in mind the position of the UK about the non-obligatory nature of CE marking, the document nevertheless *de facto* focuses on the instruments of the CPD and CE marking. Based on the assumption that not only professionals but also do-it-yourself enthusiasts might use construction products, the document does not go very much into detail on the information provided by CE marking but indicates that a CE marked product can be used and shall be accepted by building authorities (except incorrect use of the marking or wrong application in the building). (see: Actors at national level).

More specific information can be found in a document published by the authorities in 2001 (at this time the responsible unit was working for the Department for Transport, Local Government and the Regions – DTLR) on "CE marking under the Construction Products Directive", which not only provides a good overview on the framework and the instruments of the CPD but also targets all interested parties and potential users (manufacturers, enforcement authorities, building control bodies, civil engineers in general and attestation bodies) to follow the ongoing developments in European standardisation and technical approvals and to adapt their documents and work accordingly.

In addition, the UK authorities have been very active in providing information and guidance to accession countries that have to implement the CPD before joining the European Union. In conferences especially set up for the new Member States their representatives could get more information on past experience with the CPD and guidance for its implementation (avoiding the controversial issue of the obligatory nature of the CPD CE marking).

Information on specific CPD issues is distributed via the Joint Advisory Committee (JAC) to all interested parties. While the JAC has a wide range of members, it is in fact a virtual group where active participation is not required. More active parties (meaning that they might be more affected by activities around the CPD) meet in a briefing panel chaired by BRE prior to each new meeting of the Standing Committee on Construction (SCC) to discuss their positions about the latest developments and documents for the SCC. This meeting indicates the position of interested parties (about seven were reported as actively participating in the meeting) and this process allows BRE to advise the Department on which points are of the greatest interest and most pressing from the view of the other actors involved, while in the end the Department has to decide which points to take up in the SCC meeting.

The website of the Department for Communities and Local Governments provides the best overview and texts of relevant building regulations of all websites of public authorities in this study. This covers not only national or regional laws but also a description of the role of CE marking within the framework of the CPD and links to the relevant sites of the construction unit (i.e. Commission Decisions, Guidance Papers). This also includes requirements for Approval Bodies (EOTA members), "Competent Persons" (for self-certification of building works) and links to all interested parties involved. In addition, there is a link ("Planning Portal"[154]) for the general public, as well as for professional users, on how to interpret and use building regulations and Approved Documents.

Like the DIBt, BRE also puts stronger emphasis on providing guidance and promotes its services (e.g. BRE Global as Approval Body) than on providing information on CE marking (which is in any case not seen as obligatory in the UK). However, visitors to the website are informed that it becomes obligatory when entering other (European) markets outside the UK.

3.2.2.3 Austria

Based on a common political, social and administrative history, it is not surprising that Austria and Germany have developed very similar administrative structures. Austria is also a federal state with nine *Länder* and a split of responsibilities between the federal and the *Länder* levels. However, the political weight

154 http://www.planningportal.gov.uk/.

of the Austrian *Länder* is not as strong as in Germany but nonetheless causes more debate and friction.[155]

The task of the implementation of the CPD is in the hands of the Federal Ministry of Economics and Labour (BMWA) at federal level, and the *Österreiche Institut für Bautechnik* (OIB) being the coordinating body for aspects concerning the nine *Länder* and covering technical issues. As in Germany, the turnover of civil servants in the federal and *Länder* administrations is low, with only few changes of the representatives in the BMWA and the OIB at EU level. However, as a country with only one tenth of the population of Germany, it is obvious that also the resources available for the BMWA and the OIB cannot match those of their German counterparts. On the other hand, as shown below, this has been partly compensated by using the German experience and also copying some of its instruments and adapting them to Austrian resources and requirements.

Austrian Federal Ministry of Economics and Labour
(Bundesministerium fur Wirtschaft und Arbeit – BMWA)[156]

The Federal Ministry of Economics and Labour (BMWA) is responsible for implementing the Austrian *Bauproduktegesetz (Federal Law for Construction Products)*. It also officially represents Austria in the SCC. As in the German system, several construction works in the field of infrastructure are built and maintained by federal ministries or bodies and therefore the CPD directly affects the work of federal authorities – with the BMWA acting as the link between the CPD and Austrian federal bodies.

However, in most cases the building codes of the Austrian *Länder* (one for each of the *Länder*) apply for most construction works. References are made to CE marked products (based on the regional implementation of the federal *Bauproduktegesetz*) but it remains within the power of the regional regulators to define specific requirements for the use of construction products.

155 See also: Mayer: Verfassung im Spannungsfeld politischer Interessen; 2005. Differences in the interpretation of the competences of federal and regional (*Länder*) authorities when implementing the national implementation of the CPD the Austrian (*Bauproduktegesetz*) are reflected on the website where a legal "*Gutachten*" states the prior competence of the prior competence of the federal ministry in that matter.

156 http://www.bmwa.gv.at/EN/default.htm.

The Austrian Länder – the Österreichisches Institut für Bautechnik (OIB)[157]

The Austrian Institute of Construction Engineering (*Österreichisches Institut für Bautechnik* – OIB) is the coordinating body for the regional building authorities (*Landesämter*) of all nine *Bundesländer*. It is represents the interests of the *Länder* in the SCC and its Preparatory Group.

It is not a coincidence that the structure and responsibilities of the OIB are very similar to the DIBt's. Austrian authorities looked closely at the German system of implementing the CPD at administrative and technical levels and, having very similar political structures (subsidiarity of responsibilities between Federal and *Länder* levels), it seemed the most pragmatic way of copying a system that seemed to have already worked efficiently for several years.

Following the German example, the OIB is partly a coordination body, partly a representative of the nine *Länder* vis-à-vis federal authorities and in the SCC, as well as partly a research institute and provider of technical information and guidance on several aspects, including new developments at EU level (e.g. the Energy Performance of Buildings Directive and its practical impact for all relevant actors in Austria). Last but not least, it is also an EOTA member but (due to being a smaller organisation) less active within EOTA than the DIBt.

***

The BMWA and the OIB have each developed a communication system that is based more on providing information to downstream users than permanently established working groups which have all actors involved. Meetings in the BMWA depend to a certain extent on how much different actors show interest in specific issues but, in general, information is sent to the Austrian Chamber of Commerce (*Wirtschaftskammer Österreich* – WKO) to be distributed to its relevant subsections. Meetings of the OIB for representatives of the *Länder* are more frequent. Both bodies also use information events for informing interested parties and receiving feedback.

The website of the Austrian Federal Ministry of Economics and Labour (BMWA)[158] provides information on construction products, starting with a definition of CE marking for construction products. A general definition of construction products (copied from the CPD) and links to the relevant Austrian con-

157 http://www.oib.or.at/.

158 http://www.bmwa.gv.at/BMWA/Schwerpunkte/Unternehmen/Bauprodukte/default.htm.

struction products law (*Bauproduktegesetz*) and related regulations, as well as information on harmonised standards, Technical Approvals and Notified Bodies (with links to the Commission's NANDO database) can also be found. The text stays as close as possible to the CPD but also provides links to the most relevant legal text national implementations. In addition, all Guidance Papers are available on the website (in English)[159].

While the federal ministry's website provides some general information in German and English, the information available in German about the construction sector has not been translated into English.

Following the concept of a "top-down" communication approach, the website of the OIB is very thorough in providing information on the CPD, its instruments and their impact on the practical work in the construction sector. One can follow the concept of the CPD, from the role of harmonised European standards, to the use of CE marking and, finally, to all relevant standards covering construction products under the CPD (*Baustoffliste ÖE*). In general, the website provides a huge amount of information and links to other relevant sites for all interested parties involved, including downstream authorities who seem to have been a major target group (considering the large number of references to federal and regional regulations on the site). However, most information is only available in German.

Additional information is given by a frequent publication of the OIB: *OIB aktuell*, which covers technical and regulatory developments at national and EU levels. This magazine is also used for distributing information on CPD-related aspects and the interpretation by the OIB. A more direct approach was chosen in 1999 till 2001 when the OIB presented the concept of the CPD and CE marking to interested parties in conferences in all of the Austrian *Länder*.

159 However, the website gives the impression that all 500 harmonised standards are still under development which might confuse the reader when opening the link to the European Official Journal where the titles of all available harmonised standards are published.

3.2.2.4 Poland

Looking at the distribution of administrative and technical responsibilities, Poland shows several similarities to the UK[160]. Firstly, the administrative structure leaves control to national authorities, while authorities on regional level (*voivodships* – provinces, *powiats* – roughly translated as "counties" and *gminas* – communes or municipalities) are only left with executive tasks. The national Ministry for Infrastructure (*Ministerstwo Infrastruktury*) has the responsibility of implementing the national law for construction products, while technical issues are covered by the Building Research Institute (*Instytut Techniki Budowlanej – ITB*). Also similar to the UK, the ITB is more consistent in its working structure and individuals are more involved in specific tasks than those in the ministry. Nevertheless, of the four countries selected in this study Poland provides the most structured and biggest market surveillance system in the construction sector, managed by the General Office of Building Control.

Ministry for Infrastructure (Ministerstwo Infrastruktury)[161]
Ministry of Economy (Ministerstwo Gospordarki)[162]

The responsibility of the implementation of CE marking is *de facto* split between these two ministries. While the Ministry for Infrastructure can be considered as the most important authority for construction works (and also represents Poland in the SCC), all New Approach Directives (including the CPD) have been put together in a general national law, covering all common issues (e.g. the role of Notified Bodies, CE marking – in Poland obligatory for all products covered by *any* New Approach Directive) and splitting only in specific laws for sector or product-specific requirements laid down in the European Directives, and are the responsibility of the Ministry of Economy. Therefore, information on CE mark-

160 However, the contacts between building authorities in the administrative and technical field are closer to France than the UK. In fact, several members of the ministry and the ITB have been working for some years as guest of the French CSTB (*Centre Scientifique et Technique du Bâtiment*) in France. These contacts have also helped the authorities in Poland to follow closely the developments of the CPD, its implementation phase and the practical experience of the EU12 Member States.

161 http://www.mi.gov.pl/.

162 http://www.mg.gov.pl/.

ing, its role, use and control can be found on the website of the Ministry of Economy.[163]

Building Research Institute (Instytut Techniki Budowlanej – ITB)[164]

As in the other three countries, this technical institute is a support body for a national ministry, covering technical aspects of European and national policies and providing technical expertise and studies to facilitate the decision-finding process for national actors at national and EU levels. Its tasks also include the evaluation of European harmonised standards for the Ministry. Like BRE, the ITB coordinates input from interested parties and advises the Ministry for Infrastructure (including preparing for the SCC meetings).

The ITB represents Poland in the Preparatory Group of the SCC (as do the technical institutes of the other three MS) and sometimes assumes an advisory role in the SCC meetings (as for the UK). The ITB is an EOTA member, Notified Body and also an independent test laboratory and certification body for the Polish "B" mark (for products for which no CE marking exists). The ITB seems to be the most active of the Polish actors in providing information to different interested parties and receiving feedback from them. This is partly a result of its role as research institute and provider of information in general. Being less in an administrative and "enforcing" role (compared to the Office of Competition and Consumer Protection or the General Office of Building Control), it is more dependent on information provided than are the national authorities involved in construction.

Office of Competition and Consumer Protection
(Urząd Ochrony Konkurencji i Konsumentów – UOKiK)[165]

This body is responsible for market surveillance and coordinating the tasks of several specialised agencies which monitor, inspect and report on the use of CE marking for products covered by European Directives (and the laws implementing them at national level). Products not fulfilling the requirements of CE marking or products that have been wrongly CE marked are listed in publicly

163 http://www.mg.gov.pl/Przedsiebiorcy/Ocena+zgodnosci/.
164 http://www.itb.katowice.pl/.
165 http://www.uokik.gov.pl/en/.

available lists[166]. However, for construction products, a more specific body is in charge of market surveillance:

General Office of Building Control
(Główny Urząd Nadzoru Budowlanego – GUNB)[167]

The General Inspector for Building Control, as head of the GUNB, is appointed by the Prime Minister and is responsible for the supervision of construction sites as well as for market surveillance. Control and administration of construction works (buildings and civil engineering work) are split into a design part (architectural-building administration) and actual construction (building control). Both are served by a centralised approach down to local governors (for design) and county inspectors for building control.

Compared with the other three Member States in this study, market surveillance has a longer history in Poland which has allowed for a more developed system. In fact, about 400 inspectors (in regions – *voivod* – and municipalities) are active in day-to-day inspections and special investigations in case of accidents. In general, this centralised system provides a harmonised approach throughout the country, but regional differences in the priorities set by each unit of inspectors are possible.

***

As mentioned above, information on CE marking is provided by the Ministry of Economy as the one covering the national implementation of all European Directives that require CE marking on products. These laws also refer to the need of market surveillance and liability arising from wrongly using CE marking. More information on the obligations of manufacturers are published on the website of the Office of Competition and Consumer Protection (UOKiK – in general both are available in Polish and to a large extent also in English.) as well as a list of products that have been identified as not fulfilling legal requirements or which have their own declaration of performance (in Polish only)[168].

166 http://www.gunb.gov.pl/kwzwb/index.php.
167 http://www.gunb.gov.pl/.
168 http://publikacje.uokik.gov.pl/hermes_pub/WebEngine/DocumentSearchForm.aspx?CDC=PublicRWN.

Additional information can be found on the website of the GUNB (several parts there have been published in English too). While CE marking is not explicitly mentioned, the task of controlling construction products used in the works is mentioned.

The ITB as the body which is active at national as well as European levels has three main routes for distributing information to other interested parties (beside the Ministry for Infrastructure): The most comprehensive and consistent approach is the publication of documents for internal use and for the wider public. (This is done every three months). The ITB has dedicated enough resources for translation, allowing it to make available practically all relevant documents provided by European actors (the construction unit, the SCC, CEN, EOTA and the GNB) in Polish. The SCC Interpretative Documents and the Guidance Documents have not only been translated themselves but also comments by ITB experts, so as to facilitate the use of these documents.

The second route s focuses on presentations for interested parties. In particular industrial fairs (e.g. the Poznan International Fair) are used to presenting specific issues, including developments and requirements at EU level that are or will affect national actors.

The third approach is based on introducing and explaining specific issues in publications in technical journals. Considering the very central position of the ITB in Poland, they have a strong position as a provider of information and its interpretation in the construction sector.

The ITB is the most thorough in providing information on its activities at EU level, the CPD (and its national implementation) and CE marking. The main documents developed at EU level are translated into Polish and are made available by the ITB[169] – either in an electronic version or in special publications (not everything is available in an electronic version on the web, but a table of content allows a first overview – and a paper copy can be ordered from the ITB).

The ITB website is mostly in Polish but the parts covering the general position of the ITB, as well as some detailed information, are available in English ("ITB in European Union").

169 http://www.itb.pl/ue/index.htm.

3.2.3 *Federations*

3.2.3.1 Federations of manufacturers

In general, manufacturers are not only one of the most important target groups of the CPD but are also directly mentioned in the Directive. In most cases they are already organised under "umbrella" federations at national level. National federations have set up European representations, in particular the Council of European Producers of Materials for Construction (CEPMC) and most of the national "umbrella" federations are members of CEPMC[170]. In parallel, federations for specific materials or products have also been established at European level. In most cases, they follow their sector specific agenda but many of them are associated members of CEPMC too[171].

While all of these federations could contact the Commission directly (and many of them do when raising sector-specific issues), CEPMC has a unique role vis-à-vis the construction unit. From its early days on, it has been an "observer" in the Standing Committee on Construction (SCC) where the Commission has considered that only *one* body should represent the interests of the manufacturing industry. Over the years, a few additional federations have been added to the number of observers, but still CEPMC (supported by experts provided by its national members) is considered by many actors as the main representative of industry vis-à-vis the construction unit. However, this view is contested by some federations. CEPMC also participates in several working groups under the framework of the CPD (including a specific working group on CE marking), using experts from national federations to represent the federation in those discussions. While these working groups discuss CEPMC's position in specific (horizontal and technical) fields, preparation for the SCC meeting and its Preparatory Group are only done by CEPMC employees, selecting from the feedback the federation has had from its members and working groups.

CEPMC's website provides links to some of the main organisations (including the Commission and the technical specification writers) and "position papers" that have been addressed mainly to the Commission on different issues concerning CE marking, but they only indirectly provide guidance on how to interpret and use CE marking for its members. The website provides information in English, French and German.

170 http://www.cepmc.org/en/index.html.
171 http://www.cepmc.org/en/list385.html.

European Mortar Industry Organisation (EMO)[172]

Mortar is one of the most "basic" construction product, but also one that depends on the materials used in it, which are often locally extracted or produced. Also, its distribution is rather restricted because its high transport costs of transport over longer distances, stemming from its high bulk but low value.

EMO has so far been a federation of the "old" Member States, representing national mortar federations in 13 of the EU-15 Member States. As a member of CEPMC, the work between these two European federations is split between general issues covered by CEPMC and sector-specific issues dealt with in EMO. Since only about 20% of the information coming from the Commission services is specifically relevant for the mortar sector, contacts between the federation and its national members happen more on a case-by-case than on a regular basis.

EMO's website (in English) provides a good overview of the role of CE marking for mortar manufacturers (e.g. classes of attestation of conformity, information to accompany CE marking), and a list of all European standards available or under development in CEN. However, regular meetings where information can be more specifically distributed were seen as very relevant in the information flow.

European Insulation Manufacturer's Association (EURIMA)[173]

Thermal insulation products are more complex products and require more technology in the manufacturing process. This industry also shows a high concentration of big companies that operate even beyond the European Economic Area. Also, the federation itself includes members from non-EU countries.

The main focus is on the European Directive on Energy Performance of Buildings and its impact on the sector. Also the products are promoted in view of their specific performance than on specific marks: CE marking is mentioned on the federation's website (English, French, German), but no detailed information is provided.

172 http://www.euromortar.com/index.htm.
173 http://www.eurima.org/.

European Ceramics Industries (CERAME-UNIE)[174]

Ceramic products covering a wide range of products – from bricks to roof tiles, sanitary ware to high tech parts, but representing the construction sector is nevertheless CERAME-UNIE's main field of activity. Its members are themselves European federations for specific manufacturers who are again umbrella organisations for several national federations.

Its website (providing information in English) is aiming at members and less providing information for other interested parties. CE marking is mentioned but no links to other actors provided.

Tiles and Bricks Europe AISBL (TBE)[175]

Associated to CERAME-UNIE since 1991, TBE is a few decades older (founded in 1952) but with its office previously located in Switzerland (till 2002) its role on European level is *de facto* closely linked to CERAME-UNIE, given that the same individuals work in both federations.

TBE shows on its website a strong interest in "sustainability" and is clearly promoting clay products within this concept. References to CE marking are missing. Information on CE marking is, to a large extent, presented in regular or specific meetings with members.

3.2.3.2 Federations of contractors (construction companies)

Membership in one of the oldest federations (created in 1905) the European Construction Industry Federation (*Federation de l'Industrie Européenne de la Construction* – FIEC) is not limited to national "umbrella" federations (partly because in some Member States of the EU there is more than one federation) and therefore, more national members have joined the European federation.[176] FIEC has observer status in the SCC and its Technical Commission (TEC- Directives, Standards and Quality Assurance) covers CPD related issues. In addition, FIEC is the first contact for CEN and EOTA for issues concerning contractors.

Information is mostly provided via FIEC′s regular publications, but even more relevant is case-by-case information on current or new issues. This is not only providing information to members but is also used to create interest or

174 http://www.cerameunie.eu/.
175 http://www.staywithclay.com/default-en.asp.
176 http://www.fiec.org/Content/Default.asp?PageID=18.

even find members who are willing to follow specific issues at EU level – and if possible to actively participate in working groups and other activities on EU level.

A look at FIEC's website indicates that while the ongoing revision of the Construction Products Directive is clearly in the focus of FIEC, the current version of the CPD can only be considered as one – and not the most pressing – issue for this federation. Within a wide range of currently relevant issues, the implementation of the CPD has only been touched by a number of position papers (published in 2004) on the use of CE marking in which FIEC on the one hand provided a good overview on the nature of CE marking, but also raised its concerns about the practical use and credibility of CE marking for constructors.[177] While addressing the issue of the CPD and CE marking in general, no detailed explanations or guidance has been provided on the website. The website provides information in English, French and German.

3.2.3.3 Federations of architects

The Architect's Council of Europe (ACE)[178] represents the interests of architects at European level. Considering itself as a profession that is providing a professional *service* than dealing with specific products, the main interest lies with qualifications (focusing on technical universities and schools) and recognition of this specific profession and its role in the planning and procurement process (focusing on political players at EU and national levels). ACE has observer status in the SCC but in general it is not participating actively in the SCC meetings.

While the federation of constructors at least address the issue of the CPD and CE marked products, ACE's website does not refer to it at all. On the contrary, CPD is also the acronym for "Continued Professional Development". Since the CPD and CE marking have so far not been of any particular interest, the website makes no references to them or provides links to other sites. The website provides information in English and French.

ACE's main dissemination instrument is its newsletter, distributed to its members and where sometimes (general) information is published.

177 http://www.fiec.org/Content/Default.asp?PageID=23.

178 http://www.ace-cae.org/MemberN/Content/EN/wel/wel/welcome.html.

3.2.4 Certification Bodies, Test laboratories – the Group of Notified Bodies (GNB)

Certification bodies and test laboratories have to be notified to the European Commission by the Member States' responsible authorities as being organisations which are considered as the official bodies capable of certifying compliance with hENs or ETAs (and – in the case of test laboratories – testing products according to specific European harmonised standards or ETAs. Only these Notified Bodies are allowed to test the construction products covered by the CPD. However, following the same test methods is *supposed* to deliver similar results, but practice has shown that, in some cases test methods need additional clarification (e.g. how to prepare a sample for testing, special preparations for specific parts of the test procedure) to avoid that the results differs to an extent that would make any comparability impossible. In addition, national or European requirements for construction products might not have been defined precisely enough, and need clarification by EU or MS authorities.

To coordinate the needs of Member State authorities, Notified Bodies and the Commission, the implementation framework of the CPD has (like all other New Approach Directives) established a coordination body called the CPD-Group of Notified Bodies (CPD-GNB)[179]. Besides its role as a collector and distributor of information (upstream and downstream) and developer of technical guidance to the Notified Bodies, it plays a strong part in guaranteeing the compliance with hENs and ETAs (and in some cases also the comparability of test results) and therefore the reliability of CE marked products. The GNB has created 22 Sector Groups, dealing with specific product families (see below) and developing general or product-specific information and guidance documents for all Notified Bodies under the CPD[180].

On the European Commission's public database NANDO,[181] where one can get the whole list of Notified Bodies in this sector including information on which products they are allowed to certify under the CPD. Thus, one can see a quiet impressive number of about 300 test laboratories all over the EU. However, the NB are not obliged by the authorities (neither the notifying Member State

179 http://ec.europa.eu/enterprise/construction/internal/cpdgnb/gnbhome.htm.

180 By the end of 2008, 69 documents were available for all Notified Bodies, with an additional 69 still under discussion and therefore not finalised.

181 http://ec.europa.eu/enterprise/newapproach/nando/.

authorities nor the Commission services) to participate in the work of the GNB nor to follow its guidance.

Being very closely linked to the CPD, the GNB, its Advisory Group and its 22 Sector Groups depend largely on the interpretation of the Commission of open regulatory questions. Therefore, the GNB is not only an "observer" in the Standing Committee on Construction (SCC) but also one of the main "recipients" of Commission guiding documents produced by and for the SCC – like the Commission's Guidance Papers. In addition, Commission officials are regularly invited to participate in some meetings of Advisory Groups and Sector Groups. CEN and EOTA are associated members of the Advisory Group and also in all Sector Groups, because the communication between the specification writers and the certification bodies already during the drafting phase, but also when assessing the practical use of these technical specifications, was seen as essential enough to assure a more institutionalised link between these three bodies.[182] Manufacturers and other professional users are represented by CEPMC and FIEC-UEPC in an observer's role. However, manufacturers are not only present in general meetings, but are also involved (as observers) in the product-specific work of the Sector Groups. However, at this level, horizontal federations are replaced by product or material-specific federations.

The Group of Notified Bodies has developed *GNB-CPD position papers* which could cover either horizontal issues or specific, technical specifications. These documents are available to Notified Bodies (and other interested parties) on its website.[183] Also available are: all Commission Decisions concerning construction products, Guidance Papers, ETAGs, CUAPS (EOTA), and a link to the list of published standards of CEN. It also provides links to the main actors relevant for the GNB (CEN, EOTA, Commission services – including the NANDO database, CEBC, CEPMC, UEPC and NORMAPME). All information is available in English.

182 At the level of product families, it is expected that the relevant Sector Groups and the relevant CEN TCs or EOTA WGs are working closely together to avoid gaps or confusing guidance in the harmonised technical standards or ETAGs. In fact in several CEN TCs Notified Bodies are also present.

183 http://www.gnb-cpd.eu/.

3.2.5 *The technical specification writers (CEN and EOTA)*

3.2.5.1 European Committee for Standardization (Comite Europeen de Normalisation – CEN)[184]

The European standardisation body CEN (like its "sister organisations" CENELEC and ETSI) has on the one hand a y unique position, being the only organisation allowed to develop European standards (compared with there being more competition for standards' development outside the EU). Therefore, all Directives or activities needing harmonised European standards are developed under the umbrella of CEN. On the other hand, the dominance or monopoly on standardisation is a very common phenomenon in Europe, and several of CEN's national members (all national standards bodies – NSB – in the EU are also members in CEN) have got similar monopolies in their own countries. However, while National Standardisation Bodies (NSBs) are developing standards at national level and selling them as their product, CEN is not in a similar position. Standards developed in CEN are sold by its national members.[185]

National bodies are also in a strong position vis-à-vis the European organisation because they decide if they are sending experts to CEN's Technical Committees (TC), how many and whom – and therefore are able to influence the progress, quality and content of European standards.[186] To check that their experts are taking into consideration all national requirements as well as the interests of the parties involved in the national standardisation process, in most cases national standardisation bodies have established *mirror committees* at national level to provide their experts in the CEN TCs with additional expertise.

National standards bodies (NSB) are not just trying to find and support experts to be sent to CEN TCs, their involvement also indicates their interests in specific fields. In addition, providing enough resources to administer and coordinate the work in a TC is not (always) considered as a burden but often as an opportunity to have a stronger influence on the work done in the TC. While

---

184 http://www.cen.eu/cenorm/homepage.htm.

185 European standards are making reference to European standards by putting "EN" to the number of the standard: i.e. DIN EN (Germany), BS EN (United Kingdom). ON EN (Austria), …

186 For construction products, the Member States most active in standardisation work within the framework of the CPD in CEN (not counting here the new Member States joining the EU in 1995) were Belgium, France, Germany, Italy, the Netherlands and the UK.

the chairman and the secretary face the sometimes challenging task of balancing different views in order to reach consensus, they are also in a strong position to steer the TC members ("agenda setting"). Since they are also the link between the TC and the CEN Management Centre, they are also in the most crucial position to significantly improve or reduce the information flow between their TC and part of the "outside world".

However, support from relevant industry sectors is only possible if they see enough advantage in developing new standards and have enough resources to participate in the work. Not surprisingly, CEN TCs working on standards for the CPD scheme are mostly chaired and managed by national standardisation bodies (and therefore: national industries) with big national construction sectors, in particular Germany, France and the UK. All three Member States had the advantage that they have been already in the European Community when the CPD was developed and the first CEN TCs were set up. Other countries were involved to a lesser extent or joined after the working structure within CEN was to a large extent already established. Even between these three countries the expectations and approaches on the scope and detail of standards differed, which made it even more important for them to be in influential positions so as to keep as many aspects of the own national approach on board and by that avoiding later too much adaptation work on the national scheme. In addition, all actors at the national or multi-national levels could use the ongoing work at EU level to introduce or re-introduce requirements or simplifications that would improve their own position and economic gains. As we will see later, different approaches can influence the perception of new harmonised European standards if one or several actors consider these standards as unbalanced. It could also lead to strong reactions from more (public or private) parties which could seriously harm the credibility of the European standardisation work.

However, the composition of European and national technical committees are very similar: since the standards e provide guidance for the production and technically correct use of products, the actors most interested in the development of these standards are in general manufacturers and professional users of these products. Both these groups are organised either in federations, which try to follow the standardisation process and try to motivate experts from amongst their members to participate in a technical committee, or in individual companies – and here in particular the ones with enough manpower – who would send experts from within their own workforce to the TCs at national or European levels. National authorities or NGOs (like consumer protection organisations or environmental organisations) are rarely seen in these committees. This is in general not caused by administrative or organisational barriers but by the simple fact that neither of these two groups would be able to send enough experts to each TC and also because the costs practically limit their active participation to the work of a few committees which authorities or NGOs consider as high priority. NGOs are also sometimes financed to follow standardisation work at national or European levels (e.g. in CEN, the European Commission – the Directorate-General for Enterprises and Industry –supports NORMAPME to follow standardisation work from the point of view of SMEs and the Directorate-General for Environment has hired an NGO to make sure that environmental aspects are also included in the standards)[187].

In the field of construction, CEN has set up more than 60 technical committees g in most cases dealing with assessing the performance of specific construction products and, in a few cases, also with horizontal assessment issues (harmonised test methods for assessing products for their: release of dangerous substances into drinking water, indoor air, soil and groundwater, as well as for their: reaction to fire, thermal performance and acoustics). Their activities are coordinated by the Construction Sector Network (CSN) and its subgroups. To guarantee that the technical standards would cover all relevant aspects defined in the CPD and relevant national regulations, three external advisors (the "CEN consultants") were following the work in the TCs, giving guidance to them and checking the draft standards for their compliance with the CPD.

In addition to the internal coordination efforts, one person of the CEN Management Centre (CMC) is exclusively following the work in construction, and also acting as the interface between the Commission and the Standing Committee on Construction (in which CEN has observer status). In the second half of the nineties the Commission and CEN established the CEN Task Group, which seeks to facilitate the information flow between the Commission and CEN. The Task Group consists of the representative from the CMC, the CEN consultants, members of TCs (if there was a specific problem in their field) and Commission officials from the construction unit. The most relevant means of communication

187 In addition, CEN has established an *Environmental Help Desk* to support technical committees with advice and expertise in their standardisation work. The Help Desk was created by an initiative of the German standardisation body DIN and is to a large extent financed by German interested parties.

are direct letters to TCs to raise their awareness of work going on in other TCs[188] and coordinating their work – a task mostly covered by the Construction Sector Network (CSN), the CEN website and, last not least: the CEN consultants who are the technical experts following the work of each "construction products" TC.

Since standardisation under the CPD is almost exclusively focused on product standards, it depends to a large extent on the participation of manufacturing experts. The second largest group is that of the national test laboratories. In the past, they have tested the performance of construction products based on national standards and in many cases were also involved in the development of those national standards. Their involvement in European standardisation is partly linked to the work of the Notified Bodies. In fact, many members of the GNB are also sitting on CEN TCs. Less involved at the product level are the professional end users: while the Architects' Council of Europe, ACE, participates in the construction specific sector group, the federation of constructors, FIEC only follows the work on construction products indirectly. Both federations are more focused on the execution of work and design standards, only paying more attention to specific product standards if these would affect the planning or construction (execution) process.

Keeping in mind that harmonised European standards are just an instrument which allows other parties to assess products and at a later stage apply CE marking on a construction product, CEN only provides information on its own standards to interested parties via its website. It can be assumed that information on CE marking is indirectly transmitted from the Task Group and the CEN consultants to the experts in the TCs and from there to the national mirror groups and their own companies, but this can only be considered as a side-effect, not as a specific goal of CEN.

CEN's website provides a special site for standardisation in the construction sector, giving special emphasis on construction products under the CPD as well as *Eurocodes*. Since national standardisation writers are clearly the target group of CEN's website,[189] the information provided is focused on how to include the regulatory requirements of the CPD into the format of European standards, and

188 In some cases individual experts are members of several TCs, a fact which in most cases is considered as an advantage of facilitating the information flow between these TCs, and only in rare cases a "bottleneck" if this communication depends too much on one individual.

189 Since CEN does not sell the standards developed EU level, no potential customers could be addressed.

the role of CEN consultants is as advisors for CPD issues.[190] Also, the Guidance Papers have been considered as relevant enough for Technical Committees and a link to the GPs on the construction unit's website has been made.

CEN's role as provider of information on European technical standards is partly reduced by it own role as coordinator and agenda-setter but without any direct role as market actor. Standards and other technical documents developed in CEN are sold only by its national members. On the one hand, the relationship between specification writers and downstream users therefore remains at national level between national standardisation bodies and architects, civil engineers, manufacturers and contractors. On the other hand, CEN (and also its national members) promotes its own mark ("key-mark") in addition to CE marking.

At this level, the national standardisation bodies of the four Member States selected – DIN (Germany), BSI (UK), ON (Austria) and PKN (Poland) – are not covered as separate actors. In the interviews in the following chapter the "assumptions of actors at EU level" have only been included if linked to work within the CEN structure and on transnational level. More detailed information on these four NSB will be provided on the "national" level.

3.2.5.2 The European Organisation for Technical Approvals (EOTA)[191]

The European Organisation for Technical Approvals (EOTA) is an offshoot of the CPD. Based on the Directive, EOTA members assess and evaluate construction products that are not (yet) covered by a harmonised European standard, by providing *Technical Approvals* which allowing manufacturers to CE mark their products. While being so closely linked to the CPD, Member States have an extremely strong influence on the work in EOTA: the Approval Bodies (AB – in general only one per Member State) are designated by national authorities, and their membership in EOTA can also only be withdrawn by the same authorities. The important role of *national* bodies is visible in the restricted membership in EOTA (45 members, including the ones from EEA countries). However, to avoid numerical dominance in discussions by one or the other Member State, only *one* Approval Body per Member State is allowed in the Executive Board (EXCOM). These bodies have very different backgrounds and could have been involved in testing and evaluation products long before their nomination as EOTA members but could also have a more scientific or university background and still be

190 http://www.cen.eu/cenorm/sectors/sectors/construction/guidance/index.asp.

191 http://www.eota.be/.

working in the research and also testing fields. Some of them have been or still are authorities or bodies which have been delegated specific controlling and inspection tasks by national authorities. (this set-up simplifies the communication with national authorities when checking for national regulatory or administrative requirements for specific construction products. Also, the size of the EOTA members varies: some of them have only a handful of experts while others consist of several hundred employees.

Independent of their size or background, all bodies participate in the technical and administrative assemblies (the plenary meeting, the executive board and the technical board). On the other hand, only a small core of about 12 to 14 EOTA members actively participate in technical working groups and horizontal project teams (e.g. on dangerous substances in construction products, fire, seismic actions and acoustics). Again, no direct link between size and commitment can be found, but previous and current expertise in a specific field or strong interest by national industries could be a driving factor for membership in one or the other working group or project team.

Since the activities of EOTA affect manufacturers and (to a lesser extent) constructors and workers' unions, CEPMC, FIEC, AEEBC (Association of European Building Surveyors), EBC (European Builders Confederation), UEPC (European Union of Developers and House Builders) and EFBWW (European Federation of Building and Wood Workers) have observer status in the Technical Board. For obvious reasons, CEPMC is the most active observer, while others follow the work more on a "knowing what's going on" basis. But not only European actors could be involved in a dialogue with EOTA members. Since an ETA developed by one EOTA member needs the approval of the other members, all national Approval Bodies face demands for technical expertise and feedback that might not be available in-house. Therefore, mirror committees have been created by several EOTA members to discuss proposals (e.g. ETAs[192] (preferably not on individual ETAs – for confidentiality reasons) but mainly on ETA Guidelines[193]

192 Additional feedback to a national Approval Body on an ETA developed by it or another EOTA member can be useful when developing a document describing the approach how the product has to be assessed. This document – called *Common Understanding of Assessment Procedure* (CUAP) – should cover all national requirements and is sent out to all other EOTA members to check if the national requirements in their country are also covered or if amendments to the document have to be made.

193 ETA Guidelines (ETAGs) are needed if more than one manufacturer is producing similar products. (As in CEN the concept of "family of products" is also used – and preferred – when

or proposals developed at EU level) with a wider range of experts. Here, national actors are able to join the discussion (depending on the approach decided by the national Approval Body). In most cases, only federations participate in these mirror committees, not individual companies.

EOTA has had observer status in the SCC since it was established and it also (actively) participates in practically all expert groups and working groups of the Commission's construction unit, while Commission officials participate in some working group or project team meetings on a more or less regular basis.

EOTA's homepage provides information (in English only) on how and when a manufacturer might apply for an ETA. Whenever information on CE marking and other issues clearly linked to the CPD might be of interest for visitors to the website, a direct link to the Commission's website (where this issue is defined) has been installed. It also describes the scheme for developing an ETA. To facilitate the search of manufacturers to identify which products are already covered by an ETAG, the full English text of all endorsed ETAGs, with links to other available language versions as well as the list of (about 1500) valid ETAs, is provided. Certain parts (like the full text of the ETA) is only accessible for Approval Bodies.

Germany has nominated one Approval Body (*Deutsches Institut für Bautechnik* – DIBt), as has Austria (*Österreichisches Institut für Bautechnik* – OIB) and Poland (*Instytut Techniki Budowlanej* – ITB), while six bodies have been sent by the UK to EOTA (one of them the British Research Establishment – BRE) with the British Board of Agrément (BBA) as the Approval Body having a seat in its Executive Committee (EXCOM)[194]. EOTA's national members have played several roles:

- in the development of ETAGs, CUAPS but also ETAs, they have to make sure that all national regulatory requirements have been covered (therefore, taking over specific monitoring and controlling *functions of national authorities* – and to be *neutral actors* within the EOTA scheme);
- as *economic actors*, competing with other EOTA members for customers (manufacturers). In particular, when providing feedback to other EOTA

developing ETAGs). In this case, though, a more common approach has been seen as more practical, covering all similar (but not identical) products, to avoid different approaches and reduce the complexity (and costs) of the system.

194 http://www.eota.be/.

members on ETAs developed by their "competitors", they have invested resources for the financial benefit of other Approval Bodies).

3.2.6 *Other European bodies*

Most other organisations and groups are combinations of national or private actors who are members of at least one of the above-mentioned bodies. In particular, technical bodies are organised in more specific groups, like certification bodies (i.e. EUROCER-BUILDING,[195] UEAtc – The European Union of Agrément,[196] WFTAO – World Federation of Technical Assessment Organisations[197]), European federations for specific professions (e.g. European Council of Civil Engineers – ECCE)[198], organisations and enterprises focusing on research (e.g. ENBRI – European Network of Building Research Institutes)[199], or a mixture of two or more of these tasks (e.g. ECCREDI – European Council for Construction Research, Development and Innovation;[200] EGOLF – European Group of Organisations for Fire Testing, Inspection and Certification,[201] European Builders Confederation – EBC). Their aim is more to exchange information and experiences at a practical level and less to influence the discussion between EU and national administrations as such. (However, this does not exclude that they might be very active at national level vis-à-vis public and private actors). Therefore, their websites are mostly focused on the needs of their members and are partly restricted to this group. They monitor the developments around the CPD but, since they have direct links to national authorities, CEN, EOTA and the GNB, they have not applied for observer status in the SCC and only address the Commission services if issues at EU level affect their practical work. Not surprisingly, their publications and references on their websites (open to the public) are not linked to CE marking but more to very specific technical questions (with the exception of EUROCER-BUILDING which has published

195 http://eurocer-building.cstb.fr/default.htm.
196 http://www.ueatc.com/.
197 http://www.wftao.com/user/default.aspx.
198 http://www.eccenet.org.
199 http://enbri.cstb.fr/.
200 http://www.eccredi.org/.
201 http://www.egolf.org.uk/.

several comments, presentations and position papers concerning CE marking and other marks).

Two "peripheral" actors are more closely linked to the decision-making process than most others: NORMAPME (European Office of Crafts, Trades and Small and Medium-sizes Enterprises for Standardisation) and UEPC (Union of European Developers and House-Builders). The former is also an "observer" in the SCC and is more active at the political level, less in standardisation work of construction products (except for doors and windows). UEPC follows the work under the CPD, but is more attached to actors (see below) which are linked to its own interests.

NORMAPME[202] (as a subdivision of the European Office of Crafts, Trades and Small and Medium-Sized Enterprises – UEAPME) and ECOS[203] are more actively involved in standardisation work, but they cover a wide field of interests, construction being only one of them. Both bodies are supported financially by the Commission to follow standardisation work in CEN and represent the interests of SMEs (NORMAPME), as well as to make sure that environmental issues be sufficiently covered in European standards (ECOS). At the organisational level, ECOS is a "traditional" NGO: it acts as both a collector and distributor of information but as such is not bound to specific members and, due to its own specific resources (technical expertise), also acts as an independent body. UEAPME/NORMAPME on the other hand, are structured like federations. Their members are also federations, representing SMEs at national or sectoral levels. Therefore, NORMAPME is more dependent on feedback from its members,[204] such as other industry representatives, in order to provide a stronger position backed up with relevant examples or, (due to the membership of *SMEs*) in rare cases, empirical data.

NORMAPME's website strongly promotes what it called "think small first" positions, urging for standards which are less complex and more user-friendly for SMEs. The website provides a special link to the definition and background of CE marking in general and to CE marking for construction products. (How-

202 http://www.normapme.com/.

203 http://www.ecostandard.org/.

204 The network of different SME federations seems to be even closer than for "traditional" federations. Not necessarily because of closer cooperation, but also because the same individuals could work for more than one federation (i.e. the link between NORMAPME and the European Builders Confederation (EBC) http://www.eubuilders.org/who.asp?ID=whoweare), which also represents the interests of small and medium-sized contractors and manufacturers.

ever, the obligatory nature of CE marked products is not mentioned and has to be found via websites of the Commission). The information remains general (with links to Commission websites) and not very specific for SMEs but, on the other hand, the website and documents are provided in six EU languages (English, French, German, Italian, Polish and Spanish).

UEPC (Union of European Developers and House-Builders)[205] plays a more observer role than an active one compared with manufacturers, but it is active in EOTA (as an observer) and also participates in CEN work. It has observer status in the SCC and follows the work under the CPD in its own "Design and Development Committee". Links also exist to CEPMC and FIEC. Its website provides a small number of "position papers" dealing with CE marking and the CPD but, compared with other topics (e.g. energy performance of buildings, VAT), the CPD is obviously not a main concern for this federation either. The information on the website is available in English, French and German.

While building control will be analysed in more detail at the next level of the information flow – the national level – the Consortium of European Building Control (CEBC)[206] should be mentioned here as representative of de facto national activities at EU level (nearly all EU Member States are members). Like all organisations with specialised membership, the website provides only general information for the public. Nevertheless, the public domain indicates several aspects relevant for building control: they are mostly related to design and installation flaws. The quality of products (and therefore not surprisingly: CE marking) is not mentioned at all on the website.

3.3 The assumptions of actors at EU level

After describing the actors at EU level and the instruments established by them, the next question is how individuals work in this environment (at least to a certain extent) with the CPD and its national implementations. How do they see their own role and their own tasks? How do they perceive their working environment and their effect in following the requirements of the CPD and providing relevant information on its instruments (in particular about CE

205 http://www.uepc.org/uepc/home.cfm.
206 http://www.cebc.eu/.

marking)? And, last but not least: how do their networks at EU and national levels actually work?[207]

The large part of this study reserved for the results of interviews and questionnaires should serve two goals: it should help researchers to get a more in-depth picture of the worlds of different actors and, it should help practitioners in the field of construction to get more information on the perceptions of actors in other institutions, organisations and nation states. It should be stressed at this point that the following pages reflect *the perceptions and interpretations of the interviewees* and do not present facts (the same restrictions apply for the other two summaries of comments at the national and the "construction-site" levels). That some positions of different groups of actors might contradict each other highlights the different interpretations of the positions and actions of actors in this field and the risk of their misinterpretation, resulting in reactions that might even increase the complexity and confusion atn EU or national levels.

3.3.1 The European Commission

Due to the fast-changing working environment of the Commission, it was only possible to contact and interview some of the current and former officials and DNEs working with the CPD. Therefore, in most cases the interviewees have not worked in the construction unit in the first years after the adoption of the CPD. However, since many of them had still had the chance to meet and work with some of the "pioneers" of the Directive, a certain institutional memory helped form their assumptions about the first phase of the CPD. Therefore, the references to the first years in the following pages are mostly "second-hand" while the period of the last ten years, from the "interregnum" of missing techni-

207 Since I have tried to get more than one interview per each interested party, their positions are "aggregated" in the following pages. However, the roles of a number of individuals do not always fit precisely into only one of the "clusters" in this and the following chapters. Individuals could have been working on different levels and in different positions (e.g. working in standardisation in CEN and working as manufacturers in a company). Therefore, these comments are included in each group where they seemed as most appropriate and helpful for the understanding of the individual perceptions and concerns. In case individuals were referring to their experience at national level, I have excluded these comments in this chapter and added them in the one for the national level (see: Assumptions of actors on national level).

cal standards in the 90s, up until the end of 2007, is based on the individual experience of the interviewees.

A recurring theme in the interviews with Commission officials is their recollection of the phase when the structure around the CPD "had been invented practically from scratch". The text of the Directive had been developed by a few experts in the Commission and Member State authorities, but for most of the civil servants and DNEs who had to deal with the practical implementation afterwards, the CPD only provided a rough framework with all the detailed "nitty-gritty" work still to be defined. On the other hand, *too many details* would have been conter-productive. Therefore, more "general specifications" were sometimes (but not consistently) searched for. It was also mentioned that not only missing parts, but sometimes even contradictions in the text of the Directive forced the construction unit to spend a long time on discussing and clarifying CPD requirements with Member State authorities and other actors. Entering a completely new field, none of them could rely on experience but had to develop something fresh. Next to the challenge came the uneasy feeling that, even with the best intentions and cooperation, that might not be good enough.

The main problem was the lack of technical standards which for years made the CPD not only a "paper tiger" but also left much room for interpretation to Member State authorities and other actors. For some Commission officials, the slow progress in CEN – and to a certain extent in EOTA – was caused by more or less "active resistance" against harmonisation. Since many of the technical experts in these bodies were sent by the same technical bodies that might have to face a reduction in national certificates they would previously have provided (and charged) to importers into their national markets, there was no real incentive to make progress in harmonisation. It was acknowledged that this assumption did not apply to *all* experts, and in particular the people working *directly* for CEN (and the other CPD-related organisations) were considered as motivated and cooperative. But they lacked the power to encourage national members (working voluntarily and at their own expense) to participant in the work at EU level and to find solutions. Part of this lack of power was caused by CEN's inability to follow closely the work of each TC. A CEN task group, consisting of CEN representatives and officials of the construction unit met on a regular basis, where the Commission managed to keep track on any progress of the relevant TCs.[208] It was acknowledged that the CPD concept (e.g. *obligatory CE marking* and therefore a special annex ZA for the legally binding part of the standard) was very new for CEN and its technical committees. Also, identifying what the regulated characteristic of a construction product might be and how these are covered in a (national or regional) law was more challenging than previous standardisation work.[209] Both the construction unit (writing the mandates for CEN) and CEN (developing a working programme based on the mandate) were entering "uncharted territory", both "learning by doing" (in particular when discussing and defining performance levels and classes of products) without having somebody else to refer to as an experienced "point of reference".

The lack of clarity about the scope of some mandates to CEN and the work based on the mandates were considered as closely linked to this problem. The first mandates to CEN had to be invented by the construction unit and some experts from the Standing Committee with few or no useful examples from other fields in EU standardisation. Technical requirements – based on national regulations and the six essential requirements of the CPD – had to be defined in a general way in order to assure the "performance-based approach" of the CPD on one hand and to cover all products already on the market on the other. It was recognised that Member State authorities sitting in the SCC depended to a large extent on the feedback from technical bodies in their countries and could not always easily identify if the requirements were based on voluntary schemes or state-of-the-art approaches (not all covered by the CPD) or on requirements laid down in national laws or *de facto* binding administrative provisions (which are the only ones relevant under the CPD and therefore the only ones that have to be taken into consideration in harmonised product standards). Under close scrutiny, some "regulatory" requirements turned out to be voluntary agreements between national authorities and national industries which were aimed at higher and safer performance but as such not legally binding, or just on "our industry is used to it" perceptions from certification bodies. Since neither the national authorities nor the Commission had the resources to check the nature of all of these requirements, it was expected that several of the voluntary aspects slipped into the

208 In fact, this was achieved by one END who managed to be well informed about the work in the TCs as well as about the stage of each standard. However, with this END leaving, priorities (and resources) changed and the work was soon neglected. The task group meetings remain but the knowledge of the construction unit has decreased.

209 But it was also seen that some TCs avoided the problem, by ignoring the regulatory issues and continued to focus on the technical and economical aspects.

obligatory requirements. This fact left a lot of questions open for TCs and could only partly be covered in TC work programmes.

The lack of ability of Member States to provide complete data on their national regulations was seen as an even stronger obstacle to efficient implementation work. In parallel, the finalisation of harmonised product standards increased the number of complaints of national authorities that specific national regulations or provisions have not been covered in new harmonised standards.[210] These late reactions were considered by some interviewees more as a lack of interest in cooperation with the Commission than an original oversight. The fact that each of the contested standards needed *years* of development – and therefore also years for national authorities to provide complete information on national requirements, and enough time to follow the progress within CEN via the national mirror committees of the national standardisation bodies – was seen as proof of this assumption.

It was also considered that some Member State authorities interpreted the "precautionary principle" in a way that the highest possible safety levels (Attestation of Conformity classes) were *de facto* essential requirements, even if this meant higher levels than in their own national systems[211]. In the early stages, industry was mostly represented by the federation of architects (ACE) and that of the contractors (FIEC) but manufacturers were still in a weak position to argue for their interests. In fact, in the early 90s, CEPMC had not yet developed its working structure and established its position as an effective umbrella organisation. Support from the Commission, some industries and some Member States helped to "create" another actor for the discussion, but one not necessarily in favour of the highest safety classes (as the "end users") but rather promoting more balance between requirements and technical (and economical) feasibility.

To break the deadlock within some CEN TCs, the construction unit speeded up the creation of the Group of Notified Bodies (GNB) to check the technical

---

210 In addition (based on feedback from specific industry federations or companies), it was stated that certain standards were not precise enough, not even having a good definition of the product covered by the standard, or that the standards were too descriptive, excluding products already existing on the market.

211 But it was also noted that, even within Member State administrations, different positions were presented to the Commission (mostly in different Committees, where other Ministries or national bodies were representing their nation). Therefore, Commission officials became wearier about "*national* requirements" but had in to follow the position of the national authorities for construction.

practicality of the standards under development and to put pressure on them for a faster delivery. Being created and financed by the Commission, the GNB was at that stage a very unusual body. Following the concept that Member States have to notify certification bodies to the Commission services, based on the assessment criteria defined in harmonised product standards, a Notified Body (not to mention a body coordinating their work) could only exist if harmonised standards were available. Nevertheless, by introducing an additional step in the procedure – the "pre-notification", certification bodies entered the system. The Notified Bodies proved to be effective in having a close look at the work in CEN and providing the Commission with information on deadlocks and delays, thus allowing the Commission to address these issues with the relevant TCs and forcing them to proceed. On the other hand, the Notified Bodies were also seen by the construction unit as a group with its own specific interests, in particular in their own field of attesting the conformity with technical specifications but also that of testing and assessing products. National regulatory requirements rarely provided enough references to technical instruments (such as standards) to assess compliance. This left a lot of room for manoeuvre for test laboratories to "err on the side of caution" and select a more stringent, complicated – and therefore more expensive – test, by referring to the argument of safety.

As an additional instrument and to ensure that the work within the TCs was following the requirements of the Construction Products Directive, CEN hired up to three technical experts as consultants to monitor the work and advice the TCs.[212] However, their position as adviser could have been (and sometimes *was*) contested if a specific TC had its own ideas about its priorities.[213] The CEN consultants could highlight difficulties and delays, but their power to force changes did *de facto* not exist. Nevertheless, in most cases they were providers of relevant guidance when they had to interpret the requirements of the CPD. Therefore, having somebody with a solid knowledge oft the Directive was

212 It was mentioned that these consultants are *paid* by the Commission but they are *hired* by CEN, which gives national members of CEN a strong position when discussing – or even renewing – the contract of one or the other consultant. On the other hand, the Commission is participating in these discussions and had also influenced the decisions in CEN.

213 An example was the delay of publishing specific standards, because this was seen as creating a market distortion between products that could be already CE marked and others (with standards still under development) still facing different national marks. Therefore, the TC decided that *no* standard should be put forward for voting in CEN and publication before the whole set was ready (even if this could have taken additional years).

considered essential and could be found in former DNEs who were now willing to work as CEN consultants. But their involvement in CEN work was in the Commission's eyes a two-edged sword: they might have worked longer on the CPD than the Commission officials now in charge and, since they have worked at the early stage of defining range and limits of the CPD their interpretations sometimes clashed with the *current* official ones. Nevertheless, the concept as such was never seriously questioned because in many cases these consultants not only just highlighted problems but were also very active in working on solutions.

EOTA was seen as another instrument to force CEN to speed up its work. While officially a "complementary" path for CE marking, an attempt was made to use this organisation also as a "competitor" by being faster and more efficient than CEN. However, organising members in all EU countries was often as difficult as in CEN, in particular since these members also seemed to have their own interest in the CPD scheme: compared with a harmonised standard, for which a manufacturer has to test only for all "essential requirements" (as defined in the CPD) of the national markets targeted, manufacturers applying for a European Technical Approval has to test for *all* requirements in *all* EU Member States. This includes requirements that are backed by regulations, but not "essential" in the sense that it would influence the structural or safety performance of the product or the building.[214] Like the Notified Bodies, the complexity (and costs) of tests required by Approval Bodies raised the criticism that some work was not so much based on necessity for assessing a product but more on the interests of the test laboratories involved. But it was also highlighted that EOTA members were supposed to do a huge amount of work without proper (financial) incentives of doing so: while having been given the tasks of commenting on *all* proposals for ETAs by any other member (meaning that they have to check their national regulations if this product should be assessed for specific criteria and identifying the relevant test method – if existing), or developing documents for common assessment (Common Understanding of Assessment Procedure – CUAP), they were (with few exceptions) not paid for carrying these out. Only the specific ETAs that the body was issuing itself could be charged to the client.

214 "Cleanability" was given as an example of a national requirement in one Member State which was not aiming at any CPD requirements, but lead to the result that the product – no matter where it is sold in the EU – has to undergo expensive testing before it can be CE marked. On the other hand, since ETAs were voluntary instruments for manufacturers they themselves could have asked (in ETAs) to cover more requirements to document the high performance of their products.

Since the Commission only financing work of the EOTA office in Brussels and a small number of mandates for ETA Guidelines, its influence on the performance of EOTA's members practically did not exist, hoping that Member State authorities or other interested parties would provide more support for their national EOTA bodies. Additionally, the competitive position vis-à-vis CEN to speed up the work in CEN was not always considered as successful, and EOTA was sometimes even seen as blocking too much CEN standardisation work by claiming specific technical specification as its own domain.[215] By more clearly defining the framework of EOTAs tasks and developing a structure for coordinating the work in CEN and EOTA via the construction unit, another administrative control mechanism was introduced.

Contacts with Member State authorities outside the PG or SCC meetings were in general considered by the construction unit as a very useful informal tool for communication. Looking at the four Member States selected in this study, the frequencies and quality of the meetings differed significantly, though this was considered partly as result of the administrative structure and resources of a country, and partly a function of the individuals representing a Member State and the way they approach issues. For example, German authorities were definitely seen as the most frequent visitors to Brussels. This was to a certain extent due to the different interpretations of the quality of European standards and the German *Ü-Zeichen*. But while not always agreeing with each other, it was also obvious for the interviewees that the German authorities and industry made significant efforts to clarify open questions with the construction unit – or to convince the construction unit of the German point of view. The United Kingdom did not approach the construction unit very often with specific questions, but was very strong when defending its position in different working groups of the SCC or in the PG and SCC meetings.

Austria and Poland were more or less restricting their contacts to the official meetings and correspondence with the construction unit.[216] But this was no surprise. With few exceptions, Member State authorities do not have the resources to cover the CPD and to provide input on a more regular basis or even to

215 A position contested from an EOTA point of view since an ETA should be (officially) seen as »entrance« till harmonised European standards would be available. However, the definition of products and their intended use could allow for »gaps« between how and when CEN or EOTA would be dealing with these products.

216 However, they participated in most Expert Groups of the construction unit.

present their positions personally, and Austria and Poland were no exceptions.[217] Nevertheless, both Austria ("for a country of that size") and Poland ("compared with other new Member States") were considered as quiet active in so far as they could be.

While regretting these sometimes only loose contacts, the Commission officials were not "grieving" about the situation. With 27 Member States, such informal meetings were seen as extremely time-consuming, while correspondence by (e-)mail provided more time for reflection, or even the possibility that the problem would be solved before a reply had to be given by the construction unit. On the other hand, it was (and still is) not clear if the more "silent" Member State authorities were implementing the Directive in the way the construction unit intended, or if (intentionally or unintentionally) deviations had occurred without the construction unit (and sometimes also without the specific Member State authority) being aware of them.

That fact that bigger Member States have more resources to be active atn EU level is not new but, as was highlighted in a number of interviews, the current situation has also put the construction unit in a difficult position: on the one hand as "guardian of the CPD", deviations from its aims and its requirements by larger Member States were seen as more problematic than those by smaller Member States. Larger Member States might not have been as affected by new barriers against actors of other Member States, because they could have provided a large national market. Smaller MS however depended to a larger extent on exports and would suffer more from market distortions created by specific national regulations and requirements. Therefore, confronting the authorities of larger Member States should have had more effect on the efficiency of the internal market than splitting resources between several smaller ones. On the other hand, these larger nations were (and are) also the ones providing most of the experts and input for the work at EU level. While none of the interviewees denied the double role of this support (support *and* control of the ongoing work), there were different perceptions about which motivation dominates in each Member State (depending on the issue).

Similar restrictions were seen when being in contact with other stakeholders. Monitoring the correct implementation of the CPD would be impossible

217 *However, I have experienced and observed that Member States have a strong tendency to contact Commission officials of their own nationality to get feedback, advice or to discuss open questions.*

for the Commission without outside help. Since it was not seen as very likely that national authorities would bring their own failures to the attention of the Commission – as long as they could be dealt with in the national system – the construction unit depended on information from other actors. Highlighting flaws in national systems could be seen as risky by private actors vis-à-vis national authorities. Even if their position proved to be justified, they might have faced less cooperation from these authorities at a later stage (in particular if these authorities were in a position to assess or accept products on the market). Also, the process would take years to be solved, which in practice did not help either. Therefore, actors who would challenge national administrations via the Commission (and possibly via the European Court of Justice) in many cases had a strong economic position and were aiming at medium- or long-term goals, rather than trying to solve an *ad hoc* problem. This left only few actors (federations or large companies) who could provide first-hand information to the construction unit. But it was stressed that the bigger actors have established themselves already in several Member States and do not always have an interest in removing existing barriers to trade based on the requirements of national authorities. On the contrary, while larger companies have already adapted to different national approaches (having more resources to deal with them), smaller companies might face considerable hurdles when trying to cross national borders with their products. Since SMEs were mostly in a weak position in European and national federations and their contacts to the construction unit were seen as almost non-existent, it was assumed that the construction unit's picture of potential and existing problems was strongly blurred by getting mostly one-sided information from bigger MS authorities and market actors.

But not only communication with Member State authorities was mentioned during the interviews. Contacts within the Commission were also considered as not being optimal. In particular, other units in the Commission services financing *construction* projects in Member States, or working on public procurement, were seen as potential partners. But they had no regular contacts – or no contacts at all. This is not so much criticism against other DGs but more a complaint that the construction unit itself was not sufficiently "promoting its services and tools" to other EC services and EU bodies.

It is interesting to note the role of Interpretative Documents and Guidance Papers in the construction unit itself. As mentioned above, only few interviewees had already been working in the construction unit when it was seen as essential to develop Interpretative Documents to link the intentions of the Directive with the technical requirements of construction products. However, these documents seemed not to have played a significant role in their daily work. One explanation provided was that the CPD was already widely known at that stage and the additional interpretation was no longer necessary. Guidance Papers were also losing their importance for some respondents, the longer the work was going on and the more detailed specific work became. It was also mentioned that the GPs were too complex and over-loaded with details ("gold-plating") – and therefore indirectly *indicating* that the text of the CPD was not precise and useful enough, because of the many details that had to be put into these GPs. But it was noticed (sometimes even with amazement) how important *other* actors considered these papers and how often they referred to them.

3.3.2 MS authorities

A significant characteristic is the central role of Member State authorities within their national system. As the only official representatives, they play a significant role as "agenda-setters" at national level. However, creating sustainable contacts with authorities of other Member States remains an exception and for all Member State authorities in the field of construction is mostly limited to ad hoc contacts if problems occur that affects at least one other Member State. Therefore, the following comments were not only focused on national activities because of the framework set in the interview, but also because contacts and experience with other Member States (and assumptions on their positions) were not seen as significantly influencing one's own national position or activities.

3.3.2.1 Germany

The interviewees in the German administration had the advantage that they have been working with the CPD for a long period, the current vice-president of the DIBt has even written parts of the CPD himself (as a national expert seconded to the Commission). Others have seen the effects during their career from different angles within the civil service on federal and regional (Länder) levels. They also had a technical background and/or experience in common which was shown in their focus on technical aspects of the CPD and the use of CE marking.

In a certain way, the CPD or – more precisely – the implementation of the national *Bauproduktegesetz,* was considered as unproblematic in the German system. There was no need to change the administrative procedure and references to technical standards could easily be introduced in all relevant documents wherever necessary. Only the resistance of some Member States to accepting that CE marking was obligatory – which allowed manufacturers in their own country to avoid any costs of adapting to the European system if they kept their products in their own country – was seen as market distortion and therefore a significant flaw of the CPD. Therefore, the CPD was considered as a useful instrument, in particular when providing the proper harmonised framework of the Internal Market.

What was problematic for the interviewees was the technical level outside the regulatory implementation and adaptation of national and regional laws – the European standards. The focus of the interviewees was on the ability of authorities (or controlling engineers used by private contractors) to control the *performance of buildings or construction works*, based on the requirements of the regional building codes and technical specifications in public tenders (*Zusätzliche technischen Vertragsbedingungen – ZTV; Technische Lieferbedingungen*), which were providing more guidance and demanding more than just product data but also information on how a product has to be correctly installed in the building. The fact that European standards differed in this aspect significantly from the previous German system was seen as a major weakness of the European approach[218] – a position that was shared by several interviewees representing manufacturers or contractors in Germany.

The CPD was trying to combine these technical issues with economic priorities, leaving national and regional authorities with the task of finding instruments for practical implementation. It was mentioned that the German *Bauproduktegesetz* was also facing scepticism and resistance – not from manufacturers but from groups that had to buy and use these products. Such resistance was not always based on practical arguments, but rather on "uneasiness" or even "fear" of new products or new approaches in general. Information events were therefore also seen as "fear-reducing" events by moving the discussion back to a practical and pragmatic level. But it was not only vague perceptions which made the task difficult. It was highlighted that Commission documents were not providing (enough) relevant information for designers, constructors and controlling

218 Information on the correct use and installation might not be missing in a European standard, but since these parts are not in the "obligatory" part of the standard but in the voluntary part, CE marking was not seen as guaranteeing correct performance in the voluntary part.

authorities to be of use to them, and for many of them these were too long and too "bulky".

In particular, comments from the DIBt (in its role as the institute assessing products) raised the point of the technical completeness of a number of harmonised European standards, the reliability of their assessment methods and in general the dependency of the CPD approach on a commitment of all interested parties towards quality ("economic game between manufacturers and constructors", "competitiveness is mostly influenced by prices"). Of major concern was the limitation of the CPD on requirements that were based on regulations or that were *de facto* obligatory instead of taking "all relevant product requirements" into consideration.[219]

Coordination with interested parties on CPD and *Bauproduktegesetz* issues was left in the hands of the Federal Ministry, with the DIBt, as representative of the *Länder* and provider of technical input, also being present. While the role of federal bodies was limited when it came to their involvement in construction works (except in building and maintaining infrastructure works on national level like highways, waterways or railway tracks), it saw itself in a strong role as the focal point and interface with the Commission and the SCC.[220] All interested parties were provided with all documents developed at EU level and representatives of interested parties participating in these meetings were expected to provide practical input, not just stating the position of their organisation or company.

While not highlighting it specifically, it was mentioned that awareness about CE marking of construction products is only just *now* increasing. Since European standards were only published during the last few years, manufacturers, end users and authorities could only recently start to gain experience (or identifying potential problems) with the practical use of harmonised European

219 *This position has already caused several disagreements with the Commission since it resulted in (from the Commission's point of view) additional national requirements (*Ü-Zeichen*) or additional technical (DIN) standards for aspects that were not required by any national or regional law. The DIBt on the other hand considered the Commission's position as a wrong interpretation of the term "essential" requirements of buildings which are based more on technical experience and the state of the art than being precisely defined in (very general) building codes.*

220 *From practical experience and contacts with different representatives of interested parties in Germany, I have noticed that the representative of Germany in the SCC was not repeating specific positions (even the ones which have been brought forward with "lots of emphasis") but presented a balanced position of several parties.*

standards. Only actors with international or even global interests were discussing CE marking and Attestation of Conformity (AoC) issues at an early stage. Most other actors have considered themselves as "not affected at all" – or have assumed that "Brussels will *never* achieve it" ("*das kriegen die in Brüssel nie hin*").

The influence of the DIBt on the other hand can be considered as more direct (*Ü-Zeichen*)[221] and covering technical requirements for all construction work vis-à-vis other actors in the construction sector. Keeping in mind this specific role of the DIBt and the instruments it has available, it is not surprising that a strong emphasis was put in the interview on the importance of maintaining high quality for products used in construction – a quality that is ensured by the involvement of an authority to compensate for more market-driven approaches in the private sector ("price comes first – quality is only of secondary importance").

3.3.2.2 The United Kingdom

Of the four countries selected in this study, the split between the "political" and the "technical" representation in the UK system, including for construction products, is possibly the most transparent (with Poland a close second). On the one hand, because the civil servants in the ministry have changed several times (in fact, most of the interviewees in the department were just a few weeks away from leaving for other posts and positions), while the main actors in BRE have been following the CPD work practically from its beginning, the latter were therefore the ones keeping the continuity of the UK approach. On the other hand, the individuals of the ministry have been recruited from a wider background and therefore were more likely to cover the "political" part than their colleagues in the BRE who had – by definition – a technical background.

The most common aspect of both bodies involved was their strong emphasis on communication. This applied at EU level as well as for communication with national interested parties. At EU level, the opportunity of PG and SCC meetings to discuss issues was seen as a good opportunity to get at first hand the positions of other actors involved. In particular, the PG meetings provided good opportunities for exchanging different views openly and frankly. This was partly because

221 In fact, the *Ü-Zeichen* was described as "preparation" of the future CE marking; "paving" the way for its acceptance, before it became a "complementary" (DE) or "competing" (EC) mark for construction products. On the other hand, the first *Ü-Zeichen* was in its nature more a quality mark than a conformity mark (as the CE marking).

it was not considered as an official meeting and minutes were rarely provided by the Commission (if they were, they remained very general) and partly because in this forum, different positions "would not be used against you". At national level, communication was seen as even more important. Since the building codes were considered as very general, with several possibilities for architects and constructors to get additional (technical) guidance from other sources, the focus was stronger on providing information and getting feedback from interested parties than setting rules and enforcing them.

However, working on more dialogue did not necessarily mean that all interested parties were always using such an opportunity. Architects and constructors have not shown any real interest (considering themselves as not affected by it) and even national authorities (for specific fields like health issues for drinking water in contact with construction products) were rarely in contact with the authorities responsible for construction products.[222] One reason given was that, in the UK approach, authorities were also accepting other marks as equal to CE marking (since the CPD is not explicitly referring to an *obligatory* CE marking). With a wider range of possible assessment and conformity schemes, the interest of manufacturers and other interested parties might not have been strong. While recognising that the construction unit and most Member States considered the obligatory nature of CE marking as indicated in the text of the Directive, from the UK's point of view this restriction would have been an interpretation *adding* to the text of the CPD. However, it was mentioned that the ministry and BRE have tried to highlight to all interested parties that, outside the national territory of the UK, CE marking is an obligation, and therefore not following that approach might cause disadvantages of UK manufacturers and other actors in future when international trade becomes more and more important and manufacturers might move "beyond the realms of reputation".[223] Additionally, it was stressed that the new Construction Products Regulation should finally make CE marking obligatory.

Another reason for the lack of interest by most parties in the UK might have been that documents like the Guidance Papers and other documents written by

222 Most information on the work going on in the Commission's expert group on drinking water is provided by the Commission's report on the expert group (the other expert groups for fire and dangerous substances are within the responsibility of the minitry and BRE and experts of BRE participate in these meetings).

223 The minitryt, BRE and BSI have put information on CE marking on very prominent position – even before their own additional marks or services.

the Commission were written for a very small audience. Providing information to interested parties in the UK was seen as difficult when only a few of them would get useful information out of documents developed by the Commission (therefore even "supporting" the stereotype that "Brussels" is not very close to the needs of the people affected by its actions).[224] It was suggested that widening the target audience (or at least allowing them to follow the general developments) could be achieved by providing an overview at the beginning and only after that moving to more specific (technical) issues.

The UK delegation in the PG and the SCC referred most of the time to the feedback it has got from "industry" to explain its position. Few Member States have made such strong references to the positions of private actors in these meetings. However, these positions were not accepted only on face value and it became obvious in the interviews that the members of the UK authorities had a critical view of the motives of the interested parties providing information and their positions to specific aspects ("common good" versus "driving competition out of the market").

3.3.2.3 Austria

Austria's involvement in the CPD started long before it joined the EU. As an EFTA member, it had access to the documents of the SCC, via the EFTA representative in his role as an observer in the Standing Committee. But at that stage only the federal ministry followed these issues more or less closely, while the Austrian Länder were in a process of establishing a coordination body, based on the experience of the German Länder.[225]

When Austria joined the EU, other national bodies and actors, like industry federations, seemed to have shown only limited interest in this field – most of them did not consider themselves as being directly affected or were expecting

224 The Guidance Papers were mentioned once as documents where it was not always clear *why* they were written by the Commission if this small target audience could have been reached otherwise. However, it was appreciated that it was done by the Commission and not by any other actor (with more national or sector-specific orientations) and the fact that an issue has been "put on paper" for reference.

225 It was stressed during the interviews that the OIB might at first been a "copy" of the DIBt, but that the OIB had in the meantime developed its own position which was not always comparable to the one of the German counterpart. In particular, the strong emphasis of the DIBt on the relevance of the *Ü-Zeichen* was considered as conter-productive for CPD implementation.

that European harmonised standards might only come "still far away in the future".

After becoming a Member State of the EU, the Austrian authorities, the federal ministry and the newly established OIB – but still with few people working on EU issues, were busier with the *implementation* of the existing aspects of the CPD, rather than being able to contribute much to the ongoing discussion at EU level.[226] The above mentioned lack of interest in the CPD by several actors also made it difficult to get enough information and comments (or even questions) to feed them back into the discussion in the SCC. Most interested parties (including the building authorities in the Austrian *Länder* who have created the OIB) seemed to have taken the position that from now on it was the task of the federal ministry and the OIB to *handle and solve* all issues coming from Brussels, being a "shield" between EU issues and the daily work on national and regional level. Therefore, national actors expected not to be bothered with requests for additional input or strong involvement from their side.

This became even more obvious when the first mandates were developed. Lack of personnel – in particular in the federal ministry – made it difficult for the Austrian representative in the SCC to challenge decisions that were – from the Austrian point of view – incorrect. But even with the technical input of the OIB, the work of the Commission when developing these mandates was not considered as transparent and cooperative enough to allow for additional input. Work on the mandates was seen by some interviewees as too strongly dominated by industry and specific Member States – afterwards accepted by the Commission – which only left the SCC a role as an "approving body" but not as a forum for discussion.[227] Keeping in mind the difficulties of getting enough feedback from national interested parties before a PG or SCC meeting, the efficiency of the Commission in providing all documents on time became even more crucial – and its lack was felt more strongly when preparing a national position.

226 While in general the BMWA and the OIB are working together when representing Austrian interests in the SCC, Austrian actors seems to struggle with the roles and competences between federal and *Länder* level (also in the field of construction products), which can also sometimes seen strongly in both levels highlighting their competences on various occasions. (see: Bussjäger: Homogenität und Differenz 2006 p. 75ff. & S. 147 or the website of the BMWA http://www.bmwa.gv.at/BMWA/Schwerpunkte/Unternehmen/Bauprodukte/RechtFragenKonform/default.htm#%20%20kompetenzrechliche%20Grundlage%20der%20Bauprodukten richtlinie%20in%20Österreich).

227 Which might have created even less interest of downstream parties in Austria to follow the developments in Brussels.

Real interest by other actors was mostly experienced when a new standard had been published and had become a requirement of manufacturers. Information provided by the ON and the OIB (publications and information events) seem to be the tools most often used. Less information was available as to how industry (the Austrian Chamber of Commerce – WKO) was dealing with the information provided by the ministry. In some cases the OIB participated in special information events in the WKO, but there was not much feedback (questions, comments). The general lack of interest by civil engineers and architects was partly seen as a result of their general working environment: technical or legal requirements were mostly outside their scope or their abilities (manpower) to participate in the discussion on national or *Länder* levels. Therefore, the final requirements were not (openly) questioned but just introduced in their work. CE marking still seemed to be not seen very often in the day-to-day work of civil engineers and architects – not least because CE marking did not even appear in all (public) tenders (references are either to specific technical requirements or to specific standards)[228].

Another problem mentioned was the difficulty of providing enough information for downstream authorities. Regional authorities (*Bezirkshauptmannschaften*) were responsible for infringements of the *Bauproduktegesetz*. Also, local communities (about 2500 in Austria) and mayors as building authorities played a role in the implementation of federal and regional regulations. However, while being several levels downstream from the one where information on the CPD and CE marking was discussed and interpreted, these authorities faced the burden of finding a correct interpretation and enforcement (and risk to face complaints against them). Providing enough information and ensuring that it was also received (i.e. sending the OIB publications to all communities) and understood was still considered as an unfinished task.

While maybe not a very serious problem, a language barrier and the lack of resources to translate all documents into German was mentioned. The federal ministry – and to a lesser extent the OIB –distributed the original version produced in Brussels and provided (wherever required) an interpretation in German. Nevertheless, the risk remained that at downstream levels, the English texts might have been misunderstood, their significance not noticed or the documents

228 On the other hand, references to CE marking or ÜA marks can be found in contracts between contractors and distributors or manufacturers.

would not be read at all.[229] In particular basic documents like the Interpretative Documents or the Guidance Documents should have provided detailed and practical information but might be "lost in non-translation" for several actors on national, regional or local levels.[230] On the other hand, it was also mentioned that different actors did not just use Austrian sources to get information but also participated in conferences and workshops in Germany or read information material produced in Germany. This forced the Austrian side to be as precise and efficient as possible ("competition with Germany has improved the communication flow").

3.3.2.4 Poland

Long before Poland has joined the EU, the close contacts of Polish building authorities and the ITB with the French CSTB (Centre Scientifique et Technique du Bâtiment) allowed these bodies to follow the developments in the EU and in particular the discussion before and after the adoption of the CPD. Not surprisingly, the Polish system moved closer to the CPD approach and in 1994 introduced a Polish "B" mark, which showed very similar if not the same technical requirements as CE marking (product fit for use, conformity with a (Polish) technical standard, "Attestation of Conformity" system). In 1998 the transformation was nearly finished but the lack of harmonised European standards created the situation of a "CPD framework" with national instruments (accreditation of Notified Bodies, technical standards, "B" mark). With the accession of Poland in 2004 the CPD officially became the (obligatory) framework for dealing with construction products on the Polish market.

The need for industry to organise itself was considered as one of the main challenges by several public and private actors. The concept of being an independent actor who should participate in discussions at national and EU levels might have got more and more acceptance, but the actual participation as well as the ability to create federations and present specific interests in relevant bodies was not seen as well developed (Polish manufacturers managed to have a representa-

229 While it can be expected that practically all engineers and administrators have a relatively sound knowledge of English, the problem for downstream users of interpreting a legal text written in English cannot be considered as easy, keeping in mind that even between different Member States in the EU and the Commission different interpretations exist.

230 While these documents have been translated into German by the DIBt, references to these translations are missing (In addition, these translations are property of the DIBt and have to be purchased).

tive in the European federation for manufacturers – CEPMC – only three years after the accession of Poland to the EU). Therefore, the discussion in Poland was dominated by multinational companies that have acquired existing companies in Poland, while national manufacturers were less active, and SMEs were nearly not present at all.

Also civil engineers and architects were not involved in the activities of the construction products sector (the possibility of specialised expert groups interested in this field was mentioned but it was also assumed that this would be more a "private hobby" of its members than a sectoral professional interest), reacting only if problems with products or requested for CE marking occur. More interest existed for more *building*- related issues, and in particular on the structural performance of buildings and construction products (for which universities were more closely involved in the discussion of test methods in general and *Eurocodes* specifically).

A general problem mentioned was the language barrier that manufacturers, construction companies and architects might have to face. For a long time English was not the main (second) language for engineers (as compared with Germany and Austria). This made it necessary to provide translated documents as often as possible. But even with these translation activities, several documents were slipping through because of lack of funding. These including technical standards for which the financing of translation was not guaranteed. Since effective coordination of federations was still an ongoing exercise, the burden of translation and interpretation fell on individual companies, architects and civil engineers who were already struggling with adapting to the European requirements.

Therefore, in the cases where other interested parties were invited for discussions by the ITB (the Ministry itself was not seen by several actors as an initiator of this type of information exchange) participation was not very high, which left the solution-finding process more or less in the hands of the ITB.

Contacts and the information flow with actors at EU level in some cases seemed less problematic. The cooperation with EOTA was considered as the best, while following developments in CEN and the Group of Notified Bodies and getting information depended more on the individual chairing of the different Groups and Committees. However, CEN's working structure also put limits on effective participation. The split of some CEN TCs into several working and task groups did not allow for effective representation. In some cases it would have required about half a dozen experts in one TC to follow all ongoing activities. This made the ITB focus its resources in the mirror groups of the national standardisation body. Here the work of several CEN TCs was combined into fewer mirror groups which allowed even smaller (national) institutions and federations to follow the work at EU level.

But not only the need for creating representative bodies at national and EU levels has introduced changes into the working structure of several actors in Poland. The use of different quality marks has also challenged existing perceptions. Consumer demand as a relevant factor on the market had no comparable pendant in the Polish system before the European system was introduced. Keeping in mind that even in Western European countries this is often a not very precisely defined concept and even more often not easily compatible between different EU Member States, the confusion between voluntary and regulatory (as well as the concept "quality vs. costs") might be felt even more strongly in Poland than in the other MS covered in this study.

However, the interviews have also shown that at least in the ITB the developments in other Member States of the EU have been evaluated even before the accession and the advantages and weaknesses of the different national approaches on the CPD have been well identified. The confusion between CE marking as a "passport" for construction products to enter different national markets within the EU and the accepted use of these products within the technical and regulatory framework of Member States or – better – the lack of appropriate and practical information, was seen as one of the major problems in the current system of the CPD and CE marked products.

3.3.3 Federations

The strong position of EU and national authorities in the implementation process was reflected in the importance that other actors at EU (and national) levels gave to these public actors. They were the most relevant sources of information and private actors (federations, but also specification writers in CEN, EOTA and Notified Bodies) which were constantly using their contacts, meetings and conferences initiated or at least visited by representatives of the construction unit or national authorities (ministries and technical institutes) to be aware of the latest developments (and interpretations of the requirements of the CPD). This relative strong "dependency" on feedback from authorities might to some extent have been caused by the lack of clarity of the text of the CPD. The CPD was not seen as helpful and while the Interpretative Documents and the Guidance Papers were perceived as clearer and providing more guidance, these documents also had to face critical feedback.

But authorities were not only important contacts for guidance and (binding) confirmation. Also, the different working groups established by national authorities for preparing the next SCC meetings were closely monitored by practically all private actors covered in this study, even if participation was not always seen as necessary, because no issues affecting one's own interests were touched.[231] But this role of authorities was practically completely linked to national ministries and the four technical institutes. Other (downstream) actors were rated relatively low as providers of information – or even being sufficiently aware of the use of CE marking.

A characteristic of federations of *manufacturers* at EU level was the relatively few contacts with federations of architects and contractors. Communication in both directions was significantly low, but federations rarely considered these two groups of downstream users as relevant within the framework of the CPD (e.g. in standardisation work)[232]. Discussing aspects of the CPD and standardisation work on construction products clearly focused on the interests, needs and interpretations of manufacturers – *vis-à-vis* the requirements of regulators (national authorities were generally seen as important actors as "interpreters" of national requirements in standards and technical documents). However, this lack of interaction at EU level (on more *general* issues) was not repeated at national level. Here contacts have been reported more often – concentrated on *specific* questions or problems of *specific* products. This importance of "*ad hoc* contacts" to help clarify specific questions also supported an assumption by private actors at EU level that the general knowledge of architects and contractors about CE marking was rather low and their interest was only stimulated if they were not

231 Therefore, in particular federations of architects and contractors at EU and national levels were monitoring discussions in these groups, but the strong focus on products made any active participation a low priority for these organisations.

232 However, specification writers and CEN and EOTA are giving contacts with architects and manufacturers a clearly higher significance and also report more contacts. This might be influenced by the stronger role these two groups of downstream users play in national standardisation work, which would also affect the feedback from national mirror committees (CEN and national standardisation bodies) or individual practical feedback (for EOTA members as Approval Bodies) and therefore the awareness of specification writers at EU level.

sure whether or not CE marking was needed or more clarification of the role between CE marking and other national approaches was needed.

3.3.3.1 Federations of manufacturers

The representatives of manufacturers interviewed for this study have either worked directly for CEPMC or were employees of other federations linked to CEPMC as members or associated members. One would assume that these different roles would sometimes make it difficult for each individual to define priorities. Should the individual be closer to the interests of his or her federations or more supportive of a "European" solution? In fact the interviews have shown a simple but efficient approach chosen by most interviewees: individual experience in one's sector, in most cases gained by working for national companies or federations, in a specific Member State of the EU was used as a basis for finding solutions on multinational and European levels. In other words, it was more a sector-oriented approach, supporting or opposing different policies and approaches (e.g. against the interests of other sectors, – with national or company-oriented aspects still strong but of only secondary importance. On the other hand, any solutions developed at EU level had to be "translated" for national members and companies. The following comments are focused on the work with other actors at European level, while most comments at national level will follow in the next chapters.

CEPMC was seen as an information pool and information network where all relevant information about policies, specific technical approaches or even general background information on the activities of the Commission was collected and distributed. The main advantage for all members was the fact that this work has been distributed to several experts (not just the two employees with a technical background in the federation itself) who were meeting in special working groups. It was stressed that all federations had a rather small staff and would not be able to follow all developments on their own. "Knowing that at least somebody is reading all the stuff and informing us on time" was the main asset of this working structure. Documents developed by the Commission or the SCC were therefore *per se* not so important as the analysis done by one individual expert or a CEPMC working group. This allowed each member to be more selective when choosing an expert for a specific field, because it could be assumed that he or she *would* be actually working in this field and not be "wasted" in less well known technical fields.

CEPMC was also partly a playing field where each sector got better knowledge about the position of other sectors, in particular if they were competitors in a specific field (e.g. different materials used for similar products – like pipes, walling or ceiling systems). This did not exclude the possibility that a sector or even a specific company was bypassing CEPMC and addressing the Commission or the European Parliament directly. However, in general, horizontal issues were first discussed within the framework of the European federation to find a common position. It was also mentioned that it was a learning process for federations and companies to coordinate amongst themselves and find compromises even outside their own sector, e.g. seeing that a position had more weight if it was presented "with one voice".[233] Nevertheless, sometimes the option of presenting a commonly agreed position separately by each sector, federation or company to the Commission was seen as adding weight by "sheer numbers".

Employees of European federations of construction manufacturers were well aware that they could only *promote* and *support* cooperation between and within sectors, but their real effectiveness depended much on the practical support they got from their members. In general, two groups of companies were identified as having a strong interest in EU issues and presenting their position at EU level. A small number of larger companies already working at EU level and which have already seen the advantages for them, as well as smaller companies who wanted to cross national borders (e.g. either those located in smaller Member States of the EU) and whose expansion depended on entering new national markets. Those being located close to a national border, which might block any symmetric expansion, looked at distance and the cost-efficiency of transporting their products. Other companies (both bigger and smaller ones) focused on their national markets, being used to the existing system and saw its non-compatibility as an advantage to competitors entering the market from other EU Member States.

Also in common for all federations was the problem of showing their impact on developments at EU level. Finding compromises ("position papers") would only be accepted as a useful activity by their members if they could see that their positions have been taken into consideration by other actors (in partic-

233 An important argument for establishing an office or using consultancies in Brussels was for a number of interviewees "to be known" by other EU actors, in particular the EU institutions. (See also: Mazey/Richardson 2006 p. 253ff.)

ular the construction unit of the European Commission).[234] Here employees in European umbrella federations faced competition even from sector-specific or national federations because their compromise was more horizontal and abstract rather than sector- or product-specific.[235] In general, manufacturers had less interest in horizontal political issues than in activities that might term affect their business in the short or medium terms. Therefore, sector or national federations were seen as better "rooted" in their environment, their needs for information were often stronger and the specific details provided more useful for individual companies. However, it was stressed that long-term issues (e.g. emissions trading) was on the agenda of EU federations much earlier than at national level and therefore these federations had a better start in the discussion with other actors at EU level. But the efficiency of federations at EU level as well as at national level also depended on the financial resources of their members. In times of a declining economy resources were withdrawn from less essential fields first – which was in many cases active participation in federation work – and in particular the one at EU level.

How difficult cooperation might be was highlighted by the example of the end of coexistence periods for harmonised European standards and national standards (which have to be withdrawn after the end of this period). Is a co-ordinated introduction of CE marking within this period an advantage for all actors? Is it even possible to achieve that? Are potential market distortions between different Member States significant enough to justify the efforts of a coordinated approach? Discussions between different federations or sectors are trying to avoid issues of competition and rather focus on technical issues as more "neutral" ground having a higher potential of finding a common position.

---

234 On the other hand, it is less clear how and if position statements or documents are actually distributed to the members of federations and how they are perceived.

235 An example given was that the different results of the work of CEPMC vis-à-vis the construction unit of DG Enterprise and Industry and the work of EURIMA (the federation of thermal insulation manufacturers) vis-à-vis the unit in DG Transport and Energy (DG TREN) responsible for the Energy Performance in Buildings Directive. The construction unit and CEPMC cover a wide range of products, which makes it difficult to make a CEPMC position paper very precise. Any activity of the construction unit on the other hand is also very horizontal and in most cases does not allow seeing which part of the CEPMC position actually had an impact on the construction unit. Energy performance of buildings on the other hand defines more clearly the system boundaries of the issue at hand and also leaves fewer actors involved. This facilitates interaction between DG Transport and Energy (now DG Energy) and EURIMA and the influence of industry on Commission policy and vice versa is easier to track.

Representatives in CEPMC with strong links to national actors were sometimes in a difficult position when dealing with CPD issues. On the one hand, CE marking was supposed to open the different national markets, but it was not always CE marking *as such* which interested these federations. The harmonisation process in standardisation was sometimes also seen as an opportunity to "streamline" national requirements only to *relevant* requirements (from an Industry point of view) defined in national laws. It was highlighted that some technical requirements at national level have been introduced without having any technical instruments at hand to actually test products, or that authorities were not very selective when deciding on the *practical* results of these requirements (e.g. *realistic* potential risk for a building or its users) and interpreted more into the (national) texts than necessary. Therefore, European standardisation was seen as a tool to ensure more transparency and justification from national authorities and in the best (but very optimistic) case, the withdrawal or at least the adaptation of specific laws. For these issues, "the Commission" (and CEN) was seen as one actor with influence, and documents (e.g. the Guidance Papers) were used to highlight contradictions between national approaches and "the Commission's" position.

On the other hand, it was acknowledged that CE marking had so far not seen much interest from the costumers for construction products. "Brand names" and past experience with specific products were seen as more important than CE marking or national marks.[236] It was even mentioned several times that the interest in marks as such – and therefore also in national marks – was not very strong *before* the introduction of the CPD and CE marking, but only *after* CE marking became a requirement in the national systems. Therefore, CE marking has involuntarily increased the interest in national marks. This might be mostly caused by the *economic* approach driven by companies. If a mark becomes obligatory it is more interesting to know "what has to be done" than "why this has to be done", fulfilling the letter of the law more than the spirit. Keeping in mind that *national* authorities are the ones controlling and sanctioning the correct use of marks, these public bodies became the first contacts and most relevant reference points at national level. This did not diminish the role of (national) federations providing information to their members but, in case of doubt, the

236 Nearly every interviewee in this group highlighted the importance of "brand names" as one of the most essential information that is used by manufacturers and accepted by their consumers (distributors, contractors).

decisions of national authorities naturally had more weight, also more weight than "the Commission", or (in some cases) federal authorities compared with regional and local authorities ("CE marking is the "passport", but one still needs a "visa" to enter another national or regional market").

The position of federations vis-à-vis their members was also influenced by a problem partly outside their sphere of influence: the late arrival of harmonised standards. It was stressed that, after the adoption of the CPD and its implementation in national laws, most federations were very active in raising awareness in their sectors by organising information events and providing information at different levels. Education" was still seen by practically all interviewees as one of the most important tasks of their federation. However, after not only raising awareness but also expectations, the lack of any tangible results not only reduced the interest in this issue but also to a certain extent discredited any attempts to raise awareness again at a later stage (when the first harmonised standards were published). In some cases this has caused friction between federations and individual companies when the European standards were finally available and CE marking obligatory, and mostly smaller, but also big companies were late to react. Where was the gap in the information flow or the lack of cooperation? On the side of the federation or the company?

In general, CPD related issues were only followed by this handful of experts, but awareness or interest in these topics by their members (individual companies) was rather limited. General issues have been delegated and companies only reacted if they thought that a specific issue might touch upon their interests or they had already been confronted with the requirements of CE marking and/or the position of national authorities and now needed precision or advice. The above-mentioned growing interest in marks has caused some confusion about the differences between the European CE marking and national marks and questions on this issue are those most frequently put to the European and national federations. If CE marking was supposed to be a "market tool" to get into other EU (Member State) markets, the gap between "regulatory demands" and "market demands" did not create the impression that CE marking would actually improve upon the previous information flow to customers. Several interviewees in EU and national federations also mentioned that it was very difficult to explain the assumed advantages of the EU approach to downstream users.[237]

Federations were also contacted if harmonised European standards were considered as incomplete or of poor quality.[238] Both complaints were closely linked to the format used and requirements that manufacturers were used to in national standards in the past ("it is something I have never seen before"). Also, delayed information on published standards (e.g. differences between the EUOJ and the NANDO databases, late publication of references in the EUOJ) were also seen as discouraging for individual companies to be able to follow developments more closely.

In contrast, documents and requirements elaborated in EOTA and the Group of Notified Bodies were seen as too complex and "too precise", covering every eventuality instead of *essential* requirements. Therefore, federations could hardly interest their members in complex, but not very user-friendly documents developed in these two bodies. In addition, federations and their members considered themselves on the receiving end of a high level of distrust at the level of authorities, EOTA members and Notified Bodies, which resulted in bigger and bigger documents to close every potential loophole ("If you don't trust anybody, you write a whole book about everything").

Being confronted with "whole books" from "the Commission", the SCC, Member State requirements, standards, ETAGs and documents of the GNB made it even harder to transmit the information to "downstream" users who had not been involved in the discussion process and are therefore less able to identify the parts in the text that might be of importance for them. This has left federation representatives with several choices – none of them seen as efficient:

237 The concept of "opening markets" was not only confusing for downstream actors, several individuals at EU level also had problems of identifying the "added value" of CE marking. To overcome barriers created at national level – and their regulatory requirements and voluntary schemes (e.g. national marks) were in most cases seen as complementary activities to keep markets closed from competitors – CE marking should be "better than all of them". Falling short of this (partly simplistic) perception of a useful "market tool", the large number of "ifs" in the EU approach was perceived as too complex to be perceived as helpful – or worth being explained to downstream users.

238 But it was also mentioned that "some of the old nonsense has disappeared", referring to flaws in national standards that were not repeated or taken over in the new European standards.

- to summarise all documents and highlight all relevant issues. (For horizontal federations this was nearly impossible because of the wide range of the sector, but also for more specialised federations it was still very difficult);
- to select which information should be forwarded to national or individual members and keep the rest "at EU level" (which leaves the decision-making power completely in the hands of the federations, but increases the risk that the interests of members are not known to any extent that would allow for an intervention in favour for these members);
- sending everything and hoping that the selection is made at the next "downstream" level (which was considered as very unlikely because national federations and actors would feel even less secure about making this selection without ignoring important points).

While all three options were used, it was acknowledged that representatives of industry federations had to depend on their past experience and their abilities to identify what their members might need to know rather than getting feedback that would provide clear guidance on priorities. Nevertheless, feedback was seen as important source of information, but also in these cases, the representatives of federations considered it their task to *motivate* their members to provide feedback. Very horizontally operating federations even depended on national and/or sector-specific federations to provide their members – and customers – with more detailed information. But the main problem identified when it came to mobilising members to take the output "from Brussels" seriously and contribute to any discussion was the lack of targeting a wider audience *in* the documents. They were seen as reference documents for authorities and sometimes for specification writers and Notified Bodies. Manufacturers could not see the relevance in these complex documents "before it was too late", since they lacked useful simple descriptions that would have allowed making correct decisions when monitoring and participation would have been relevant and necessary ("secondary guidance for 'Mrs Smith'"). Lacking simple documents to explain the EU approach ("few, but relevant data"), providing information to customers (contractors and architects) was often seen as a serious problem. Even more than for manufacturers, the practical implications of CE marking were rather limited and would have complicated the information flow. Therefore, it was left to downstream federations and companies to decide for themselves if and how to present information about CE marking to customers.

Scepticism about the work of authorities was also voiced when it came to the obligations of Member State authorities to guarantee the quality of Notified Bodies. Often being subjected to a "third-party control" by Notified Bodies and their prominent position when defining the number and complexity of tests considered as necessary, Notified Bodies were seen as essential but Member State efforts in keeping a high level of quality were less certain. A large number of Notified Bodies in a country (Germany was mentioned as example) was not seen as very reassuring that they would be sufficiently monitored. Moreover, bad performance by less controlled Notified Bodies might "taint the whole system". Concerns about the quality of Notified Bodies (outside one's own Member State) were frequently brought up by actors at national level and therefore gave national authorities a reason to introduce additional requirements at national level (for products – not the Notified Bodies). That Member State authorities were not putting more efforts in ensuring the quality of the system, as well as not removing less performing bodies again from their national lists, was considered as a major flaw of the European approach caused at national level.

3.3.3.2 Federations of contractors

There seemed to be a wide gap between the discussion about the implementation of the CPD and the actual use of CE marking, at least as far as the European federation FIEC was concerned. It followed the ongoing activities of the Commission services from a distance and even the amendment of the CPD was seen as only partly affecting constructors at EU level. Even more, *when* information was provided, FIEC's members have not shown any real interest in CE marking. One of the main reasons for this lack of interest could have been the slow development of harmonized European standards which had only recently had any visible impact on the market for construction products, in particular since references to CE marking were now appearing in national public tenders. It was assumed that, used to national marks and an established system between product standards and design and use standards, constructors were now trying to link the new CE data with "corresponding" previous marks and standards. In particular, linking data on *product* performance to *building* performance was seen as difficult and (depending on if and how much a product sector or authorities are providing additional guidance) adding additional "translation work" to the existing day-to-day tasks. Only if "something goes wrong" constructors might contact their (national) federations for clarification or guidance. Keeping in mind that previous national standards or quality marks and the current European standards and CE marking were in some cases clearly serving different purposes, it was expected that more and more constructors might contact their federations, which would finally turn to FIEC. But for the time being, CE marking seemed more to be a rumour ("I have heard about it – am I affected by it?") than a practical tool.

As for the manufacturers, "brand names" were assumed to play a strong role in the selection process for constructors, but for this group it was not just the quality of a product and/or the price that gave certain "brand names" their advantages against other products, but it included reliability of delivering on time and being able to get replacements in case of complaints and, last but not least, information on how to use the product correctly. In particular, the last issue was not – or only partly – covered by European standards, which was a drop in quality compared to previous national standards.[239] CE marking was not considered as useful for the practical work of contractors, because compliance with a law was always considered as a fact.

Like all federations, FIEC faced the problem of getting its members interested in participating in ongoing work in the Commission, CEN and other European bodies. Few national federations were active at EU level (namely Belgium, France, Germany, The Netherlands and The UK) and in most cases only big companies had the resources to provide experts for specific issues. Therefore, networking with CEPMC and the Group of Notified Bodies (one representative is also *rapporteur* for FIEC) was considered as the most efficient way of being informed without "wasting" resources in fields only partly relevant.

---

239 One interviewee described it as "taking one part (the product performance) out of a complex system, replacing it by a (different) European approach and than putting it back into the system and hoping that it will work." Another interviewee from national authorities on the other hand commented that compared with the previous mix of product quality and installation rules in national standards, the approach of a purely product-oriented approach of the European standards has clear advantages. The performance of a building (or a part of a building like a wall) is now separately defined and product data has to adapt to these requirements instead of creating a "package" (product and installation) which is tailor-made for a product to which the designer has to adapt.

It was also mentioned that several Member States were moving from descriptive requirements to more performance-based approaches, which were either new or not accompanied with more guidance how market actors should adapt to the new situation ("just shifting enforcement to market actors"), or even worse: changing terms and definitions frequently from document to document used by different actors.

3.3.3.3 Federations of architects

Due to the small number of representatives of ACE in Brussels and the only architect arriving in the Brussels' office only a few years ago, the CPD as an instrument of harmonising assessment methods for construction products, was not considered by them as a priority at all. Struggling with a common acceptance of qualifications and requirements for this profession, sustainable construction and energy efficiency had clearly more potential to raise the interest of architects in Europe. In fact, the CPD and CE marked products only came back "onto the radar" of ACE when a representative of FIEC highlighted in an informal talk the developments in standardisation. Still, the question remained as to how relevant this work would be for architects, even with more and more CE marked products on the market, which might in future raise more awareness by the customers of architects. It was acknowledged that architects faced a dilemma: on one hand they should be as creative as possible (in particular during their training at university), and the strong focus on artistic and aesthetic design has shifted the knowledge and experience with materials, products and their technical use more and more to civil engineers, who were now sometimes seen as dominating the design and construction process, due to a certain lack of interest by architects in the engineering part of construction. On the other hand, the more pragmatic needs of owners of houses or authorities (or the interest of an architect to "play it safe" in practice) were limiting the practical implementation of the artistic part of their job. CE marking was seen as lacking credibility as a certificate indicating the safe use of products which would have been the most important added value (reducing search costs and providing assurance for architects).

ACE's newsletter has provided (general) information in the past, but so far, no feedback from any reader has been received. The current lack of interest by architects created another problem. To identify aspects that might be relevant for architects, one of ACE's members has to spend a significant amount of time and resources in following the work in this field. But in a profession with nearly only micro-enterprises this would hardly be acceptable without any real indication in the first place that any interests of architects were touched.

Therefore, it seemed more pragmatic for ACE to stay in contact with European federations which were more closely involved with the CPD, in particular CEPMC, but also FIEC and EURIMA, than investing scarce resources more needed in other fields.

3.3.4 Certification Bodies (Notified Bodies) – the Group of Notified Bodies (GNB)

Despite the clearly defined goal that the Group of Notified Bodies should ensure a close and efficient exchange of information between the different Notified Bodies, active participation was limited to only about 50 Notified Bodies (of about 300 in total). Their experts exchanged information and worked on general guidelines in the Advisory Group as well as in the specific Sector Groups. The lack of interest shown by several Member State authorities to participate actively or passively in the work of the obligatory GNB was considered as one of the major problems in guaranteeing that the services of all NBs were comparable and could be used at European level, without doubts by authorities, manufacturers or constructors.[240] It was even assumed that some NB could not follow the work at EU level efficiently, because these NBs consist of only *one* single expert. This also raised the question as to how well authorities could brief and prepare these Bodies to fulfil their tasks within the CPD-Notified Body framework. While the UK was considered as highly efficient in providing information to existing and future NBs (partly linked to the individual engagement of one specific official responsible for this task), doubts were raised if the German authorities could have achieved the same high level of quality considering that they have notified a large number of these micro-enterprises to the Commission. Even more importantly: how can the "quality" of Notified Bodies be ensured? In particular given that no reactions by national authorities could be seen, even after being informed about the lack of cooperation (e.g. not being active in the Group of Notified Bodies or even downloading reference and guidance documents produced by the GNB to ensure consistent work by all Notified Bodies)[241] by indi-

240 Since both the GNB and CEN were only providing a platform but could not "enforce" participation, individuals active in Notified Bodies and CEN TCs both highlighted the problem of sufficient and balanced participation, continuity of individuals participating in the ongoing work ("starting the discussion all over again") and the risk of low acceptance of actors outside a GNB sector group or a CEN TC after a compromise has been found.

241 Another point raised was that some Notified Bodies seemed to have not issued even *one* certificate since they have been notified by Member State authorities, which in several cases was done years ago. If these Bodies have never been active at all (and therefore gained experience in a sometimes highly complex field of technical expertise and regulatory requirements under the scope of the CPD and its national implementations), how could national authorities consider that these bodies are (still) capable to fulfil their tasks as Notified Bodies under the CPD?

vidual Notified Bodies, was considered and criticised as a lack of interest by national authorities to take their own responsibilities in this field.[242] This criticism did not stop at Member State authorities at national level, but also the construction unit and MS authorities in the Standing Committee on Construction were not seen as active in solving this problem. While it was raised by the GNB and discussed in the Standing Committee, practically no (specific) decisions or clear commitments by Member State authorities were taken.[243]

Concerns were also raised about the "quality" of CE marking. By trying to cover as many options as possible, the Commission has "opened CE marking too wide" (in particular Guidance Paper M provided less clarification than insecurity). Also by focusing on the Essential Requirements, CE marking did not cover all information requirements of the market, which led to insecurity and provoked requests for additional certificates or quality marks. As economic actors, it was seen as difficult to promote CE marking against other "quality marks" if the "added value" for the customers of Notified Bodies – manufacturers – vis-à-vis *their* customers – architects and construction companies, was hardly visible at all. The Guidance Papers were mostly considered as useful but there were also some doubts of their practical use: they were sometimes too complicated, but even more important, the last updates of these documents have been a long pastime ago, again leaving updates of technical developments or administrative interpretations (mostly by the construction unit) often to *individual ad hoc* interpretations.

Also in this group of actors it was mentioned that there was not so much interest in national schemes and quality marks *before* the introduction of the CPD and the first CE marks appearing on the market. Being confronted with a scheme of testing and attesting conformity forced manufacturers and also certification bodies to address the issue of relevant information provided to consumers (business-to-business as well as do-it-yourself enthusiasts). Did the performance

242 It was stated that national authorities did not decline their responsibilities but demanded explicit proof before taking any action. This reluctance created the impression with some interviewees that the burden of proof has been shifted from national and regional authorities to Notified Bodies or to the Group of Notified Bodies to an extent that could not be fulfilled without having the powers of public authorities.

243 Keeping in mind that Member State representatives in the SCC did not come from national market surveillance authorities, the reluctance of the SCC to commit to another authority at national level was not completely unreasonable. On the other hand, it reduced the role of the SCC to being a "problem solving" mechanism for practical issues.

characteristics used for CE marking really address the needs for constructors and planners? Or did the CE characteristics define in a harmonised product standard really describe the potential of a product in a way a manufacturer would like to see it? While it was not always clear who started it – it seemed clear that new quality marks were more and more frequently entering the market. (See also: Assumptions of actors on national level).

Another problem highlighted was the "lost in translation" factor: the construction unit's website as well as practically all documents have only been available in English, which has forced some Member States and national bodies to translate them into their own language to reach as many interested parties as possible. Even with the best intention and the best resources used, the risk with this has been that messages might be change, which might create confusion between interested parties in different Member States and also outside the EU. It was suggested that the construction unit should provide all relevant documents in all official languages in the EU and Member State authorities and EU and national organisations should only refer to the "official" interpretation.

While the GNB was practically always present in the meetings of the Standing Committee on Construction (and reported in every meeting on developments in the GNB or problems encountered by its members), and its representative reported back to its members, the guidance provided by the SCC was not always seen as clear and helpful enough for the practical work of Notified Bodies. The Guidance Papers provided some information, but were sometimes considered as too vague ("written by and for civil servants") to by useful. But more relevant was the lack of decisions taken in the SCC on questions and issues raised by the GNB or other actors relevant to Notified Bodies. It was acknowledged that the results of discussions in the SCC were "diplomatic" but it was difficult to identify clear conclusions at the end. This again left room for different interpretations within the GNB and other national actors.

Closer links existed to CEN´s Technical Committees. However, these contacts were mostly based on individuals (from Notified Bodies but also manufacturers being active in both organisations) being members both of TCs and Sector Groups of the GNB, not on an established approach between these two organisations. In these cases, information on developments of technical standards were passed on to the Sector Groups with feedback also moving in the opposite direction. Nevertheless, not all TCs or Sector Groups had these links and it was highlighted by a number of experts from Notified Bodies (not only in the interviews of this study) that draft texts of standards were received at a very late stage, allowing only limited input to these technical documents.

Since Notified Bodies were in direct contact with their customers, feedback that NBs got and could provide in meetings of the different working groups of the GNB was more practice-oriented, but it was also sometimes difficult to develop a useful *common* solution. Their closer contacts to practical downstream users might be one reason why their perception of downstream users in general, and architects and contractors in particular, as to their awareness and knowledge of CE marking was more positive (while still not very optimistic) than those of manufacturers' federations.[244] Additionally, they saw more CE marking as more relevant for these downstream users. Anther difference is the relevance the NBs gave the "political" level (in particular the SCC) and the role of (EU and national) authorities in their day-to-day work. In general, the Notified Bodies created weaker ties to the EU level, but they remained in closer contact with national (practical) actors – a characteristic that was also found (although less pronounced) when looking at the work of specification writers.

3.3.5 The technical specification writers (CEN and EOTA)

3.3.5.1 CEN

Pressure on CEN was increasing in the late nineties and the first years of the new millennium from several sides because of the slow progress in developing harmonised product standards. However, some aspects were outside or at least partly outside the control of CEN as a standard-setting organisation. Mandates for CEN were developed at a late stage. The first Interpretative Documents (ID) gave an idea about the scope of future standardisation work, and in fact CEN started the work on standardisation in anticipation of mandates. These mandates were also to a large extent written by the construction unit and Member States representatives and only later were CEN TCs or CEN consultants (for construction products) allowed to bring in their expertise into the drafting process, which was considered as creating an unnecessary gap between regulatory demands and CEN's ability to develop technical solutions.

244 On the other hand, compared with federations of manufacturers, NBs and specification writer in CEN and EOTA were more careful when attesting manufacturers' (in general) sufficient knowledge about CE marking.

When mandates were given to CEN, some TCs faced the problem that they were sometimes vague ("difficult to understand the mandates"). In particular, the task of a standardisation body was to identify all regulatory requirements in all EU Member States or include requirements for which even in national (When standardisation started, there were already 12 MS and their laws to be checked. However, the first standards were not finalised even when three additional countries joined the EU and all new harmonised standards – as well as all revisions of existing standards – now have to identify all relevant regulations of 27 Member States). The quality of mandates and the possibilities of different CEN TCs to respond varied significantly, depending on the products targeted. In general, it seemed that interested parties (mostly the relevant industry sectors) were easily able to mobilise to provide resources for "big" products, meaning products that were widely used on national and European markets, while products with less circulation, less influential or economically weaker manufacturers received less attention. In many cases, voluntary standards existed either at national or CEN levels and should have allowed an easy transition from the purely voluntary standard to a harmonised European standard with the obligatory part in annex ZA. However, the "obligatory" aspect made more actors alert and definitions and approaches already agreed were again subject to new discussion. In addition, the time for response to the mandate – the work programme of the TC(s) should be provided to the Commission within six months – was considered as insufficient to provide a useful reply. It was mentioned that for a serious approach one "has to be already half way through with the draft standard" before replying to the mandate. This was practically impossible and could result either in a very vague work programme or long delays in providing it. In most cases the latter was the final outcome).[245] Also, the wide range of products and combinations with other products and materials that are required for product standards by the CPD made it difficult to predict the actual workload and to assure that the future standards will cover "everything".[246]

---

245 In contrast to several of the interviewees from the construction unit, the interviewees from CEN believed in general that the different product TCs do have a strong interest in finalising product standards. However, they acknowledge that in some cases companies (that have bought companies in other Member States and were therefore avoiding adaptation costs for operating in this new market) have already adapted to the different national schemes and were less eager to make it easier for competitors that were just starting entering new national markets.

246 A very illustrative example was given for bricks and mortar. Standards can define the properties and performance criteria for bricks (which has already been achieved). However, it is not

Since CEN depends heavily on the support and cooperation of its national members for providing experts, chairmen and secretaries, it was highlighted that practically the expenses for the management of the different TCs were covered by five members: NBN (Belgium); DIN (Germany); AFNOR (France); (Italy) and BSI (UK).[247] Naturally, the background of these standardisation bodies – their priorities, approaches on content, quality and quantity of a technical standard, and – sometimes even more important – the interests of specific (national) industries in the outcome of a standard, could influence the way a Technical Committee performed its tasks, defined its work programme and included or excluded technical aspects in standards or technical reports.[248] The risk of an unbalanced representation of interests in a CEN TC, and therefore an

the brick as an isolated product that has to be taken into consideration to assess its performance in a building. It is laid in mortar (for which additional standards are developed) and only the combination of the performance of both products gives an indication of the performance of the wall. Unfortunately, the number of mortars used within the EU is extremely large and each has to be combined with each specific brick in a harmonised European standard. Therefore, standardisation work as needed under the CPD is seen as an endless story, while manufacturers and contractors are either left with an infinite number of options (or financing expensive research work on several combinations) – or need to fall back to the combinations used in the past, therefore remaining on the "safe side". Data on most used combinations in one Member State are usually available in specific tables. However, this is limited to experience on national level and on combinations assessed by national manufacturers. Products imported from other Member States are most likely not covered in these tables and would therefore need additional scientific proof.

It is interesting to note that this example was given by an interviewee in the UK (not attached to manufacturers or authorities) and it fits with the argument of German authorities about the limits of CE marking in construction works.

247 From the group of "newer" Member States (beyond the EU 12) only Austria, Finland and Sweden were considered as putting more resources into the standardisation work in CEN. One explanation given for the limited participation of the central and eastern European Member States was that many companies in these countries have been bought by enterprises of the "old" Member States. Therefore, several of the representatives already participating in CEN work were now also representing manufacturers of the new MS.

248 In one interview the efforts of an industry sector with a specific product (so far not covered in a work programme of any TC) were described to become involved in standardisation for their own products (due to the requirements of one Member State). While there was no problem from the side of the CEN Management Centre, the actual work of finding the "right" TC, *convincing* the chairman of the TC to be working (as task group) in this TC, finding experts and working on the standards for the product was left to the industry sector. It was stressed that it was more the support of *individuals* already working in the TC (and coming from the same sector) than of one of the sector specific federations or the CEN structure that facilitated for the members of the new task group to understand the system and how to work in it.

unbalanced result in its standardisation work, was seen as higher than in some systems of national standardisation bodies.[249] However, there were different opinions about how influential the chairs and secretariats of TCs actually were and, if not, how the TC as a collectivity of a specific sector might have played a larger role when deciding on its work programme and interpreting Commission mandates and the CPD. Whoever might dominate in the discussion process of a CEN TC the CEN Management Centre (CMC) was always "outnumbered" by the numbers of experts and financial input of its national members.[250] Therefore, CEN´s employees could only restrict themselves to general advice and – with the support of the CEN consultants – only partly influencing the work of more than 60 TCs (including their subgroups, working groups and task groups which sometimes splits the work into a very large number of working items).

Often more relevant than the role of chairmen and secretariats was the continuous participation of experts which allowed for progress in technical discussions and a stable composition of the group itself. The main problem for CEN, its national members but also for industry federations or federations of architects and civil engineers was to convince experts to join a TC and contribute to the work or at least to follow it. Manufacturers were in general in a better position to "spare" an expert for a limited period of time but this willingness for cooperation depended on the economic situation of the company and shifts in policy and interests. Professions like architects and civil engineers and the large number of SMEs and micro-enterprises made continuous participation even less likely (if a volunteer was found at all). A number of interviewees mentioned

249 One interviewee mentioned that there is more interest in balancing „national" interests (meaning improving the participation of different nations) than balancing interested parties of producers, authorities and users.

While all national standardisation bodies were highlighting their efforts to keep the composition of their technical committees as balanced as possible, the German DIN provides a type of official "fail-safe point" preventing the acceptance of a standard against the expressed opposition of at least one group of actors ("interessierte Kreise") (DIN Präsidialbeschluss 4/1996).

It was also mentioned (not only by NORMAPME as "representative" of SMEs) that CEN standards could create barriers for Small and Medium Enterprises, since they are not able to be effectively involved in the standardisation work on EU level (often also not on national level) which leaves the power of definition and interpretation to a few "strong" actors in the field.

250 In addition, while spending a large sum on standardisation, the Commission is only paying for a part of the actual costs (in particular the amendments of standards are not paid by the Commission), which gives the national members again a stronger position against the CEN Management Centre.

their "enlightened" companies that allowed them to work on European issues (standardisation or policy) on a regular basis, but it was also highlighted that continuation was often achieved by employing retired experts, which guarantees good technical expertise but does not touch the actual working pool of a company. But some interviewees considered the change of individuals as even worse than no participation at all. Each new expert could reopen discussions or could introduce new positions in already finalised parts of a standard. This could create a downward spiral of delaying the development of a standards which would increase the chances of experts dropping out and new ones joining, which could in turn reopen agreed parts of the standard, which would delay the finalisation, … etc.

However, working at CEN level was not always seen as a difficult (or even frustrating) experience. The "added value" of participating in standardisation work at EU level was also reported several times as being rewarding – by entering new networks of knowledge and expertise. Information on other approaches, experiences and solutions was – while only partly used in one's own (national or sectoral) environment – valuable input and created a better understanding and trust in the positions, expectations and reactions of other actors in a TC. This was often highlighted as compensating for other shortcomings of the work at international level. But these levels of trust were disturbed when new individuals and, even more importantly, – new concepts and (political and technical) approaches – were introduced into the system of a TC.

The main contact for actors in CEN to "regulators" was by definition with the Commission services (in particular the unit responsible for standardisation work and – for the CPD – the construction unit), since it was this body with which CEN has a contract and which was issuing mandates to CEN. In the late nineties, the construction unit had put most of its resources into following the standardisation work in CEN, providing input and – wherever necessary – putting pressure on specific TCs to improve their progress. This was seen as very fruitful, but the quality and quantity of the input from the construction unit also depended on its resources and interest in providing information and guidance. It depended in particular on: the specific technical field and/or individuals involved on the construction unit's side, if and when feedback was provided to CEN, thus leaving the responsibility of decisions to some extent to the CEN consultants (see below). Sometimes individuals leaving or newly taking a post in the construction unit changed specific perceptions and guidance from this unit. These were in most cases horizontal issues or interpretations of Guidance

Papers[251] that forced CEN employees (and in particular again the CEN consultants)[252] to interpret and explain the new "Commission position" to the TCs.[253] The role of the construction unit was strengthened by the fact that Member State authorities rarely addressed CEN when identifying potential problems in standards under development, butrather contacted the construction unit directly. This made the construction unit a "filter" for MS intervention, but also added another layer of communication between the ones who have identified a "gap" in a technical document and its authors (the relevant TC).

The CEN consultants were seen as another "link" *and* "filter" to the "outside world". Even more relevant than the construction unit (since the contacts with the consultants were more regular and more often), they had to provide the TCs with guidance, but here there were different expectations by the interviewees about their specific roles. Everybody agreed on the role of the consultants as checking the compliance of (draft) standards with the mandates, but there were differences as to how much their role included providing guidance to match the requirements of the CPD and how much the consultants should be involved in the technical details of the standards. Some consultants were seen as being "too fussy" about editorial issues while partly neglecting the technical work. This was considered as slowing down the progress of work in favour of less relevant issues rather than what the TC considered as its primary task. The inputs from consultants were welcome when they helped to put the results of the

251 The Guidance Papers were seen as a good starting point, but have now lost some of their relevance because the general knowledge has increased in product TCs over the years. It seems that they were mostly used by consultants for backing up their arguments than by TCs themselves. In particular the volume of these documents and the complexity of them ("What do they want to say?") often discouraged their use.

252 Like for bilateral approaches by Member State authorities, direct contacts between TCs and the construction unit included the risk that solutions were developed, but only a small group of individuals were aware of it. In particular if CEN consultants were not involved or informed about new decisions, the discrepancy between positions and approaches of different TCs could increase.

253 *Once a new term was introduced by me into the discussion of standardizing test methods for dangerous substances:* "regulated *dangerous substances". This was done to solve a problem within the Commission services in the most pragmatic way. However, several weeks later I got from different interested parties documents with different interpretations why "the Commission" has introduced this term. While very flattering for me (all of them assumed that I put much more and deeper thoughts into it than I actually did), they triggered several (long) discussions in several groups which in some cases distracted them from the relevant tasks at hand.*

technical discussion into the right context with the requirements of the CPD (e.g. format and content of annex ZA that is determining the obligatory requirements).

However, individuals could change and with new consultants or officials in the construction unit, the interpretation of requirements, mandates and Guidance Papers could change. Since some CEN TCs were only meeting twice a year, even sporadic changes could leave the impression that positions were "changing week by week". Guidance Papers should provide more stable information, and it was acknowledged that in particular the first ones provided a more reliable framework for everybody who was not always involved in all discussions about the CPD ("we finally got something in plain English"). But also some comments refer to several of them as "too sophisticated", "written by lawyers, not engineers" and in a "typical Commission jargon". They were seen as tools for administrations to highlight their positions than providing guidance to "implementing" actors.

On the other hand, experts in CEN TCs did not consider themselves as purely passive parts in the information flow. Several mentioned that, if needed, they were actively searching for additional information on websites of the Commission, federations or even the European Parliament. (However, most of the experts interviewed had several functions in the construction sector at EU and national levels and their different roles – in particular more political ones as representatives of federations – required a more active approach) Nevertheless, the best combination that was available to all members of a TC, according to most interviewees, was the use of Guidance Papers and useful complementary information and interpretation by the CEN consultants.

While universities were not involved in standardisation work as independent actors, they were sometimes very active in the discussion on test methods in specific product TCs (in particular for testing the structural performance of products in a building) and advising them and providing data of their research. Questions on structural performance and the related product and design standards were seen as the only ones where architects and constructors have so far shown open interest and participation in the standardisation work. But this seemed to be not so much the starting point of more involvement of this profession but more the only field where the interest would be strong enough to encourage participation.

Member State authorities as such were not present in CEN Technical Committees. This did not mean that they could not significantly influence the work in the TCs: It was their input which set the requirements laid down in national laws and administrative provisions. However, mandates were sometimes seen as too theoretical. Again the assumption that they were more written by and for lawyers than for engineers and manufacturers. Later requests for specific requirements by national authorities were also perceived as more caused by administrative needs than technical relevance, in particular when it was considered as relevant only in one Member State while all others were using the "NPD option" ("no performance declared")[254] ("the work for nothing"). Even worse, the standards met serious objections from national authorities after their finalisation in CEN. But even without external objections, slow administrative procedures were mentioned as another frustrating factor. Finalised standards have to undergo a procedure before being officially binding documents.[255] Sometimes, this procedure took months – or even years. Therefore it had a similar fate to the CPD that, after finalisation and awareness raising, the actual use – and therefore the interest of downstream users – had already significant diminished) which made it even harder for individuals in TCs (or federations) to present the final outcome as achievement.

However, the focus of individuals working in CEN was practically completely on manufacturers as the relevant group of downstream users. Cooperation with other actors in the private sector (contractors and architects) was rare or non-existent in the actual standardisation work and also information to these groups was not provided on a regular basis, but only when individual questions were brought forward. Mostly, it was perceived that these downstream users would not directly benefit from the introduction of harmonised standards and that they would not have the manpower to go deeper into the subject anyway. Therefore, providing information was left to individual manufacturers and their specific contacts with their customers. Since experts in TCs were mostly seconded from manufacturing companies, it was not surprising that the assumptions and approaches were similar to the ones of the manufacturer's federations. The only exceptions in this rather closed environment of product standardisation were national authorities who ranked prominently in the information chain (as the

254 This approach leaves the concept of national regulations intact, while restricting their use to specific Member States. Outside European countries that are regulating, manufacturers do not have to declare any performance values or classes for these requirements. In some cases, this could lead to a requirement which has been covered in a harmonised European standard but is demanded in one Member State only.

255 The title of the standard has to be translated by CEN into all official languages in the EU, and afterwards published in the Official Journal of the EU.

ones accepting standards and therefore as an important group to explain the scope and use of the final harmonised European standards).

3.3.5.2 EOTA

Generally, EOTA members were often more closely attached to national authorities or even partly fulfilling tasks of public bodies which were delegated to them. Therefore, comments were often influenced by this other role and its obligations. Interviewees were aware of the complex situation and potential problems of this combination of public actor and economically driven actors, but the "public role" seemed to be the most relevant reference point. Since the Approval Bodies depend in their work on cooperation with other Approval Bodies, their EU and (partly) national activities will be covered in this chapter and not repeated in the chapter of actors at national level.

The fact that most EOTA members (three out of the four Member States in this study, except The UK) had a unique and monopolistic position in national markets did not necessarily indicate that competition was not an issue for these organisations. Cooperation under the umbrella of EOTA (e.g. providing information for another EOTA member when this body develops an ETA for a customer and asks for information on regulatory requirements in other Member States) was on the one hand seen as essential. On the other hand, it also produced costs which could not be directly compensated. Most interviewees asked themselves the questions: how much effort was put into providing data for other EOTA members? How sufficient in quality and quantity this information was. However, it was not assumed that the data were flawed. It was more the concern that less obvious – and less relevant – requirements "might escape the scrutiny" of an Approval Body).

In several cases being closely involved in the work of national authorities at EU level as their "technical advisors", or even representing regional interests (as for Germany and Austria), these bodies considered themselves as being used as important information points about CE marking by downstream users. Also, the scope of their work on a relatively small number of products not (yet) covered by harmonised European standards allowed them to be more focused and to provide more detailed information and guidance to manufacturers when the questions arose as to if and how CE marking could be used. This product-specific approach (even with European Technical Approval Guidelines sometimes in place, which could be seen as rather similar to a harmonised European standard) was also seen as an advantage compared to the CEN approach because it allowed more precise assessments of specific products – and therefore better service to customers. However, these customers were in most cases manufacturers and (regional) authorities. Again this linked more closely to their role as "technical advisor" for authorities). Architects and contractors were not seen as target groups for providing information and only ad hoc (case-by-case) contacts were reported.

Compared with the Group of Notified Bodies, the small number of EOTA members was seen as an advantage in being able to know all other actors and to learn to work with them. Also, the transit of individuals working in different working groups was relatively low, which allowed for consistent approaches. However, the changes of individuals of other actors, in particular the construction unit, was seen as increasing difficulty, if positions and interpretations were changed and if the new positions were not consistent with documents (e.g. Guidance Papers) still considered as valid by EOTA members. These Guidance Papers, aiming to a large extent at EOTA as one of their most relevant target groups, were reported as having been used relatively frequently as references. Having also ensured that officials of the construction unit participated often in meetings of EOTA working groups and project teams, the direct access to information was better than for several other actors. However, at the same time, the risk increased that the information received could be confusing or contradicting previous positions.

***

While being active at EU level, one question was put forward in the interviews and questionnaires: what would individuals working for private bodies (federations, specification writers, NB) consider as relevant factors for downstream users to choose specific products? In practical all responses, CE marking was not seen as a very important. Practical aspects (e.g. price, data availability, past experience) played a stronger role and even national marks were seen at least as equally relevant for buyers' decisions. Notified Bodies were stronger "defenders" of CE marking, but even for them certification was assumed to be a peripheral aspect for downstream users. A little bit surprising was the feedback from federations which in general have been more positive about most aspects of the CPD (e.g. improved transparency, quality and quantity of control by manufacturers). They seemed not to put too much expectation on the role of CE marking vis-à-vis their customers. As will be shown on the next two levels, this was a realistic assumption.

3.4 Conclusions at EU level

Due to the number of roles some individuals had to cover at EU level, it might not always be possible to draw a precise line between the "EU level" and the "national level". Nevertheless, some structures and interaction procedures *are* specific for the environment at EU level, forming perceptions and reactions on this level which might affect national actors or could be influenced by national input. These specific aspects will be analysed in this chapter.

3.4.1 Working at EU level: The "power" of the few ...

Practically all actors at European level had one thing in common: they were very few in number and had an agenda covering a wide range of issues. "The Commission", "Member States", "industry" and the management of other European organisations officially dealing with the CPD were in reality no more than between two to half a dozen engineers, lawyers and other experts in each public body, federation or organization. All in all in the EU organisations and the four Member States selected in this study, about 20-30 people in public bodies and private organisations were spending a large part of their time on CPD-related issues. This had three main implications. Firstly, each individual was (due to a "lack of competitors") in a very strong position to decide on the quantity and quality of information provided to downstream users (e.g. other authorities, members of federations, companies, test laboratories, technical bodies) and therefore of set the framework of their own work and also influencing the work of actors on this level and downstream levels. Secondly, each individual was *responsible* for the quality and quantity of the information he or she provided and the practical usefulness of the developed framework. Thirdly, they depend significantly on their abilities to create information networks at EU and national levels to get and to provide enough (technical) expertise or influence vis-à-vis other actors.

All three aspects could again be seen from two different perspectives. The first one would follow the assumption that "Brussels" is a tightly knit community of civil servants and lobbyists, making decisions far away from those who are most affected by them. Considering the very special position of these individuals, they would be in the perfect position to act as the *homo economicus* – focused on their own individual gains in the first place (see: "Stayin' alive ..."): The possibilities of downstream actors monitoring and sanctioning their actions is extremely limited and reaction might often come too late – it indeed they were aware of any situation where they should react at all.[256]

The second perspective focuses less on the *potential power* of individuals or this small group at EU level and more on the *burden of responsibility* and the *practical implications* of having only a few individuals as creators, interpreters and distributors of information – information that could have serious legal effects for different interested parties. The above-mentioned dependency of downstream actors put a lot of weight on documents and interpretations delivered by actors at EU level, sometimes even the choice of a single word could created confusion at downstream levels, which could "back-fire" onto actors at EU level, who have to defend not only a result but even their own position in the process. To find the right balance depended on certain expectations that other (downstream) actors are using the same norms when interpreting results and reacting vis-à-vis national or EU actors. Presenting and defending a position also depends on the assumption that other actors at EU and national levels of other Member States or federations were not working against the result, and as a result leaving other actors in an even weaker position defining a system that has obviously already "failed".

Both assumptions – the closely knit community "in power" and the "burden of power" – are at least partly correct and the image of the profit-oriented actor in a very specific and powerful position might at first glance seem to dominate, in particular when looking at the small number of individuals involved. Not least because several actors at national or federation levels have in the past been employed by the Commission, CEN, EOTA or a Notified Body and *vice versa*. In addition, most members of this small "community" in Brussels *were* (and are) facing only limited control by their peers and other actors because most of them

256 Good examples for the dependency of downstream actors on information from EU level are documents summarising the outcome of meetings (e.g. minutes or voting tables). In several cases, actors at EU level insist on taking their position down in these documents to prove their activities and compliance with the expectations of national actors, which increases the size of these documents significantly. Documents only focused on the results of the discussion are shorter, but they are making it more difficult for actors atn EU level to demonstrate that they were strongly following instructions or expectations from downstream actors.

have been in contact with each other for several years and a common understanding has been developed which made open (and therefore *visible*) confrontation less likely than efforts to solve differences at a low-profile level before they were brought up in a more open forum. Since some individuals also (officially or *de facto*) represented different interests, they were to a certain extent their own controllers, because none of the actors at home could demand complete compliance with their own goals if they had to "share" their expert with other actors.[257] Additionally (as often voiced by actors on the "construction-site" level), "Brussels" was for many national actors too far away to be contacted directly. Contacts with the Commission or the Parliament were not known, the stereotype of the "Eurocrats" as being too aloof to be of any help might have been another restraining factor and, in most cases, the dependency on the established lines of communication (based on and promoted by the "select few") might also have discouraged any individual approach to actors at European level others than the ones already known. This gave individuals acting as an interface between the European and national levels even more power in selecting what information should be provided (to the national level and vice versa to the other European actors), without having to fear too much interference, correction or criticism from other actors in their own sphere of influence.

Promoting and explaining the CPD was (and is) an ongoing process because different actors were only now becoming aware of the requirements of the Directive and were beginning to experience difficulties on a more practical level. E.g. "What are the solutions for problem X, according to the text of the Directive (a specific Guidance Paper, a document discussed and accepted in the SCC)?". Based on their specific interests, different actors sometimes interpreted the content of official documents or feedback from the construction unit (or other actors also working at EU level) in a way that was not foreseen by the construction unit and might even have been seen as contradicting the original concept. Since the Directive was *de facto* written by the construction unit, individuals in the unit might have seen themselves as the ones that had the most accurate and relevant interpretation of it, and felt obliged to defend it against other (opposing) interpretations. However, "convincing" actors was and is focused on Member State

257 It was also mentioned several times in the interviews that a selection of information is done not only on a technical level but also to "create" a positive or even supportive reaction from "downstream" members to allow the actors at EU level to represent at least a cooperative and not a defensive or outright negative interest group.

authorities and other actors at EU level (like CEPMC and other federations of manufacturers), and the strong involvement in monitoring and "pushing" CEN TCs to finalise European standards did not allow for thoroughly addressing all relevant actors. In particular, contacts with actors who could provide a more first-hand account on national perceptions and needs (e.g. architects, contractors) were rare and were leaving the construction unit in a state of strong dependency on feedback coming from public authorities and representatives from manufacturers at EU level.

Due to the fact that the Commission's construction unit has outsourced the technical work to CEN, EOTA and the GNB on a contractual basis, it followed relatively closely the discussions and developments in these bodies. While giving CEN, EOTA and the GNB leeway in their technical work (because the construction unit did neither have the power nor the resource or technical expertise to interfere), it was often aware of deviant interpretations and actions within these technical bodies and so tried to influence the work of these organisations. In addition, the importance of having CE marked products on the market as soon as possible (after the long delay) was an even stronger incentive for the construction unit to concentrate its resources on the control and guidance of the work on these two bodies and in particular on CEN. Several interviewees have mentioned their concern about the lack of control the CEN Management Center (CMC) and the Commission services could establish on different Technical Committees and the way these TCs were able to accept or to ignore requirements and guidance from the Commission. Their independent role and the lack of coordination and cooperation experienced with some TCs ("private kingdoms") raised the perception that specific actors were dominating the development of technical standards to their own advantage, forcing the construction unit even more to monitor developments in CEN at the price of having fewer resources available for other tasks within the framework of the CPD.

Additional "outsourcing" approaches like the support of the development of CEPMC, as the representative of manufacturers or the early introduction of the Group of Notified Bodies and involving EOTA as a "competitor" to CEN, seemed in some cases to have speeded up the work in CEN, but it has introduced new actors with their own priorities, which now forced the construction unit to follow *their* activities more closely so as to avoid any dominance by specific actors in these bodies. Not being able to do this on a permanent basis or even to cover most of the essential work of all actors involved, a different path was chosen to increase transparency. Several Guidance Papers and other "explanatory" documents were written by the Commission (and "adopted" by Member State representatives in the SCC), which provided more information on the administrative framework and even technical details on how specific actors have to perform their tasks under the CPD. This guidance was seen as an instrument to support the management levels of the European bodies (CEN, EOTA and the GNB) in creating a common approach within their organisations, and also as an instrument to facilitate peer-group control and peer-group pressure on actors moving too far away from these guidance documents.

Member State authorities supported many approaches of the construction unit, because the goals were often very similar. Like the construction unit, Member State authorities had reasons to watch the work in CEN and EOTA quite skeptically. While having a strong position in the "regulatory" part of the implementation of the CPD by having voting power in the SCC, their influence on standardisation works in CEN and EOTA was even more limited than that of the Commission services. Not being presented in CEN Technical Committees and (due to a lack of manpower) only partly involved in the work of the "mirror committees" of their national standardisation bodies, they experienced a huge gap between the phase of writing or amending a mandate to CEN or EOTA and the final publication of their work, a period in which they rarely have any direct influence. Since in three out of four Member States, active market surveillance did not *de facto* exist, the previous (only) controlling power of national authorities in these countries, by controlling their national manufacturers, was removed when European standardisation was introduced, thus leaving them more or less "blind" when defining and enforcing the quality and use of construction products in their countries. Not surprisingly, much effort has been concentrated on the text of these mandates, putting as many requirements as possible into these documents, and also supporting the development of additional documents (in particular Guidance Papers) that defined system boundaries for technical specification writers and technical bodies (like the Notified Bodies), so as to "regain" influence in this field. All these documents caused long discussions (adding several points to close potential "loopholes") between EU and national authorities before they were accepted in the SCC.

Besides stressing the obligations of private actors in these documents (as a relatively resource-saving approach), national authorities have not shown any strong initiative to compensate for their relatively weak role, for example by creating closer bilateral or multilateral cooperation. There seemed to be no regular or frequent exchange of information between national authorities outside the SCC, but only *ad hoc* contacts (mostly if they were confronted with problems). While it was mentioned in the interviews that knowing each other from SCC meetings facilitated later contacts outside the SCC framework, no need was seen for closer and regular contacts. Keeping in mind that the national representatives were mostly in a coordinating role but not actually implementing the CPD, this would also support their own impression that contacts to implementing authorities were rather sporadic ("when something went wrong"). This left the construction unit in a more powerful position as an "agenda-setter" but also reduced the potential of the SCC as a "problem-solver", because issues were largely only dealt with during SCC meetings, leaving the follow up mostly to the construction unit and its limited resources.

Federations at EU level were playing several – and more reactively than actively – roles. They were *de facto* "collectors" and "distributors" of information on the CPD and CE marking issues. Being officially "powerless" in the discussion in the Standing Committee on Construction, they were nevertheless not completely without influence. In particular the construction unit had supported their developments or their role at EU level – mostly to balance the power of specific actors, like Member State authorities or other federations or technical bodies. The federations were aware of their mutual dependency with the construction unit when providing support as well as lobbying for their own specific interests. Cooperating with the construction unit was seen as providing more advantages than disadvantages for industry. Since in general the construction unit and industry were aiming for removing national barriers to trade, they had also strong mutual interests. Additionally, the construction unit was a strong "agenda-setter" within the framework of the CPD, and therefore more likely able to effectively influence positions of Member State authorities.

But not only had the construction unit needed (technical) input from market actors. In fact, specific industry federations have simultaneously played a role at EU level (via the European federations – providing information to the Commission and to the SCC), at national level (providing information to the national authorities) and finally at the level of the technical specification writers, by providing experts to CEN TCs. These roles will be discussed in more detail at the "national level". The same possibilities were open for bigger companies using their resources to "bypass" federations. Like federations they could have been active at several levels, *and* used their strong position in federations to influence their positions in favour of stronger individual actors.

Maybe surprisingly for the most openly profit-oriented actors (and therefore, *the* typical *homo economicus*) in this system, European federations seem to belong to those actors heavily dependent on cooperation within the concept of *homo sociologicus*. Compared with most other actors, federations were routinely using networks of actors from different federations and professions to get and to distribute information. Sharing the workload of monitoring activities of the Commission and national administrations at EU level was seen by all interviewees as essential for their own efficiency. One could hardly argue that this approach was completely voluntary, keeping in mind the limitations of these federations in manpower and information. Also, the fact that despite the large number of "lobbyists" in Brussels, the actual environment for federations in the field of construction made them a rather small community, thus generally allowing for deviant behaviour to be identified easily.

Moreover, *European organisations* were – no matter how big the organisation might have been in theory – often "one-man-armies", or at most "platoons", in that they had only one person or a few individuals dealing with CPD and CE marking issues. Compared with public authorities and their "institutionalised" networks, these organisations *depended de facto completely* on the voluntary input of their national members. In addition, CEN and EOTA – as the most visible *European* organisations – were positioned between regulators (the construction unit and MS authorities) on one side and federations, individual manufacturers and test laboratories on the other. Each side showed quite some distrust about the goals and the influence of the other in the work of technical standards and ETAs and so tried to limit the influence of the other. (National standardization bodies and industry, because it allowed them to exercise their influence in standardisation; national authorities because they could *not* significantly influence it.

Last but not least: The "real downstream users" of construction products – architects, designers, civil engineers and contractors – have *de facto* been missing during most of the phases of the implementation of the CPD. This was partly due to a lack of interest by the other actors (the construction unit, MS authorities, manufacturers, specification writers and Notified Bodies) who were more focused on the development of harmonised European *product* standards and finding compromises on interpreting the CPD and national regulatory requirements. But it is also true that interest at European and even moreso at national levels (as the one providing experts and feedback), of architects or civil engineers was nearly non-existent. Here, the lack of resources (SMEs and micro enterprises as members) was even more significant but also the lack of understanding by all sides to seriously link the requirements of buildings (design, implementation) with the requirements of products, significantly affected the communication and cooperation of all actors.

3.4.2 ... the real input of the few ...

No matter if one focuses more on a "power" scenario or a "cooperation" scenario, both depended on several factors:

- the political and practical *priorities* of the individual actor (which might have been in competition with the goals of the implementation of the CPD and the use of CE marking and/or might influence how resources could be used);
- *available* resources (manpower, time, technical means, financial means);
- quality and quantity of *existing* working and communication *networks* with other interested parties;
- if the *priorities and goals of all interested parties* were compatible with the use of CE marking or contradictory to it.

The **priorities** were the most difficult to identify and to verify in this study. European and national authorities were supposed to know all relevant laws touching their field of expertise and should be aware of political developments. However, past experience by a number of interviewees and the author has shown that knowing the legal requirements *in general*, did not necessarily lead to the correct link between (sometimes very general) laws and the specific technical issues at hand in standardisation under the CPD. In fact, monitoring the work of specification writers had so far been more passive and reactive, with only few resources being spent by public authorities on guaranteeing proper input from national standardisation bodies (their mirror committees) or checking the final version before the official publication, which resulted in a quite frequent phenomenon that national authorities became aware only at a very late stage of the standardisation process that harmonised standards were not covering all relevant national requirements. In several cases this was seen by some Commission officials as "intentionally forgetting" these relevant requirements. However, it highlighted the strong dependency of EU *and* national authorities on correct feedback from national actors.

In particular the feedback from the federations of architects and contractors has highlighted another problem for actors setting their priorities vis-à-vis Commission regulations and policies: the lack of priority setting by the Commission (services) for *all* its policies and regulations affecting the construction sector. While the Commission services sometimes try to coordinate all their activities *between* them (or at least to avoid overlaps), there is no clear declaration for actors *outside* the Commission on how these different activities fit together, and how the different target groups are supposed to comply to them simultaneously (or set priorities). Actors are in general supposed to "create their own awareness" (the "early-warning system" mentioned before), but in reality the Commission services are "competing" with each other for this awareness – and compliance. Since resources are limited for all public and private actors, and more prominent policies and their instruments have been developed since the adoption of the CPD (e.g. energy performance of buildings – to reduce the threat of "global warming"; "sustainability" criteria – for acting against the loss of natural resources and bio-diversity), the CPD can only expect to catch the interest of the actors directly involved in construction products: manufacturers, certification bodies and (to a lesser extent) national, regional and local authorities.

After the first implementation phase the actors involved in work on CPD issues have in many cases experienced a decline in available **resources**, in particular fewer experts were seconded to this task. The fact that only during the last few years the awareness about CE marking requirements for construction products by manufacturers and authorities has increased (because only *now* products are covered by harmonised European standards) seemed not to reverse the trend. The "newcomers" in the family of Member States (in this study: Austria and Poland) had a certain advantage that the time of the publication of European standards fitted together with the process of creating or organising the necessary administrative or technical bodies. In their cases, availability or lack of resources depended more on the original interest and assumptions about the potential workload, and it remains to be seen if more European product standards or potentially more need for guidance and clarification would affect the recourses available for the task, or if there too resources will be redirected to other issues.

For private actors it was even more difficult to adapt to new developments at EU level and to decide if they should participate in the implementation process or not. Some comments addressed a certain "jargon" used by EU actors (i.e. specific terms or definitions) which was harder for actors further away from the discussion process in "Brussels" to translate and to interpret. In particular, if new topics or working groups have been introduced at EU level, it was not always obvious (from short titles or short descriptions) if this was of interest and if experts could be identified and motivated to participate. Therefore, national federations but also smaller ones with only limited contacts to the construction unit, were often dependent on information and interpretation from more "experienced" or larger federations.

A similar lack of balance could be found in the composition of actors working in CEN and EOTA. Several actors – like architects and contractors – were not actively involved in product standards, focusing instead on design and implementation standards. Also getting experts from companies seemed rare (coming from "enlightened companies"), which reduced the chance of getting first-hand experience in all TCs on all the different aspects needed, and considering all the potential aspects of construction products, without a clear link to design and implementation standards, made the concept even more difficult. All of these limitations made the request of the Commission and Member State authorities of taking all regulatory and technical requirements into consideration extremely unrealistic.

Networking seemed to depend strongly on national "traditions" as to how important networking was seen for specific issues, but also on how often formalised or informal structures are preferred by different actors or even individuals. Therefore, variations even within Member States or industry sectors were common, and individual preferences have at least in some cases played a significant part in how networks have been developed and evolved.

- The national ministries responsible for representing their country in the SCC had (at least in theory) all structures in place to distribute information to other interested parties and to receive feedback from them. In The UK and Poland the technical aspects were discussed in BRE (UK) and the ITB (PL) which gave these bodies a stronger role in selecting relevant issues and "filtering" them to their ministries. On the other hand, since this included also more options, the official representatives in general had a wider range of choices on how to proceed during the discussion in the SCC (actively used by the UK delegation). Compared with his UK counterparts, the civil servants in charge in the German Federal Ministry had to cover tasks of receiving, evaluating and selecting information received from all interested parties – including the position of the German *Länder*, represented by the DIBt (but still leaving most of the detailed technical issues to the DIBt).

Austria had a very similar system but active feedback from industry (or the Austrian *Länder*) was rather scant. It seems that this was partly caused by the assumption of industry and *Länder* authorities that the issues discussed either did not affect them or should be dealt with at Federal and EU levels anyway.

- Industry networks were mostly based on sectoral interests, supported by different national communication structures. Industry and authorities seemed to have very much in common when comparing the level of interests and involvement in EU issues. In The UK (where CE marking was not the only mark allowed) the need for the Commission as provider of guidance or European federations to represent industries interests was less strong than for the other three Member States in this study. The work was closely followed but the need for clarification from EU actors was rather low or at an informal level. More emphasis was put on standardisation work where The UK (via the British Standards Institute – BSI) was one of the most active countries. Germany considered CE marking as obligatory which demanded more preciseness about its use and the instruments in place to guarantee the reliability of CE marked products. Not surprisingly, more contacts with the Commission or European bodies and organisation have been sought. A very specific aspect of the involvement of German actors seemed to be the view that discussions or actions at EU level might help to strengthen specific positions at national (or regional) level or to change them. For authorities (mostly the DIBt), this has meant that a specific technical approach was taken over at European level, as unchanged as possible by technical specification writers. For industry, the European level provided the opportunity to question specific approaches or specific limit values used in Germany as to their practical usefulness. While the relevance of the European dimension was uncontested by both parties in Germany (much stronger than in Austria and The UK), both sides were also struggling if it was a different (multi-national) level as such or just a different level to re-discuss existing national approaches. In Poland, industries were still working on developing strong and efficient networks at national and EU levels. Still under development, industry depended more on the input from authorities (also because of the centralised structure in Poland) and on the experience of individual companies – often linked to or owned by companies with their headquarters in the "old" Member States.

Looking at **priorities of other actors**, one faced one of the major problems of the CPD: very different interpretations existed about the role and the usefulness of CE marking of products. While everybody agreed on the official definition that the CPD should remove barriers to trade and that CE marked products should be allowed to be placed on the market in every Member State of the European Union, the last years have shown that this did not cover the whole problem:

- one of the most relevant difficulties was based on the different approaches of the Commission and the construction authorities of the Member States: The Commission in general and the construction unit as enforcing body considered the market aspect as the main goal, leaving any decisions of the real (and legally allowed) use of the products more or less completely to the "downstream" users.[258] If at that stage Member States would have had delegated experts from ministries or public bodies covering market issues to work in Brussels, maybe some of the existing confusion might have become visible and might have been avoided. However, (construction) authorities with a more general agenda were charged with the task of cooperating with the construction unit and were approaching the issue from a different angle: the building performances laid down in national building codes. This created a major dilemma. The CPD tried to include *all* products already on the market. Building codes (in particular in the 80s and 90s)[259] *de facto* aimed at *excluding* products from being used in specific buildings, conditions or intended uses (practically always based on safety requirements). Some of the interviews and also SCC documents like the Guidance Papers were highlighting the confusion and uneasiness caused by these different approaches. This has led to the over-complexity of several documents and positions, trying to cover all aspects and, in particular, the ones that could have been interpreted in different ways. Paradoxically, this did not remove the criticism of "over-regulating" on the one side and at the same time of "watering down" on the other side.

258 Following the assumption that a wider choice will encourage users to be more selective, which would not only give them the chance to use different products, but would also increase competition and fewer "protected markets" at national level.

259 Since the late 90s more and more Member States are trying to change their building codes from more descriptive and detailed documents to a more performance-based approach.

- National actors compared their current national systems and standards with the CPD approach and European standards, which produced the expected, but from their point of view uncomfortable solution that significant changes have to be introduced to adapt to the new system. However, in many cases no reflection on the national approach took place. The possibility of evaluating the national system, removing flaws and improving national approaches and standards were rarely seen in the Member States in this study (with the exception of Poland where more changes have taken place). Instead, the focus was nearly always on identifying flaws in the *European* approach and standards. The undeniable advantage was the stricter scrutiny of European standards (not always followed by similar strict and fast adaptations). But on the other hand, this lack of self-reflection kept flaws in national systems. While sometimes removed in CEN standards, they were sometimes reintroduced by national actors in CEN (or EOTA) work and were therefore affecting the technical specifications at EU level.[260] Attempts to remove them in the standardisation process have been seen as another attempt of "watering down" specific requirements and therefore again negatively affecting the perception of the quality of European standards.
- Another problem – more addressed at the national level – was the lack of market surveillance, which on the one hand was the cause of much of the distrusts with other systems, but did not result in more efforts at national level to introduce more efficient systems. This is even more surprising, considering that the text of the CPD refers to the obligation of Member States to ensure the correct use of CE marking on their territories. In addition, the construction unit and in some cases Member State representatives in the SCC, have tried to get more information on the different national approaches and to strengthen this element of the implementation of the framework of the CPD, but only since the discussion on the future Construction Products Regulation (where market surveillance was introduced as an obligation) more activities on Member State level to provide resources for active market surveillance could be seen.

260 This sometimes created the situation that specific flaws in European standards were objected by national actors but the same flaws could be found in national standards of the same Member State that raised the objection.

3.4.3 ... *and the output*

After having identified some of the major issues for actors at EU level and their effects on the interaction with other actors, one should not forget that none of the different positions and activities would have any practical meaning if it would not lead to actions on the next "downstream" level. Even more importantly: they should have *facilitated* the work of "downstream" actors at national level. Based on this assumption, what have the different actors considered as output and how were they receiving and working with feedback?

3.4.3.1 Organising the information flow to and from "Brussels"

For most of the time, the construction unit was torn between speeding up the development of technical specifications in CEN and EOTA and promoting the CPD approach vis-à-vis national representatives in the SCC and private actors. However, the wide range of products covered by the CPD, as well as a vague concept about the role and interest of professional actors when selecting products, never allowed a clear focus on specific target groups. Focusing nearly exclusively on the other EU actors CEN, EOTA and the GNB, guidance for downstream users remained vague and have shifted the actual responsibility to federations and national authorities. Since the national public and private representatives were not direct users of CE marking, guidance developed at EU level was in the end often more reflecting specific interests of actors at EU level, rather than providing practical guidance for downstream users.

The Standing Committee for Construction was more an "information point" for presenting and monitoring new initiatives of the construction unit than a "problem-solving mechanism". This statement (which most likely would have been contested in most interviews if presented as such) is based on several observations and some comments in the interviews given by national actors: the construction unit had a strong position as an "agenda-setter", while initiatives of Member State authorities of introducing additional issues (if they are not complaints about European standards) were rather rare.[261] Sometimes requests for getting an overview of approaches of other Member States for specific issues

261 On the other hand, one should not forget that MS representatives also have to work with few resources. Reacting on the (draft) agenda proposed by the construction unit for the following meeting might already require a large part of these resources to get feedback and coordinate a national position, not leaving much for additional proposals.

were raised, but the follow-up (encouragement by the construction unit or – even more important – feedback from other Member States) was often weak, late or even forgotten. Member States have not used the SCC to develop stable networks to exchange information but have used it only for facilitating *ad hoc* contacts (on the other hand, individuals working in the expert groups on CPD issues were often creating additional networks for projects or exchanging information). This more "defensive" role vis-à-vis the construction unit, the focus on national positions and the lack of well established transnational networks, gave the SCC and its meetings more the role of a "ritual" than an active instrument. While actors outside the decision-making process might have focused on the work of the SCC, most discussions and solution finding took place in bilateral meetings between the construction unit and one Member State. This made it even harder to follow developments and strengthened the role of national administrations that had "direct access to the Commission".

The wide range of products covered by the CPD made it difficult to assess how much information has not only been received but also used by downstream actors. In theory, "by now, everybody should be aware of CE marking" – a position taken by several interviewees of public bodies. At the same time, it was acknowledged that this assumption was mostly based on the knowledge that individuals of other interested parties have been informed and are aware of the issue, not so much that the information has been successfully passed on. Additional confirmation or feedback mechanisms were not considered as necessary.

After the first wave of information provided, resources – but also interest by other actors – were declining. Whoever has not followed the introduction at that stage (or has forgotten between the first information provided and the first standards available for a specific product) might be at a disadvantage. This also included downstream public authorities (local authorities and market surveillance). But in particular the practical users were rarely seen during the "introduction phase" and general doubts were expressed in all four Member States that architects (and to a lesser extent: contractors) were actually aware of CE marking and taking it into consideration.

3.4.3.2 Technical standards: market instrument or technical instrument for the construction sector?

By focusing on product standards and practically ignoring design and implementation standards, the CPD approach has picked out only one aspect of a system of different requirements and different types of standards that were generally used by national actors in the field of construction. This has confused several federations representing designers and contractors when trying to understand the practical use and implication of this approach. Considering that new "reporting formats" for products could not (significantly) affect their work, CE marking was seen as "irrelevant", and input from these "downstream users" was mostly not received and did not affect the EU decision-making level (the SCC, CEN and EOTA).

While European standards were often seen as "weaker" than previous national ones, feedback was mostly based on individual (expert) opinion rather than on consequent and frequent monitoring of developments, problems encountered and solutions found. In several interviews (at EU and national levels) it was not clear if the negative perception was based on a real technical problem or highly influenced by the fact that the new approach was different and therefore individuals felt less secure when working with it. It should also be noted that most of the interviewees at EU level could only provide second-hand experience, based on feedback from their members or other actors which made it even more complicated to pinpoint problems (except for individual examples given). This blurred the picture and made it more difficult to identify real problems caused by harmonised European standards. But also the construction unit had to depend on second-hand information. This lack of first-hand knowledge helped create the problem of over-complex documents developed at EU level and so discussions were often at a very abstract level. This often widened the scope of potential problems even beyond reasonably expected difficulties. Equally important, it often ignored the problem-solving capacities of "downstream" actors (architects, civil engineers and contractors). Preparing for the "worst-case scenario" in discussion and documents developed at EU level covers administrative and legislator's interests, but the output rarely provided practical guidance. ("The number of regulations is increasing – acceptance is declining".)

Last but not least: the above-mentioned problem of getting precise feedback on the quality or flaws in harmonised European standards could be expanded to the question if somebody knows what the impact of the CPD has been so far and if its goals have been achieved. Can products enter the market faster and in a less expensive and time-consuming procedure? At this stage (early 2010), this remains a big question mark at EU level but also at Member State level. It is interesting to note that, during the "stakeholder consultation" on the CPD (for getting information on flaws in the Directive to be solved in the amended CPD or – as it became clear at a later stage – the new Construction Products Regulation), the general support for maintaining a European approach was again based on (national) "expert opinion" – Empirical data was (and is) still lacking.

3.4.3.3 Reaching the national level

The most obvious difference was the status that Member States have given CE marking in their national systems. The UK did not consider the use of CE marking as obligatory (a point of view that was contested by the Commission services). Poland on the other hand has made all CE markings covered by different (New Approach) Directives obligatory. Germany and Austria have adopted the position of the European Commission that only CE marked construction products (if covered by the CPD and harmonised European standards were available to allow for an assessment that could lead to CE marking) were allowed on their markets.

However, when it came to providing information on CE marking, public and private actors first mentioned CE marking as conformity marking before referring to other national marks (BBA). Poland also provided information on CE marking, but since this was covered by a framework law for all New Approach Directives, raising awareness was linked to a larger scheme than just one for construction products. Information on CE marking could also be found in documents, presentations and websites of Austrian public bodies but, as will be seen in the following chapters, it was rarely mentioned by other downstream and private actors. In these four Member States a rhetorical split has been made between building requirements and requirements for construction products. This allowed seeing the EU approach for products as complementary to the requirements of national and regional building codes. The German approach of most public and private actors on the other hand was largely focused on *building* requirements. Therefore, CE marking was mentioned but *de facto* presented as the least relevant aspect when describing and implementing certification and approval schemes, which were dominated by the German *Ü-Zeichen*.

Within the framework of the CPD, additional aspects also played a significant role: both The UK and Germany had another advantage that they have been involved in the development of the CPD right from the beginning and therefore they have also been active in the "first implementation phase". This allowed on the one hand "shaping" the CPD, which might have given a strong incentive of stronger involvement, but also being able to "shape" the work of organisations around the CPD. The national standardisation bodies of Germany (DIN) and the UK (BSI) were always amongst the national members that provided most of the chairmanships and the secretariats of CEN technical committees. Less obviously linked to the early involvement was the fact that the German DIBt held the presidency of EOTA and the UK's BRE has provided the secretariat for the Group of Notified Bodies. The presidency of EOTA is based on a vote of all its national members and the secretariat of the GNB is based on a public tender of the construction unit of the European Commission. Nevertheless, it could not be denied that the resources available in these two organisations, but also their experience in these specific fields, could have been strong incentives for both organisations to apply for these positions and for other actors to accept their application.

The involvement of German and UK actors in prominent positions did not necessarily indicate less interest or involvement by actors from Austria or Poland. The national standardisation bodies ON and PKN can refer to (at least nominal) participation in several technical committees in CEN, ISO and in the work of EOTA. The "newer" member of EOTA, the Austrian OIB, also held the presidency of this organisation (before the DIBt). However, they were late for applying for "agenda-setting" positions and it was mentioned in some interviews that a lack of influence (or a dominance of the UK or Germany in specific fields) was experienced by Austrian and Polish individuals working in EU committees and organisations. Also, participation was not evenly spread in the different EU organisations and committees. Only where specific interests were affected (mostly the interests of large industry sectors or companies) were enough efforts made to find experts and to participate in the actual work. This created different "centres of gravity", depending on national interests and even allowed for in specific tasks which were dominated by actors of the "newer" Member State actors.

But joining the EU at a later stage did not only create disadvantages. The fact that more significant change had to be made in the two "newer" Member States to adapt to the requirements of the CPD seemed to have influenced them to select a slightly different approach when implementing the requirements of the CPD at the technical and communication levels. While interviewees in Germany and the UK thought that no significant changes in their national systems had to be made, and therefore left these systems practically unchanged, national authorities in Austria and Poland have indicated that they have seen *their* approach more as introduction of the common European approach into their national system rather than just trying to "translate" all these EU requirements into the national system. While not ignoring the needs of national actors, the emphasis was nevertheless on introducing and explaining something *new* to these national actors, whenever necessary.

Another view of the four national approaches covered quantity and quality of information provided *to the EU level* and *to the national level.* Providing information to actors on EU level seemed to have caused the official representatives of the UK and Germany less difficulty than their counterparts in Austria and Poland. Having a large number of experts in different positions at EU and national levels allowed for faster and more efficient networking and facilitated the work of national representatives to present a common position, or at least a very complete picture of the national situation. But here again, other factors also influenced national approaches. In Austria regional authorities or regional federations (*"Kammern"*) did not show strong interest in European activities if their practical effect was not clearly evident. Polish authorities and the ITB had similar problems getting feedback from actors in the private sector, but this was due to the still ongoing process of industry and professions to organize themselves in more efficient networks and organisations. In both countries, authorities and their technical institutes reported that private actors were strongly focused on national and international standardisation work, more as a means of monitoring and influencing (regulatory and private) requirements than on the implementation of regulations per se.

Providing information back to actors at national level is again regrouping the four Member States with The UK as the most "consumer-friendly" in providing information in a format that allows even non-professionals to use it efficiently. Documents and websites of public and private actors were going to great lengths to provide easily comprehensible step-by-step guidance and practical examples. On the other hand, the UK system had also left most of the responsibility of the correct implementation of its laws to the owners of buildings, which made its approach more a necessity and obligation than an additional service to the public. Germany has developed the most stringent "top-down" approach of the four Member States. Most decisions (e.g. the acceptance of a construction product for specific intended uses – the German "*Bauregelliste*") have been made by authorities (in several cases with the agreement of national federations). Therefore, information was less intended for individual interpretation but more as a reference either to the regulatory framework or to authorities that were given the tasked of providing technical and administrative approvals. This left downstream actors (architects, contractors, local authorities) with less freedom of making their own decisions, but it also relieved them from their responsibility when selecting specific products, because if and how they can be used had to a large extent already been defined by "the authorities". Austria and Poland – visibly trying to explain the new European approach in their documents and websites – could be found between The UK and the German approach. While also highlighting the regulatory framework and the role of different public actors (or approval schemes) there was a strong attempt to provide a comprehensive picture of all aspects of the system to a wide range of (professional and also non-professional) downstream actors.

Compared with all the above-mentioned efforts to provide information to downstream users, the main question – how much is CE marking actually used (following the law or actually getting additional useful information out of it)? – could hardly be answered by actors at EU level. Lack of market surveillance made any empirical assessment difficult and even federations and individuals closer to the actual market and construction works could often only refer to their own experience or – like public actors – consider a lack of complaints as an indication that in general CE marking was correctly used (affixed, checked and interpreted) by all relevant actors. More cynical comments highlighted that "something that is not known cannot be missed". But even here assumptions and not data had to be used to develop these positions.

3.4.3.4 Trust at EU level?

At first glance, the EU level did not present the image of a structure of trustful actors. Complex guidance produced at this level, trying to cover all potential "worst-case scenarios", as well as reactions to reported problems at national level. Since no empirical research has been done by actors at EU or national levels, singular cases, "feedback" in general and expert opinions had to be used to illustrate specific concerns and as basis to add more precautionary measures to the EU approach. Adding more actors into the system (as practised by the construction unit) has widened the "range" of input, but it has also decreased the influence of Member State authorities, which in turn created even more need for guidance produced by the construction unit and these authorities. Feedback from federations at EU level already indicated that the complexity of the documents have not raised the interest and understanding of the CPD approach but has even convinced several downstream users about the over-complexity of the approach.

Despite this, 14 of these documents were developed by the construction unit and the SCC, indicating that authorities remained concerned about the actual behaviour of private actors.

But a second glance shows more positive developments too. After a first phase of "defensive reactions", several actors started to (better) understand the position of other actors at EU level, in other Member States, and in their own country and became more flexible when interpreting the positions and reactions of others. In particular, interview partners who have been in the field for a long time acknowledged that often "resistance" and skepticism of some (national) actors resulted less from *specific* problems, but more from the *perceptions* of potential problems, worries about the adaptation costs and in particular the phase of insecurity of the implementation phase which would cause most of the confusion and potential financial losses. The CPD (and also its national implementations) rarely fitted with the interest of most actors in the field of construction and *confusion* added more to the negative perception than any *intentional* resistance. Therefore, in a second phase (and for the two newer Member States Austria and Poland right from the beginning) the focus was stronger on *convincing* than just presenting neutral ("sterile") facts, with only few links to the actual working environment of the actors involved. Also, getting more familiar with the interpretation of the CPD on the one hand and the actual interests and concerns of downstream actors allowed these individuals to provide clearer answers and therefore improve their role as competent providers of guidance. Increasing the trust in their own position indirectly influenced the trust in the approach (at least reduced the skepticism if these individuals had a relatively positive attitude to the CPD approach). In addition, while still rather rare and mostly initiated if problems have arisen, contacts to representatives of other Member States were increasing to find solutions already at a low-key level.

It can be said that the weak position of nearly all actors at EU level, when it comes to the availability of data and feedback from national levels, has been a major factor in the rather "economical" distribution of trust. The push for additional documents to steer downstream users has been very strong in the phase where only theoretical assumption and no practical experience were available for these individuals. The more these actors could fall back on their experience and on their own networks providing practical feedback, the more they could improve their role as competent actors at EU and national levels and the need for additional guidance documents dropped (moving strongly to the role of "corporate actors"). While not showing *lots* of trust (at EU and transnational levels), the situation is slowly changing to accepting that other actors are following common rules and (at least to a large extent) the same goals. However, it remains more a trust in and between *individuals* and informal networks than in institutionalised structures.

3.5 The national level

Compared to the EU level, where a relatively small number of actors (authorities, federations and organisations) were active in the field of construction products and CE marking, the number of national ministries, regional authorities, federations on national/federal or regional level and certifications bodies increase on national level.[262] For pragmatic reasons it was no longer possible to cover *all* of these actors but to select the ones which were assumed to be in a direct line of the information flow: authorities responsible for building laws as well as planning and building control, national members of federations selected at EU level, and national organisations being linked to authorities.

It is characteristic for many policies developed at EU level and implemented at national level, that Member States are not creating new structures but using existing organisations and networks (see: "After the dust has settled"). As seen at EU level, several actors in the UK and in Germany did not consider that their existing system had needed much adaptation to implement the requirements of the CPD into national law and into the structure of public administration. Austria and Poland on the other hand, have seen more changes in their working structure: Austria has copied several parts of the German approach (i.e. by creating the OIB based on the German experience with the DIBt) and Poland's "transition phase" after the fall of the Iron Curtain and the accession to the EU made the requirements of the CPD "just" another part of it.

While national administrations were still in important decision making positions (being even more important vis-à-vis other actors than on EU level), the

262 In this overview of actors information publicly available such as documents, guidelines, presentations and – last not least – websites of these actors have been included to provide a picture of the priorities of these actors and the instruments they have used to distribute information (on CE marking). This data was collected between mid 2008 and mid 2009. Changes might have occurred in the meantime on quantity and quality of these publications.

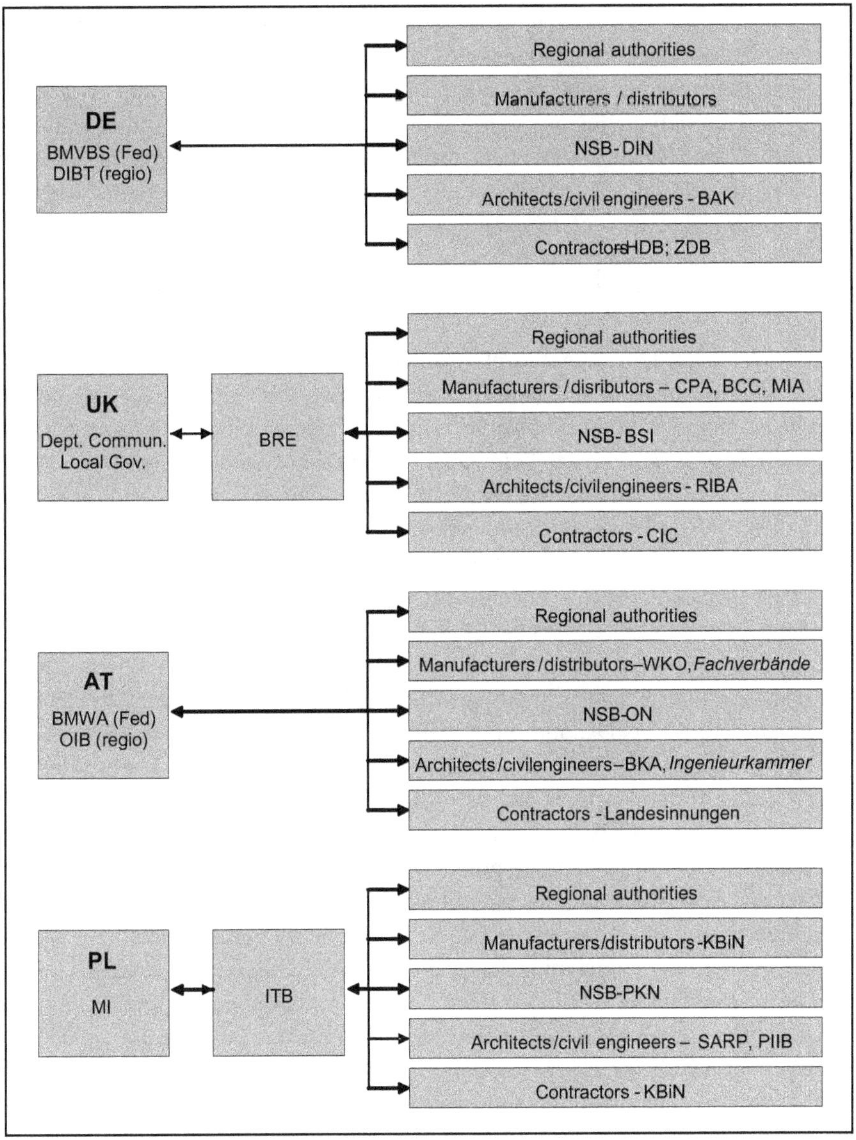

Figure 3: National actors – overview

Commission services (and here in particular the construction unit) were no longer playing a very significant role. Direct influence on national level – like providing specific information – was rather rare and mostly the result of specific requests from national actors than a pro-active approach by the European civil servants. This lack of involvement was partly caused by the principle of *subsidiarity*, leaving several tasks completely in the hands of "downstream" authorities. But also the lack of resources and practical instruments to enforce their policies and laws (compared to their national counterparts) left the power – but also the burden of implementation – in the hands of national, regional or local actors.

Arriving on the national level, one could find many "known faces" – sometimes literally, because the same individuals who are representing national or organisational interests were also in charge of implementing or informing about decisions made on EU level. In particular public administrations were very consistent and left the responsibilities at least in the same public body if not in the hands of the same individuals. Federations on the other hand were providing a slightly different picture. European federations consist mostly of national members (federations or individual companies), and their role as provider of information stops in most cases at national level where national organisations are taking over. However, since the national members were often providing experts for discussions at EU level, some individuals played a major role in distributing information to national actors and "translating" it for them.

The national level also introduces new actors or at least different roles for individuals or organisations active at EU level, in particular architects and constructors and their federations which are playing a stronger role in national standardisation work and on the product market than on EU level. Also national federations, national standardisation bodies and private bodies tasked with technical/administrative issues that are *de facto* obligatory requirements have sometimes significantly different orientations and working procedures than their European equivalents. While some of these actors have been in one way or the other involved in activities on EU level (either by active participation or by providing information for EU level actors), the national background can be seen as the major reference for individuals and organisations when facing new requirements developed on EU level. The introduction of new actors or new roles for actors reflects the different *distribution of tasks* compared to the EU level. Getting closer to the "construction site level", the specific technical and regulatory requirements on construction works are adding more actors on the administrative level covering specific parts of the national administrative approval procedure. Also more technical aspects have to be taken into consideration (e.g., calculation of the structural or fire performance of buildings) as well as the monitoring and controlling of the actual construction work.

Significant is the change which laws are mostly used as guidance and reference: At EU level, the Construction Products Directive was seen as the starting point, using national building laws and building codes as complementary regulations providing the technical input. At national level however, more laws and documents were of obligatory nature for different actors, also shifting the power of interpreting laws and monitoring compliance from the construction unit to national authorities. The position of national administrations was even stronger considering that also in previous national schemes they were the public bodies that all other actors had to consult and had to refer to their interpretation:

- In all four MS of this study market surveillance which should ensure that only these products are put on the market that have been produced and sold by applying national legal, technical and administrative procedures (mostly involving CE marking and national quality marks) has been delegated to regional or local authorities. As next step building control (partly done by authorities, partly by private actors) should ensure that only these accepted products are used in construction works. As will be shown, these monitoring and controlling tasks often depended more on monitoring done *within* the market by competitors than on an *active* market surveillance system established by national authorities.
- Also mostly delegated to downstream actors is the control of the design and the actual construction work. This is often in the hands of regional or even local authorities and even private experts could fulfil this task (either for the owner or for public authorities). In fact, building control seems to move more and more from the public to the private sector of specialised and certified experts.[263] National building laws and building codes are setting the framework for the design, the construction works and the control of both. Here the CPD and its national implementation became in most cases just a paragraph defining which products are allowed to be used in construction works. But while products are playing a less prominent role in building laws, these laws (and their regional or local interpretation) are more relevant

263 Building Control Report (CEBC) 2006 p. 5.

for the "construction site level" – the architects, the civil engineers and professionals on site and the controlling engineers. Therefore, these buildings codes will be assessed in this chapter (when they are relevant for accepting or assessing construction products) to allow a better understanding for some positions of national actors and later the final "downstream users" on a construction site.

Not surprisingly, private enterprises and their federations on this level are often more focused on developments initiated by *national* actors because they are more likely to influence their day-to-day work than initiatives at EU level. But also "providers" of information like regional and local authorities or national or regional federations are clearly focused on *national* actors. At this level, publications in other than the official national language are very rare and mostly only cover very general information, which makes it more difficult for actors from other countries to get and compare information.

Another group is becoming relevant at this level: Distributors are in general the link between manufacturers and "end users" of construction products. In this function, they have two roles: as "gateways" into national, regional or local markets – and as "gatekeepers" by selecting which products they will distribute to their customers. In addition, their abilities (and responsibility) to ensure timely and sufficient supply could influence the selection and continuous use of specific products by downstream users. Therefore, their interests were mostly focused on transport and distribution networks than on specific qualities of products *per se*. The responsibility for the quality of a product remained with the manufacturer. But they were also in many cases the first contact when "end users" consider products as faulty, and therefore the interface between manufacturers and "end users".

3.5.1 Member State authorities

3.5.1.1 Germany

The responsibility for implementing the German "*Bauproduktegesetz*" makes the Federal Ministry for Transport, Building and Urban Affairs (*Bundesministerium für Verkehr, Bau und Stadtplanung*) the main actor at Federal level. However, market surveillance, setting legal requirements for buildings and construction products as well as controlling the work on construction sites is the task of the building authorities of the *Länder*. The responsibility for building laws, access to land for construction works, urban planning and other construction-related policies and regulations are in the hands of the *Bauminister* (ministers for construction) of the 16 German *Länder*. For this overview, the ministries responsible for construction of two of the *Länder* (Baden-Württemberg and Nordrhein-Westfalen) have been selected, being two of the bigger regions and (partly due to their size) also better equipped to follow developments at EU level. The Ministry for Economy of Baden-Württemberg covers also all regulatory and administrative responsibilities for construction works in its state. Via the *Bauministerkonferenz* (see below) and the DIBt, the ministries of the *Länder* receive information from federal and EU level.[264] This information is distributed to downstream building control authorities. The public website[265] refers to regulatory and administrative frameworks and requirements for applications and control of construction works, and covers also specific technical (and also social) issues like accessibility of buildings. Specific information on products or CE marking is not provided.

As mentioned before, the *Länder* are in several political and administrative fields independent vis-à-vis Federal authorities. Therefore, additional structures (i.e. the annual conference of these ministers – *Bauministerkonferenz* – ARGE-BAU)[266] have been established to allow an exchange of information and a common approach for specific issues. For construction products, it was decided to develop common certificates (*bauaufsichtliche Zulassungen*), a task that was handed over to the (in 1968 established) *Institut für Bautechnik* – the predecessor of today's DIBt.

Other tasks, like the coordination of market surveillance or setting common technical rules for construction works and construction products have also been delegated to the DIBt. Published as "guidance papers" ("*Leitlinien*") these common technical rules are *de facto* obligatory since all regional building authorities are not only using them but even demanding compliance with these guidelines before allowing products to be used in their territory. Compared to the EU level,

264 In fact, the *Länder* authorities have established different networks to monitor and react to developments on EU level. These could consist mostly of other national and regional authorities (often in specific technical groups – "*Arbeitskreise*") or could even be managed by private actors (i.e. federations in different field including urban planning and house owners).

265 http://www.wm.baden-wuerttemberg.de/infrastruktur---planen-und-bauen/62332.html in German.

266 http://www.bauministerkonferenz.de/.

where the DIBt is representing the interests of the *Länder* but having the Federal ministry as main representative vis-à-vis the Commission services and the SCC, its role on national level is significantly stronger. While the building authorities of the *Länder* have reduced their own workload (not just for developing new requirements for buildings but also for communicating and coordinating them with the other *Länder*) by shifting it to one single body, they have also delegated – to a certain extent – the power of defining technical and obligatory requirements to the DIBt. This delegation to experts and one specific "expert body" should reduce conflicts between the *Länder*, reduce their administrative costs and strengthen their position vis-à-vis Federal administrations and policies. The DIBt is also the major source of information on any developments on EU level. Additionally, it provides technical input and in particular the German "*Bauregelliste*" indicating products that need additional certification and approval to be used in construction works (in several cases including CE marked products). Nevertheless, the formal decision remains with the authorities of the *Länder* to accept this proposal in an expert committee ("*Fachkommission Bautechnik*"). The roles both of the DIBt and the ministries for construction is defined in the regional building codes[267], indicating that the final decision of demanding additional information is taken by the building authorities ("*Oberste Baurechtsbehörde für Bauprodukte*") but also clearly states the important role of the DIBt in the selection and decision making process.

The DIBt plays also a major role in assessing potential certification bodies (*Prüf-, Überwachungs- und Zertifizierungsstellen – PÜZ*), proposing their acceptance to the Federal or the *Länder* authorities (depending on the products and the competence of Federal and regional level) or can even accredit them itself (based on the competence delegated by the German *Länder*). Not only in absolute figures but also in relation to the size of the country Germany has more certification bodies under the CPD (more than 200) and under the regional building laws (*Landesbauordnungen* – LBO) – about 350 – than any other Member State of the EU. Certification bodies for construction products on EU level (the Notified Bodies) have been notified to the Commission and are operating under the umbrella of the CPD and the national *Bauproduktegesetz*. For products not

267 E.g.: the building code of Baden-Württemberg – §17-§20 http:/+www.baurecht.de/landesbauordnungBaden-Wuerttemberg.html#Bauprodukte & http://www.peterknoedel.de/lehre/V0309_FH-KA/Projekte/Baurecht_BW/P_Baurecht_BW_05-09-25.pdf, and for NRW §20-§23: http://www.bauordnungen.de/html/nrw1.html & http://www.mlpartner.de/Download/Merkblatt_ZIE.pdf.

covered under the Federal law, the *Länder* could require additional assessment and certification. But here too, all the certification bodies and their competences (at national level) can be found in official publications.

Actual building control (including the issuing the building permit) however is a task for local authorities.[268] In addition, private experts ("*Prüfingenieure*") have taken over most of the technical building control tasks (in particular the structural design and calculation, public safety and quality standards) and have the same liability as any building authority.[269] The requirements for becoming a "*Prüfingenieur*" are very detailed and require next to technical qualifications (e.g., structural calculations, design, knowledge of materials) experience in this field of more than 10 years. If all requirements are met, the Federal State's Supreme Building Authorities appoints *individuals* (not *companies* as in the UK) to represent de facto public (local) building authorities. Today, the majority of the technical controls are already in the hands of private civil engineers acting on behalf of the authorities. The local building authorities (including the "*Prüfingenieure*") should control the structural (load-bearing) work (before it is covered by other construction products). Also foundations, sewers, roof constructions, staircases and chimneys are considered as main parts that require inspection. But it remains within the power of the building control authorities to decide which parts of the building would need control and how often inspections have to be made. If any of the (main) installations do not correspond with the agreed plans, they have to be changed or could be demolished by order of the building control authorities.

Building codes

On federal level a *Model Building Code* ("*Musterbauordnung*" – MBO) provides since 1994 a common format and examples of how specific requirements could be addressed in regional building codes. The aim of introducing this horizontal model was to harmonise the different approaches on *Länder* level, but leaving it to the regional parliaments and administrations how close they want to bring

268 In fact, the highest authority for *building supervision* is in general a Federal ministry. However, this task has been delegated to *Länder* authorities and passed on to the authorities of smaller regions (*Landkreise*) or municipalities.

269 In fact, civil engineers acting as public authorities have a long tradition in Germany and in Austria. German *Prüfingenieure* are acting in this role since the 1920s. (See also: Eurocer-Building position paper 2005 p. 15)

their laws to the MBO. The *Länder* have taken over the complete technical part and deviate only in specific procedural aspects from the common format. Therefore, the MBO can be seen as a unified approach on technical level applicable in all sixteen German *Länder*. Building control depends at several stages on permits that allow starting or continuing construction works. At each stage planners or contracting companies have either to present the design to the authorities for approval or show on site that the actual work complies with the plan and regulative requirements. In some cases, specific experts (e.g., fire departments) might also be involved and responsible for specific controls. The main aspects of building control related to the control and acceptance of construction products are:

- Notices and plans: providing all relevant plans and necessary certificates (at the beginning of the works as well as certificates provided after assessing the final works);
- Control of building work (structural parts, testing of drains and private sewers, selection, use and sampling of construction materials/products used);

The assessment of plans and the practical work on a construction site is to a large extent based on technical standards – in the field of design still dominated by national standards. These technical standards (developed in DIN) are playing a very specific role in the German system. Since DIN had (even after the introduction of harmonised European standards) a national monopoly on standards in the field of construction, its standards were considered as the main reference for evaluating the quality of the design, the structural work and the quality of construction products. Federal and national laws as well as provisions by the German *Länder* (i.e. requirements for subsidies) or guidance documents produced by the DIBt are often referring to specific DIN standards (now partly replaced by European EN standards). However, while being essential parts of regulations, they are not freely available and have to be purchased from DIN. This does not only makes the availability of *obligatory* information more complicated, it also puts DIN as private organisation in a position of providing *de facto* obligatory guidance.[270]

270 This can be seen as a basic complication of several national approaches: Laws are publicly available, but they are often very general in their description while technical guidance is developed outside the regulatory framework and has to be purchased by users to know and to fulfil obligatory requirements. Other approaches (like the one that the UK has chosen) give a choice of different routes to prove compliance with the requirements of building codes to designers,

3.5.1.2 The United Kingdom

In the UK too no major changes of public actors between the EU level and the national level has been considered necessary. The Department for Communities and Local Government is also the central building authority in the UK (since the 1980s when the responsibilities for building regulations were centralised) and the British Research Establishment (BRE) provides technical input.

Planning control is solely the responsibility of local authorities.[271] However, local authorities and private actors – *Approved Inspectors*[272] – can be appointed to undertake the responsibility of ensuring compliance with the Building Regulations, Building Control and Approved Documents (see below). The *Building Control Bodies* check plans and inspect the work to ensure compliance. *Approved Inspectors* are required to send an *Initial Notice* to the local authority which will accept (or reject) that the responsibility of the building control has been passed to the inspector. Local authorities retain responsibility for administering the requirements of other legislation such as Local Enactments and Bylaws that operate in parallel with the Building Regulations.[273] *Approved Inspectors* could be specialised companies but also individuals with the necessary technical qualifications and all are required to carry Professional Indemnity Insurance.[274] Nevertheless, private *Approved Inspectors* are becoming more common in the system. Local authorities are still empowered (but not obliged) to make inspections on sites controlled by *Approved Inspectors*. Unlike Local Authorities, Approved Inspectors do not have any enforcement powers. Should the construction work not comply with the requirements of the Building Regulations and the builder unwilling to comply, the Approved Inspector will cancel the Initial Notice and the job will revert to the local authority which can take enforcement action.

---

architects, constructors, manufacturers and other interested parties. On the other hand, this implies higher search costs for finding the most useful solution.

271 Meijer/Visscher/Sheridan: Building regulations in Europe Part I 2002 p. 42ff.; Tricker/Algar: Building Regulations in Brief 2007 p. 15 ff.

272 These inspectors are approved by the Construction Industry Council (CIC) for the Secretary of State. The assessment of the technical competence is carried out by the Construction Industry Council (CIC) on individuals and companies who have to apply for a licence in the first instance and apply for renewal every 5 years.

273 See also: Tricker/Algar: Building Regulations in Brief 2007 p. 3 ff.

274 Meijer/Visscher/Sheridan: Building regulations in Europe Part I 2002 p. 42ff.; Tricker/Algar: Building Regulations in Brief 2007.

Building codes

The *Building Act* can be considered as the framework law for the England and Wales (not Scotland and Northern Ireland) and covers building control (i.e. methods of inspecting and reporting, not only of the building but also the products and the equipment used). This act also introduced the Building Regulations and *Approved Documents* (see below), which are providing practical guidance on specific aspects of the *Building Regulations* related to requirements.

In addition, the Department for Communities and Local Government has developed a set of *Building Regulations* for England and Wales (Scotland and Northern Ireland having their own building regulations). Similar to Germany, in the general regulatory framework several tasks of building control are linked to the design of construction works and construction products used:

- Notices and plans: providing all relevant plans and necessary certificates (at the beginning of the works as well as certificates provided after assessing the final works);
- Control of building work (structural parts, testing of drains and private sewers, selection, use and sampling of construction materials/products used);

The previously very prescriptive regulations were changed into more performance-based requirements in 1985 resulting in the developments of *Approved Documents* (first published in 1985). Depending on the function of specific parts of the building or the whole building, *Approved Documents* vary in how much guidance is given or if the reference documents mentioned are more focused on design standards, codes of practice or product standards.[275] In general, the emphasis is on design references, leaving the choice of product standards more to the users of the Approved Documents. In the following, one of these documents has been selected to give a better picture of the structure and potential links to the European activities:

While the Approved Document to support regulation 7 – material and workmanship – defines the regulatory requirement:

275 http://www.planningportal.gov.uk/england/professionals/en/4000000000001.html.

Building work shall be carried out:

(a) *with adequate and proper materials which:*

    (i) *are appropriate for the circumstances in which they are used;*

    (ii) *are adequately mixed or prepared; and*

    (iii) *are applied, used or fixed so as adequately to perform the functions for which they are designed; and*

(b) in a workmanlike manner.

Section 1 for materials leads directly to technical standards – starting with national standards used for testing, assessing and accepting construction products used, to the European standards which are mentioned to eventually replace existing national ones. Also European Technical approvals and the role of CE marking of products are described and states that a CE marked product can be used and shall be accepted by building authorities (except incorrect use of the marking or wrong application in the building).[276]

3.5.1.3 Austria

Austria's approach in the construction sector is very similar to the German one. The Federal Ministry for Economics and Labour (*Bundesministerium für Wirtschaft und Arbeit*) is in charge of the implementation of the Austrian "*Bauproduktegesetz*", but the practical implementation is delegated "downstream" to the authorities of the *Bundesländer* and even authorities of smaller administrative units ("*Bezirkshauptmannschaften*"). Selecting two of the bigger Austrian *Bundesländer* (and therefore being able to provide a wider range of expertise within the building authorities – which could – at least in theory – follow European developments more closely than smaller authorities in the other *Länder*) the Viennese *Magistratsabteilung 37 – Baupolizei (MA 37)*[277] and the *Baupolizei* of Lower Austria[278] are the main bodies, with dependences on district level. The main information provided by these authorities is linked to the general approval procedures and building related requirements (i.e. energy efficiency). While the contacts to the OIB (specific expert committees – *Sachverständigenausschuss*)

276 In official and private guidance documents CE marking as an instrument of showing compliance with the Building Regulations is not only mentioned, it is in most cases indicated in first place, before references to national (BSI) standards or national certificates are made.

277 http://www.wien.gv.at/wohnen/baupolizei/ in German.

278 http://www.st-poelten.gv.at/Content.Node/buergerservice/lebenslagen/bauverfahren_start.php in German.

have provided individuals in these authorities with information on CE marking (which was forwarded to the controlling authorities at district level via presentations, distribution of documents or "info points" within the services) this information was not publicly available (i.e. no information is published on the websites of these authorities).

The Austrian Institute of Construction Engineering (*Österreichisches Institut für Bautechnik* – OIB) was founded as a "copy" of the German DIBt concerning the developments at EU level but also as coordinating body for the Austrian *Länder*. However, the Austrian *Länder* have kept more of their original tasks as building authorities in their own hands. While on federal level a common format for building codes (like the German MBO) has been developed, the different building codes still vary in what technical requirements are defined and how detailed they are in the legal text. Together with the authorities of the *Länder*, the OIB has developed guidelines ("*OIB-Richtlinien*") that can be used by the regional authorities to harmonise their building codes. These guidelines are structured in six parts, in line with the six essential requirements of the CPD (see chapter: The Construction Products Directive). Another essential reference for national actors are the two lists for construction products ("*Baustoffliste*" ÖA – for products not covered by harmonised European standards – which should (relatively similar to the German *Ü-Zeichen* approach) be tested and certified with the Austrian *ÜA-Zeichen*, and ÖE – for products covered by CE marking) which sets rules for the use and performance levels of products in Austria. These lists are part of the building laws of the Austrian *Länder* and therefore obligatory for all actors.

The Austrian system too uses private independent experts for planning and building control during the construction phase (sometimes with specific restrictions depending on the project in question and on the *Bundesland*). The Austrian private experts ("*Ziviltechniker*")[279] are architects or civil engineers who have to pass a specific test ("*Ziviltechnikerprüfung*")[280] before their application is decided by the Federal Ministry for Economics and Labor (BMWA). Comparable to the German system, only individuals could become "*Ziviltechniker*", but as individuals, they could work together in companies covering the tasks of this

279 The term "*Prüfingenieur*" is also used in Austria, but it refers in general to "*Ziviltechniker*" or authorised experts in specific fields ("*gerichtlich beeidete Sachverständige*").

280 The application is sent to the Austrian Federal Ministry for Economics and Labor (BMWA) via the Austrian Federal Chamber for Architects and Consulting Engineers. (http://wien.arching.at/index.php?cid=199).

specific role. Like the "*Prüfingenieure*" and the *Approved Inspectors*, "*Ziviltechniker*" are not only advising on design, planning and building control issues, or being allowed to provide specific services (i.e. providing statically calculations for the structural design), but could also act as representatives of public authorities (mostly assisting the local building authorities).[281]

Building codes

The Austrian federal state foresees the development and enforcement of building codes as the responsibility of the Austrian *Länder* (except for specific federal construction works – e.g., infrastructure works for railways). As a result, in each of the *Länder* specific building codes exist, varying in format, volume and specific technical requirements. The development of guidelines ("*OIB-Richtlinien*")[282] is aiming at a more common approach for technical requirements between the different Austrian regions. Four out of nine Länder have adopted all *Richtlinien* in their requirements, the others have so far introduced only the guideline for energy performance.[283] The Federal Ministry for Economics and Labor has initiated another approach by following the concept of Germany and presented in 2004 a *Model Building Code* ("*Musterbauordnung*") for Austria.

3.5.1.4 Poland

In its approach, Poland is closer to the centralised approach of the UK than the German and Austrian approach of distributing not only administrative tasks but also the political power of defining and enforcing requirements on buildings. The building code[284] has been developed on national level and its enforcement is the responsibility of the Ministry for Infrastructure and the General Office of Building Control (GUNB).

In one specific aspect Poland is the exception of the four Member States in this study because it does not delegate the approval of plans to private indepen-

---

281 § 4 Ziviltechnikergesetz 1993, BGBl. 1994/156.

282 These guidelines are grouped in accordance with the six "Essential Requirements" of the CPD, but – since they have been developed as guidance for more similar building codes – they are covering requirements for construction works as well as for construction products.

283 The general acceptance of this specific aspect is most likely based on the adoption of the Directive on "Energy Performance of Buildings" which requires the assessment and declaration of the energy performance of (new or renovated) buildings up to a defined size.

284 http://isip.sejm.gov.pl/PRAWO.nsf/4326b1a242fc14fd412563d20069fee3/f605058099f31ff2c125667200294f6e/$FILE/D19940414Lj.pdf.

dent experts. The administration of the architectural part of the building (architectural-building administration)[285] is delegated to provincial governors or to local governors (*starosts*). This part includes the correct selection of construction products. Control on the construction site remains with the county inspector of building control (or in specific cases even the province inspector of building control – who is also the authority responsible for construction products being placed on the market)[286]. On the other hand, the completion of the construction works does not require a certificate by the authorities but is declared by the owner, architect or constructor.

The horizontal approach of Poland to cover all EU Directives introducing CE marking resulted in a specific law for construction products 2004,[287] defining if and how products can be placed on the market, the role and tasks of market surveillance and how national administrations have to work in this field.

Building code

The national building code is defining the performance of buildings, using the six essential requirements of the CPD, but is also extending it to other performance characteristics (i.e. accessibility). Controlling the use of CE marked products is explicitly mentioned as an obligatory task and annual reports have to be provided for the President of the Office of Competition and Consumer Protection (UOKiK). Building permissions are given by local authorities (with technical assessment partly done by public geodesists) who are checking the plans on compliance regulatory (i.e. zoning maps) and technical requirements. Building control remains in the hands of county inspectors, who have the power to control construction sites and even demand special tests to assess the quality of building parts and construction products (e.g., load bearing capacity)

285 Polish Building Law Act 7 July 1994

286 The provincial inspector is tasked with scheduled and *ad hoc* controls and is also participating in controls carried out by the GNUB.

287 http://isip.sejm.gov.pl/servlet/Search?todo=file&id=WDU20040920881&type=3&name=D20040881Lj.pdf
http://isip.sejm.gov.pl/servlet/Search?todo=file&id=WDU20021661360&type=3&name=D20021360Lj.pdf

3.5.2 *Federations*

Most federations at national level had been established before any European legislation was directly affecting their day-to-day work, or the need for European representation was seen as useful. The roles of national ("federal") federations are very similar to their European "offspring": monitoring regulatory developments by national or regional governments and administrations, lobbying for the interests of their members and promoting the products or services of their sectors or professions. And like the European federations, they depend on the resources (data, expertise, manpower) of their members to be effective. On the other hand, some differences between federations on these two levels are visible: It can be easier to mobilise members' support for national issues because they are "closer to home" and have already got the attention of national members. It is also easier for national members to identify relevant actors, therefore being able to address issues and follow the developments and the activities of their federations. "Brussels" on the other hand is further away and the dependency increases on information provided by federations, but might also reduce the willingness to be "involved" in these issues. Another difference might slightly favour European federations: For getting additional expert input, European federations might be lucky and could profit from the expertise of at least one of their national (federation) members. National federation however might have no additional layer in between and have to communicate directly with the end users (manufacturers, designers, construction companies). This could provide more *practical* input, but in case of economically tight phases, companies are more reluctant to provide their manpower for "political" issues instead of using them within their own company (which in case of an economic crisis affecting all Member States would also "dry out" support for EU actors).

One significant difference between the three "older" Member States and Poland is the longer tradition of official representations of professions and industry sectors in Austria, Germany and the UK. The UK authorities retain close contacts with its industries, but it is Austria and Germany where contacts between public administrations and public bodies on one side and private bodies and federations on the other side are embedded in a "corporate society" even with an "institutionalised" cooperation between these two groups of actors. In these three "old" countries the current situation is the result of social, political and economic developments that have been relatively constantly developed. Poland experienced more significant changes in this process till the end of the

20th century which is still visible in the struggle of its industries and professions to establish similar networks of federations and their links to public bodies and the scientific community. Like most of the Central and Eastern European Member States of the EU, the involvement of private federations on European but also on national level has just started. However, Polish federations in the construction sector show some specific characteristics (only to be found to some extent in the UK): the three main national federations are covering a wide range of actors – manufacturers, architects, contractors, distributors – with slightly different priorities for one or the other profession.

3.5.2.1 Germany

Hauptverband der Deutschen Bauindustrie
(Federation of the German construction industry – HDB)[288]

Based on the federal structure, the HDB represents its 15 regional members vis-à-vis federal institutions but also in national standardisation works. It is also member of FIEC and following developments on EU level. In addition, HDB has its own office in Brussels, collecting information from FIEC but also other actors at EU level. A second line of communication is the VAEG – Preparatory Committee EC-Harmonisation set up by the German Federal Ministry for Transport, Building and Urban Affairs (see: "Actors at EU level") for general and policy issues, while contacts to the DIBt provided more technical information (i.e. *DIBt Mitteilungen* and *Bauregelliste*).

The website provides general information (including statistical data) on the performance and its economic importance to all interested parties and links to sector specific or regional federations and offices. Information on CE marking and its use is not provided (but there is also no reference to any other mark). The information is available only in German.

Zentralverband Deutsches Baugewerbe
(Federation of the German construction profession? – ZDB)[289]

Similar to the HDB the ZDB is also a federation representing industry interests vis-à-vis public authorities and political institutions at federal level. It is also

288 http://www.bauindustrie.de/.
289 http://www.zdb.de/.

represented in the VAEG and member of FIEC. The main difference between these two organisations seems to be their membership: While the HDB is representing fewer but larger companies, the ZDB consists of 34 federations (regional federations and sector specific ones) and about 40.000 enterprises of whom the majority can be considered as SMEs.

Every two months a publication is sent to all members to provide an overview on political, technical and administrative developments. The website of the ZDB does not provide any information on conformity or quality marks. The site is published in German only.

Industrieverband WerkMörtel e.V. (Mortar industry federation – IWM)[290]

Representatives of this federation are also active at EU level (in the European federation EMO) and are therefore also in close contact with other European federations like CEPMC (links are provided on the website of IWM). The website (providing information in German) is focused on practical advice (use of mortar in different circumstances/materials) which also includes three documents describing the role and use of CE marking. These documents (one of the best guides provided by national actors selected in this study) are following a very user-friendly approach: One document summarises in five pages the changes of standards to be used after the introduction of harmonised European standards, including where and how national implementation standards should be used. It gives a good overview of CE marking and the link to the German *Ü-Zeichen* to "translate" the European standard to the existing practice (see "assumptions of actors"). Two more elaborated documents are leading step by step from the concept of harmonised standards and CE marking to the practical documentation of product performances in the new system for all relevant product groups.

Bundesverband der Deutschen Ziegelindustrie e.V.
(Federal federation of the German bricks industry)[291]

This federation is active on federal level (and member of CERAME-UNIE and TBE) and also acts as umbrella organisation for four regional federations. Three of these regional organisations cover several German *Länder* (*Fachverband Nord, Fachverband Nordwest, Fachverband Südwest*) while the last one specifi-

290 http://www.iwm.de/.
291 http://ziegel.de/.

cally covers the interests of Bavarian manufacturers (*Bayrischer Ziegelindustrieverband*)

On the website two documents have been published on the use of CE marking of bricks. The first one provides detailed information on CE marking in general, the other is more focused on the practical implication of CE marking for users (customers of manufacturers). Following a description of CE marking and the relevant European standards, references are made to German implementation standards ("*Anwendungsnormen*") and German complementary standards ("Restnormen") which have been developed by the masonry industry and the authorities ("*deutsche Bauaufsicht*") to cover additional aspects of German masonry products. Information is only provided in German.

Bundesverband der Prüfingenieure für Bautechnik
(Federal Federation for Controlling Engineers for Construction – BVPI)[292]

The BVPI is the federation of the regional (*Länder*) federations of the "*Prüfingenieure*" in Germany, representing not only the interests of this profession vis-à-vis the Consortium of European Building Control (CEBC) or vis-à-vis German political actors and authorities, but is also contact point for federal and regional building authorities (i.e. ARGEBAU, *Oberste Bauaufsichtsbehörde*). In some cases members of the BVPI were also participating in standardisation work on national and EU level. It also provides guidance and training for its members and information on the regulatory requirements in all German *Länder*.

Its website (in German) provides links to all building codes and other regulatory requirements and also some basic information for building owners (*Bauherren*). The focus is on the performance of *buildings* and calculation methods to assess this performance. No direct reference is made to the performance of construction products and CE marking (or other marks) is not mentioned.

Bundesarchitektenkammer (Federal Chamber of Architects)[293]&
Bundesingenieurkammer (Federal Chamber of Engineers)[294]

As federal organisation the *Bundesarchitektenkammer* consists of federations at *Länder* level. It is a member of the European federation ACE but is also monitor-

292 http://www.bvpi.de/.
293 http://www.bak.de/site/214/default.aspx.
294 http://www.bundesingenieurkammer.de/english_content.htm.

ing all developments at EU level which were considered relevant for its members (i.e. energy efficiency, professional qualifications, *Eurocodes*) in its office in Brussels (established in 2002) together with the German *Bundesingenieurkammer* (Federal Chamber of Engineers). Sharing the offices with the Austrian body for architects and consultants (*Bundeskammer für Architekten und Ingenieurkonsulenten* – see below) and the European Council of Engineer Chambers (ECEC).[295]

The website of the Federal Chamber of Architects is providing information on the CPD, harmonised standards and the role of CE marking (in German). The federations (*Länderarchitektenkammern*) in Nordrhein-Westfalen,[296] Baden-Württemberg[297] and Bayern[298] did not provide information on construction products, CE marking or references to other marks. Also the website of the Federal Chamber of Engineers or the websites of its regional members (*Ingenieurkammern* in Nordrhein-Westfalen,[299] Baden-Württemberg[300] and Bayern[301]) were not providing information on CE marking or construction products.

3.5.2.2 United Kingdom

Construction Products Association – CPA[302]

This association is the umbrella organisation of 43 federations of UK manufacturers, as well as large individual companies. Its Technical Committee is following the developments under the CPD and standardisation work. CPA is also a member of CEPMC and a representative of this association is often participating in SCC meetings as representative of CEPMC. CPA is also following other activities at EU level affecting the construction sector and provides a regular update via e-mail to its members. CPA's website (in English) does not refer to CE marking and it seems that only within the ongoing discussion on the new CPR is CE marking playing a relevant role.

295 This organisation covers several Central and Eastern European countries, including Austria, Germany and Poland (there was no UK member listed) http://www.ecec.net/.

296 http://www.aknw.de/.

297 http://www.akbw.de/.

298 http://www.byak.de/.

299 http://www.ikbaunrw.de/.

300 http://www.ingkbw.de/.

301 http://www.bayika.de/.

302 http://www.constructionproducts.org.uk/.

British Ceramic Confederation (BCC)[303]

The CERAME-UNIE member BCC covers ceramic products from tableware to construction products (tiles, bricks). The federation promotes products as consumer goods, and in the case of construction products it provides examples on its website of how these products are used in buildings (using specific projects in particular for presenting the aesthetic and architectural value). References to specific certificates or regulations are not provided. The information is only available in English.

Brick Development Association (BDA)[304]

Closely linked to TBE on European level and the CPA on national level, this association represents specific actors in the national bricks industry (manufacturers and installers). The association is also active in national and European standardisation work for their products. While providing some very specific and detailed guidance on the use of bricks, references to specific quality marks and CE marking could not be found.

Mortar Industry Association (MIA)[305]

MIA (member of EMO) informs its members in its "datasheet no 19" about the change from British standards to harmonised European standards, highlighting the difference of the performance-based approach chosen for the ENs while the previous national approach was based on prescription (the recipe of a specific mortar indicating the proportions of materials). It also provides some information on the CPD-specific terminology (e.g., initial type testing, attestation system), but also stressing that CE marking is not obligatory in the UK. After the general introduction the data sheet provides information on how the new European standards have to be used (e.g., the classes of attestation of conformity required for mortars). Links are provided not only to the European Mortar Organisation (EMO) but also to the federation of products that are used with mortar (e.g.,

303 http://www.ceramfed.co.uk/Index_files/Main_files/Main.html; http://www.brick.org.uk/index.html.

304 http://www.brick.org.uk/.

305 http://www.mortar.org.uk/.

aggregates, bricks) and the BRE. Data sheet no 9 lists document developed in the BRE and the Brick Development Association.[306]

Construction Industry Council (CIC)[307]

CIC is an organisation of a wide range of members of organisations of architects, designers, researchers (like the BRE), contractors and professionals closely linked to construction work. Compared with the membership of federations in the other three Member States of this study, CIC in its heterogeneity differs significantly from the German and Austrian schemes, but seems rather comparable to Polish construction federations. Different to all three Member States is its role as approval body for Approved Inspectors in the UK. Based on the *Building Control Performance Standards*[308] developed by the Department for Communities and Local Government (see: Actors at EU level), CIC members and *Approved Inspectors* will assess any application for becoming an *Approved Inspector* and decide on the qualification of each applicant. CIC's website provides information on the application procedure, research in the UK construction sector, general developments (e.g., sustainable construction) and training opportunities. Construction products are not specifically mentioned on the website. Information on CE marking or other marks is not directly available (but could be covered in one of the technical publications mentioned on the website). Links are only made to UK organisations and actors, references to EU actors are missing.

Royal Institute of British Architects (RIBA)[309]

One of the two UK ACE members, RIBA, provides information for architects and for the clients of this profession (specific "client's guides"). In its own publications (i.e. "Clerks of Works and Site Inspectors Handbook") references were made in the field of "quality assurance" to several certificates (including BBA certificates and the "kitemark"), depending on the materials and products in question. However, CE marking was not mentioned. Also as a platform for exchange of information for architects by providing links to product manu-

306 The BDA website provides no information on CE marking or other marks but links to CPA, TBE, BCC, BSI and the BRE.

307 http://www.cic.org.uk.

308 http://www.planningportal.gov.uk/uploads/br/bcpi/building-control-performance-standards_june06.pdf.

309 http://www.architecture.com/TheRIBA/Home.aspx.

facturers ("ribaproductselector"), no direct reference to CE marking could be found (in fact, "CPD" is read as "Continued Professional Development"). However, several manufacturers promoting their products used the reference to CE marking on RIBA's website (in English).

3.5.2.3 Austria

Austrian Chamber of Commerce
(Österreichische Wirtschaftskammer – WKO/Geschäftsstelle Bau)[310]

The structure of the Chamber of Commerce is based on the federal structure of Austria. Being the national representative vis-à-vis other national/federal organisations and institutions, it nevertheless depends on the cooperation of the chambers at *Länder* level. There is also a distinction between different industry sectors following developments on national or EU level.[311] In the case of construction products, the *Fachverband der Stein- und keramischen Industrie.* This sector-specific unit is keeping the contacts to European federations, in particular CEPMC and other material or product specific federations.

Next to the Chamber of Commerce additional federations ("*freie Verbände*") represent specific sectors (e.g., bricks and ceramic products: *Verband Österreichischer Ziegelwerke*)

Fachverband Bauindustrie/Landesinnung Bau[312]

Also the federation for contractors is a member of the WKO (and linked to its website) and the representing regional federations (*Landesinnungen*). While the website of the WKO is not providing information on CE marking or the Austrian *ÜA-Zeichen* but provides links to the OIB for construction products marked either CE or ÜA (*Baustoffliste* ÖA & ÖE) and to the Federal Ministry for the proposal of a new common building code (*Musterbauordnung*). Information is provided in German (the more general information on the WKO is also provided in English)

310 http://www.wko.at/fvbi/.

311 In fact, the WKO as umbrella organisation for several industry sectors is not member of a European federation in the construction sector but member of the European federation of chambers of industry and commerce EUROCHAMBERS (associated in 1974 and becoming full member after the accession in 1995).

312 http://www.bauinnung.at./

More information is provided via specific (monthly) publications or sector specific meetings. While many of these meetings mostly deal with regulatory and political issues, technical questions have been handed over to sector specific federations (and the "*freie Verbände*") which are considered to provide more specific technical information and guidance to their members (see below). The federations are also the ones sending experts to ON for national and European standardisation work.

Österreichischer Ziegelverband (Austrian Brick Federation)[313]

While links to the relevant Austrian authorities (the BMWA and the OIB) exist via the Austrian Chamber of Commerce, they are mostly limited to meetings once or twice per year. The main source of information is the participation in standardisation work on CEN level and mirror committees at national level.

This federation is promoting a product, defining and explaining the use and advantages of the products of its members, references to CE marking on the other hand are missing on its website (see: "Assumptions of actors on national level") which provides information only in German.

Federal Chamber of Architects and Consulting Engineers (Bundeskammer der Architekten und Ingenieurkonsulenten)[314]

The Federal Chamber of Architects and Consulting Engineers represents the interests of these two professions at federal level and is also member of the European Council of Architects (ACE). Like its European counterparts the Federal Chamber does not consider CE marking as the most pressing issue for architects and civil engineers. While being in contact with the Federal Ministry (BMWA) most information is directly handed over to the regional members (*Länderkammern*), but so far feedback has been rather low. Specific information on CE marking is not available on the Chamber's website.

313 http://www.ziegel.at/
314 http://www.arching.at/

3.5.2.4 Poland

Confederation of construction and real estate
(Konfederacja Budoznictwa I Nieruchomosci – KBiN)[315]

KBiN is the Polish CEPMC member, but compared to other federations working with CEPMC, KBiN covers and promotes the interest not only of (federations of) manufacturers, but also actors in the field of real estate and construction. Established in 1995, its membership remains voluntary. While the KBiN has as created a special Committee of Producers and Distributors of Building Products, it website (in Polish) does not make references to CE marking.

Architects (Izba Architektów Rzeczypospolitej Polskiej)[316] and
(Stowarzyszenie Architektów Polskich – SARP)[317]

Two main national organisations exist for architects in Poland: *Izba Architektow Rzeczypospolitej Polskiej* has a similar role as the chambers of architects in Germany and Austria as legal representative but is also the controlling body for the performance and services of its members, and also as umbrella organisation of regional federations. It is also a member of the European federation ACE. A second body, *Stowarzyszenie Architektow Polskich* (SARP) has set its focus on training and promotion of the role and services of architects. Information on CE marking is not available on the websites of either organisation which are both in Polish only.

Polish Chamber of Civil Engineers
(Polska Izba Inżynierów Budownictwa – PIIB)[318]

The PIIB is a federation of civil engineers (again, like in Germany and Austria, with compulsory membership). This body officially represents the interests of civil engineers vis-à-vis public and private actors, providing technical expertise, but also controlling and sanctioning the technical and ethical performance of its members. Information on CE marking is not provided on the PIIB website (which is with few exceptions only in Polish).

---

315 http://portal.kbin.org/.

316 http://www.izbaarchitektow.pl/index.php.

317 http://www.sarp.org.pl/.

318 http://www.piib.org.pl/.

3.5.3 The technical specification writers

3.5.3.1 Standardisation bodies

Playing a very central role as national standardisation bodies in a *de facto* monopolistic national position, several standardisation bodies were also active as certification bodies – or even Notified Bodies under the CPD. This puts these organisations in a difficult position if they have to work on harmonisation at European level and being potential competitors to European certificates. On the other hand, a dual role as specification writer and Notified Body could partly facilitate the combination of technical requirements defined in a standard and the practical feasibility of the test methods selected in these standards – or it could again create a conflict between selecting test methods that impose the least burden for manufacturers – and the economic interest of more complex and therefore more expensive testing. Three of the national standardisation bodies (DIN, BSI and ON – the Polish PKN is not acting as Notified Body under the CPD) have made a split in their organisational structure between the organisation responsible for writing technical specifications and the certification body.

German Institut for Standardisation (Deutsches Institut für Normung – DIN)[319]

DIN is one of the oldest national standardisation bodies in Europe and has a monopoly as standardisation body in Germany. DIN is in general open to all interested parties to become members in the organisation, not only as providers of expertise and manpower but also as financial contributors in its standardisation work. The Federal government plays a major role as guarantor of DIN's monopoly as standardisation body in Germany but also as initiator of standardisation work and controlling authority for this work linked to political and regulatory requirements.[320]

As CEN member it has created mirror committees for the standardisation work under the CPD following the work and voting on the results of it. DIN is also the testing and certification body for several products covered by European Directives and is also providing its own certificate ("*DIN-geprüft*") – but not for construction products.

319 http://www.din.de/cmd?level=tpl-home&languageid=en.

320 Laid down in a contract between the Federal Government and DIN, it is also stated that DIN has to ensure that any obligation of Germany to remove barriers to trade will not be hindered by DIN standards. http://www.din.de/sixcms_upload/media/2896/Vertrag_BRD_DIN.pdf.

The website developed for DIN includes references to New Approach Directives and CE marking. There are no specific references to CE marking of construction products. The website provides all information in German and English. A special part is reserved for members to distribute and discuss more detailed information on ongoing standardisation work.

British Standards Institute – BSI[321]

BSI proudly states that when established it was the world's first standards institute (in 1901). BSI is open to all interested parties to become members of the organisation. While also dependent on financial support by the UK authorities for parts of its standardisation work, the government has not introduced a monopolistic position of the BSI.

Also on BSI's website CE marking is addressed as marking that is needed for several European Directives (links provided). For the construction sector, the BSI *kitemark* (a quality mark) is the first one mentioned, with CE marking as second option. In both cases BSI is declaring its ability to perform the testing – under the CPD as Notified Body – offering in some cases a "package" covering both certificates in one. There is no link to the Commission's website or other Commission's documents under the framework of the CPD.

The website provides information in several languages (including FR, DE and PL) but the part about construction products and CE marking is published in English only. Members are also informed on specific issues via a restricted part of the website.

The Austrian Standards Institute (Österreichisches Normungsinstitut – ON)[322]

Like the other national standardisation bodies selected in this study – ON has a double role as being a member of CEN and therefore developing European harmonised standards and as a national standardisation body working with and for national actors (e.g., authorities, industry). Its monopoly on standardisation in Austria is based on a Federal law (*Normengesetz* 1971).[323] Like in Germany, ON is in general open to all interested parties to become members in the organisation, not only as providers of expertise and manpower but also as financial

321 http://www.bsi-global.com/.

322 http://www.on-norm.at/publish/home.html.

323 Bundesgesetzblatt (BGBl.) Nr. 240/1971.

contributors in its standardisation work. Here too the Federal government is playing a major role as guarantor of ON's monopoly as national standardisation body.

Being also a Notified Body under the Construction Products Directive, the ON keeps its role as certifying body ("ÖNORM geprüft", ÖN-CERT, "Keymark") for construction products on national level.

Following a corporate approach, ON is trying to prevent any domination of one or more actors (e.g., specific industries or companies) in their technical committees and the mirror committees following the standardisation work in CEN, and at least 75% of a committee have to agree on a position to be accepted under ON rules. Inviting all interested parties is done via the national federations (e.g., WKO), but also scientific bodies, certification bodies and national and regional authorities can participate in standardisation work. New developments at EU level (new mandates, changes in work programmes) are transmitted to all parties/federations, leaving it to them to nominate (motivate) experts.

ON's website presents its role as standardisation writer, as provider of information and training and as the certification body. Therefore, reference to CE marking of construction products (providing an overview on the concept of CE marking and if and how it should be applied) is also linked to certification for specific performance limits defined in ON standards (quality requirements), offering a whole package to manufacturers of construction products. An internet platform reserved for members only facilitates the distribution of new information related to the ongoing standardisation work. Nevertheless, ON has published a guidance document (*ON-Regel 20000*) aimed in particular at its own members and experts participating in technical committees on how to introduce the requirements of the CPD (e.g., how to develop annex ZA or other specific instruments and terminology).

The role of CE marking and its used is described (or linked to EC websites) and this information is available in German and English.

Polish Committee for Standardisation (PKN)[324]

The PKN is the national member of CEN, sending experts to CEN technical committees and introducing CEN standards into the national system. Different to the other standardisation bodies, it is still mostly financed by public authorities.

---

324 http://www.pkn.pl/index.php?lang=en&pid=en_strona_glowna.

Also slightly different is the smaller role of national standards (about 1 percent of PKN's standardisation work) vis-à-vis European or ISO standards. It seems that the focus is stronger on participating at international level and implementing the results at national level, rather than creating additional national standards.[325]

The website (providing information in Polish and English) does not provide specific information on construction products, but its annual reports refer to CE marking, highlighting that it is not a quality mark but a conformity mark. References are also made to the CEN "*keymark*" as providing more clarity for manufacturers and customers. It is highlighted in the annual reports that more and more information is now searched for and found on the website. However, PKN has 14 regional standardisation information points (SIP) which are still in demand for specific (technical) questions by customers.

3.5.3.2 EOTA – national members

Even more than national standardisation bodies, EOTA members (national Approval Bodies) could cover a wide range of functions at (EU and) national level. While working on European Technical Approvals (ETAG) or Common Understanding of Assessment Procedures (CUAP), their role is closely linked to national regulators and administrations (or if they are responsible for evaluating and notifying certification bodies as Notified Bodies to the Commission, they are *de facto* holding powers of national authorities). Selling European Technical Approvals (ETA) on the other hand is a commercial activity. The commercial part could even be extended if these organisations are also providing national certificates (to indicate that specific products satisfy national regulations – as the "agrément certificate" of the BBA) or if they are also Notified Bodies.

EOTA's national members in the four Member States selected are organisations that are also playing other roles on EU and national level:

- Germany's EOTA member is the DIBt which is also *notifying authority* for Germany and representing the German *Länder* in the SCC
- The UK has six members nominated with the British Board of Agrément (BBA) as Approval Body (see below)
- The OIB is Austria's EOTA member, and additionally represents the Austrian *Länder* in the SCC.

325 However, apart from European and ISO standards PKN explicitly mentions German and US standards as being sold on to their national customers.

- For Poland the ITB has been introduced as Approval Body

Of these four examples, three organisations (the DIBt, the OIB and the ITB) are also involved in research activities for authorities and private actors.

As shown in their description as actors at EU level, their websites and other publications reflects their dual role as provider of scientific and technical information to national authorities (making them at least closely linked to law-making actors) and as market actors in the field of technical assessment within a private and profit-oriented environment. References on their websites are clearly focused on regulatory requirements on national or regional level, their role as coordination bodies or at least as providers of common solutions between actors at national level. Nevertheless, the role as certification body – for ETAs but also including certification under national (or even self-created) schemes – is highlighted and promoted (see: "Actors at EU level").

The British Board of Agrément (BBA)[326] plays a significant role as certifier in the UK by providing its own voluntary (national) *Agrément Certificate*. The BBA is also one of the UK's Approval bodies allowed to issue European Technical Approvals (ETA) and represents the UK in EOTA as spokesman body. In addition to issuing ETAs it also provides complementary "CE marking Application Guides" (CEMAG) linking information provided with CE marking with national regulatory (and sometimes also voluntary) requirements. Its website focuses on BBA's role as national testing and certification body, but there is also some information available on CE marking (for ETAs). Links have been provided to EOTA and the Department for Communities and Local Affairs. The website provides information in English, French, German, Italian and Spanish.

3.5.4 Notified Bodies

Since there is no limit for notifications by national authorities for assessment or certification bodies under any European Directive, more than 300 Notified Bodies for products covered under the Construction Products Directive can be found in the Commission's NANDO database. A closer look reveals several organisations that are also active in other fields within the scope of the CPD: In

326 http://www.bbacerts.co.uk/.

particular the national standardisation bodies DIN (DE), BSI (UK) and ON (AT) can be found as Notified Bodies for several construction products. However, the organisations might be the same, but different individuals are dealing with these specific issues of technical assessment.

Some of the Approval Bodies of these four Member States have also another role as EOTA members (DIBt, OIB, ITB). In case that they are not Approval Bodies but Notified Bodies (like the BRE)[327] they could even expand their activities from testing a product to certifying it. While this would reduce conflicts of accepting or using test results for certification, it provides a certain advantage for actors in this double role by providing a (less expensive?) "package" for customers compared to actors with only one role within the framework of the CPD.

An additional role of Notified Bodies is linked to their previous (or continuing) work within the national system as part of market surveillance on national or regional level.

3.5.5 Other national bodies

In addition to manufacturers, designers and contractors, another group is setting requirements for buildings, both on the technical and on the economical level: Developers and house builders (selected here for the four Member States: *Bundesverband freier Immobilien- und Wohungsunternehmen e.V.*,[328] the *Verband Privater Bauherren* (VPB), Home Builders Federation (HBF),[329] *Österreichischer Verband der Immobilientreuhänder* (OVI),[330] *Polksi Zwiazek Firm Deweloperskich* (PFZD)[331] – all members of the European federation UEPC). However, as final (professional) customer of the services provided by the other private actors in this field, they can easily refer to general clauses in their contract requiring the necessary competence and construction works based on commonly accepted technical requirements. This includes the quality of con-

327 BRE CERTIFICATION LTD., INC. BRE CERTIFICATION, LPCB & WIMLAS is a separate organization within the structure of BRE.

328 http://www.bfw-bund.de/.

329 http://www.hbf.co.uk/.

330 http://www.ovi.at/de/verband/index.php.

331 www.pzfd.pl.

struction products used, but seems not to be explicitly mentioned in contracts with architects or construction companies.

As distributors of construction products national federations are playing a strong role as coordination bodies for individual companies. In this study federations of three of the four Member States have been selected, due to their membership of UFEMAT: The German *Bundesverband Deutscher Baustoff-Fachhandel*,[332] the Builders Merchant Federation[333] in the UK and the *Verband Österreichischer Baustoffhändler*. Clear priority in the information provided to their members (via websites, regular publications and specific working groups) were logistic and price issues as well as information on energy efficiency activities (political, regulatory and product specific). Also for customers the main focus of information provided was on developments in the field of energy efficiency, potential financial support by public and private actors for measures in this field and references to insulation performance of several products. CE marking or other national marks were (with very few exceptions) not mentioned.

3.6 The assumptions of actors at national level

As highlighted in the previous chapter, the number of potential actors at national level is much bigger than the few authorities, federations and organisations selected. However, not all of them have in the past been active in the field of CE marking. Therefore, the sample is relatively small and comments from interviewees (contacting larger regional authorities or federations as representing actors *knowing* about CE marking) reflect individual expertise and experience and did not *necessarily* reflect a view commonly shared in each professional group.

As mentioned previously, not only the same institutions and organisations might busy at EU and national level, even the same *individuals* might be active at both levels. Due to this dual role, some interviews with individuals working for European organisations or representing national and organisational interests on EU level showed this interdependency of both levels and provided both insight into the networks of "EU actors" as well as into the working structures

332 http://www.bdb-bfh.de/.

333 http://www.bmf.org.uk/index.cfm?mode=browse&page=14&CFID=519490&CFTOKEN =c07aafeb1e3cb8d3-8291CFC0-D408-A386-67F18C8294621107.

and experiences of "national actors". It was not always possible to make a clear cut between these two levels, because some aspects were more or less the same (mostly originated from national systems and transferred to the European one, but also sometimes adapting national schemes to a common European approach). Interviews with "purely" national actors helped to identify what could be considered as "national" positions and approaches.[334] To avoid on one hand repeating everything mentioned "at EU level" but to show both similarities and differences between both levels, references to similar structures, positions or experiences might be indicated but no longer explained in detail as at the previous EU level, and the focus will be on specific "national" aspects.

A problem of public and private actors responsible for distributing information about CE marking always was to evaluate how effective they actually have been. If individuals in authorities or federations were not considering CE marking as of much relevance for downstream users, their interest in assessing compliance was naturally low. But actors with a strong interest, had difficulties identifying how much awareness about and use of CE marking has increased. While safely assuming that awareness has increased (this was highlighted by practically all interviewees), specific data was not available.

3.6.1 Member State (national and regional) authorities

At EU level, national technical institutes were supporting their national ministries representing national interests vis-à-vis other Member State representatives and EU institutions and organisations. In the case of Germany and Austria, they also got an additional role as coordination body and representative of the interests of their Länder. Nevertheless, all four of them were more focused on technical issues and therefore were more closely linked to national actors planning, constructing and monitoring construction works – in particular because at this level, technical questions and interpretations were becoming more and more important than administrative and regulatory issues (which are more horizontal by nature and mostly not providing enough detailed information).

334 This "national" level is showing the same "overlaps" with the next level defined in this study as "construction site" as the EU level is linked to the national one, because it is actual planning and construction work is closely embedded in the regulatory and administrative system on regional and national level.

While being embedded in different national schemes, interviewees of all four technical institutes were in several cases highlighting aspects that were very similar in all four Member States: The most significant one was the clear focus on the (overall) performance of buildings or civil engineering work. Downstream authorities were more interested in the "final product". To a large extent planning, construction and the selection of products was based on either professional experience (in particular in Germany) or on careful selection by (non-professional) house owners (as in the UK). Therefore, practically all other public and private actors were looking at the national or regional building codes as main reference, while additional national legislation (like on the quality of products) was considered as complementary.[335] This assumption was common in all four Member States, independent of the national approaches – from defining the tests necessary and defining the acceptable use via a de facto regulatory list for construction products in Germany ("Bauregelliste"), a slightly similar approach in Austria ("Baustoffliste"), the use of a large public market surveillance network in Poland, to a more "laissez-faire" approach in the UK by leaving the power of decisions but also the responsibility to a large extent outside the administrative structure.

Being more interested in building performance and requirements set up at EU or national level (like energy performance and energy saving potentials of buildings or accessibility for all users of buildings), it was not surprising that most actors (except manufacturers) showed only limited interest in new instruments to assure the correct performance of construction products used. It was also acknowledged in all four countries that while at least all downstream authorities should be aware of the existence of CE marking and the correct interpretation of the information that this marking is providing, little was known if and how these downstream authorities have received, interpreted and used information on CE marking.[336]

---

335 Which largely explained the absence of architects or their federations in discussions on construction products and the low response from contractors.

336 In several cases interviewees of public or private bodies raised their concerns that local authorities have to carry the burden of most tasks identified at EU or national/federal level while not being given enough information or resources to deal with all of them. The task of market surveillance was highlighted a few times as being most challenging for local authorities ("the poor devils") when even at EU level (or national level) different interpretations existed.

However, except for Poland, no empirical data was collected by national authorities and references to or estimates of known cases of wrong or misleading use of CE marking were rare or could refer only to very few examples (in product-specific sectors the numbers were ranging

It should be noted that when providing information, national authorities have focused on active professionals, but did not include universities or technical schools as regular target groups. Keeping in mind the limited resources and manpower of the authorities, limiting their efforts to the most relevant actors (as the ones selecting and using construction products now) was reasonable, but it also left the responsibility of informing the "next generation" of professionals to a large extent to private actors and – as in most cases indicated by several interviewees: individual commitment of civil servants and private professionals lecturing at universities and technical schools to be up to date as well as willing and able to explain new requirements in their fields.[337] These individuals who were on one hand lecturers and on the other hand still active "in the field" were in all four countries an essential link providing practical expertise to public and private education and training systems.

3.6.1.1 Germany

The split of responsibilities between federal authorities and the building authorities guarantees the role of the *Länder* as *de facto* regulators on land use, urban planning and construction works on buildings. In Germany the regional ministries for construction (*Bautenministerien*) are on the highest level of coordinating and decision making. Practical planning and building control was often delegated to downstream authorities at regional or local level. Compared to the strong position within the national system that these competences will remain on regional level, there were few signs that the regional ministries were planning to play a more prominent role in the communication with authorities of *other* Member State in this field. Most links were maintained between national authorities (the BMVBS and the DIBt) with few if any (regular) contacts to other Member State authorities or even the Commission services. Sometimes being critical about the "dependency" on these trans-national active bodies and the quality and quantity of information provided by them, it was also acknowledged that the limited resources of the regional authorities (including reducing the number of civil servants in regional administrations) would be stressed too much (in par-

between 1-3 per year; interviewees of regional authorities in Germany and Austria were estimating up to three cases per year had happened to their knowledge.).

337 Interest was mostly seen for practical planning and calculation issues as for the evaluation of the fire performance of buildings and products or the *Eurocodes* as calculation methods for structural performance.

ticular in the smaller *Länder* with even fewer resources) if they would try to monitor and react to all developments at EU level in their sector. It was highlighted that for regional authorities (often more concerned about activities of the Commission on regional and urban planning)[338] it remained difficult to follow different initiatives by different Directorates General which gave the impression that on one hand more and more responsibilities were taken over by the Commission but at the same time the Commission lacked any internal co-ordination of these activities.

Comments from interviewees working for regional authorities contradicted slightly the perception of actors at national/federal level that the implementation of the German "*Bauproduktegesetz*" could be considered as "business as usual" (see: "Actors at EU level"): Market surveillance had to be established in the following years (20 years after the adoption of the CPD) by the *Länder*[339] and also the introduction of European standards was sometimes perceived as a drop in quality compared to the existing national scheme. Reference to "bad experience" was based on feedback from several actors, but it was less clear where the standards *have* actually reduced the quality of construction products. References to the previous national approach indicated that this system might not have been less prone to flaws (products of poorer quality); but that *information was distributed faster* between actors and different bodies (e.g., certification bodies, authorities) could react faster. It was assumed that DIN standards were more practically-oriented and had been tested in practice, while hENs were new and one could not find enough indication that they were providing that level of assurance for users. Following this assumption, harmonised European standards did not seem as an improvement but as an additional burden to cover the specific interests of the building authorities by other means. Therefore, *Ü-Zeichen* were seen as "bridging the gap" between a performance-based declaration and clear

338 This political and technical field seemed to be of higher importance and the German *Länder* have invested more of their resources in this field. It was also mentioned that cooperation with the Federal level was seen as more constructive as well as the opportunities of the regional actors to play a more active role was higher and more promising than in the field of construction products.

339 Like for the UK and Austria, active market surveillance was achieved by manufacturers monitoring the market and their competitors. However, it was mentioned that lack of CE marking might have been seen by manufacturers more as a possibility to act against competition than actually identifying flawed products or wrong declarations of performance (with the exception of imports from outside the EU which were by most national actors (in all four Member States) seen with more suspicion).

indication where and how the product can be used.[340] However, both the perceived weakness of harmonised European standards and the ongoing work on the "*Bauregelliste*" was seen as additional strain on the limited resources of the *Länder* since the costs of maintaining and updating the "*Bauregelliste*" had to be covered by them with no indication that these costs would be reduced in future (by getting standards of "higher quality" and therefore a shorter "*Bauregelliste*"). On the other hand, despite the significant workload for the authorities, it was acknowledged that it was not clear if all "downstream" users were familiar with CE marking *or* the German *Ü-Zeichen*. In particular architects might not have been sufficiently aware of the nature and use of these marks.

The interviewees from German authorities were significantly more sceptical about market actors and their responsible behaviour than their counterparts in the other three Member States. While not denying the efforts of these actors of reducing costs as logical and in general necessary, doubts were raised that this would stop on "reasonable" cost savings but could also lead to cuts in the quality of the products selected and the final performance of the building. To compensate against this risk more guidance has to be given by public authorities allowing all actors to refer to a commonly accepted quality (of products and buildings). The use of regulatory instruments to make these requirements obligatory was seen as additional assurance for all actors that everybody is using "the same rules". It was also stressed that while these decisions were made by the regional building authorities (based mostly on a proposal of the DIBt), other actors were also often consulted before a final decision was taken. Despite this strong involvement the information flow seemed to be more one-sided (from the authorities to specific target groups) while feedback remained rare and very general (actors were asking for guidance if they have to demand or have to affix CE marking)[341].

340 Also seen as instruments to "repair" weaknesses and technical flaws in the harmonised European standards ("*Reperaturzeichen*").

341 It was mentioned that in most cases concerning the wrong application of CE marking this was often due to a lack of understanding the details of this approach rather than deviation on purpose. Manufacturers were reported to have been grateful for more information and guidance.

3.6.1.2 United Kingdom

It did not seem that CE marking had a significant impact on the work of authorities on a purely national (regional, county or district) level. "Business as usual" could be more easily maintained because CE marking is officially one of several means to provide information on a construction product. Having dealt with different systems simultaneously in the past has made CE marking *another* instrument that one has to grow accustomed with, but which did not affect the overall scheme of planning, approving or controlling in the construction sector. CE marked products have to be generally accepted by local authorities or *Approved Inspectors,* since the *Approved Documents* published by authorities (which are seen as one of the most important source of information for controlling authorities and *Approval Inspectors*, but BBA Agrément Certificates were more often used and accepted (because they are seen as providing more relevant assurance for specific uses)[342]. The limits of CE marking as providing only an attestation that the product has been tested according to harmonised European standards was seen as a disadvantage compared to quality marks used in the sector, but it was also stressed that even products certified by the BBA did not necessarily cover all requirements or allows a product to be used in all foreseeable ways in a building. Therefore, building control bodies (local authorities or *Approved Inspectors*) were regularly dealing with different requirements and approval systems which depended to a large extent also on practical expertise to correctly assess the information provided by house owners, planners or contractors. However, the responsibilities of market actors (including developers and house owners) were in the eyes of UK actors helpful to distribute the burden of decisions and control to several actors (in particular compared to the strong commitment of German authorities).

3.6.1.3 Austria

Austrian authorities were facing a slightly more complicated situation than their German colleagues. While similar in their structure (see: Actors at EU level), manpower was significantly less available in Austria. Therefore, the Federal

342 The control of construction products used included the check that the same products that were indicated in the plans were used on the construction site (not substituted by "cheaper" products), by comparing product names and if the products were marked according to regulatory requirements (national or CE marks). Product testing remained (like in the other three Member States) the exception.

Ministry for Economics and Labour (BMWA) depended more or less on the work of one individual and even the OIB only had few experts in its organisation. Additionally, the question of competence for construction products has created some friction between the Austrian Länder and the Federal Ministry (as products or as components of buildings) for years[343]. Even more significant, other actors seem to be less active and cooperative vis-à-vis the BMWA and the OIB, assuming that developments on EU level were less relevant for their day-to-day work.

Despite the fact that the corporate structure of Austria in general not only facilitates the involvement of actors of different fields in discussions but can be considered as one of its most significant characteristics, communication between different actors or downstream authorities was seen by several interviewees as satisfactory at best – but also noted that in some cases communication was actually improving. While a certain lack of interest about developments at European level might explain some reluctance of a number of actors on national level, some comments indicated also that the "official" lines of communication might not have reached the right target group but only a level in between. Also the small number of potential contacts (e.g., building authorities in Austria are in most cases significantly smaller than in Germany, were directly responsible for more tasks than in the UK and being less centralised than in Poland –the decisions were left to these smaller bodies) was considered as one explanation by actors in the Austrian administrations why communication was time-intensive and not always rewarding.

The main reference point for regional authorities was the OIB – and here in particular its expert groups ("*Sachverständigenausschüsse*") which were discussing specific questions that were put to regional authorities and were providing binding guidance as well as its guidance papers ("*Leitfäden*")[344] which were also used as reference in interaction with other actors (civil engineers and architects) as relevant guidance documents. The lists for construction products ("*Baustofflisten*") were also playing a major role as reference documents, but it was mentioned as a drawback that these lists were not freely available (compared to

343 See the position of the Federal ministry on its website: http://www.bmwa.gv.at/NR/rdonlyres/9376D54F-26EE-48FC-A382-B0A2711C0574/0/GutachtenendgBauprodRLGA.pdf and the position from the *Länder* point of view in Bussjäger: Homogenität und Differenz 2006 p. 157.

344 This refers to documents developed by the OIB. The Guidance Papers developed on EU level were hardly known and not used as reference.

the building codes and other relevant documents which were available on the public RIS database – "*Rechtsinformationssystem*").

On the other hand, Austrian actors had the advantage that in their larger neighbour country Germany similar discussions were taking place and additional information and documents (i.e. the translation of the Guidance Papers into German) were available. But this additional input was seen as a mixed blessing when it came to the specific German approach of adding the requirements of the German *Ü-Zeichen* into the system. With close links to the German market for construction products, Austrian (public and private) actors saw clear advantages in the CE marking concept, and therefore considered the use of the *Ü-Zeichen* as *de facto* new "barrier to trade" that should have been removed with the adoption of the CPD and its national implementations and not been reinforced by public and private actors in Germany. While having a national mark for the Austrian market too (the *ÜA-Zeichen*), it was stressed that this mark was not used *in addition* to CE marking but only for products for which CE marking was not possible (either because it is not covered by the CPD but considered as construction product by the Austrian authorities, or because harmonised European standards were not yet available)[345].

In general, experts in regional authorities were aware that the continuous development of technical standards at national and European levels has put a major burden on practical users (architects and civil engineers) who have to follow these developments – a task that SMEs and micro-enterprises could hardly fulfil. CE marking was also seen as causing some confusion by other actors, because the assumption that CE marking would be a quality mark was quiet common. On the other hand, as a rather "conservative" sector, it was assumed that products were in most cases selected because of past experience and the

345 *Similarities like the same language, a very similar administrative structure, nearly identical technical requirements for buildings and products and also technical qualifications of national actors that are easily comparable between Germany and Austria are making the neighbouring country a logical target for extending the market for actors in both countries. At the same time, competitors from the "other country" have easier access to previous national domains. The struggle between German and Austrian authorities and private actors to find common approaches and removing (real or assumed) barriers was not new when Austria joined the EU (and can be found between several countries with strong similarities – like Belgium and France or the Netherlands), but it highlights the limits of the CPD which should already have solved this problems at EU level.*

"brand name"[346] which would decrease the risk of selecting and installing products not fit for the intended use. However, since CE marking was in some known cases not covering a whole part of a building or civil engineering work but only some of its components, it was mentioned that CE marking was seen by several actors as only partly useful ("failing in the overall performance assessment") and therefore diminishing its acceptance.

3.6.1.4 Poland

Similar to interviewees in Germany, the UK and Austria, interviewees in Poland mentioned problems in communicating with other actors in their country. But here the differences experienced were more between authorities and private actors than between national authorities and downstream authorities on regional and county level. The top-down approach within the civil administration and the obligation for downstream inspectors to report on an annual basis was seen as providing a reasonably transparent picture of the findings on different administrative levels with regard to CE marked construction products. However, since market surveillance was only "focused on the market" control of products *actually* installed in buildings was still seen as a weak point in the national approach.

In interaction with private actors the perception of CE marking by private downstream actors was seen as leaving room for improvement: CE marking was used by these actors, but actual knowledge about the use of CE marking and the information provided with it (in particular for SMEs and micro-enterprises) was still seen as low ("used to follow the law" – "important on ′invoice day` to prove that all obligations were fulfilled"). However, references to CE marking in (public) tendering were considered a successful approach to increasing the relevance of CE marking within the national system.

Being another neighbour to Germany, the German market was considered as relevant for Polish market actors (and German DIN standards are explicitly available by the Polish standardisation institute PKN) but the approach on how

346 For products of widely known manufacturers ("brand names") a pragmatic approach was mentioned in one interview: Since well-known companies have the resources to follow all developments on regulatory requirements and standardisation and their risk that mistakes could have a negative impact of several regional or national markets, it was assumed that these companies "could not afford the risk" of not having all relevant certificates. Therefore, these products were more easily accepted when indicated in plans than products of less-known manufacturers where additional checks if all certificates could be provided was more likely.

to deal with construction products and CE marking was closer to the French one than the German one. This seemed not to be caused just by the close connections between the Polish authorities and the ITB with their French counterparts. The advantages of the French systems and their potential use in the Polish system were highlighted and explained by the interviewees themselves.[347]

Documents developed by the construction unit and the SCC were seen as important guidance, but also critically assessed (in particular by interviewees working in the ITB). As certification body, the institute was one of the target groups addressed by the Guidance Papers and specific websites (like NANDO) were clearly used. Based on this experience it was stressed that the complexity of documents developed on EU level was difficult to transmit to downstream users on national level. Also information provided by electronic means was sometimes difficult to find for actors who were not familiar with the EU systems on a day-by-day basis ("*one* place where everything could be found"), but who on the other hand have legal responsibilities (like civil engineers and architects during the planning and tendering phase).

3.6.2 Federations/ standardisation work

The advantage for other actors at EU level of having a European federation as interaction partner is that these organisations are supposed to represent the common position of their sectors. To achieve that they have to "aggregate" different national or sectoral positions. This common position (if it can be achieved) hides the fact that in each Member State slightly different or very different schemes have been developed. In case of Poland the system of representations of professions can still be considered as being in transition, where most actors have to get experience and to develop a framework that will satisfy their needs as well as

347 *In both of the "newer" Member States interviewees were showing a certain pride in not being just at the "receiving end" of the system (like following the* acquis communautaire*) but being proactive actors. Austrian actors highlighted that while they were following the German system at the beginning, they have by now developed their own approach and considered that their approach now is more "European" and less "national" than the German one. Polish interviewees were keen to highlight how much they have prepared themselves years before Poland joined the EU (on organisation level but also on individual level) – therefore having been able to easily adopt the EU system (of the CPD). In both cases the emphasis in the self presentation lied with the ability to act European (international) than purely national.*

the requirements of external actors[348]. But also the corporate nature of the systems in Germany and in Austria has formed their understanding of networking and communicating with different actors which is different to the more "individual" approach in the UK.

The interview partners at this level were selected from national federations, but also the points of view of individual manufacturing companies were added here. This is often due to the fact that many individuals had several roles at the national level: While being employed by individual companies, they could also be working for EU or national federations, being members of specific CEN technical committees or in one of the mirror committees of CEN's national members (DIN, BSI, ON, PKN), or being observers in CEN, EOTA or in the Group of Notified Bodies. In their different roles, they were also often participating in the information networks of the national authorities preparing a common national position vis-à-vis the construction unit of the European Commission. Being able to participate in different working groups, technical committees or directly in the management of national federations depends on the ability and willingness of a company to share the expertise – but more important: working time – with other private or public actors at national level. Not surprisingly, practically all interviewees were working in rather large companies which were considering national (or European) developments as relevant enough to have some of their employees monitoring and influencing these developments (or as one interviewee put it: "enlightened" companies). However, some of the federations (in particular for architects, contractors, developers and house builders) were only partly following the work on construction products and could not provide any particular experience or indicate any specific interest in this issue. In some cases knowledge about CE marking was more the result of individual networks which brought it up on one occasion or another, than professional need or professional interest. Also documents produced on EU level – like the Interpretative Documents and the Guidance Documents were either not known or never distributed to downstream users (federation members) because they were seen as too complex and not practical enough to provide guidance in the interaction between manufacturers, planners, contractors and authorities on the

348 Difficulties in communicating and interacting with Polish industry representatives or companies have also been mentioned by interviewees of companies operating in several EU Member States (including Poland).

"construction site" level, which again highlights the limits of interest and use of CE marking.

3.6.2.1 The "added value" of CE marking

The "added value" of CE marking was questioned in several interviews. The advantage of not repeating tests in each national market or the "recognition factor" for contractors working in different countries of the EU was clearly recognised, but there were different perceptions about what could be considered a "barrier to trade" or an opportunity to show the high quality of a product. In slight contradiction of European federations, national federations and actors had fewer problems with regulatory or market requirements as "entrance fee" to a national market. In their own market, it was seen as "protecting our levels of quality" (this was mentioned in all four Member States) and assuring that competitors are playing "by the same rules". While being more critical about the need for other requirements in other EU Member States, they were not completely dismissive. However, these were comments from individuals working in companies that were operating in several Member States – this does not indicate that SMEs would have the same point of view.

Another position that interviewees in federations and companies had in common was the use of CE marking as proof of conformity vis-à-vis customers and authorities. Considering that market surveillance was not seen as efficient by interviewees in Germany,[349] Austria and the UK ("left to industry"), an added value of CE marking could only be achieved by explicitly highlighting its existence in contact with customers. But the consumers were not *asking* for CE marking – manufacturers had to *promote* it to raise the awareness among architects, contractors or non-professional customers.[350] This seemed to have created a curious situation (according to the information provided by public and private interviewees) that in particular in the UK *promotion* was made for CE marking

349 It was also mentioned by an interviewee from a Notified Body that products manufactured in Germany and covered by the CPD was not always CE–marked, which would indicate that even with so much information provided by different actors in Germany the risk of unawareness or deviation from obligatory requirements could never be completely avoided.

350 Also highlighting that distributors are practically never really interested in specific marks, leaving this aspect of communication and trust between manufacturers and consumers in the hands of the manufacturing industry. On the other hand, manufacturers thought that distributors are extremely worried about their liability, where therefore following the letter of the law, but not going too deeply into the philosophy behind it.

(in one case even "selling" it as "quality mark") by some manufacturers and sectors; *Austrian* manufacturers were using it, but were not promoting it, Polish manufacturers were fulfilling the requirements of the law and in *Germany* the *Ü-Zeichen* was seen by manufacturers as essential to promote their products. It was also mentioned that applying CE marking was seen as making the position of the manufacturer or the professional user "watertight" against future risks of being sued for not using a CE marked product rather than using it for checking the conformity with regulatory requirements (which was – in general – taken for granted) or getting information on the product performance (which was "covered" by experience with often-used products or the selection of products by "brand name" – see below) – CE marking (or other marks) was asked for "if something went wrong" – or after the works had been finished (for documentation).

3.6.2.2 Standardisation work

Interviews with individuals commenting on their experience in standardisation work can be grouped in two different types of actors: those working directly for national standardisation bodies (mostly in charge of coordinating technical experts and committees) and those who have been active as experts in specific CEN TCs or mirror committees at national level (being mostly seconded by companies to the technical committees). Both were moving between the EU and the national level and could report on their experiences of standardisation work on both levels. Some of the interviewees had been interviewed in the first part of the study, but additional experts in the field of standardisation were contacted at this level and added more positions and details (the questionnaires covered aspects relevant at EU level as well as other aspects referring more to experience within a national environment).

In general, the perception of the work in CEN and its output depended much on the national background of the interviewees. The lack of balanced representation in CEN TCs was seen as a crucial flaw of the CEN system for German actors (highlighting that this has been achieved in DIN). The Austrian and UK actors were not contradicting the German position, but they were sceptical that a balanced TC would always be possible (either on EU or on national level). In fact, comments from individuals active in DIN, ON or BSI acknowledged that the dominance of stronger federations or companies cannot be completely avoided. In the end, much depends on the "diplomatic skills" of the chair to maintain a level playing field in a national or CEN TC.

Independently of any national background however were comments about the practical use of harmonised standards for downstream users. Some interviewees active in one of the standardisation bodies thought that several European standards were trying to cover too much at once ("Everything that is already on the market"),[351] making them sometimes too general to be of practical use or so complicated that their correct use might be doubted.[352] In particular in these cases where the information provided by European standards was not seen as sufficient, the development of complementary application standards was not only seen as temporary solution till the flaws in the European standards were solved, but as an essential instrument to make them functional and applicable at all. Also the large number of standards for one product family was considered more difficult to explain to downstream users, in particular to small and micro enterprises ("How do you explain to an architect that he has to use – and buy – 12 different standards when he had to use only one in the past?").

But harmonised European standards were not only receiving criticism, it was also acknowledged that harmonisation has (at least partly) resulted in more transparency and created the feeling that with CE marking everybody was now playing on the same level playing field. Also several flaws or over-complicated approaches in the previously national standards have not been repeated in the new European version.

For the non-English speaking countries an additional aspect was mentioned of finding experts who would be willing and able to communicate at *international* level.[353] The problem seen was not so much in having a certain knowledge

---

351 While at the same time it was mentioned that for several product families large numbers of European standards have been developed which makes it difficult (and expensive) for users – in particular SMEs – to follow and to comply with all requirements correctly;

Another aspect raised was the introduction of other national regulations into the standardisation work under the CPD, adding requirements (i.e. for workers protection) that were not relevant for the "in-use phase" of a product (meaning the performance of the product after it has been installed in the building).

352 On the other hand, they also acknowledged that these are always risks for standards of the first generation and similar problems have occurred with national standards in purely national systems.

353 Working language in CEN TCs is not exclusively English (e.g., the members could agree on another language or have translation provided) but on one hand, English is the language most often used for technical discussions, and on the other hand the draft standard distributed to all

about the English language, but being confident enough to participate in a discussion – in particular "against" English native speakers. While not being explicitly afraid of being disadvantaged by using another language, there seemed to be a certain uneasiness that oneself or a representative being sent to "Brussels" might not be completely accustomed to finer details in a discussion ("not the text worries but what is between the lines") and might miss aspects important to national actors at home (who might also not know about this because it was not reported back to them). *While not explicitly mentioned by the interviewees, this could also be seen as an indication that standardisation remains to an extent a "political" struggle of having enough power to influence specific interpretations which might result in advantages and disadvantages for (national) actors.*

3.6.2.3 (Private) actors in Germany

The corporate system seemed to be a very important national characteristic and guiding principle for many German interviewees. The fact that German actors could develop common positions for discussions on EU or national level was often highlighted as important achievement, avoiding contradictory positions, defending the specific national approach (the official declaration of fitness for the intended use via the German Ü-Zeichen), but sometimes even more important: being better coordinated to convince other actors at national and European level of the advantage of a national position.

When working at European level the system of accepting solutions based on qualified majority votes – like in CEN standardisation work or in the SCC (compared to a veto-right for every actor) – was sometimes seen as an improvement against "stalling tactics" of actors to improve their bargaining position or slowing down specific solutions (a "joint decision trap")[354], sometimes it was considered a disadvantage for actors who might be seriously affected by majority decisions without being able to influence them effectively. The former group of interviewees mentioned that insistence on a "common position" was often a "common defence line" against external approaches and changes, blocking serious discussions about potential advantages vis-à-vis a "we have always done

CEN members for comments and approval have to be written in English. Therefore, additional language skills might be helpful, but in most cases not essential when presenting and defending a crucial position.

354 Risse/Cowles/Caporaso: Europeanization and Domestic Change, in: Cowles/Caporaso/Risse (eds): Transforming Europe 2001 p. 9.

it like this" position. It was highlighted that resistance was mostly caused by lack of knowledge (or lack of attempts to get more information) than outright rejection of the goals and instruments of this new approach. The latter group was more concerned about the decrease of trust in a system where positions could be "ignored" by stronger actors. In particular in the field of standardisation where changes in the composition of actors (not individuals) in CEN TCs or national mirror committees were very unlikely and therefore keeping the dominance of specific actors, weaker actors might be "trapped" in a position where their participation would give the system credibility without giving them enough power to seriously influence the outcome (this view was more common for contractors who were wary that their needs would be ignored during the development of CEN standards – a position that was partly reflected in their European federation FIEC[355]). As the CEN system was not viewed favourably by several interviewees on the user's side ("you have to participate because you have to avoid worse") it created a general wariness about CEN standards and a wide-spread perception that the new standards were weaker than the previous DIN standards.

But also at national level the actual results of this corporate approach were viewed very differently. The framework created by the Federal ministry (the preparatory committee VAEG) was seen as an important focus point to present and explain positions, but on the other hand, actors responsible for distributing information, collecting views and presenting them were more inclined to see their work efficiently done than actors who could only contribute information or positions but had only few means of monitoring or influencing the actual discussion in the decision making process on EU or national level ("in Brussels it sounded very different"). However, it was acknowledged several times that the official German position and the outcome of developments at EU level (in particular the SCC meetings) were rarely assessed as *combination* of several (different) interests but only from the point of view of *one's own specific interests*.

There was also some scepticism that the existing scheme of providing information from "Brussels" via the German authorities to other interested parties was still providing "anything new" that would peak the interest of federations or companies in the sector any longer. Some interviewees considered the CE marking as fact, but not being extremely relevant in their own specific busi-

355 See also: Eurocer-Building position paper 2005 p. 8.

ness, because additional market requirements made it obvious that more information than the one provided by CE marking was needed:[356] Next to practical (positive) experience with a product ("brand names"), the question of how to use (install) a product was considered more important for a contractor and therefore also more important for the manufacturer to provide this type of information or specific guidance.[357] Some interviewees were also sceptical about the role of market surveillance or the role that public authorities claimed to play in this system. It was stressed that it was still private actors in the construction sector itself (manufacturers or contractors) who were observing their competitors and therefore the most important – if not the only *efficient* – instrument against illegal use of construction products. Public authorities were seen only as secondary (reactive) instruments to sanction deviant behaviour within the sector.

In general, direct control and direct involvement in (national or European) standardisation seemed to be more important for manufacturers than any decision-making processes at EU level. Developments "in Brussels" were monitored by national federations via their European umbrella organisations but this information rarely made it beyond that level, and interest in upstream developments were more often based on individual interests and curiosity than strategic company interests. Therefore, some experts in federations saw themselves as kind of "ambassadors" for keeping interest in EU affairs alive and presenting positive developments ("instead of just complaining about *Brussels*"). However,

356 Examples given in the mortar sector indicated that European standards were excluding specific criteria that were relevant for specific products to be competitive in the market (allowing for thinner layers of mortar and therefore using less material and reducing costs for consumers). Additional guidance for application – provided by *Ü-Zeichen* – removes the disadvantage and keeps the product in use. (see also: http://www.iwm.de/content/cesonder.pdf).

357 The potential advantage of the CPD approach of moving from specific products to performance requirements in tenders was viewed sceptically by interviewees on the contractor's side (in Germany, Austria and the UK): Planners (architects) were seen as mostly micro-enterprises who could hardly afford the time-consuming process of going deeply into specific performance criteria and therefore they remain vague in their tenders. As a result, products could not be compared sufficiently which includes the risk of later complaints between planners, contractors and manufacturers. Therefore, German actors in particular welcomed public or private (federation) initiatives which "re-translated" product declarations to the known national schemes and facilitated communication between contractors and architects. In addition, (more) precise guidance was in general provided in tenders written by public authorities (or they were considered as the most likely actors to provide more detailed technical requirements). This strengthened the positions of public authorities as defining technical – and therefore: "market" – requirements at national level.

motivating their members to provide feedback was very difficult and it was more the establishment and use of *individual* networks, rather than the existence of organisation networks that kept the information flow alive.

Another point raised by authorities (and to a lesser extent by all other actors) was the absence of distributors in discussions on national level. While considered by end users as an important interface with manufacturers, the whole system (manufacturers dealing directly with contractors but delivering via distributors) was not seen as very professional when it came to the distribution of information on products ("economists managing these companies and not engineers who would understand these issues"). Manufacturers on the other hand, did not put too much emphasis on the role of distributors, using them only for simplifying financial aspects, but leaving the information flow of technical data to manufacturers and their contacts to designers, architects and contractors. Despite this assumed rather low awareness level, CE marking has held strong interest for (at least for the federations of) distributors, in particular in the field of marking products and ensuring correct and useful documentation.[358] While here too, the role of "brand names" and past experience were seen as important factors in the decisions of professional users and do-it-yourself enthusiasts, another aspect was highlighted: the complexity of buildings and building parts did no longer allow for an infinite combination of products but favours whole systems of clearly defined products combined in the most efficient way.[359] Therefore, certification of components (single products) was seen as falling short on demands for practical information, and could be one of the main causes of why "end users" have not (specifically) asked or controlled CE marking (or other marks) on construction products.

One exception however was highlighted: contractors crossing national borders and faced with different products on the market. Here CE marking

358 Since the distribution chain demands different forms of documentation (i.e. "Lieferschein", product information, bills) and changing responsibilities (liability) of each actor involved it became important to ensure that obligatory information was correctly provided and not "lost" in the process to the "end user".

359 For example, the strong emphasis on energy efficiency (not to mention regulatory requirements) have resulted in more complex approaches for walls or roofs, selecting a specific combination of products to optimize the performance of this component of the building while remaining as economic as possible. Since planners and contractors are moving more and more between very narrow margins of improving performance and reducing costs, individual combinations were seen as more time- and resource-consuming and therefore less and less attractive for these "end users".

became more interesting because it was a familiar reference for companies. In particular, when only smaller quantities of specific products were needed or transporting well-known products from one's own country/manufacturer to the construction site was no longer cost-efficient. However, several products were already crossing borders too (brought with the contractors) or manufacturers expanded by buying companies in other Member States. In these cases, the "brand name" became once again the more relevant reference.

As said above, technical universities or schools were rarely involved in activities of construction products other than assessing product performance or working on test methods (which puts them closer to the group of test laboratories and certification bodies). Manufacturers and their customers (civil engineers and contractors) have only reported sporadic contacts and cooperation, considering sector-specific training as the domain of federations or individual companies. In fact, there were two different approaches by universities, depending on the scope of their activities: As pure institution for training and research, the involvement of universities was rather low. But some technical universities used their facilities as test and certification bodies in the market. In these cases (as Notified Bodies) they were closely following developments at EU level (including the GNB), but also creating a stronger incentive to keep contact with other universities in this specific (economic-technical) field. Similar to "pure" Notified Bodies, the complexities of standards ("several pages of references to other standards") and of EU reference systems (i.e. NANDO) as well as the duplication of work by two parallel schemes – the EU and the national approach/ standardisation were considered as major problems for practical work as certification bodies. The transfer of knowledge about certification (including CE marking) to the training programmes of future civil engineers and architects was rather rare. This was partly seen as result of the general training programme that put emphasis on product performance *per se* but not on specific certification schemes, and partly because a lack of interest by students in this field.

While architects and contractors were only in some cases actively participating in discussions and developments in the field of construction products at national level, several interviewees of other professions mentioned the increasing role of these two professions in guaranteeing the performance of buildings and therefore also their responsibility of selecting the best (and still affordable) construction products. This is nothing new within the German system, but the current developments were experienced as continuous withdrawal of authorities (and to an extent also the "*Prüfingenieure*") as actors actively controlling construction sites and products to more "administrative monitoring" (i.e. checking documents provided by actors in different phases of the planning and construction work). At the same time the complexity of regulatory and technical requirements was increasing, leaving these two professions with a heavier burden of ensuring quality with less "backup" (and "shared responsibility") by regional or local authorities.

Compared to this "external" perception by manufacturers and authorities, feedback from architects highlighted again the dilemma of the lack of resources (micro-enterprises) and the growing number of activities initiated at EU and at national level. In particular the different policies at EU level were seen as not very coordinated (different Directorates General were initiating their own policies but hardly trying to present them in a context with other Commission initiatives[360]) and therefore shifting the burden of identifying intended (and unintended) links and interpreting of their importance to downstream users. Similar to distributors, the lack of *active* participation of architects in several fields did not necessarily mean that the federations were not aware of specific developments. Developing and maintaining a network of actors in different professions and federations[361] was seen as most efficient way of maintaining a reasonably steady flow of information, selecting relevant topics and transmitting them to downstream users (the regional federations – *Länderkammern*). However, it was acknowledged that information "from the EU" was mostly considered as irrelevant by national actors. Raising awareness even at regional level was not an easy task (but the general perception was slowly changing and more actors becoming aware that developments at EU level could – via national laws – influence their policies and day-to-day work).

360 Not only German actors have mentioned this problem. A major policy field – "sustainability" – was used by several units, directorates and Directorate Generals of the Commission but their scope and the instruments developed differed significantly and thereby forced downstream actors to adapt to similar, but nevertheless incompatible approaches and instruments.

361 Not only at national level, but also for the office of the BAK in Brussels, contacts to other German actors were seen as more helpful than to European federations. While a common language and a common background might have facilitated the creation of these contacts, it seemed that it was more the number of potential sources of information that was supporting this approach. European federations were seen as having even less resources available and therefore only one – but not necessarily the main – source of relevant information.

3.6.2.4 (Private) actors in the United Kingdom

The fact that the CE marking was not considered as obligatory in the UK by its national authorities created a situation where European standards (and even CE marking) were of less concerns in the sector. References to a product has been CE marked could be found in several sectors promoting their products even on the national market, while confusion about combining it with (additional) national marks seemed to be of less relevance.

Like their counterparts in other Member States, manufacturers in the UK had to face the dilemma of deciding when to prepare for developments at EU or national level. The adoption of the CPD at EU level clearly indicated changes for exports into other EU Member States (however, most products were shipped to Ireland where CE marking was also not obligatory), but it was less obvious if this would also affect their national markets. The lack of published standards made CE marking relatively quickly a theoretical issue and manufacturers and their customers regarded their system of known products ("brand names" or well-known products)[362] or competition on prices as more relevant than specific marks. This has put manufacturers preparing for CE marking at a disadvantage because the resources were spent too early, while on the other hand, the risk for less "advanced" companies remained that without constant monitoring of developments they might react too late. Nevertheless, other activities moved more into the focus of private actors in the UK: A special characteristic of the UK (compared to the other three countries of this study) was that customers had a stronger interest in "social responsibility" and ISO 14000 (or at least ISO 9000) certificates. Other marks were rarely promoted, with CE marking clearly of less importance[363] than the *kitemark* or the BBA certificate.[364] However, it was acknowledged that architects were sometimes giving more precise product specifications, including specific (BBA) certificates, while public authorities were putting more emphasis on CE marking.

362 It was mentioned that specific regionally-used products remained the most used for a large number of craftsman, even when other products exceeded the performance of these "traditional" products. Being familiar with a product still played a major role in accepting or rejecting products for a number of professionals.

363 It was assumed by a number of interviewees that the majority of sales people of larger companies might not even be aware of CE marking.

364 Surprisingly, since BBA certificates were often seen as expensive, the less expensive CE marking was sometimes considered a reasonable alternative.

The importance of familiar products or certificates was also highlighted when it came to the control of markets and competitors – in short: market surveillance. From the manufacturer's point of view the general choice of national, regional and local authorities to use the "fire brigade" approach and also to delegate several responsibilities to individual or company market actors made this part of the construction industry more sensitive to market demands and sanctions if products did not perform accordingly to the manufacturers declarations. Therefore, professional actors were less inclined to trust rigorous monitoring by the authorities to protect the overall trust in the behaviour of all market actors.[365] Instead, the past experience (one's own or the information one got from informal networks)[366] of existing products, the reliability of punctual delivery and getting advice if specific handling was needed was seen as most important for their work. As mentioned above, "brand names" were playing a major role while additional marks (including the BBA certificate[367] and CE marking) were considered more as "commercial" aspects rather than as actually providing much (additional) technical information to any customer[368] (an assumption also made by distributors – highlighting the factor of "being familiar with products" as more important for selecting products by professionals and DIY-enthusiasts).

---

365 However, building regulations and Approved Documents developed by governmental bodies were considered by all interviewees as the most binding framework for all actors.

366 This approach was not only used by architects and contractors but also to an extent by federations of home owners. This information was not seen as "permanent" assumption but as experience that has to be (more or less regularly) checked for its accuracy ("even familiar good products could "go bad").

367 Which still was in all interviews considered as more informative and useful for other actors than CE marking – in particular when giving architects and contractors clear information where and how a product can be used ("extra form of assurance").

368 Here some comments differ significantly to the official position of the UK in the SCC: While the UK delegation with reference to unnecessary burdens for manufacturers was strongly supporting lower classes of attestation of conformity (AoC – class 3 and 4 – declaration of the manufacturer without additional control), some manufacturers highlighted the need of third party control by test and certification bodies (in higher classes of AoC obligatory) for insurance purposes and to improve the trust of their customers in their products. Therefore, additional certificates were considered as necessary market tools and were explicitly mentioned in product advertisements (where one can also find reference to CE marking).

Similar remarks were made by Austrian interviewees that low classes of Attestation of Conformity (self declaration) were more seen as difficulty for an individual manufacturer to know what to declare and how, while higher classes were not only increasing the credibility of a product but also relieved the individual manufacturer by providing a common and comparable format for his declaration.

The role of harmonised European standards as "market instruments" for providing a level playing field was acknowledged, but also that they were just *one* aspect for selling products on the UK market or any national market in the EU. In particular the fact that these standards were extremely complex made them difficult for many *manufacturers* to use to check product performance. Other parties were most likely not able to use them at all. (This seemed to be very accurate, considering that contacts with architects, civil engineers and contractors were reported as rare, and mostly initiated by manufacturers to promote their products)[369]. This "casual attitude of the builders" not only shifted the responsibility for producing *quality* to manufacturers but also to a large extent the task of monitoring the market for "cowboys" within the system. While the (local) *Trading Standard Office* was responsible for market surveillance none of the interviewees could name a case where industry itself brought problems to the attention of the authorities.[370] However, this was seen by most as the most efficient way, because the technical and practical knowledge for identifying problems was in the hands of industry, while authorities were providing "judgement and sanctions".[371]

Manufacturers were also seen as the driving force behind the involvement of the British Standards Institute (BSI) in European standardisation. Some sectors were taking a strong involvement in the standardisation work as guarantee that the European standards were "good" in the sense that existing quality

369 It was in one case even stressed that CE marking was (indirectly) promoted as "quality mark" to make customers aware of it and increasing the demand of CE marking within the sector. This was achieved by putting enough requirements into the standards (of manufacturers) being tested according to a harmonised standard indicated already that the product has been tested for a wide range of performance criteria. Another comment highlighted that it would be too complicated for manufacturers to explain the difference between "quality marks" and "conformity marks" (CE marking) to customers. Therefore, nobody objected if CE marking was perceived as "quality mark".

370 It was also mentioned that the Trading Standard Office is in general financed by local authorities/communities – linking the possibilities of starting investigations, their duration and their completeness to the financial abilities of these communities (see also: Laylock/Graham/Fewings: The effective implementation of the Construction Products Directive (CPD) 1995 p. 122).

371 An interesting argument was provided by an interviewee on the interest of manufacturers to bring a "bad" product to the attention of the authorities: In general it is distributed by the same company that is selling the products of the manufacturer who might consider starting a complaint against the competitor. "Hitting" the competitor would also hit ones own distribution line.

requirements were taken on board and not "lost in translation". [372] Moving to the European level was not so much seen as a "cultural change" at the administrative and technical level – just slower when it came to the frequency of meetings and deadlines for producing final standards ("decisions are so hard to get"). However, the differences started when the requirements of the CPD were introduced by CEN consultants and Guidance Papers. The perception of the Guidance Papers depended on one hand on how closely they were related to open questions for specific product standards ("Guidance Papers were used if nobody had a better idea") and on the other hand, how "theoretical" the discussion became ("Do we need the wide picture to write a simple standard?"). More confusing were changes in the interpretation of the text of these GP or positions taken by CEN consultants or "the Commission" (since these were more indirect information being provided via CEN consultants or the CEN Management Centre), in particular when the individual contacts to the TC changed.

While industry provided the technical expertise, the interest of some sectors participating in standardisation work did not always match their abilities to provide enough experts over a period of several years. Keeping in mind that as long as these experts were not retired (an option that was often used by several industry sectors and national standardisation bodies in the EU to keep the expertise of former employees without splitting their work between standardisation and the work in the company), these experts were "lost" during this time to their companies. Being torn between "different masters" experts were facing two different dilemmas: Too many meetings could reduce the willingness of an employer to spare them for standardisation work (in particular in times of economic difficulties), too few meetings on the other hand did not allow for consistent work. Long gaps between meetings or if experts were changing, the risk became even higher and discussion points would be re-opened and jeopardizing the planned finalisation of a standard.

372 It was stressed that the actual costs for the development of (national or European) standards are very high for all parties involved and only the chance of keeping a certain level of quality (or keeping competitors producing lower quality out of the market) justifies the involvement in the first place.

3.6.2.5 (Private) actors in Austria

National federations have split their work, leaving much of the political tasks to either the Austrian Chamber of Commerce (WKO) or the regional chambers of commerce, while sector specific federations were covering technical issues – like standardisation work. It was also to a large extent their responsibility to provide either additional information for their members (guidance handbooks) or request additional design/use standards developed in ON. In general, there was a certain concern that standardisation work in the mirror committees was not always looking for the most pragmatic solution but adding to requirements of the mandate and to the work in CEN ("gold plating").[373] Via the federations feedback from the experts participating in the TCs in ON was flowing back to the WKO, which gave these federation a stronger position in influencing the content of standards but also provided them with an additional source for information other than WKO meetings (about 1-2 per year) with representatives of the federal ministry and the OIB.

While the information flow to and from ON was considered very good, it was mentioned that information from the BMWA on the work of the SCC (SCC documents and additional comments) did not provide much specific information for the different sectors and was not relevant for their daily work. The lack of progress on market surveillance was seen as a more pressing issue and a major concern for industry. However, it was also mentioned that feedback to the WKO from its members (i.e. for mandates to CEN) was low but might have been dealt within the sector specific federations or specific enterprises.

Closer to the level of specific products, the relevance of *regional* building codes requirements of local customers became more visible and more significant. Several products were produced and distributed locally which gave public and private actors on the regional and local level more weight compared to any input from national bodies or European requirements. That *national requirements* and *national marks* existed was considered as a fact – in particular since most local actors were focused on the building code of the region (*Bundesland*). The important role of the interpretation of the regional building code was closely followed by the experience of planners, contractors and authorities with existing products

373 There was a strong emphasis on more transparency on what requirements were set by the mandate and "what has been added by national actors". Otherwise, the harmonisation is seen as a useful instrument to improve transparency and better communication between different actors.

("brand name"). Specific performance criteria and values were of less interest, since they were considered as given in an existing product (as the performance has been satisfactorily proven by past experience). In particular customers who were building their own homes were interested in very few criteria. Tendering authorities and other commercial actors had a more holistic approach, but they too relied more on known criteria and performance values than actually controlling every criterion and value given with a fact sheet or CE marking. Distributors (covering 80-90% of the transactions between manufacturers and customers) were seen to be even less interested because they lacked the technical background which would help them to put CE marking and the information accompanying it into use ("it has to be there, but nobody knows exactly why – and nobody cares"). Therefore, CE marking was not seen as essential part of consumer interest and (as in the bricks industry) not explicitly highlighted in advertisements or in contacts with customers. However, it was mentioned in a number of interviews with different actors that Austrian actors sometimes lacked an interest in being aware of developments on time ("lack of strategic precaution").

As a smaller neighbour of Germany and therefore being affected by the developments in this country, the intensive use in Germany of the German *Ü-Zeichen* and its promotion by authorities, manufacturers and test laboratories was considered by several interviewees (not only manufacturers) as "inflexibility" of the German system and protection of the interests of specific actors. Reference was made to the more "EU-conform" implementation of the CPD and CE marking in Austria.

But as in Germany, the relevance of CE marking (or other national marks – including the Austrian ÜA and ÜE mark) seemed to lose its relevance at the distribution level. While being aware of the role of CE marking (getting the information via the Chamber of Commerce –WKO), it was seen as an obligation (products have to be CE marked to be distributed to customers – therefore, the first responsibility was with the manufacturers)[374], but not very useful at a practical level – a fact highlighted by the nearly complete lack of interest, ques-

374 It was also mentioned that distributors in general expect and trust their (usual) manufacturers that they do comply with all obligatory requirements, rather than introducing extensive control instruments when receiving and selling products. This seemed not a large risk for distributors because in cases of serious damage caused by flawed products (it was highlighted that these cases were very few in practice, because in most cases damage was caused by wrong application by do-it yourself enthusiasts) *manufacturers* had to provide advice or compensation.

tions of feedback by customers of distributors (on CE marking and any other mark). Here again, past experience with specific products, "brand names" or specific requirements (which would be found on the data sheets provided by the manufacturers) played a much stronger role when selecting products than "external" certificates.

Better contacts between Austrian and German actors were reported from the academic field: Like their German counterparts, Austrian technical universities were sometimes expanding their scope beyond training and research and were also active as certification bodies (Notified Bodies), therefore combining the role as market actors and researchers. Exchange of knowledge and expertise between technical universities was therefore more likely, in particular when universities have specialised in specific aspects of products and product performance. Also similar to the experience of their German colleagues (maybe even stronger) was the reported low interest when trying to provide more information to companies. Here too communication was better between one's own specific group (as Notified Bodies or as technical universities) than improving awareness and communication to other actors. On the other hand, references were made to a different information route: Since several companies were operating in more than one country (or getting their raw materials or components from more than one country), the main offices were often more closely linked to federations (or monitoring developments on EU and national level themselves) and were providing information to all their "daughter companies" and other relevant downstream actors. In particular the close links of Austrian companies to the German market (with more transnational companies active) might have had a positive impact on the quantity and quality of data received by Austrian actors (Nevertheless, the general awareness by Austrian private or public actors was not considered very high).

Besides the Federal ministry and the OIB, the Austrian Standards Institute (ON) was one of the main bodies coordinating the position of interested parties on a technical level linked to specific standards. While all interested parties were allowed to participate, keeping a balance between different interests and interest groups (manufacturers, designers, contractors, bigger companies and SMEs) was considered as a main and also difficult task of ON. Bigger companies, federations and authorities were in general more often represented in TCs than SMEs, architects or civil engineers (who were more interested in design standards and *Eurocodes*). This was partly seen as a result of the abilities of bigger actors to follow developments in standardisation at EU and national level closer than smaller companies. The information flow also depended on individuals acting as interface between ON, federations and their members and their abilities and interests in transmitting information in both directions. Also the awareness of national actors that European standards would influence the national construction sector was still growing. With more and more standards becoming obligatory in the national market, more sectors and companies were now trying to comply within the coexistence period – but not always succeeding. In this situation ON was also facing complaints (unjustified in the view of ON) that the sectors were not informed on time.

However, there seemed to be a difference between the approach and the information flow starting from the Commission's construction unit and CEN and its consultants on one side compared to the previous solely national one on the other: While in the national system, either ON or Austrian (public) bodies were providing binding guidance or positions, more actors were now in a position to define or to interpret targets set down in the mandates to CEN: The Guidance Papers written by the construction unit were seen as mixed blessing. It seemed that they played a relevant role in most discussions in CEN and mirror TCs. On the other hand, there was still room for interpretation and individuals with a more profound knowledge about their content had a major advantage in a discussion – Not always because of their interpretation but because of the *de facto* binding role that the Guidance Papers were perceived to have.[375] "It is written in the GP" sometimes stopped a discussion right there and then. This would not have been a major problem, were it not that sometimes interpretations and the texts of different Guidance Papers or other technical standards were seen as inconsistent. Following one "set of rules" did not necessarily guarantee that the final standard would not be contested based on another interpretation.

It was also seen as difficult if different documents and positions (e.g., mandates, GP) were of a *technical* and a *political* nature. While mandates on EU level and Guidance Papers were not always carefully studied during their development, the practical work showed later that not all requirements could be tackled by technical testing but were more based on "political/administrative" assumptions and goals. In addition, the interpretations by the authors (in particular the construction unit) could change, which could make ongoing work based on previous interpretations redundant.

375 While provided by the Commission only in English, the German DIBt has translated them and is selling them to interested parties – including Austrian actors.

Also a certain “unreliability” of the European system was confusing actors in standardisation: Examples of standards that were contested after their finalisation by national authorities at EU level created a feeling of uncertainty and resignation (“Was the investment in particular standardisation work useful at all?”). Even worse, if these contested (and withdrawn) standards were already referenced in other European standards large parts of finalised standardisation work had to be “reopened” again[376].

In its dual role as standardisation body and as certification body (Notified Body), ON was facing requirements for standards, but also for an equal treatment of products on national markets. National manufacturers or their federations might complain about different starting times of the introduction and use of CE marking within a certain range of products – criticism and complaints that were also directed at the certification body ON. On the other hand, lower levels of attestation of conformity (AoC levels 3 and 4) defined under the CPD, were shifting the responsibility of deciding on quantity and quality of a declaration about the performance of a product (e.g., how factory production control should be performed) completely to manufacturers, and therefore leaving the certification body “outside the loop”.

3.6.2.6 (Private) actors in Poland

Despite the fact, that Poland was not only a *new* Member State of the EU but was also still developing its economic and administrative structure (not only to comply with the CPD), the comments are very similar for private actors in the other three Member States: The focus on buildings made the introduction of a performance based approach of construction products more confusing than providing more practical transparency (“The CPD created a virtual market”). National actors were used as a clear link between products and their use in a building given in national standards or other guidance. However, Poland’s actors were not completely taken by surprise when the CPD was introduced in the national regulatory system because a very similar system was established before joining the

376 This is even more problematic when only ON, EN ON or ISO ON standards are allowed to be used in Austria. Based on this dependency on these standards (not to mention the trust in them by national actors) questions about their reliability and acceptance have a stronger influence than on markets where users could move to other alternatives.

EU[377]. Also larger companies buying Polish manufacturers brought knowledge and experience into the system. Nevertheless, following developments at EU level were seen as a mixed blessing:

The standardisation was taken to the European level, which – while access to CEN TCs was open to all actors – allowed only few actors to participate in these activities – mostly authorities ("scientific officials"). This work was also seen as dominated by stronger actors pushing for more detailed standards (closer to production issues than their intended use) and therefore creating new barriers for other (weaker) actors.

Documents written by the Commission (in particular Interpretative Documents and Guidance Papers – which were all translated into Polish) were considered as partly helpful, but the impression remained that the authors of these documents were only addressing actors of "their own kind" (officials addressing officials, certification bodies only writing for certification bodies) instead of providing information for all actors to follow and to know what they could expect from other actors[378]. However, it was mentioned – after one has put some efforts in studying these documents closely – that the documents could be used by private actors in discussions vis-à-vis public authorities. In these cases, the documents carried considerable weight and were accepted by authorities as reference and providing guidance for all (public and private) actors.

The introduction of CE marking was on one hand seen (and strongly supported) by manufacturers as a possibility to enter other EU markets ("the key to other markets"),[379] on the other hand in contact with other actors (architects, contractors, distributors) CE marking was more seen as an legal obligation: All

377 However, private actors did not consider that national authorities (with the exception of the ITB) were very active in promoting the CPD approach and CE marking. "Being even more liberal than industry", authorities were reportedly avoiding any restrictions harming the growth of the economy, and therefore putting less emphasis on enforcing compliance when it would support the interests of industry (against imports from outside the EU).

378 It was mentioned that federations were involved in drafting national regulation in the past – developments at EU level would put more burden on federations to monitor and follow all developments at this level to retain their position at national level compared to actors on national level (with maybe better links to EU actors and more accurate information).

379 Here the opinions differed between assumptions that SMEs are supporting the introduction of CE marking, their abilities to comply with all requirements, or if they were not "lost in the system". Larger companies (with more resources to adapt) were more optimistic about the general acceptance, while representatives of authorities were more worried that smaller enterprises might have difficulties in identifying if and where the CPD approach is affecting them and to adapt (on time).

downstream users were thought to be aware that products have to be CE marked (with some confusion which ones actually *could* be CE marked within the framework of the CPD) and market surveillance played a role when ensuring compliance, but knowledge rarely went beyond knowledge of the existence of CE marking. Certificates were generally known by architects and contractors but they just demanded that the product was certified. Further checks or additional requests for documentation were rare or non-existent. The perception of CE marking as "quality" mark was wide-spread and even market surveillance inspectors only checked if a CE marking was affixed, but hardly actually controlled products placed on the market.[380]

Also similar to their counterparts in other Member States, customers of construction products were seen as having a specific trust in manufacturers, suppliers and products they were familiar with or which had already a good reputation ("brand name", known performance of the products, price, availability/ delivery of products). A characteristic of the Polish approach is the strong emphasis on certificates in general: Products are promoted not only by reference to their technical performance (in technical data sheets or price sheets). All information is accompanied by reference either to the CE marking (even with detailed information – e.g., used on hENs) or another certificate indicating that the product has been following specific assessment procedures.

3.6.3 Certification Bodies/Notified Bodies

As an economic actor, their contacts to downstream actors – even beyond manufacturers – were more often mentioned. Based on their high expertise on certification issues, they were (next to the technical institutes DIBt, BRE, OIB and ITB) one of the major contact points for most downstream (architects, contractors) users to get clarification and advise how to use CE marking (or other marks) most effectively. In particular compared to responses from CEN TCs where the focus on manufacturing is strong, Notified Bodies reported more requests for clarification but also ranked these practical users higher as relevant contacts, and were not that pessimistic about the overall knowledge of these

380 Like their counterparts in the other three Member States, manufacturers were in particular worried about imports from China, having a *very* similar CE mark affixed (which is supposed to be read as "Chinese Exports"), which allowed several (even inferior – but anyway wrongly declared) products to "slip through the net" and be used by downstream users.

downstream users about CE marking (but in many cases still did not consider them sufficiently well informed).

As market actors, Notified Bodies were also monitoring the market for illegal competition and were (after manufacturers) the second group alerting authorities (and the SCC) about the incorrect use of CE marking. However, like manufacturers, their experiences with national market surveillance authorities were rather mixed. Sometimes the lack of information on national, regional or local level was seen as reason why authorities on these levels were rather reluctant to tackle the issue (on the other hand – supporting this assumption – it was also mentioned, that market surveillance authorities have shown a great interest *if* information was provided – in particular if specific and practical issues related to their work were addressed). Less interest was received by building authorities, which was partly seen as a question of manpower but also of technical qualifications. Larger public bodies (with enough resources and engineers in their ranks) were better able to take additional information into account, but the fact that in many cases building control was delegated to local authorities with a small staff (maybe not even a sole employee delegated to construction issues), made product certification less relevant for their day-to-day tasks. In general, only few cases of wrongly-marked CE construction products have been reported to the GNB by its members, but it was assumed that more might have been found and national authorities have been informed by a Notified Body, but no information has been transmitted to other Notified Bodies (which is not absolutely required – but was seen as making the "real" situation more transparent).[381]

381 Even more difficult for Notified Bodies: manufacturers are not always demanding *one* certificate for their products, but are carefully planning where they want to put a specific product on the market. Products for national markets where regulatory requirements are usually high will be assessed according to the highest Attestation of Conformity (AoC) class indicated in the harmonised European standard and covering more performance characteristics of a product. But if another product is foreseen for sale in Member States where less stringent requirements are in place, the customer of a Notified Body also aims for the less expensive AoC class or testing for fewer characteristics. The confusion starts when the same product is tested according to different AoC classes or a different number of characteristics. Since some of the classes also demand the control of the production line by a Notified Body (in the CPD called "factory production control" – FPC), and bigger companies are manufacturing their products in different countries, reducing costs in some countries might be an interesting alternative to having a product always assessed to the highest AoC class required.

On the other hand, it was also mentioned that bigger companies aim for higher AoC classes to impose higher requirements on their competitors. Here the mix between the use of

The task of Notified Bodies under the Construction Products Directive vis-à-vis "demands of the market" and national requirements was seen as one of the major difficulties. On one hand, national marks guaranteed compliance with the requirements of building regulations ("*accepted* for use") which was more than CE marking could ever provide ("*fit* for use" – a seemingly minor but in fact significant difference). Trying to compensate for these different needs for information, Notified Bodies were sometimes developing "Application Documents" at national level to bridge the gap between the information provided with CE marking (performance of the product) and its "translation" into the requirements of national or regional building codes. On the other hand, their role as certification bodies sometimes encountered competition by "quality marks" introduced by other actors – manufacturers or distributors. Additional performance criteria and claims that products were fulfilling them, did not only made a CE certificate less interesting for users, it also challenged the role of Notified Bodies as competent bodies when assessing products (in particular if a specific claim was not even "backed up" by an assessment of an independent body but consisted only of the declaration of a manufacturer or distributor). It was also questioned if these declarations were in fact "market demands" or more "marketing tools" to impress customers.

Feedback on the experience with national acceptance of CE marked products and market surveillance indicated that CE marking was as such (even positively) accepted – but its practical use often depended on more than the "official" acceptance.

- Germany was seen (in the group of these four Member States) as the one that was relatively openly "restricting" the use of CE marked products. Additional requirements – covered in the German *Ü-Zeichen* – were commonly accepted in the German market and were *de facto* neutralising the concept of market access of CE marked products. In addition, it was mentioned that certification bodies (Notified Bodies under the CPD) have difficulties being accepted by the German Approval Body as certification body for the German *Ü-Zeichen.*[382]

CE marking as "conformity" mark and a "quality" mark (as "marketing tool") becomes more visible, intentionally used by market actors.

382 This complaint was used by several actors on different occasions and repeated in the interviews. However, clear evidence of discrimination could not been provided.

- The UK generally accepted CE marking and it was acknowledged that most public and private actors relevant for providing information on building and product requirements were mentioning and highlighting the role of CE marking. However, it was noted that the costs for the approval of construction works could depend on which mark has been attached to the product – making the mark of the BBA sometimes more accepted – and therefore: less expensive, while more scrutiny was exercised for CE marked products (which increased the costs for approval)[383].
- In Austria the role of regional or local authorities and also of different federations (*Kammern, Verbände*) was considered as playing a strong role when accepting products in construction works. Leaving building control to local or regional authorities has also shifted the burden to them to accept or reject products used. The above mentioned difficulties of providing or recruiting enough technical expertise could reduce the acceptance of products to the "well known" ones. Federations on the other hand were providing (technical) guidance to their members which could also better reflect the experience with *familiar* (national) products than a thorough assessment of products *available* on the market.
- Information on the situation in Poland was more difficult to get and it was not clear how efficient the system of market surveillance operates or how much the Polish B-mark has actually been withdrawn with the introduction of CE marking. However, it was stated that while Poland (of the four MS) had the most developed market surveillance system in place, wrong declarations of performance were still slipping through the net.

3.7 Conclusion at national level

Reaching now the level between "Brussels" as the *policy making level* and the "construction site" (where the *practical use of products* and its performance in a building plays the most important role), the "national level" could– at a first glance – be considered just as an interface between the other two levels. Looking closer, the picture changes: Structures at the national level were (in most cases)

383 On the other hand, it was mentioned by an Approval Inspector in the UK that CE marking is rarely seen, because all actors considered that a BBA certificate confirms compliance with the Building Regulations (in England, Wales, Scotland and Northern Ireland).

not only older than the one at EU level, all relevant instruments and the distribution of tasks between all actors on this level have been established long before the national implementation of the CPD became relevant. At this level, building laws and building codes were the most relevant reference documents for all actors involved. In addition, based on established requirements and working structures these actors have developed national networks and markets that were in several cases different to the ones established "in Brussels". Therefore, orientations, values and procedures developed over decades on national level have formed the perceptions and working structures of national actors. This provided them with certain security on how other actors might react and how this would be dealt with within the national system. Since national markets were still the main reference for most actors (even if some actors are covering more than one)[384], following the rules and procedures of these national environments was still dominating the roles and actions of EU/national actors. The European system on the other hand was seen as less clear – not necessarily because it was less transparent, but because most actors were less experienced with it and the outcome was therefore less predictable for them. Several comments in interviews have shown that actors had relatively accurate assumptions about the positions, potentials and limitations of other actors (if compared to the self-descriptions of these actors in interviews) in the *national* environment (professions, upstream or downstream users). Even distributors – considered by most actors as not really aware or interested in the discussion around CE marking – had a very realistic picture about other actors and their tasks as intermediate link between manufacturers and "end users".

In these national environments, national actors who were also operating at EU level have to present decisions made "in Brussels" to downstream actors, to get useful feedback from them and to transmit it back to the European level. But roles and tasks were often changing after some actors were "re-entering" the national level, or at least their importance changed. In addition, new actors with different interests and incentives for cooperating with EU (or national) approaches were appearing. This gap between different systems of control and trust (at EU and national level) will be the main focus of this chapter.

384 While some manufacturers and other market actors might be active in several EU Member States, they have (if no harmonisation on EU level has taken place) adapted to different national requirements. Therefore, they *are* transnational but at the same time their different national *dependences* are operating within a given national framework.

3.7.1 ... and still: the "power" of the few?

Starting with actors whose task *is* in fact monitoring and sanctioning, the number of actors in public authorities has partly significantly changed: Instead of the Commission services, national ministries have taken over the role as coordinators and as interpreters of the national laws implementing the CPD vis-à-vis other national authorities and private actors. Like the Commission services – and here in particular the construction unit – this competence was carefully guarded, but was facing sometimes competing interpretations from other actors, closely involved in the decision making process: The technical institutes (DIBt, BRE, OIB, ITB), supporting the national ministries at EU level and in their national environments, were still to a large extent in an advisory role, but their importance as providers and interpreters of information has significantly increased. The four national technical institutes were also the most influential actors (following here the top-down approach) which were "multiplying" information coming from the EU level. While national ministries were still closer to "one-man-operations" when it came to the implementation of the CPD, information has to be spread to more individuals in the institutes dealing with different technical aspects of buildings and construction products. The fact that these institutes were often sending experts to different committees and working groups of the construction unit (e.g., the PG or topic specific expert groups) helped to get as much information as possible from different sources and to have more experts with "first-hand knowledge" within their own organisation. Still, the actual number of individuals working on CPD issues was still relatively small and depended on the internal structure for information to be distributed. The "institutionalised" German approach made participation in the exchange of information more "obligatory" and seemed to have positively influenced the interest of actors to participate and therefore also influenced quality and quantity of information provided upstream and downstream. The same seemed to be the case in the Polish approach when dealing with downstream *authorities*, but less so with private actors. The UK and Austrian interfaces between the EU level and the national level depended more on voluntary cooperation. The individuals were providing the framework of discussion and exchange of information but putting less emphasis or *indirect* "pressure" on other actors to join. Still the number of individuals working in these four institutes was rather small. In addition, the general focus (including the distribution of resources) was in many cases not on the CPD or CE marking but often on more current developments at EU and national level – like energy efficiency or "sustainability", keeping more resources on these topics than on CE marking (which was in particular in Germany and the UK but also partly in Austria considered as "rather well known by now").

Being responsible for "translating" general regulatory and administrative requirements into technical terms became more essential, because at this level more actors (architects, contractors and manufacturers) were close to the *practical technical work* of designing and constructing and their need for information as well as their feedback was more in the field of *technical implementation* than *regulatory interpretation* of given laws. The position of these four bodies was additionally strengthened by their role as EOTA members and by providing and cooperating on European Technical Approvals for manufacturers also being in an interaction with economic benefits for both parties.[385] Here they changed their profile from being (neutral) providers of information for public authorities and private actors to being *market `btors* themselves. By becoeing a market actor, the int%rest in providing information on CE marking depended also on their involvement in promoting and using national marks, and the role they gave to these national marks. If the link to national marks was already close, CE marking became only an addition to the nathonal approach but did not beplace it. Also their links to the national standardisation bodies made them more aware of developments in this field than national/federal or regional (*Länder*) ministries – developments that might have strong effects on manufacturers, planners and contractors. All of these activities were placing these institutes closer to the downstream actors (and allowing for more practical feed-

385 However, their role as "national certifiers" has partly changed: In the past certification bodies at national level issued certificates indicating that a product was fit for certain uses in the country and, possibly also indicating that it responded to certain regulatory national requirements. Thereafter the certification procedure also contained one or the other form of the continuous surveillance of the product. This was performed in a one–stop-shopp principle usually by the same body. Under the CPD the "certification", as exercised by certification bodies, meant something different: "only" conformity to a TS; there is now a clear division between TS writers and certifiers, which usually did not exist at the national level (this is why so many Approval Bodies were still considered "certifiers" at national level). This is to some extend a logical development because an ETA (and related CE marking) does not mean that the product is universally fit to satisfy all national requirements due to the variety in regulatory national obligations; at the level of the non-standardised products this shift in responsibilities for the certifiers and in the certifying processes is usually an issue of utmost confusion for various actors.

back) but were also demanding more efforts to keep these different tasks and interests apart.

With the exception of Poland, where a strong market surveillance system and a strict top-down-approach made downstream authorities (at least in theory) obligatory recipients of information on the European approach for construction products and CE marking, downstream authorities in the other three Member States were not showing very strong interest in these issues. An explanation for the two "older" Member States would be that "everything is known by now" and downstream actors are already used to these requirements. However, this assumption was contradicted by statements from some of the downstream authorities and in particular from other private actors.

Looking at federations of manufacturers, the task of assessing information on EU level was left to European federations (and hardly used at national level) or to the same individuals active at EU level were also distributing information at national level. The larger number of federations at national rather than at European level (in Germany, the UK and Austria) did increase the number of recipients of information, but in most cases this did not necessarily result in more or better feedback to the individuals acting as provider and "interpreters". It also seemed that the high level of cooperation *between* federations at EU level was not always copied at national level. Exchange of information was not impossible – and depended on the specific sectors in question – but in general a stronger competitive approach characterised the situation in the four Member States. The corporate system in Germany and Austria provided a more "neutral" platform for exchange in the coordination meetings organised by national authorities (see: "Actors at EU level"), and in particular German actors mentioned the importance of a balanced approach. However, this approach seemed less corporate in nature than "institutionalised" (like the coordination meetings initiated by public bodies), allowing for monitoring other actors rather than creating more (voluntary) cooperation.

While harmonised European standards and rules for using them for certification were developed in organisations at EU level, national Notified Bodies and national standardisation bodies (NSB) became the main if not the only contact or reference points for most national actors. Since the CPD (and its national implementations) gave in particular Notified Bodies (and the bodies that were evaluating their competences as Notified Bodies – the Approval Bodies – which were in German the DIBt, in Austria the OIB and in Poland the ITB) a strong position vis-à-vis national actors (in particular manufacturers), this position has attracted significant interest of national certification bodies. However, the lack of active members in the Group of Notified Bodies and even the lack of continuous contacts with the large number of Notified Bodies raise the question if the number of well-informed receivers, interpreters and distributors of information had really increased at national level or if only the number within a virtual administrative system had increased.

The national standardisation bodies on the other hand have most likely naturally increased the number of actors (at least in general) familiar with the CPD and CE marking for construction products. Nominating experts to CEN TCs, creating mirror committees at national level, or working on design and "implementation" standards, the national standardisation bodies needed a large number of internal and external experts to cover all these tasks. On the other hand, the same individuals could be active at both the EU and the national level, and therefore the *real* addition in interested and knowledgeable individuals still seemed to be rather low. In most aspects, the NSBs were facing the same environment as CEN when it came to expert input: Providing experts at national and European level also was always straining the resources of enterprises and federations (which might in particular reduce their willingness and their abilities to be active at the *European* level).

3.7.2 ... the real input of the few ...

One can safely assume that (like at EU level) at the national level of national/federal authorities and national federations, only few individuals were interpreting and distributing information on construction products and CE marking to upstream and downstream users ("corporate actors"). This was partly due to the small number of officials or representatives of economic and technical actors working on this level, but also the competition with other EU policies (e.g., energy efficiency, "sustainability" or "accessibility") which attracted the interest of more actors and was more directly affecting the day-to-day work of more professionals in this sector than the assessment of construction products or CE marking. Another reason for the lack of interest (besides the long time since the (theoretical) introduction of CE marking) seemed to be the stronger focus of all actors on *buildings and civil engineering work* – covered by national or regional building codes. While Interpretative Documents (see: Actors on EU level) were supposed to bridge the gap between the requirements of the CPD and requirements on buildings and engineering works, when the first harmonised standards appeared these documents were already partly outdated and also reported as too long and too theoretical to be actually used by downstream actors. Lacking the clear link to practical questions related to construction works, it depended much on the interest and abilities of individuals acting as interface between the EU and national level if and how information was distributed and how much downstream actors could be motivated to react.

While introducing national or regional building laws and building codes, the main differences between the EU and national approaches on requirements for construction products became more obvious. They were highlighting the practical and political priorities of *(other)* national actors, which were becoming more important at this level to influence the positions and reactions of purely national actors and the ones representing interests at EU level:

At EU level, all possible ("intended") uses for a specific construction product have to be taken into consideration and have to be covered in a harmonised European standard. Discussions between authorities at EU level (the construction unit and MS authorities) and to a certain extent the text of the Interpretative Documents and the Guidance Papers indicate that at EU level not only *known* uses but also *potential* uses were seen as relevant ("we don't know how manufacturers in other MS might produce them, designers might include them in their planning and contractors will install them"). As seen at EU level, the struggle between experience (by CEN TCs) and assumptions of "worst case scenarios" (by MS authorities) was not only keeping actors at EU level busy, but it has also affected the acceptance and publication of harmonised European standards.[386]

National building codes, national standards and technical guidance documents on the other hand were not dealing with such complex assumptions. Based on common training, common knowledge and common experience, the complexity was reduced at national level to agreed practices. The actors at this level did not have to cover *all* eventualities but only risks that seemed reasonable in the given national environment (e.g., code of practice, "everybody knows how this has to be done"). Building codes, technical documents and technical standards could (partly) refrain from addressing specific scenarios because they trusted all

386 However, while the need of authorities for covering all potential risks seemed to have influenced negative assumptions about the quality of European standards, the national representatives of the SCC have also very often (thanks to feedback on national level) acted very competent when assessing these standards on technical level – a task for which the construction unit was completely lacking resources.

actors that they would operate only within the agreed framework (referring to the "technically competent" and "workmanlike manner" in which planning and building works have to be carried out). In addition, in all four national frameworks planning, installation and product standards were tightly interwoven (sometimes all aspects were even covered in one standard) with technical guidance – and sometimes even the texts of the national and regional laws – closely linked to (national) standards in a complementary way. These national systems were clearly *building oriented.* It was also mentioned by several interviewees in different professional fields that the focus on planning and construction works instead of products was based on practical experience that problems in finished buildings were more often caused by design flaws or incorrect installation (or use of materials) than by the product and its quality[387].

This observation raises the question again of the use of CE marking for downstream actors (as consumers of products being put on the market). As market instrument, its use seemed to be more in the *exceptional* case of a product entering another national market for the first time, not so much for the day-to-day needs of architects, contractors and controlling authorities. But even then, professional actors were looking for information linked to the technical requirements set down in daily practice and building codes. These "interpretation costs" were seen to be shifted to them with the introduction of CE marking which increased the complexity instead of reducing it – with the rather rarely-experienced advantage of selecting new products. An indication of this "lack of practical relevance" might be that downstream authorities or market actors were rarely reported for asking for advice or guidance or for providing feedback on their experience.

This left public and private actors at the "interface level" – in particular the DIBt, the BRE, the OIB and the ITB – in the difficult position of having to bridge the gap between the CPD and the needs of actors closer or directly involved in construction works by providing guidance (and translations of documents). In general, at national level, they were more familiar with the different actors with whom they had to interact. Established networks and sometimes even long-term contacts not only facilitated communication between actors, it was also easier to know about potential resources in one's own organisation and those of other actors. As mentioned before, the technical institutes were becoming more important at national level as focus for information net-

387 See as example: http://www.abcmeldpunt.nl/.

works of technical professionals, leaving national ministries more with the role of interpreter of legal issues and the organisation within the national administrative framework (e.g., competences at different levels). For the two Member States with a federal structure, the quality of the networks established by the national ministries and the technical institutes differed even more significantly since the German DIBt and the Austrian OIB were also important actors for regional building authorities (and according to the feedback of several actors) the most important – if not the only – sources of information and guidance.

The additional level of CEN allowed all actors to work on two levels to "correct" assumed or real errors in national or European standards. Either by reopening some questions on the solutions provided in national standards in the European forum of a CEN TC or by challenging solutions found in CEN TCs in the mirror committees established in the national standardisation bodies. Bigger actors were often active at both levels, smaller ones were concentrating their resources at one level where they would think that their position was more likely to be accepted and included in a technical standard. In both cases, national standardisation bodies were providing the interface and therefore remained in a strong position within the framework of the CPD. But neither the discussion in a national standardisation body nor in CEN necessarily clarified the "added value" of CE marking becoming more attractive for downstream users (or – in the worst case – defending it against criticism by other national actors).

At the same time, the "interface" actors were the target for demands of "translating" or even "adjusting" the CPD approach of CE marking to national requirements – which should reflect "business as usual" at national level as much as possible. Here national approaches differed significantly at the level of national/federal authorities and federations (see below). In all cases the CPD approach was "overshadowed" by other (EU or national) policies, national building codes and specific technical interests which left the CPD and CE marking a "sideshow" in the eyes of downstream users and therefore also affected the position and interest of "the few" to promote CE marking at national and regional level – and in most cases excluded the local level as being too difficult to reach.

In this complex situation several national authorities have found a way of keeping their own image intact vis-à-vis other *national* actors, even when facing criticism about the CPD approach and CE marking: In some cases they were downplaying their role as "interfaces", and in particular their role as codeciding actors (in the SCC) giving the impression that they were "defending" interests of national actors. In presentations of their role the emphasis could also be shifted to only "transmitting" decisions made by "the Commission". In both approaches the own contributions (or responsibilities) were rather "downplayed". However, while this tactic seems to be solely for "self-preservation" it keeps the role of these actors as "neutral" or even supportive, which provides this individual in general with enough trust to present the specific national positions at upstream levels. Being entrusted with support of (critical) national actors, the power of selecting which issues should be brought forward at EU level and how they should be presented on this level remained in the hands of these few individuals. In many cases this allowed the actor to present positions in a balanced – and often less aggressive – way when arriving at EU level, which made it easier for other actors at EU level to react in a constructive way to the national input. While these changes were nevertheless noticed at national level ("it sounds different in Brussels") the competence of the "interface" actors remained intact and was keeping the communication lines open in both directions.

3.7.3 ... and the output

At this first level downstream the committees and working groups at EU level, information was clearly received and the knowledge of "purely" national actors (who were confirming several positions of national actors as interfaces between the EU and the national level) about the CPD and CE marking was still relatively complete. However, they have shown much more scepticism about the usefulness of information developed at EU level for downstream actors (their own members – individual companies, architects or local authorities): The Interpretative Documents and the Guidance Papers were more seen as documents useful for EU and national *officials* to focus on and find agreement ("written by civil servants *for* civil servants"), while the practical use for downstream users outside public administrations was often questioned. In particular the lack of clear guidance made it difficult even for the main target groups (technical specification writers in national standardisation bodies, EOTA members and Notified Bodies) to extract useful information for practical questions or even explaining sufficiently the roles of actors created by or working within the framework of the CPD. This left much of the interpretation work to these bodies, but also to public administrations that had to give a "national" interpretation. More often, it seemed that the documents were used more for a "later check" if the chosen approach was in compliance with these documents (therefore a "reinterpretation" to make the guidance fit with the solution) than using them as important guiding documents. But no matter how much importance these documents were given by this first level of "purely" national actors – these documents did not go beyond this small community. Being considered as too big and too complex, it was assumed that first downstream actors would not have the time to read them,[388] and their complexity would even harm the acceptance of the CE marking approach.

More (practical) guidance was provided on websites or specific documents of technical bodies and federations, and it was obvious that some have put much effort in making this guidance as practical as possible (e.g., using practical examples, providing a step-by-step approach). However, the general trend was clearly moving from pro-actively informing interested parties (which was often done years ago, after the implementation of the CPD, but unfortunately also years before the first harmonised standards could be used as practical examples) to providing information on demand. So far, most interviewees (authorities or market actors) could not claim that there was a strong interest in that information by downstream users. CE marking (according to the interpretation of the interviewees) was either well enough known not to cause additional questions – or not relevant enough for manufacturers and users to bother too much with details ("they are just affixed on the product and everybody is happy").

One interesting aspect should also be mentioned at this level when moving from an international environment where language skills are considered essential and expected from all actors, to the national level, where experience with foreign languages to an extent where even small nuances are noted and correctly interpreted can be less taken for granted: Industry actors and engineers were supposed to understand in general requirements laid down in English – keeping in mind that several documents have been translated in Germany by the DIBt and were also available in Austria and Poland. Civil servants on the other hand were not only required to "get the big picture" but to make *legally binding decisions* based on the documents available (in English, or German or Polish). Here the risk of misinterpretation played a stronger role and was strengthening the position of "upstream" public bodies, but it reduced the chance that downstream authorities (e.g., local authorities responsible for market surveillance) would risk making

388 In addition, specific terms or phrases have been developed by actors working with the CPD, which have been used in documents produced on EU level ("EU jargon"), which were also considered unhelpful to users outside the few representative working with the CPD on a regular basis.

decisions in a field where even national authorities and "the Commission" might have different interpretations.

Being closer to the practical effects of developments at EU level, national actors were not only in a more important position to affect the perception of downstream actors, they were also closer to the *reactions* of downstream actors. Since downstream actors were practically in all cases not involved in the decision making process at EU level, they had only the final outcome as a basis for their perceptions and reactions on these input from the EU (and partly national) level. This included that problems at EU level were seen as more critical and caused more reluctance in putting too much trust into the CPD scheme: Standards contested, amended or withdrawn after their official publication have not only caused confusion but have also raised doubts about investing in adaptation at an early stage. Confusion about the competence of Notified Bodies (not only at a technical level but also in cases where technical specifications were available but no Notified Body was officially notified or accepted) added to this dissatisfaction. Keeping in mind that investing in *trust* in the CPD scheme includes investment in *monetary terms* for a large number of actors, even a small number of drawbacks experienced (or even only being informed about them by other actors) could create a negative perception. While the national scheme might not be seen as perfect, the "investment" in it has already taken place and includes fewer risks of losses in money, resources and trust.

3.7.4 Technical standards, CE marking and other marks: "market instruments" or practical instruments for the construction sector?

Technical standards can without any doubt be considered as one of the most important instruments for actors on this level. Standards (like at EU level) were always seen as an instrument giving the "skeleton" of regulatory requirements the "flesh" of specific technical definitions and technical values to be achieved. They were also (again: like at EU level) a possibility for manufacturers (and for product standards much less for designers or contractors) to influence the final scope of requirements they would have to face in product production and product performance.

One cannot claim that standardisation work in national standardisation bodies was always closer to the needs of their final users (designer, contractors, tendering or controlling authorities), but they reflected more the national environment and (voluntary or informal) agreements between national actors. Therefore, they provided more "security" for national actors, because their strengths and weaknesses were better known. Based on that knowledge, it was easier for different actors to compensate in practice for any "disadvantages" created by these standards (e.g.: which part is relevant, which part has to be fulfilled and which part is most likely never checked by building or planning control at all). What has been mentioned repeatedly was the use of (national) standards to show and protect high performance of national manufacturers (however, these performance criteria were in many cases defined by the manufacturers themselves and depended on where they considered the performance of their products better than of their competitors). Standardisation work could be considered not only as codifying existing practice and performance requirements but also as instruments for excluding (national or external) competition.[389] Based on national agreements of performance parameters and values, fulfilling the requirements of national standards was generally seen as protection against liability claims at a later stage. If needed, additional (national) certificates could provide even a better position vis-à-vis authorities and customers.

Not surprisingly, the main criticism against harmonised European standards highlighted that harmonised European standards and CE marking were not covering – and therefore not harmonising – some of the criteria and information downstream users need ("only one part of the system"). In particular not providing assurance for the safe use of products was considered by some national authorities but also by architects and contractors as missing very relevant information. Also manufacturers supported this claim, but they were more concerned with a lack of differentiation between the *qualities* of products, because "everybody could get a CE marking". Not denying the need for comparable performance values or the fact that the European standards have in some cases removed errors that were to be found in previous national standards, the market value of harmonised European standards and CE marking was for most interviewees not seen as significant ("CE marking is not absolutely wrong – but what to do with it?"). In at least one case CE marking was even "pepped up" as a quality mark to make it more attractive for customers. But not only the fact that

389 While interviewees of national standardization bodies stressed their efforts to provide a balanced playing field for all actors, they also acknowledged that larger companies had more resources to participate in standardization work and could therefore also strongly influence the content of technical documents and standards.

CE marking was not directly helping to identify "good" from " bad" products was seen as problem by manufacturers – since national authorities mostly neglected market surveillance competitors could easily use CE markings without a high risk of facing negative consequences (a problem which is also true for national quality marks).

It seemed that in general CEN has achieved the goal of removing (national) standards as instruments of market exclusion by presenting a framework on what product information has to be provided and the necessary format for making it comparable. However, standardisation in all four Member States was also aiming at reducing the complexity of the information provided to customers ("it has fulfilled the requirements of the standard – therefore, the product will not be rejected by the authorities"). For nearly all interviewees this could not be achieved by European standards; neither could CE marking provide more security for planners and contractors against liability claims. This brought additional quality marks into the system. They existed before, but according to several comments, demand for these marks increased, after one mark – CE marking – became obligatory. From that moment on, starting with the question "Do I need CE marking?", marks became more relevant to show the positive performance of ones own products, and to compensate customers for the "loss" of trust in their products which was provided previously by national standards ("CE marking creating its own competition").

But the need for additional certification seemed to be more complex than just being caused by a different approach as presented in harmonised European standards: Practically all representatives of manufacturers, architects and contractors agreed that relationships between producers and users of construction products depended significantly on previous positive experience ("brand names") with the product performance (no later damage and therefore liability claims and repair work – "quality means fewer complaints/repairs – therefore quality marks were more useful to keep everybody's mind at rest."), punctual delivery and additional information if using the product was causing problems. Also public authorities could not provide any data (if available at all – since market surveillance rarely existed) of significant numbers of claims of wrongfully-declared performance values or faulty products. Finally, most interviewees (including bigger property owners) thought that most damage in buildings was not caused by faulty products but by incorrect installation.

But if products did not seem to be a major problem for the safety of construction works or their durability, why is there still this strong insistence for national actors to use additional certification? There are several explanations at national level:

- The construction sector was rather conservative when dealing with new approaches[390]. The assurance of acceptance of products tested according to a (national) standard by national, regional or local authorities reduced the complexity of communication between manufacturers, contractors and authorities. This situation has been reestablished (at least in theory) by introducing or increasing the use of quality marks[391];
- Still *national markets* and *national networks* were more relevant to all actors in the sector, which supported maintaining or even strengthening national approaches because they were providing more security for all actors;
- CE marking was (and still is) rather unknown by downstream actors, or just used to fulfill the letter of the law but not the spirit;
- CE marking was (and still is) not seen as providing any real added value in the communication between actors at national, regional or local level and was therefore rather ignored;

It should be added that none of the interviewees could provide any figures on how often manufacturers wanted to enter a new national market and if and where they were seriously blocked. This does not indicate that this is not happening, but the problem remains that there is a gap between individual cases reported to European or national authorities and federations and a reliable empirical overview. There is also no data available on how often designers and contractors have decided to try new (foreign) products.

---

390 This was a commonly-shared assumption from actors in public administrations and federations. However, it was also highlighted that the small differences in prices (of products on the market and therefore leaving practically no flexibility of prices vis-à-vis one's customers) makes also wrong choices of products (cheaper at the beginning but expensive for maintenance or repairs) a significant risk that is avoided as often as possible by all economic actors.

391 Independently if it was introduced or strengthened by market actors (mostly in the UK and Austria) or by public authorities (Germany).

3.7.5 National approaches

Despite the fact that **Germany** is the "oldest" Member State in this study and has (at least in theory) a headlong start in growing accustomed to adapting to developments at EU level, a first glance at the German system created the impression that in the field of construction products public and private actors have made less efforts to introduce the European approach (compared to the other three countries in the study) but have focused on "reinterpreting" European input into the existing national system. No matter if one looked at the information provided by the DIBt or industry federations (see: Actors at EU level; Actors at national level), CE marking was presented as *additional* information while the *Ü-Zeichen* was the most relevant mark for any professional user to accept and use construction products. Therefore, not only actors in decision-making positions have agreed on this German mark for accepting products in construction works, a common position presented in publications and websites provides downstream users with information referring to *Ü-Zeichen* as the really relevant mark.

At second glance however, the picture slightly changes: The discrepancy between the acceptance of CE marking and the *de facto* insistence by all actors on additional *Ü-Zeichen* was caused by combining two steps which were separated in the systems of the other three Member States (and most other Member States in the EU): The first step was the *accessibility of a national market*, which was not contested by German actors. The second step however was linking products allowed on the market with *providing security for its users* against later law suits. The above-mentioned interest of authorities, designers and contractors in avoiding later liability claims on one hand and keeping to a minimum the costs for assessing a product for the intended use on the other hand, made the *Ü-Zeichen* for these actors more relevant in the practical environment of planning and constructing a building than a more abstract conformity mark. While the other three Member States have more clearly separated these two steps– and have therefore also separated the different actors affected by CE marking on one hand and the technical requirement of actual construction works on the other – the approach of getting consensus of a large number of actors ("collective actors") which is characteristic for the German system included already at an early stage representatives of downstream users who are affecting the perception of the use of CE marking and the solutions finding process to fit the European approach into the known national system. Therefore, German actors introducing the CPD approach at national level (be it that they are active at EU *and* national level or on national level only) were facing demands that were not necessarily *contradicting* the goals of CE marking but nevertheless highlighting its limitations, and had to find a way to combine the requirements of actors at EU and national level – which resulted in keeping the German national approach as untouched as possible and shifting the "translation costs" (in both directions) to the "interfaces" between these two levels – on the technical level mostly to the DIBt.

This approach created two characteristics that were more prominent in Germany than in the other three Member States: The acceptance of the intended use of a product was shifted to an authority. This removed the *responsibility* from manufacturers to a certain extent when declaring its intended use to their customers. It also provided downstream users with the assurance of a public body – closely linked to controlling authorities at regional level (and therefore providing an assessment which would be highly unlikely to be challenged by other authorities) – and removed insecurity when selecting and installing a product. On the other hand, the weak point of this approach was the clear and *de facto explicit* focus on the German *Ü-Zeichen*. None of the actors at national (authority and federation) level were mentioning the acceptance of other marks as equivalent, and were therefore creating the presumption that only *Ü*-marked products *can* be used. Here the security aspect of the German approach seemed to neutralize not only the CPD approach but also innovative approaches and the selection of products that have not been through the *Ü*-marking procedure.

Actors in the **United Kingdom** had the advantage that CE marking was not considered as obligatory in the official interpretations and therefore left the choice of investing in "interpreting" the use and added value of CE marking to federations, but often also to individual companies. The actors in the UK seemed to be the ones most used to different approaches and therefore they were also more flexible when accepting new ones. However, here too the main interest of all actors was *security* provided by declarations of manufacturers – not only on the product performance as such but also on the proper installation and acceptance of these products for specific uses. National marks (i.e. the BBA certificate or *kitemark*) did not lose their appeal. On the contrary, they were still useful instruments for communication if new products were introduced and promoted to architects and designers. Since the coordination and interaction between actors in the UK seemed to be less "institutionalized" and more initiated on a case-by-case basis, agreements across several sectors were less relevant and left the interpretation and use of CE marking and other marks more to sectors or individual companies than to a centralised common position.

When introducing the CPD approach and CE marking, **Austria** was starting with copying the German approach, but moved soon to a scheme that very much separated the market instrument "CE marking" from specific building requirements laid down in regional building codes. While the problem of providing *security* for downstream users remained the same as in Germany, there might be two (complementary) explanations for the different Austrian approach: One is based on the observations of a number of interviewees that feedback from downstream authorities and users was harder to get (the "corporate actor" scheme existed also in Austria but in the field of construction it did not reach the level of cooperation and "institutionalisation" as in Germany), and while information was distributed to the next levels in the communication flow, it was more difficult to see how much it was used and incorporated in the day-to-day work of public and private actors. In fact, it seems that in particular practical users (see the "construction site" level) met the introduction of CE marking rather with indifference and therefore did not consider the same problems as relevant (or relevant enough) to initiate similar "translation" activities as in Germany.

Another explanation for developing a different approach to the German one would reflect the stronger dependency of Austrian market actors on exporting products and services – traditionally with a strong focus on the German market. CE marking as "passport" for entering market had more appeal for actors who were facing a rather small national market. In addition, the strong emphasis of German actors on the German *Ü-Zeichen* (seen as a *barrier to trade* by Austrian actors) seemed to be another incentive for supporting the transnational approach of the Construction Products Directive to get easier access to the biggest and most important foreign market for Austrian actors.

Since there were fewer responses from **Poland**, an analysis of the situation in this country on national level has to be treated even more carefully than for the other Member States in this study. There were two different positions to be noted during the interviews: One was based on the established and institutionalised system of working with CE marking and market surveillance. While one could argue that Austria as an accession country has already put more emphasis on preparing itself for EU requirements, Poland (joining even later) clearly outclasses all three other countries in its efforts to adapt to the EU approach *and* adapting on time (instead of "readjusting" European requirements to their national schemes). The political and economic changes during the last 15 years in the country have most likely facilitated this approach (not to mention the close contacts between the Polish public actors and their counterparts in France) but nevertheless, Poland showed the best-developed structure for dealing with the CPD (and its national implementation). However, the economic changes in this country have also created new situations for all actors which made it more difficult to evaluate how efficient the official system works. In particular the ongoing efforts of coordinating national actors – in particular economic actors – do not allow for confirming or contesting the image of a more efficient implementation of the CPD based only on public authorities. As already seen for the other three countries, economic actors were influencing (in cooperation with national authorities or independently) national approaches by contesting, accepting or ignoring some requirements of the scheme.

Despite all organisational changes in the economic environment, professional actors were also using past experience ("brand names") as essential reference point for their decisions – a position practically identical for actors in the other three Member States.

3.7.6 Trust at national level?

When moving from the EU level to the national one, the importance of (CE or national) marks changed significantly for professional users (designers, architects, contractors, craftsmen). While discussion at EU level (in particular between the construction unit and representatives of German authorities and private actors) were focused on the use of CE marking and national marks, most interviewees did not consider that as particularly relevant when it came to the interaction between manufacturers and users (mostly via distributors). Here past experience and trust in products ("brand names") and knowledge about their correct use, prompt delivery and additional advice from manufacturers when necessary was seen as much more important than any marks developed and provided by upstream actors. CE marking was often seen as a demand created by authorities which were fulfilled to avoid later complaints ("only if something goes wrong, one will check if the marks were there") but with rather limited practical value for downstream users. This was also seen as the major difference between purely private marks and marks that are at least supported by national authorities (including the CE marking): The former could or could not survive market demands and acceptance in the Internal Market. Their acceptance depended on the useful information they could provide. CE marking and some national marks strongly supported by national authorities on the other hand were seen as having *forcibly created* new markets for marks but have not (necessarily) harmonised or improved the existing ones.

In addition, the *de facto* lack of efficient market surveillance in three Member States in this sample[392] would be another explanation why CE marking did not rank very high as information tools used by downstream users. Lack of monitoring or sanctioning, marks could be affixed correctly or incorrectly without giving actors on the "construction site" level too many possibilities to ensure their correct use. Ironically, the same problems seemed to exist for national marks (*Ü-Zeichen*, BBA certificates, *ÜA-Zeichen*, B-mark) which put much emphasis on controlling production and declarations of manufacturers, but lacked the structure for monitoring the next steps from the gate of a manufacturer to distributors, buyers and finally the construction site – therefore diminishing their practical use for the end user on a construction site. No matter if EU or national marks, these last downstream users have to fall back on past experience with products and established contacts – and *trust* – with manufacturers rather than on European or national schemes developed by public authorities.

The dilemma of the CPD approach (CE marking) with partly-overlapping additional (private or official) requirements or information provided by private or official actors already highlighted by actors at EU level was not originally introduced by the CPD. National and regional schemes too were facing these problems (even when being confronted with the new CPD approach) and sometimes have not found efficient solutions. The combination of public and private approaches (the law has to be fulfilled – but to do this, one has to buy technical specifications developed in (private) national standardisation bodies) was generally accepted within national environments, where the needs and requirements of but also limits of execution by all actors were relatively well known. However, due to a lack of knowledge about actors in other Member States, moving this approach to the European level has made general assumptions about other actors more risky (resulting in the need for more detailed agreements/guidance on EU level to reduce this risk – which would lead to complex and voluminous documents). Therefore, two different strategies were used by national actors:

392 See also: Eurocer-Building position paper 2005 p. 14.

- Trying to get a strong influence in the standardization work in CEN (in the hope that one's own national scheme will therefore remain relatively intact in the harmonised European standard – which would increase the trust in the European standard in one Member State, but might decrease it in others).
- "Translating" technical specifications and documents developed at EU level into a format that would fit into the national scheme and maintain certain levels of trust between national actors. (which would *de facto* maintain the *status quo* for all national and external actors).

Obviously, both approaches were aiming at *maintaining* a level of trust between national actors, but not *investing* in trust in actors from other European countries.

However, even when highlighting problems of the CPD approach or practical flaws in the implementation (caused by the construction unit, MS authorities or other private or public actors) and showing preferences to more "familiar" (national) schemes, most interviewees stressed their uneasiness with the duplication of work caused by two schemes existing in parallel with neither of them covering all requirements of all actors involved. This deadlock of lack of trust while at the same time carrying the burden of operating with two schemes could be (at least partly) removed by *investing* in the trust of actors in other Member States. Ironically, these national actors – who could win the most when investing in trust – were also the ones with relatively few links to actors beyond their national border. Actors at the "construction site" level were even more disadvantaged by having even fewer links but being even more liable for any selection of construction products. But as will be shown in the last chapter, this level also provides some options to deal with this dilemma.

3.8 The "construction site" level

At the "construction site" level two specific aspects significantly shape the environment of all actors involved:

First, even more than at the national level, the focus is on the building or the civil engineering works as *the final product*, while construction products are only *components* in the whole planning and construction process. National or regional building laws and other regulatory requirements set already the framework for the performance of buildings and civil engineering works. But it is the specific nature of the work at the "construction site" level that all the professional work has to be organised in all phases (planning, tendering and construction) to comply with all (legal, technical and economic) requirements (e.g., structural performance, energy performance, but also the most efficient use of products, timely completion) to create the final product: buildings or civil engineering works.

Nevertheless, information on construction products is required at the "planning phase": The technical plans developed by designers, architects or civil engineers have to indicate at least the material used for specific parts of the building (e.g., ceilings, structural or non-structural walls, chimneys) for contractors and controlling authorities or controlling engineers[393]. Reference to specific products (including "brand names") depends on regional or local practice in the planning control process.

In the "tendering phase" more details are needed and reference to very specific product performance (e.g., energy-saving performance, load bearing capacity) will be indicated. Specific quality marks could be mentioned as a possibility of proofing a specific performance, but (for legal and economic reasons) they should not restrain actors from selecting alternatives which would provide a similar or even better performance.[394]

The "construction phase" includes the use of products and the considerations on how much experience workers have with a specific product, or how easily they could get additional information and guidance in case of problems in the installation phase or later.

The *second* aspect is the legal framework that encloses all actors involved on the construction site. Here the building codes remain important background, but knowledge and compliance has to be taken (more or less) for granted. More important are the *individual contracts* between the different actors: Between (future) building owners and planners and contractors; between planners and contractors; and between contractors and suppliers (manufacturers or distributors). Specific requirements, as mentioned above – including product performance – are laid down in contracts and technical documents accompanying these contracts. These documents are in general the most important reference points for all actors in the planning and construction phase.

393 This information might of course also be interesting and relevant for the future building owners or tenants. However, since the focus of this study is, for pragmatic reasons, on the information flow between professionals, the role of non-professional actors will not be assessed in detail.

394 This includes considerations of the quantity used (e.g., thicker or thinner walls), economic ratios (performance to price) or availability (short delivery times).

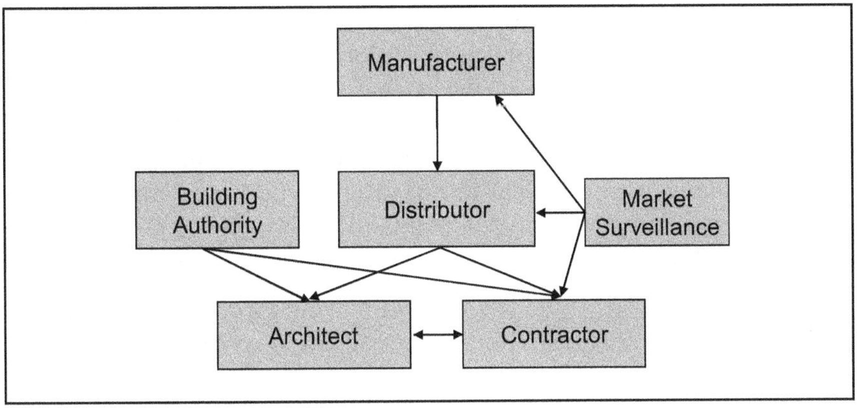

Figure 4: The "construction site" level

The "construction site" level can be roughly defined as all activities from the planning/design stage of *specific* buildings or civil engineering works to the actual construction work and all activities of authorised engineers controlling these phases. This includes:

- Architects and designers (in procurement and as controlling engineers on construction sites)
- Civil engineers (in procurement and as controlling engineers on construction sites)
- Specialised civil engineers (e.g., for structural calculation)
- Planning control
- Manufacturers
- Distributors
- Contractors
- Building control

However, in this study the specialised engineers as well as actors in the field of planning and building control were not specifically targeted. Going deeper into the work of specialised engineers would have widened the scope of the study too much (introducing different tasks and technical standards) without adding significantly to information and selection process. Actors in the field of planning and building control are partly included, but in this study their feedback has been covered mostly at the national level. Another exclusion is based on the shift of most of the responsibility for product quality from public bodies (in Germany, the UK and Austria) to architects and contractors (they have to declare the use of products compliant with all (regulatory and technical) requirements which leaves only an administrative role to public actors (building control authorities were covered in the chapters on national actors). Planning and building control in the hands of private actors with delegated powers indicates that these actors belong in general to the group of architects and civil engineers (who have an even a stronger responsibility to ensure the quality of products used). Therefore, their experience will be included in the comments made by these two professions.[395] This leaves four major groups of actors at this level:

- architects/civil engineers (in procurement and as controlling engineers on construction sites),
- manufacturers ,
- distributors,
- contractors.

While federations and public bodies are providing a framework for representing specific interests as well as receiving and distributing information downstream and upstream, the "construction site" shifts the major role to individuals or individual enterprises. All of them fulfil a specific role in the system and their assumptions and reactions are based on these roles and supporting background structures (providing guidance or clear orders for specific situations and activities), but in the end, they often have to make *individual* decisions to select, accept and use construction products. How well they can follow established paths developed in their environment or developed on their own and how construction products fit into their work will be established in this chapter.[396]

395 Architects and civil engineers could have several *controlling* functions in the planning and construction phase. Starting as having delegated powers of planning and building control authorities, they could have the same function in the private field as representing the owners of the buildings or civil engineering works. In this function they play an additional important role when evaluating the final building for their customers – which is very similar to the "official" control function of *Approved Inspectors* and "*Prüfingenieure*" (which makes both systems – the more privately organised UK scheme and the scheme more based on public control in Germany and Austria – more comparable).

396 At this level, no specific references are made to specific companies, planners of civil engineers. As for the other levels in this study, these comments represent only a small sample and are only highlighting specific points, but might not (despite the best attempts focusing on common and representative comments) always be representative for a specific profession.

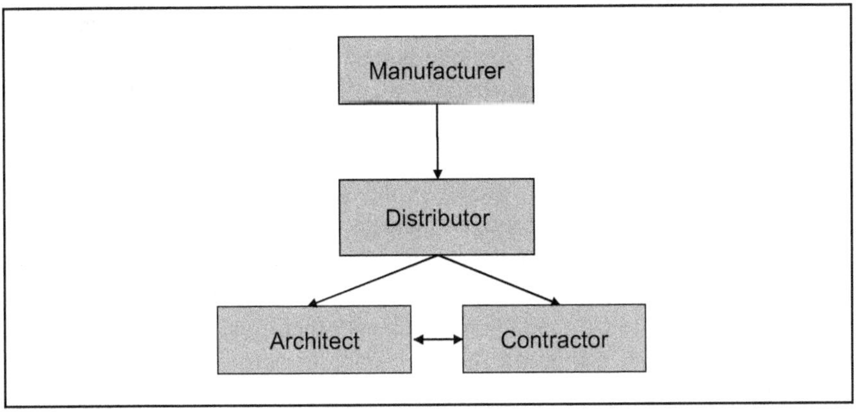

Figure 5: The "construction products" level

At this level, construction products are no longer theoretically discussed targets of regulations and administrative provisions, but real products selected, bought and installed in buildings and other civil engineering works. The various actors at this level are also not (so much) involved in discussions on regulations and technical standards, they are *working* with them, but they are hardly in a position to influence discussions and decisions made by upstream actors on regional or national level.

Architects are the first actors who – by designing a building – are setting certain parameters and defining materials to be used. They have (protected by national laws) in all four Member States specific positions as planners and they are (compulsory) members of specific bodies (chambers of architects) which provide information about requirements and developments at EU and national level. More than any other profession at the "construction site" level mentioned in this study, technical university training is required (which would make universities another important distributor of information on product performance and quality). Also more than the other groups, architects are mostly micro-enterprises, with few larger enterprises.

Technical standards are important technical information, but here the emphasis lies in design and specific uses of buildings (e.g., accessibility) rather than calculation methods or product standards. For architects the knowledge and expertise of planning and building control authorities or individuals with delegated official powers are an essential source of information, not only for the current regulatory requirements but also for interpretation in each specific case.

Manufacturers are the most important target group when implementing the CPD at national level and on applying correctly CE marking on products. As shown at national level, some federations were very active in providing practical information (some even using a step-by-step approach) for their members, helping to understand the scope of the information provided with CE marking and how it has to be declared and affixed on the actual product (or its packaging). Individual contracts with distributors indicate the obligation of manufacturers only to deliver products in compliance with all regulations and official documentation also cover CE marking. However, there was a huge difference in how manufacturers are use CE marking for promoting their products. In several cases CE marking was not mentioned (here larger or transnational companies were referring to it in a general way, mentioning "compliance with all requirements"), while information on the technical performance was given priority.[397] Others were combining regulatory information with other (from their point of view essential) information, while in at least one case CE marking was actually "presented" as a quality mark, showing compliance beyond the essential requirements. Polish manufacturers (and distributors) have shown the strongest emphasis indicate compliance with regulations in their data sheets and price lists, providing for practically *all* products reference to either a CE marking or to another mark.

The main instrument to assure a common understanding and compliance between manufacturers but also other actors as architects, contractors and authorities were technical standards. Therefore, technical standards were the first line of (general or specific) information, with complementary information coming from federations on specific approaches on how to used these standards, and finally feedback from end users on how useful their products actually were at a practical level.

Two different main groups of **distributors** were of interest in this study: builder's merchants ("*Baustofffachhandel*") distributing construction products to professional customers (architects, contractors) on a large scale, and large-scale

397 Product information was provided in all four Member States with datasheets, and even proposals for how these products should be described in tendering documents were placed on the companies' websites. References to CE marking are in most cases missing. http://www.heidelbergcement.com/uk/en/hanson/products/bricks/quality.htm; http://other.baumit.com/front_content.php; http://www.wienerberger.de/servlet/Satellite?pagename=Wienerberger/Page/Start05&sl=wb_de_home_de; http://www.rockwool.at/sw16718.asp; www.knaufinsulation.pl.

distributors serving do-it-yourself enthusiasts ("*Baumärkte*"). In all four Member States, distributors were largely SMEs, which often organised themselves into networks of distributors, but also some larger companies could be found. Their main role was to *provide* products by either delivering them to customers (construction sites) or having them stored for collection. Therefore, their main interests were distribution networks and logistics.

Distributors played a very specific role in all four Member States. On most professional projects, products were delivered by them to construction sites and they charged customers (do-it-yourself enthusiasts, professionals and construction companies). However, direct contact between technical experts on the performance of products, their proper use and other technical aspects were in general communicated between manufacturers and customers without the involvement of distributors[398]. The main advantages seen by the other two parties involved were to have one contact point taking care of the logistic and most aspects of the financial transaction, but also knowing more (and delivering to more) potential customers. Manufacturers did not have to worry about being paid, because they were paid by the distributor who had to deal later with the customers. Customers on the other hand had one focal point to inquire if and how products were available, which reduced their search costs. This gave distributors a very significant role in providing access to a local or regional market.

Another role of distributors was their possibility to offer customers *combinations* of products. Since several products need complementary products for their installation or efficient functioning (e.g., mounting and fixing products, glues), manufacturers were (and are) trying to find the best combination, often in cooperation with the providers of these complementary products. While both sides were still selling only their own product range, distributors could easily offer these combinations to professional users and DIY enthusiasts. An additional advantage for downstream users is the combined delivery, which reduces the risk (due to different manufacturers and providers of each product) of having only some parts of a consignment delivered on time.

398 The UK had even a specialised group of actors – "factors" – who were in particular providing a link between small manufacturers and (smaller) customers by promoting their products in direct contact with architects, planners and contractors. This role was reduced when mergers created bigger companies that were more and more relying on their own sales force.

A screening of websites of distributors in Germany, the UK, Austria and Poland has shown that in none of them CE marking was mentioned, either in general or for specific products.

Companies tasked with the actual construction work were under the scope of this study defined as one of the most relevant "final end users" of construction products.[399] These **contractors** could cover all types of construction works (only this group has been selected in this study) or could provide services for specific installations. Other companies have specialised in *organising* construction works (sometimes including the planning phase) but are no longer involved in actual construction work themselves. In particular for the first group, technical competence has to be proven (e.g., technical training in technical schools or universities) to be legally accepted as contractor at national level. These companies could be active in several Member States, but there is also a large number of SMEs in this sector.

Contractors are largely responsible (based on each contract) for the selection of *products*, ensuring compliance with all regulatory requirements as well as any additional requirements set by the design, a special environment or new technical developments, and the most efficient installation in the building. Like architects, information on their services is focused on buildings or civil engineering works. References to construction products (with very few exceptions for specific products promoted by the company) were not provided.

3.9 The assumption of actors at the construction site level

To get a better impression of the needs of actors on this final practical level and how they would interpret the role and use of CE marking, This study has been following two different routes: One was a continuation of the approach used for the other two levels by asking architects and civil engineers about the current knowledge and experience. The second route was simulating a type of "bottom-up" approach, where downstream users were asked to try to get information about CE marking and judge it by its usefulness for their daily work. Publications of technical bodies, or even the worldwide web in general were often the

399 Do-It-Yourself enthusiasts are for pragmatic reasons (large target group but difficult to reach) generally excluded from the study. Only in thecontext of experience of distributors will they be mentioned in the following chapter.

starting point, and produced interesting, but not always helpful information. Both approaches will be presented in this chapter, to show the effects of information passively received and actively searched for.

At the "construction site" level, the differences between different Member States (at this level, feedback from Polish actors became the exception, which mostly left actors from Germany, the UK and Austria as sources) seemed to be less obvious and relevant to make a clear distinction between actors of different countries necessary. Therefore, the following comments were aggregated from all four Member States. Only if comments reflected specific national or regional circumstances or were significantly different in one or the other Member State, were they highlighted as specific "national feedback".

3.9.1 Manufacturers

In general, CE marking had a clear advantage for transnational companies because the certificates could be used for a specific product range in several countries (except where specific factory production control by a third party is required). Poland has the most open approach to certificates in general: The majority of transnational manufacturers producing in Poland have been operating in the "old" EU 12 and EU 15. Therefore, certificates were already issued for their products, before they started production of these products in Poland (by either establishing a new factory or by taking over existing national manufacturers), and were mostly written either in English or German.[400] Certificates in Polish appeared mostly for European Technical Approvals (issued by the Polish ITB) – allowing for CE marking for not (yet) standardised products (manufactured in Poland). This would indicate that either all requests for information were coming from actors who could master all these languages well enough, or that there have been few if any requests for information about the content of the CE marking certificates provided in foreign languages. According to the feedback from manufacturers, the curiosity of their customers was low, which would be consistent with the comments from companies in the other three Member States. The Polish example would even provide additional proof of the low relevance that CE marking has for actors at the construction site level because not even information provided in another language (most certificates in German; in

400 http://www.knaufinsulation.pl/pl/documents/overview/certyfikaty.

general, certificates given by certification bodies in Germany, the UK or Austria were available in their national languages only) has caused more requests for clarification.

Comments from the other three Member States indicated that in general, CE marking was used and affixed to products, because it was a legal requirement ("to have a "paper trail" in case of complaints"). The practical use as a declaration to customers, on the other hand, was rather dubious for two reasons: One, the information provided with CE marking was either more or less the same as previously. Therefore, it was more a question of whether compliance with "third party control" by a Notified Body was less expensive than using (previous or still existing) national approaches and certificates than if CE marking was considered by manufacturers as an improvement on the quality and quantity of information provided. Second, since CE marking was not giving any guarantee of "safe use" (as presumed to be provided by other "quality marks") it was seen as of little use to customers. In fact, the sole acceptance of certificates as "quality assurance" by professional downstream users lead manufacturers to the pragmatic approach of either not contradicting the wrong assumption of architects or contractors that CE marking was a "quality mark" ("It takes too much time to explain to them the difference to "performance" certificates") or of supporting it. However, there were two main exceptions reported: Larger property owners and public authorities were at least asking for documentation – in particular for whole systems of products (e.g., thermal insulation systems). In general, feedback from "basic" or "traditional" products (e.g., bricks, mortar) practically never raised concerns or requests by other actors that the declaration of product performance would need additional proof. Newer products, but in particular complex products were, on the other hand, more often targeted by planners, contractors and authorities to provide certificates to show their compliance with national or regional regulatory requirements.

New "consumer demands" were mentioned as introducing new requirements (for declarations), but were only partly covered by a technical approach: "Social responsibility" was reported in the UK as one of these new requirements (and certificates or declarations of manufacturers were prominently displayed on packaging of specific products). Also compliance with ISO 9000 and ISO 14000 standards was seen as information worth transmitted to customers. "Recycling" was more an issue in Germany and Austria, and information that waste would be recovered was something that was visibly promoted (size and position of pictogram on products and packaging) compared to a more "neutral" presentation of CE marking and national (Ü and ÜA) marks.

3.9.2 *Distributors*

Feedback differed, from having a very good idea about the role and use of CE marking for downstream users to not being aware of its use at all. The general perception was that manufacturers were obliged by contracts with distributors to ensure the quality of their products and compliance with all relevant regulatory requirements. In contact with professional actors, the necessity for CE marking was not explicitly mentioned, but appeared in contracts as basic requirement. However, specific questions or requests for the marking were not received. This was also reported for other national marks. It was a practically unanimous reply that professional actors were not specifically interested in CE marking but were in most cases focused on "brand names", familiar products[401] or specific (combination of) products.[402] This was explained more in economic terms, because professional customers were prepared to pay a little bit more for well-known products because the risk of flaws in the products and later complaints were minimised: also manufacturers of these products were seen as professional (fast and experienced) in giving advice in case of problems.

In Germany, do-it-yourself-enthusiasts were even more oriented towards a "brand name". The company name was perceived as guarantee of compliance with technical and legal requirements. It was even highlighted that products from the *same* manufacturer without a "brand name" were less accepted by customers and lower pricing did not change the preference for "brand names". Distributors in the UK and Austria on the other hand said that the price of a product seemed to be more important for non-professional users, trying to get less expensive products. Similarly, in both countries, specific marks (CE marking or national

401 It was mentioned, not only by distributors, that "conservative" behaviour by professional users could keep products on the market because they were well-known and used even after products have been developed which have shown better performance than the traditional ones.

402 More and more manufacturers are trying to improve the performance of their products by selecting and adapting them for the most efficient installation and use (e.g., specific plaster or mortars as binding materials). Since the margin of product quality is getting smaller, these combinations with supporting/complementary products are often seen as market advantage against competitors. Distributors, as well as architects and designers were reportedly looking more and more for these performance-enhancing combinations.

marks) did not play any role at all for DIY enthusiasts.[403] Quality was checked with specific product declarations of the manufacturers (data sheets) but in fact, only few parameters (1-3) were actually taken into consideration (also because the technical knowledge to interpret the information provided with the other parameters was missing).

In most cases, the employees and managers in distribution markets were generally informed about the obligation of having CE marking affixed on products. However, here too, CE marking was not thouthe to provide too much useful information (in at least one case it was clearly seen as "bureaucratic nonsense" of authorities, in a failed attempt to protect European or national markets) for customers. Therefore, CE marking was an *administrative* obligation being passed on to manufacturers (they have to deliver only CE marked products) and professional customers (who should have this requirement mentioned in their product descriptions).

In general, complaints by customers varied between professional users and DIY enthusiasts: Professional users had fewer complaints because they were mostly selecting products they had used in the past and therefore had experience of. They knew how to install them; which products and materials were compatible or for which installations more preparations (e.g., preparing the base, insulating specific products or materials) were needed. DIY enthusiasts hardly had the opportunity to gain such experience, and were reported to make more mistakes when installing products – or even selecting the wrong product for a specific application. These complaints and problems were mostly solved by the distributors themselves, based on their practical knowledge. In only few cases (for DYI enthusiasts and professionals) had they to refer the complainants to the manufacturers.

403 Distributors in the German *Bundesland* Nordrhein-Westfalen were approached. This part has borders to Belgium and the Netherlands which are both relatively stable markets. The Austrian distributors approached in this study were operating in Vienna and Lower Austria. The close proximity to the markets of a number of newer Member States (in particular the Czech Republic, Slovakia and Hungary) has created a still-fluctuating market or at least a market that has only recently seen significant changes.

3.9.3 Architects/designers

This group has sometimes several different roles, depending partly on the national and regional regulatory definition of their profession, but also on the individual contract with their customers which could extend or limit their involvement – in particular in the construction phase. They might be only responsible for the design, but they could also follow the project as controlling technical experts for the building owners till the finalisation of the project.[404] *In these cases their obligations also covered the control of the progress of the work and the materials and products used by other contractors.*

Interviewees who were not only responsible for the design, but also control functions during the construction phase, were (partly) aware of CE marking of construction products. It seems that (recent) training was an important factor in the dissemination of information to practical users: While CE marking or other marks were rarely the main topic of training sessions (training or information events organised by federations mostly covered other aspects and only included information on CE marking), nevertheless, they have been included occasionally as additional (background) information. General information provided by national or regional federations seemed to have played a lesser role, or was not received.[405] In Germany and Austria the perception of CE marking as a "quality mark" was strong ("What else would its practical use be?"), and CE marked products were *generally* seen as "fit for use". But even with this assumption, the practical use was questioned when coming to specific product declarations: As many performance indicators were declared in technical classes which were not always found in each product class but in other general product standards or horizontal test standards – but also the fact that European standards have changed compared to the previously-used national ones – forced (at least in theory) all actors in controlling functions to buy "all" European standards to get

404 All these functions could also be taken over by construction companies, keeping control of the planning and the construction phase in the hands of one actor. In addition, specific actors (of either profession) could be in charge of management of the project beyond the technical part, covering also the later use phase and its economical aspects.

405 However, it was acknowledged that this information might have been distributed at a time when it was not considered relevant by individuals and was, therefore forgotten.

this relevant information.[406] The additional burden of getting information to fulfil regulatory requirements was also raised several times: To comply with (regulatory or technical) performance values (e.g., energy efficiency,[407] fire resistance), architects and designers could not just refer to publicly available documents but had to buy them (in particular technical standards – the obligatory part of annex ZA – and the "*Baustofflisten*" in Germany and Austria) from different private actors (national standardisation bodies) or semi-official/semi-private actors (technical institutes). It was criticised that these actors were playing two different and conflicting roles as setting requirements that were obligatory at national or regional level (and therefore part of the regulatory power in a Member State) and at the same time were market actors who got part of their income from selling these documents – *and* amending them several times which forced users to purchase each new version.

But in several cases architects found it possible to bypass these financial burdens: Manufacturers were often not only providing product information – they also developed texts for tenders with detailed product requirements, which could be used by their customers (architects and contractors). These texts could be relatively neutral by using "aggregated" performance characteristics and values (mostly used for public tenders), or very specifically defining their own products (mostly for private projects where product specific tendering is allowed).[408] Again, trust (in the manufacturer) allowed the use of this support, assuming that the manufacturer has been aware of all relevant requirements and that they were all sufficiently addressed in the text. In these cases, references to CE marking or other (national) marks were completely left to the manufacturer.

As a profession that defines itself to a large extent by its artistic skills and input in the construction sector, architects are also the ones most likely to be searching for new products fulfil the specific requirements of their designs. Selecting new products might force manufacturers and planners to provide more

---

406 In fact, not all of the planned 500 harmonised European product standards would be necessary to get this information. Nevertheless, the large number of standards was seen as an unnecessary financial burden for a regulatory requirement.

407 In addition to regulatory requirements, architects also referred to the pressure of complying with demands created by new policies at EU and national level. On one hand, this allowed faster individuals and enterprises to compete and/or to specialise for specific issues, but it also put a greater burden on micro-enterprises to monitor a very wide range of new developments.

408 Which would have still have left a competitive angle (for distributors) in the approach, but at the same time it would be ensuring the use of the manufacturer's product.

information on their potential use and performance which could be cost-intensive and time-consuming. For these cases, it was highlighted that proven acceptance of these products by authorities – via national marks – clearly created an added value, not least because new products might not be used in *every* new building design, but they could be a significant part of the costs. Having a certificate that included specifications that covered other possible intended uses could be advantageous for their actual selection.

3.9.4 Contractors/construction companies

Since contractors share in several cases very similar responsibilities with architects as professional providers of services and products (the final building or civil engineering works), their expectations and uses of products and certificates provided by manufacturers were also often similar or at least complementary. Architects might select specific products that contractors have to buy and use, but there are many cases where the materials are defined or products are described in general (technical) terms, leaving the selection of specific products to contractors.

Contractors – as the actors installing products on the construction site – were *the* actor at this level responsible for selecting construction products and checking the information on their performance and compliance with regulatory requirements. Keeping in mind the large number of products used – as well as the different potential uses of these products – contractors try to reduce complexity by using known products and used by their workers in the past.[409] Since customers (architects as well as building owners) could request the use of different products, or products , which the workforce has no experience of, the close and efficient link to distributors and in particular to manufacturers was seen as

409 One interviewee also referred to the effect of "familiarity" with specific products and the acceptance of any changes that might occur and create resistance from workers on construction sites: A manufacturer who has delivered a specific product for years to a construction company was bought by another company. While the new owners were leaving the production line and the product completely unchanged, the product was now packed in plastic bags of a different colour (using the colour code of the new owners). This caused confusion and complaints about a "new and un-known product" by the employees who had to use it, reflecting their concerns that now the installation might be different and could cause problems (damage) which would fall back on these workers. It took some time and explanations to increase the acceptance of the "new/old" product.

another important "fail-safe point", providing fast and precise information and guidance from manufacturers on the correct use of specific products. Unanimously, contractors declared that direct cooperation with manufacturers was essential to get specific information which could not be found in product standards or application standards.

Compared to these practical information flow, quality marks or CE marking was not seen as very important. Even when perceiving CE marking as a *quality* mark (responses from Germany and Austria), practical interest was very low. Following the letter of the law, the reference to CE marking was introduced in contracts with manufacturers or distributors, but since this information was already provided in the past in data sheets provided by manufacturers, additional marks were not considered as an improvement on the quality of the data provided. In some cases it was mentioned that national marks provided more security for contractors when using them, but it was not so much the *technical input* that was seen as added value but the shift of the *legal liability* to national or regional authorities which have declared the product as safe.[410] It was highlighted that in general, it was taken for granted that the products selected by the contractor himself were safe (since the product has to fulfil the performance values or classes declared by the manufacturer – and this declaration would also have been used in court)[411], and the additional involvement of authorities was more "to justify their existence" than significantly improving the quality of products as such.

Liability and future costs for repair work were also mentioned as criteria for selecting well-known products and "brand name" products, even if (in most cases) they would be (slightly) more expensive than other products on the market. Damages and later complaints would bind the working force (one of the most cost-intensive parts of construction works for buildings) for repair work in already "finished" projects instead of allowing them to be used in new projects.

410 It was also highlighted that the future private or public owners would require complete documentation – including all certificates. But again, this is done at the end of the construction works (as kind of „paper trail function"). CE marking (or other marks) were not influencing the decisions of an intended use, nor was much thought given to the quality or quantity of the data provided with these marks.

411 Contractors also saw distributors (in particular larger companies) as „really European" – indicating that these actors were operating at transnational level and could purchase and provide products from other countries too – outside the field of experience of contractors. Product performance and confidence that the distributor is following all legal requirements therefore becomes more relevant than individual checks of product certificates.

The financial difference in purchasing these products was seen as easily compensated for by reduced (successful) complaints from their customers.[412]

However, the factor of being "familiar" with products or certificates was not always to the disadvantage of CE marking. In contradiction to first assumptions of the advantages of CE marking for *products* crossing national borders, the opposite seemed to give CE marking some recognition: *construction companies* crossing national borders might not always be able to get well-known products in other countries they operate in. While often larger companies have expanded into several countries – and therefore are able to provide their products in several Member States, some products might not as easily be acquired or (cost efficient) transported by the contractor from the country of origin. When selecting new products, CE marking had a certain "recognition factor" which was seen as useful. However, here too, the assumption that CE marking was *de facto* a quality mark influenced these perceptions.

Also (like the architects) having to pay for documents setting regulatory requirements (the "*Bauregellisten*", but also technical standards) was criticised by several actors. In particular compared to building codes which were seen as relatively "stable" and only occasionally amended, standards and other regulatory requirements were changed more often, and therefore increased the costs also for small and micro-enterprises for relatively little additional information in exchange. Following all developments on time was seen as unfeasible because national approaches were not seen as very coordinated which made it difficult to focus on specific actors (authorities, national standardisation bodies or technical institutes) which could develop new requirements or approaches for downstream actors.

Also the complexity and the volume of technical standards were mentioned several times. The new standards were often compared with the previous (national) ones,[413] and a significant increase in pages was rarely seen as provid-

412 It was mentioned that problems highlighted by customers were rarely a matter of flawed products but more often caused by other factors in the actual use of the building by its occupants (i.e. high humidity because of low air exchange rates).

413 Like for manufacturers, technical standards were the basis for understanding and using products (both parts, product definition and guidance for product application, were often combined in national technical standards and other technical specifications.), combined with more specific information provided by manufacturers or technical publications as well as direct contact with manufacturers if special questions occur (i.e. combination of different materials, special needs for fixing products on other parts of the building).

ing more precision but as “being more complicated than necessary” (“Previously, the standard had 10 pages, now it is 100 pages”). However, the differences between a new *European* standard and the old *national* standards were not always realised. In some cases, the rather large number of new standards and amendments previously produced by national standardisation bodies had created a more critical view of the work of these bodies, and any new developments were seen as continuation of a national problem, rather than caused by input from EU level.

3.9.5 www.CE – The invisible actor on the “construction site” level

The role of the internet as source of information became clear in several interviews and contacts with actors (architects and contractors) at this level. In a number of cases where CE marking was not known – or at least not *well* known – one of the first reactions was to search the web for information on CE marking. *Wikipedia* provided basic information, but trying to get information on CE marking in general proved to be trickier. There was no lack of websites informing about CE marking, its role and use. However, most sites (set up by companies offering their services in advising and helping manufacturers to get CE marking for their products) were providing information on CE marking *in general* – focusing on the “real” New Approach Directives. Sometimes – but not always – the CPD was specifically mentioned and differences to other approaches highlighted. But in several cases there was no differentiation made. In particular the aspect of the New Approach CE marking that a product has fulfilled all safety requirements was seen as the most impressive characteristic of the European mark – but also the most misleading.

However, the risk of interested individuals getting wrong information on the “CPD CE marking” was rather low. These steps to the “general www” were seen as an *informative* excursion by all interviewees, and precise information was not expected. The main reference point was always the technical institute (DIBt, BRE, OIB and ITB)[414] or the building control authorities.[415]

414 The technical institutes were clearly the top reference for architects and civil engineers. Manufacturers too depended to a large extent on information provided by these bodies, but were also (in particular in Germany) searching on the websites of their specific federation(s).

415 *One should keep in mind that the reference to national technical institutes is easy for actors already established and familiar with the system of an EU Member State. More confusing (and here I am also referring to my own experience with non-EU actors) is the split between New*

Complementary to comments from these institutes and other national actors, this "bottom-up" approach practically stopped at the "website level". Getting a general idea about this mark (or any other (national) marks) was considered as sufficient background information, since the correct use of CE marking was seen as the responsibility of manufacturers and distributors. Products might be checked in future if CE was affixed on products arriving at the construction site, but any check on the correctness of this declaration was not seen as responsibility of the "end users" of construction products.

3.10 Conclusion construction site level

The good news at the "construction site" level was that CE marking was *de facto* affixed to construction products – in general as described in Guidance Paper D. On the other hand, except for manufacturers, interest in and awareness of CE marking was very low in all other professions. But even within the group of manufacturers the feelings about the practical use of CE marking for construction products were rather mixed. It is a downside of this study that all interviewees were either working for manufacturers only covering (more or less) *one* national market or were already active in several Member States. It might have been interesting to get the experience of manufacturers which had recently moved significantly into other national markets or were planning to do so. For the "national" and "transnational" actors, the requirements under the national construction product laws were not so much increasing the quality or quantity of the product information they provided, but (at least for some interviewees) increased transparency of other actors entering *their* markets.[416] The confusion of their customers about "conformity mark" and "quality mark" was seem as problem in all four Member States, and manufacturers tried to neutralise the

Approach Directives and the CPD for actors who are not so familiar with these differences and could not fall back on a body that would have enough information and experience *to provide useful feedback and guidance.*

416 It was already mentioned on national level that – due to a lack of active public market surveillance in several Member States – manufacturers were monitoring their competitors. While complaints against competitors in their own country were seen as "two-edged swords", products entering from other Member States, but in particular from outside the EU were seen as more promising and more successful. Here the lack of CE marking was already an instrument to act against competition.

problem by either supporting (or at least not contradicting) the assumption of a "quality" CE marking ("too difficult to explain the difference") or by not mentioning it to customers.

Not surprisingly, other actors were not interested or even not aware about the role of CE marking. This has created a type of "vicious circle" of architects and contractors not aware of it, therefore not participating in discussions – or even standardisation work – therefore not being considered as interested by manufacturers (who were dominating this specific field of standardisation) and therefore not actively informed. Of course, the relative absence of downstream users in the information chain and their lack of awareness cannot be reduced to such a simple explanation. In fact, the rather "conservative" selection of products and suppliers used played another important role in the interaction between downstream users, distributors and manufacturers. Using mostly familiar products and also getting these products in most cases from the same supplier over years, created a level of trust in the performance of these products ("We expect that the manufacturer/supplier fulfils all regulatory requirements"). In addition, local authorities or private planning and building inspectors ("*Prüfingenieure*", *Approved Inspectors*) were also more likely to accept familiar products than ask for more quality assurance (by using certificates) for less-known products. It seems also that even with regulatory requirements in place only few indicators were actually checked – again more closely linked to practical requirements of planners and contractors than to specific regulatory targets. CE marking and national marks were therefore sometimes even an "information-overkill" compared to the practical needs of public and private downstream actors. References to specific certificates, be they national "quality" marks or CE marking, was of secondary importance and more used for correct documentation than getting more information on the product. Here again, the size of or the consumer group targeted by an enterprise had slight influence on the awareness of CE marking: Since public projects were regularly demanding CE marking (but here again, more following "the letter of the law"), companies and architects working for public authorities were more accustomed to additional requirements. But even in these cases, these actors had very different perceptions of CE marking, in general considering it as "quality mark".

At the "construction site" level – "far away" from the EU level and its actors – the perception of national and European approaches became more and more blurred. While not always being aware from *where* specific regulatory or technical requirements originated, interviewees at the "construction site" level commented very similarly as their counterparts at national or EU level regarding advantages and disadvantages of regulatory and technical approaches,[417] indicating a general wariness about new requirements, which were often not seen as facilitating their work but to set requirements based on theoretical assumptions. As a result, downstream actors reacted defensively to new requirements and put even stronger preferences on familiar system (even if downstream actors were critical about existing schemes; they were considered as less complex and less burdensome than new approaches), or even ignored specific requirements when it was known that they will not be controlled and sanctioned.

It should be noted that "end users" (architects and contractors) were aiming for *pragmatic* solutions ("low risk of problems in any part of the building") while actors at EU level (and the reactions at national level) were often focusing on the "worst case scenario". The actors in between these two "extremes" have to balance between concepts ("the spirit of the law") and (partly highly complex) instruments and the need for simplification at downstream levels. Considering the large number of SMEs and micro-enterprises, it is hardly surprising that in most cases a pragmatic approach was chosen and only *general* information was provided (if at all), leaving knowledge of details (including documents produced at EU and national level) in the hands of national authorities and federations, only to be used for specific questions and individual requests for more detailed information.

417 The different roles of the four leading technical institutes (DIBt, BRE, OIB and ITB) as public and private actor were mentioned before. However, the strong influence of the CPD on strengthening the position and role of the DIBt and in particular the OIB were not realised and only seen as "purely" national developments.

4 Conclusion: Lessons to be learned?

> We have not been able to answer all of your questions. In fact, by answering some of them we found new questions to be answered. Therefore, we think that we are as confused as before – but on a higher level and about more important things.
> (Unknown author – Department of Sociology/University of Vienna)

The last chapters have analysed positions, expectations, problems and solutions developed at three different levels. What was at the beginning of the study more a pragmatic approach of splitting the work between different levels has proven to reflect very much the different legal, administrative and practical approaches of all actors involved. Seeing the different needs of actors at each level and in each Member State, it is not completely surprising that the goals and the usefulness of CE marking changed and finally practically disappeared in the information flow to downstream users.

In this chapter, I will try to put the results of the analysis of the different levels together. It should be stressed again that the aim of this study was the evaluation of *the information flow* at three different levels, with public and private actors involved. The critical comments on the practical use and therefore the practical impact of CE marking raised on practically every level would lead to a different question about the impact and the scope of the CPD (or the future CPR) approach. However, such a discussion would clearly go beyond the scope of this study. Therefore, this conclusion considers the CPD as basic legal framework, and also the recommendations of improvements to interaction between different actors in the next chapter are based on the existing *working environment* of the current CPD, and are not focusing on potential changes of this Directive. It would also not be correct to assume that a study that has – for pragmatic reasons – limited itself in general to four Member States and three different product groups, could provide a picture of the *overall* impact of the CPD. However, these comments highlighted some of the limitations of the CPD which should not be ignored in this analysis.

4.1 "I had a dream ..."

The main goal of the CPD was its contribution to the policy of an Internal Market of all EG/EU Member States. Products should circulate freely between countries, providing consumers with a wider range of products (trade effect) – and therefore more freedom to select the products most suitable for their specific needs – by harmonising the technical assessment methods used for all criteria laid down in national regulatory requirements.

By creating more competition, it was also expected that manufacturers would put more emphasis on adapting to consumer needs rather than just "pushing" their products on a (national) market (competition effect). While at that time only few sectors were facing competition from other countries within the EC/EU or outside this economic area, concerns were voiced within and outside the Commission that a strong focus on national markets and attempts to "close" them against imports would reduce the flexibility of market actors to react in time to challenges coming from even further than the EC/EU. "Learning" flexibility and competition with actors which were not so comparable to the existing national ones within Europe seemed to be a good preparation for growing international interaction – the so-called "globalisation" (restructuring, rationalisation).

Also promising was the concept of only *slightly* interfering with (national) markets by only providing a tool (harmonised product standards and CE marking) that would make declarations of product performance generally trustworthy, but restricting itself at the same time to requirements set by national authorities, and therefore leaving additional "market demands" untouched. Defining in this concept "market demands" as "consumer demands", private actors should have enough room for manoeuvre to define their own needs and to make their suppliers adapt to them. Therefore, CE marking would have opened markets in the interests of the consumers by keeping their "power" intact while at the same time increasing the number of products available to them.

However, right from the beginning, the goal was very ambitious:

- Keeping in mind that the construction sector consisted (and consists) of only few large companies (mostly manufacturers) and a large number of SMEs (construction companies) and micro-enterprises (architects), the CPD approach included the high risk that any representation of these actors at EU level (e.g., in the SCC, CEN, EOTA) would be asymmetric, if not – due to a lack of human resources – impossible to achieve at all.

- The approach covered a very wide range of products – from those consisting of only one material (e.g., natural stone) to highly complex products using several substances and materials and chemical processes to create the final product – and all different combination how these products could be used and combined. Also, no distinction was made between products that were already generally traded across borders (and facing barriers to trade), products *potentially* traded across national borders, and products only used within a national, regional or local environment. In addition, since it was envisaged that *all* products could be put on *any* national market within the EC/EU, even products distributed within a limited radius (e.g., "low-cost" products like gravel or cement which would economically not justify transporting long distances,) had to be covered in an EU-wide scheme. In other words, for an extremely wide range of products and their uses, the most complex system (practically a "worst case scenario") had to be taken into consideration to cover all eventualities.
- This wide range of products and their intended uses also increased the risk of failure when identifying the relevant regulatory requirements in the field of technical specifications (at the beginning, in particular, of harmonised European standards). Essential for any effective measure against such failure would have been resource-intensive, continuous and efficient monitoring and coordination by all actors (the construction unit, Member State authorities, CEN and the relevant industry federations) to make sure that the first tangible results – the first harmonised product standards – would be complete and useful enough to not face serious objections by (national) actors.
- On one hand, the CPD approach should facilitate the choice and use of construction products by all downstream actors (designers, architects, contractors, public and private inspectors, market surveillance and do-it-yourself enthusiasts), but on the other hand, the *only* specific needs of most of these actors *covered under the scope of the CPD* were *obligatory requirements* laid down in national or regional regulations. Since building codes were often very general when defining technical requirements, and in some cases requirements of downstream users were already higher than laid down in national or regional laws, covering only the regulatory part was often not providing enough information and security for using them for

private actors which would leave only the small group of market surveillance inspectors as realistic target group for CE marking.

- One of the main characteristics of the construction sector was (and is) the strong role of national authorities – not only as creators of regulations but also as market actors. Their investment in construction works (e.g., infrastructure works, public buildings) also made them one of the strongest customers: They were formulating the rules (in laws and administrative provisions), could add requirements after the finalisation of national standards and could sanction the performance of other market actors at different levels (e.g., planning and building control, monitoring of projects, certifying products or buildings, market surveillance) – again based on regulatory frameworks that have been developed by (sometimes the same) national or regional authorities. Not surprisingly all private actors (industry, certification bodies, standardisation bodies, architects and contractors) were frequently in contact with national authorities, to be aware of any changes of the national or regional framework. Also national technical institutes were in some cases playing different roles as actors providing technical input for authorities, and as market actors, as Approval Bodies (EOTA members) or Notified Bodies. Therefore, the theoretical clean cut between "regulatory requirements" and "market demands" was ignoring the fact that in several Member States national authorities and not private actors were *de facto* strongly influencing the definition of "market demands" and therefore blurring the line between "regulatory" and "market" demands.
- Finally, the CPD approach only covered *components* of the final product – buildings and civil engineering work, which were covered by specific building regulations. Since the performance of buildings was only indirectly dealt with by the CPD, and therefore architects and contractors were only to a small extent interested in this work, the link between construction products and buildings was left mostly to authorities and technical specification writers (dominated by manufacturers and certification bodies/test laboratories), not the final users (however, the SCC developed Interpretative Documents to explain relevant building performances which should be tackled in harmonised European standards).

4.2 "Brussels" – setting the stage

At the (in)famous centre of EU policy and regulations – "Brussels" – the above mentioned actors were coming together and trying to coordinate their positions and actions. At this level, EU and national authorities were the most influential actors within the institutionalised part of the system – the setting of regulatory requirements via the SCC:

Naturally, it was the first task of the construction unit in the Commission to introduce and to maintain a functional framework for the implementation of the CPD at EU level. Due to a lack of experience in this field between market regulation (the later New Approach) and obligatory instruments, the following "learning by doing" approach showed some promising results, but also the first problems with the CPD approach in general – and some more specific issues:

- The idea about the target groups of the CPD remained ambiguous during all phases of the implementation of the CPD. In addition, at no stage of the development or implementation of the CPD had the construction unit taken any empirically-sound efforts to get a clear indication of the actual interests and requirements of end users. The involvement of "downstream users" was more an information exercise than an actual search for feedback at a practical level about the utility of CE marking.
- To cover all products under the CPD, two approaches had been chosen at the same time – covering practically *all* products in one common approach, and splitting the work into several product groups ("product families") – but handed over to different actors:
  - The necessary split into different products and product groups was *de facto* delegated to the European standardisation organization CEN. While the construction unit and Member State representatives in the Standing Committee on Construction were defining product groups and regulatory requirements (in mandates to CEN) *in general*, the decisions on a practical technical approach (specific definition of products and their intended uses) were then left to CEN and its Technical Committees.
  - Since standardisation work was outside the control of national administrations or the Commission, and – to be more precise – on national regulatory requirements (see below), general guidance was provided by the construction unit and the national representatives in the SCC by

developing the Interpretative Documents and the Guidance Papers for the CPD. It was tried to cover *all* products, their intended uses and potential risks in one document, which made them highly complex for any actors not directly involved in their development – and often resulted in the development of *another* document (mostly at national level) to cover additional (potential) gaps.

- While the Commission and in particular the construction unit succeeded in adding actors into the system (i.e. CEPMC, NORMAPME, GNB, EOTA) to allow for more differentiated input, manufacturers became the dominant group of actors outside public administrations, inadvertently shifting the focus from consumer needs (due to the lack of participation of consumer representatives, the "pull factor" of contractors, architects lost their influence) to putting products on the market (the "push factor").

The construction unit had a strong role as main partner for other European organisations (CEN, EOTA, GNB) which needed (more) precise and detailed information for implementing the requirements of the CPD in their work and providing practical guidance for their members. Therefore, the construction unit was bundling its (few) resources to the fields where it could effectively influence developments, with the result that more or less all Guidance Papers as well as most databases developed for CPD issues (most of them not publicly accessible) were aimed at providing guidance for specification writers (CEN, EOTA) or certifiers of construction products (GNB). Here *general* information was no longer useful, and several Guidance Papers started with specific questions raised by experts in these European organisations. By trying to solve these problems, but also providing general guidance for *all* products and scenarios (including most possible "worst case" scenarios) introduced by national authorities, the construction unit and other actors influenced the quality and complexity of the Guidance Papers. Being highly complex on one hand and sometimes too general on the other reduced their practicality for their target groups, but even more: anybody outside this smaller group could rarely profit from the efforts put in these documents.

So far this summary has been following a typical "top-down" approach, giving the impression of "the Commission" as playing an active part and an agenda setter[418]. This is to an extent a reasonable reflection of the real situation, because most of the activities were based on laws and contracts with CEN and EOTA at EU level. However, the dependency of the Commission (the construction unit) on the input of other (national) actors was also very obvious. All actors, be they Member State authorities or representatives of federations or other organisations introduced into the implementation scheme of the CPD, were (and are) essential for the construction unit to get data and feedback about (national) approaches, positions or problems. Without them – and due to the lack of any previous empirical research in this field – the construction unit would be relatively "blind". The same argument applies to the other European organisations CEN and EOTA. From this point onwards, input provided by national authorities and other actors was significantly influencing the positions and activities of the construction unit, CEN and EOTA[419] and networking was clearly an essential tool for all actors to reduce the dependency on one source at the risk of not receiving input at all. This forced all actors to use at least a minimum of trust to remain operational: By the construction unit and by representatives of national bodies and industry federations that that the information received was reasonably reliable, and achieved agreements would be honoured by all actors. However, this strong position of downstream users as providers of information and therefore their chance to influence discussions and decisions at EU level seemed not to be realised by them. Like the upstream actors in the SCC, they were mostly *reactive* and missed the chance of an active and creative role of the "bottom up" approach.

But also national representatives were hampered by similar problems: They too had nearly no useful empirical data at national level. Most positions, questions or problems presented at EU level were not based on aggregated or representative empirical data but on general "expert opinion" and individual examples. "Embedded" in a national system or a national organisation, these assumptions and examples could have relied on specific norms and experience commonly shared by national actors which made it easier for these actors to

418 This study is only looking at the *implementation* of the Directive. During the creation of the CPD other actors – and here in particular Member States (via the European Council) – had a different and stronger position.

419 Unfortunately for several actors, being the interface between the EU and their national level, the fact that there might have been 27(!) different positions and a compromise could be seen as a clear success of communication and cooperation, the actual evaluation done by downstream (national) actors was often based on the "survival rate" of a national position.

assess and accept or reject them. While the results of several interviews from different levels seem to indicate that the general perceptions about other levels were relatively accurate, many actors at EU and national level had nothing more than isolated examples reported to them and had to form their position based on their individual judgement as to their relevance. Finding reasonable positions and compromises was in most cases left to these few individuals acting as interface between the two levels, leaving them between the demands of the Commission and their national actors.

While representatives of national authorities often remained in their position even during the long implementation phase of the CPD, private actors were less able to keep the same individuals in their places. Delays in the field of standardisation have shifted interests and resources to other fields and policies made at EU and national level. At the beginning of the 21st century, the construction sector was more in the spotlight when its impact on "global warming" and its contribution to energy efficiency and energy savings was discussed. Naturally, most actors were moving more and more resources from CPD issues to these other fields.[420] Also actors which had not been very active in the field of construction *products* – mainly architects and contractors – were more affected, interested and participating in these new policies. This did not necessarily reduce the role or the power and influence of national representatives or representatives of federations within their system (in particular if they were also active in these other fields), but by losing its rather "unique" role as sole EU directive in the field of construction. This aspect explains the small number of actors and the time they spent dealing with CPD issues at EU level and on the interface level today. But while "older" Member States have already covered CPD and CE marking issues, newer Member States had to split their resources and the CPD was right from the beginning "competing" with other policies and directives for interest and sufficient resources to be provided by national public and private actors.

Nevertheless, the national transpositions of the CPD – and more precisely, the publication of harmonised European standards and CE marked products –

420 This development highlights the problem of authorities creating their own "competition" by opening activities in several policy fields: Since public authorities might not be able to cope with all developments at the same time and with enough resources, the risk is even higher that downstream users will have even less resources at their disposal, which reduces the chance for compliance even when downstream actors would (like to) support a policy and its instruments. By default priorities have to be set which would differ in a sector as heterogeneous as the construction sector which will make the approach even less coordinated.

were affecting national systems. By introducing obligatory marks for products, at least authorities (linking these product-specific requirements of the CPD with national building codes and other laws) and manufacturers (being concerned with the quantity and quality of data that has to be provided with CE marking) had to react. Therefore, the only official "construction" committee at EU level – the SCC – remained *the* instrument for Member State authorities to monitor and react on activities of the construction unit in this field. This *monitoring* aspect was also reflected in the selection of national units or departments to be sent to "Brussels". The authorities representing their country in the SCC were in most cases not the ones who would *use* or profit directly from the CPD and CE marking, while other national or regional institutions and agencies were actually contracting construction work (public procurement), setting requirements on product performance and were controlling the construction works (e.g., infrastructure, national buildings). It could be argued that national administrations have considered competence of collecting and distributing information as more important than specific technical competence,[421] but this argument was not always convincing, considering that "practical users" within the national administration seemed to have only partly actively participated in the discussions on the use of CE marking at national level. Reactions at the national level ranged from being interested at a more general level ("one has to fulfil the letter of the law, but it has only low impact on the practical work") to considering the developments "in the EU" as something that is not directly affecting them and therefore leaving all issues in the hands of specific actors (e.g., public or private bodies tasked with monitoring and reacting to EU initiatives). This left the individuals coordinating national positions with two heavy tasks of *raising interest* and *guaranteeing cooperation* of national public (and private) actors. If feedback was incomplete or non-existent, these individuals could even find that a position taken by them at EU level was at the same time challenged and contradicted by other authorities at national or regional level.

With all these practical restrictions and the number of tasks of individuals representing national or sectoral interests, it is not absolutely surprising that in interaction with the construction unit or in the SCC, national representatives were rarely pro-active – except where serious interests of national actors were at

421 In several cases the same department, but often even the same individuals are representing their Member State in a wide range of committees and working groups on EU level with a similar wide range of technical expertise needed.

stake. Also the main official instrument for exchanging information and finding common solutions – the SCC – was (and is) *de facto* a *reactive* committee. Most of the information flow was going in *one* direction from the construction unit to the representatives of national authorities and other actors. "The Commission" was *reporting* on activities or was presenting draft Commission decisions or documents of less regulatory nature, while most national actors were *reacting* to this input. The few attempts of some Member States representatives (or the construction unit) to initiate a more informal information flow between *all* actors ("How is something done in other Member States?") were mostly met with indifference and provided little if any feedback. Also questions raised by other actors (authorities, specification writers or notified bodies) did in several cases not receive answers quickly – and in some cases they did not receive any answer at all. However, this criticism was mostly directed at the situation in the late 90s and beyond. At the beginning of the implementation of the CPD the SCC had also been trying to provide additional guidance to specification writers, Notified Bodies and industry in general by producing the Interpretative Documents as link between the CPD and building requirements as well as Guidance Papers for more detailed information on the practical implementation. But here too, the approach was not so much to develop communication between different actors in *both* directions (downstream and upstream) but as a "top-down" approach. Here again, feedback or the comparison of results (in different Member States, sectors or CEN TCs) was not actively pursued by the SCC (again, individual attempts excluded). Considering its reactive nature and an information flow significantly below its potentials, the SCC can be described as an institutionalised "*action generator*" (see: "Knowledge, lack of knowledge and trust") rather than as a "*problem solver*". Positions, problems or questions were fed via established paths into the system (the procedure of the SCC or specific regulators/expert/working groups) and "have been discussed in the SCC". However, the problem has been shifted to the EU level which reduced the risk of conflict between actors at *national* level and also provided a justification for national or federation representatives for implementing a decision "made by the SCC" or "the Commission" ("politics of blame avoidance")[422].

Outside the SCC, national authorities were only in some cases active in transnational networking (within the framework of the CPD). This could be partly explained by their specific role as purely *national* actor. Being embedded in a

422 Weaver cited in: Schimank p. 163.

national system had clear advantages when it came to their special role as regulators and their access to administrative resources and expert input by national actors – in particular if "in-house" resources were relatively easily available. It was therefore not surprising that individuals from national authorities were also the ones with the least contacts with other actors outside their national system. On the other hand, this reduced their possibilities to identify and learn from solutions found in other (national) systems. But even when national representatives were more interested in stronger transnational cooperation, they were also aware that feedback was mostly based on individual cases. Initiating activities based on such weak data would have been too risky which only left them the option of a relative passive national position.

Industry representatives on the other hand, have selected a different approach. Having no institutionalised networks at their disposal which would have guaranteed at least passive participation in the information flow, they dependent on voluntary support and input. Facing in addition declining interest of members if their focus and their (economic) needs were changing, they used more often contacts outside their own organisation or federation by networking with other federations or organisations (active in the construction sector) to get enough information and analysis on time. This more open and flexible approach of networking was a characteristic of private (industry) actors, but not in all fields. This higher level of cooperation worked relatively well for representatives who had to monitor and to react to policy and administrative activities of EU actors. The more specific the issues became – with standardisation and certification work as the most technical part of the system – more specific interests were becoming dominant and influencing quantity and quality of the communication of "expert" actors.

While only being partly involved in discussions in the SCC (having only observer status), industry sectors found a different route of introducing their positions, experience and technical expertise into the system: the standardisation work at EU and national level. Having the clear advantage of more technical expertise and experts available for this technical work than authorities, standardisation and certification work gave these private actors a strong role in the practical implementation as well as allowing them to be active in a field that is often more directly affecting their work and interests than more general regulatory requirements. Here again, sector specific (economic) interests or even specific national interests did not always allow for a united approach in the field of standardisation but made work in CEN (as previously in national standardisation bodies) sometimes a place for introducing more than technical expertise in this work. Since (lack of) awareness about developments on EU (CEN) level and the need for resources to influence them created an even more asymmetric situation in EU organisations, scepticism about the work at EU level as neutral and balanced was often voiced by *national* industry actors.

In addition, to increase interest in the private sector, the tendency to see the CPD and CE marking as not only removing *administrative* barriers (e.g., additional test methods in each country) but removing *regulatory* barriers (changing national laws) became and remained strong within EU federations. Therefore, they were also partly adding to the imprecise information on the actual use of CE marking, and by raising the expectations also increasing the disappointment of downstream actors when the actual (limited) impact of CE marking became clearer.

An aspect that has put CEN and EOTA into the spotlight was their roles as the only ones which had to produce (technical) *practical* and *tangible* results: European standards, ETAGs, CUAPs and ETAs. These technical specifications were seen by most private actors as having a much stronger economic impact than most of the results of the work of any other actor at EU level. While documents produced by all other actors (the Commission services, MS authorities and industry representatives) were of a more general nature (except for Commission Decisions) – which were also only partly used by downstream actors – European technical specifications were naturally closely examined by national actors, compared with previous national specifications (which were already known and used at national level) and critically assessed. Considering the complexity of the tasks for some of the standards and the vague guidance from authorities about relevant regulations, the complaints about the time the development of these specifications needed and the final quality (practicability) were not surprising. Following the principle that success has many fathers, failure has none, despite the large number of actors involved in the process of developing technical specifications, blame was left with the European bodies. It should be noted that here too, criticism was mostly based on "examples" and assumptions – not on empirical data.

The difference between CEN and EOTA – when it came to criticism – was mostly caused by their specific memberships: CEN needed experts for its technical committees which were to a large extent provided by *manufacturers*. Challenging the results of their work was mostly done by *national authorities*. Either, because they themselves had objections to standards (mostly the case in Germany, Austria and Poland) or specific industry sectors addressed national authorities with their concerns (more often seen in the UK). EOTA's members were either bodies with some *delegated official powers* or very closely linked to public authorities. Here *manufacturers* and their federations had been at the forefront of critics.

4.3 The information flow to (and from) national actors – setting the national level

With the CPD introduced in national legislation, the construction unit, national authorities and various federations in the construction sector were facing the task of "selling" the new approach and CE marking to downstream users. Since EU actors have no or only limited power to "enforce" compliance by national actors, practically all of them (CEN, EOTA and the GNB – excluding the construction unit as part of the EU administration) had only a role as coordinator and distributor of information and as reference point while their national members (in particular national standardisation bodies) had the task and responsibility of providing clear interpretation to downstream actors on documents and decisions made at EU level which increased their importance and their input into the scheme. Often seen as an advantage: The same individuals active on EU level were often trying to explain the CPD and CE marking concept to downstream actors.

Like at EU level, information spread by EU and national authorities was not focused on a *specific* target group but provided general information on the official website of the authorities, some information events and participation in conferences and other events organised by other actors (e.g., conferences of industry federations, construction fairs). Authorities active at EU and national level were collectors and distributors of information but not actual users of "the CPD" and CE marking. In all four Member States of this study, national authorities had tried to raise interest, but on the other hand they were also not (or: no longer) *pushing* – assuming that awareness and interest would grow when more standards were available and therefore more practical examples would allow a more practical discussion – which would be dealt with by national technical institutes (DIBt, BRE, OIB and ITB). The main problem at that general level was again the wide scope and the complexity of the CPD: It was easy to explain the *general* concept, but providing enough information on how the scheme would work for *specific* products or on a more practical level which would have raised interest in downstream users (who were already considered as rather "conservative" and sceptical about new approaches) was difficult if not impossible without existing technical standards.

Since building codes were for most actors at national level the most relevant legal and technical documents, Member State authorities have often considered technical organisations (technical institutes) as more competent in providing useful technical data and guidance. Also industry federations at EU level often depended more on efforts at national level to interpret (or even translate texts into the national language in the first place) documents produced at EU level and to provide practical and pragmatic guidance for *their* downstream users. Nevertheless, national actors often kept a system of continued information flow, which was linked to activities at EU level: preparing for meetings of the Standing Committee on Construction and its Preparatory Group provided enough incentive to keep national actors interested and aware of developments at EU level. Germany and the UK had the most "institutionalised" structure of preparatory committees in place to receive feedback from downstream actors. The limits to this became apparent in the actual participation which depended on how much actors felt affected by these developments on one hand, and how much their positions were based on empirical data or "expert opinions". The relatively weak position of downstream actors (they had to be invited to these committees and the hosts had no *obligation* to present their positions) forced national actors to act as an interface to develop what they considered the most realistic (and balanced) position of all national actors. In all four Member States the route of bilateral discussions with the construction unit was also (to a different extent) used.

No matter if EU or national authorities, organisations or federations (also completely independent of their national origin), most of them were following the same approach: A first strong "push" of providing data, raising awareness (if possible), and then waiting for feedback and questions. The choice of distributing information to a large number of potential recipients without putting strong emphasis on information for specific users seemed to be partly caused by a lack of knowledge even at the level of distributing actors on what downstream users might need, where their interests, potentials and limits might be. Since in most cases no or only few reactions were received (except mostly general scepticism), communication was reduced to continuous distribution of documents whenever they were considered as relevant or interesting for other downstream users (due to the lack of feedback: based on the assumptions of the distributing individuals).

Federations in general were even more dependent on *voluntary* feedback from their members. Compared to national administrations, these federations had even fewer individuals working at EU and national level, monitoring developments at these levels, interpreting it, distributing it and coordinating positions of their members. In several cases being "one-man-armies", their workload and responsibility was increased by being both active at EU *and* on national level at the same time. Not surprisingly, these individuals were often very selective about the quality and quantity of information they were passing on. Information that seemed not to affect their members directly was often kept at EU or national federation level to avoid an "overkill" of information to SMEs and micro-enterprises. On the other hand, information of more technical nature (e.g., technical standards) was of strong interest for these actors and efforts were made not only to provide this information to all downstream actors, but also to provide interpretation and guidance to facilitate the practical implementation. Again, mostly federations of manufacturers had been active while federations of architects and contractors had shown only limited interest in this topic and rarely distributed information (to avoid the above-mentioned "overkill") and also received few if any questions or feedback.

However, the main challenge for authorities and private actors was to describe how the new approach would fit into existing schemes. "Selling" the CPD approach depended on its added value for downstream users which would justify the adaptation costs, or showing that even with the new scheme no significant changes would be necessary. The "natural weakness" of the CPD as providing product information but not giving any guarantee about its safe use involuntarily supported a "natural" advantage of any (national) scheme that declared a product safe for (specific) intended uses. Providing only complementary information, several actors at national level decided to pass on only basic and essential information on CE marking.

4.4 The "construction site" level – The quest for the "missing link"

From the level of national federations and coordinating authorities "downwards", the role of CE marking of "opening" markets was for most downstream users relatively irrelevant and remained therefore only knowledge at federation level. Again, the lack of conclusive empirical data made any assumption difficult but it seemed reasonable to err on the side of caution: Despite the fact that CE marking was more and more used by manufacturers, its role as *successful* "push factor" for construction products into new markets was difficult to prove. The wide range of products covered by CPD-CE marking did not allow for any conclusions if and where CE marking had produced tangible positive effects (This did not stop federations of manufacturers in general supporting the introduction and use of it).

This lack of relevance of the CE marking *per se* for downstream users (architects, contractors) reduced also the relevance of the information passed on, and CE marking remained rather unknown, or it was seen as type of "quality mark" guaranteeing the "safe" use of CE marked products. Here a major dilemma for manufacturers and consumers became more visible: Practically all marks in the market are somehow indicating (justified or unjustified) a performance or use that would set the certified product apart from competing products. Therefore, all marks can be seen as simplified *declaration of improvement* – including the CE marking for construction products. But since even low performing products would easily get CE marking (since CE marking is only indicating that it has followed a harmonised system of declaration), competitors could easily "catch up" in consumer perception with high quality products. Contradicting the scheme of reducing complexity by using marks as simplified information, consumers (architects, contractors) have on one hand to forget about this approach and to compare technical data and link it to their intended uses, while at the next step they could fall back on simplified information by checking for additional quality marks. Not surprisingly, manufacturers and their customers had problems clearly identifying the differences between these two approaches (or the added value of increasing the complexity for them) and often decided to invest the minimum of efforts to fulfil their legal obligations).

But CE marking *did* leave its mark in national markets in a different – and unintended – way: By introducing an *obligatory* mark into the European and national construction products market, more and more manufacturers and downstream users became aware that there were some obligations to be fulfilled. While CE marking provided only part of the information that would have *facilitated* the choice of products, the interest in certifications that could be used for customers got a new appeal. Also awareness raising activities by certification bodies (promoting combination packages covering the requirements for CE marking and "market demands" in the widest sense) has "pushed" (national) actors in the direction of using marks – or at least "pushed" them to check if a specific mark was now officially or *de facto* obligatory to remain competitive in their market.

Nevertheless, marks of any type (including CE marking) remained more a concern for manufacturers and certification bodies (and depending on how strongly national authorities insisted on additional certification – public authorities too) than for users at the "construction site" level: Compared to the complex systems of responsibilities assumed and discussed at EU and on national level, at the level of practical implementation the links between different actors shortened to few actors involved (contractor/architect – distributor – manufacturer) which allowed for more direct contact and also a clear distribution of tasks and responsibilities. Also the relevant requirements were different to the ones discussed at EU level: While technical performance was still important, additional requirements were undisputable priorities when selecting products:

- easily to be used (experience with the product, clear instructions),
- easily available (provided by distributors) and
- with no or only low risks of liability in case of later damages (product quality and confirmation that the planner and contractor are only responsible for selecting the correct product and the correct installation).[423]

Playing devil's advocate and assuming that the CPD has "provided products (technical specifications), but not solutions"[424] for actors in the construction

423 While manufacturers, specification writers and authorities were often considering the "price" as the most relevant criterion, this could be considered as over-simplification. While not denying its economic relevance, one has to take the *overall costs* into consideration – including how difficult and time-consuming the installation would be (costs of the workforce – not to mention the risk of flawed installation), how fast products could be delivered (costs for delays on the construction site) and repair work (additional costs of binding the workforce on a theoretically-finalised project). Also more intense competition would allow only limited differences in prices of products, which would make these practical/technical criteria even more important.

sector, the question would arise about the "missing link" between the goals of the Internal Market and the actual planning and construction work. Lacking evaluation of the needs of the end users of CE marking even 20 years after the creation of the CPD, most actors at EU or national level could only provide vague assumptions about the practical added value of CE marking. Therefore, the CPD approach was *de facto* only facilitating opening markets to CE marked products. How easily a product could be used and how much information and support manufacturers were providing to their customers was outside the scope of the CPD and remained more or less completely in the hands of market actors and their competition. Leaving such an important factor out of the CPD approach automatically reduced the practical use of European standards for downstream users (whether as market instruments for manufacturers or technical instruments for architects and construction companies).

The last bullet point addresses the most difficult requirement and highlights the gap between the intentions of the CPD and the "construction site": Providing information on products was not only sensible, it was the usual approach in practically *all* national systems for selecting and using products by planners and contractors (including guidance provided in technical guidance documents on EU level – like the GP, ID, Approval Documents and others). However, the CPD was only focusing on *regulatory* requirements which in most cases were not giving precise guidance on how to achieve specific performance criteria. In fact, national or regional building codes *depended* on *additional* technical experience and guidance given by professional actors (universities, federations of manufacturers, contractors or specific professions in the building sector) to fulfil the "state of the art" requirement. This additional information – resulting in the *assurance* that a product has been correctly used – was and is essential in any professional selection process. The fact, that CE marking was not providing all relevant information but on the other hand became obligatory (in most Member States) created even more so the impression of that something "has to be fulfilled" rather than provide additional help.

In this gap other (national) marks were moving in as instruments claiming to provide assurance and therefore reducing search costs and the costs of interpreting the information provided with CE marking. However, the comments of the "final users" were indicating that these problems were already mostly

424 Bonchek/Howard: "The Power to Convene" in: Heckscher/Adler (eds): The Firm as a Collaborative Community 2007 p. 517.

compensated for (without any specific use of marks) by experience and trust in existing structures of getting information and buying products from known and reliable sources (e.g., "brand names").[425] Therefore, additional national marks were also not often perceived as extremely helpful but as an additional certification and documentation layer. In fact, they were often only seen as useful *after* the purchase and the installation to have a "paper trail" in case of later complaints, and could only partly (if at all) contribute to buying decisions. This was not surprising, because for most products used in construction all national marks (and like CE marking) were introduced *after* these products (or similar types) had been on the market for several years and users had already had their experience of them. Most "market decisions" were already made and (even) national marks were only providing a late approval ("I know it is safe, but now even the authorities are confirming it" – and taking the responsibility). Only planners and contractors working outside their own national environment highlighted a certain relevance of CE marking (but again, the reference to known and used products remained stronger). This lack of added value highlights a general problem of the strong focus on product standards by several EU and national actors: Most downstream users expect that the requirements laid down in product standards *are* met by manufacturers, no matter if they are of national or international standards. Expecting that downstream users at the construction site level are actually checking all data was (and is) not a realistic assumption of the time and resources available for most downstream actors.

The lack of interest could also be partly explained by the experience of most actors that damages in buildings (and therefore expensive maintenance and repair work) were rarely a question of poor quality construction products but caused by design flaws or mistakes during the installation phase. But I would argue that one of the main reasons why certification marks were playing a rather insignificant role in active selection and buying decisions were the limitations that these marks had to *establish* trust. In a system that has to rely strongly on trust, CE marking and national marks were "competing against each other" too much,

425 An interesting perception of actors at national and "construction site" level turned the argument of improving acceptance of products by introducing CE marking or other marks around: besides positive experience or feedback on "brand name" products, they were supposed *to have all certificates anyway*. Only smaller and less known companies were actually checked if they complied with all *regulatory* requirements. Following this perception, CE marking would not play a major role for *entering* a market (which would clearly depend on "market demands" from private and public actors) but for *remaining* there.

which resulted in more confusion and distrust than increasing trust (in CE marking or another mark). Since all changes included the high risk of disturbing established systems of trust, these systems reacted rather defensively, following the letter of the law but not its spirit. The importance of experience and trust was also to an extent caused by the lack of active market surveillance which forced planners, contractors and other professionals to rely more on their experience and feedback within the market than on marks and certificates.

It might be a little bit reassuring (at least for the Commission) that not only CE marking but also national marks could not claim to have made a *major* positive impact (in fact, it was considered as having an impact "in a subtle negative way"), and that discussions on EU and national certificates and acceptance were maybe less relevant at the "construction site" level. On the other hand, this point of view cannot hide the fact that CE marking for construction products has over the whole phase of its (theoretical and practical) existence been introducing and strengthening the "push factor" (obligatory CE marking and its acceptance on all national markets) to put products on markets, expecting these markets to accept them[426], but no significant "pull factor" has been searched for, established or supported by any actor at EU level – including the construction unit.

Following this argument, the "missing link" between the CPD and construction work will remain "missing". Providing only *some* essential information minimises the value of CE marking for planners and contractors. The important "added value" that CE marking could provide to downstream actors – the *reduction of complexity* – was only partly possible and this approach has created the *image* of an additional burden, creating more confusion and being a "challenge" to the existing national scheme. The original (and familiar) reference points for actors at the construction site level – building codes and individual contracts with suppliers or manufacturers – became even more important the more the confusion increased. It did not matter that most assumptions about the efficiency and quality of national or sector specific approaches were in fact lacking empirical data to prove these assumptions right. The fact that most actors *expected/ trusted* it to work this way already reduced interpretation costs and decreased the level of insecurity and complexity. Creating *trust* that this product can be *safely used* was outside the CPD and CE marking and these interpretation costs (which

426 See also: Adler/Heckscher: Towards Collaborative Community in: Heckscher/Adler (eds): The Firm as a Collaborative Community 2007 p. 32.

had been at least partly removed in previous national schemes) have been (partly) reintroduced for downstream users.

However, the confusion between CE marking as an information tool for planners and contractors or as a pure market tool for manufacturers and market surveillance authorities has in some cases been solved in a very pragmatic way:

- A simple, but important step was the split between *accepting* CE marked products in a (national) market and *the actual use* of these products. While not in agreement with the interpretation of the construction unit, the acceptance of CE marking in general in the UK but not considering it as *obligatory* followed the spirit of "opening the market". Also Austria and Poland made a relatively clear split between the obligatory use of CE marked products and the actual use in buildings and civil engineering works. The fact that Austrian manufacturer's federations rarely provided additional information on CE marking for their customers but focused on technical performance criteria and values instead also indicated the *relative* value of CE marking as communication tool between manufacturers and customers. The German case is only partly different from the other three examples: The German "*Bauregelliste*" was combining the acceptance of CE marked products in general with providing additional (binding) information on their safe use. Here two relevant steps were taken in one document: official acceptance of products *and* reducing the complexity for planners and contractors by defining the scope of technically (and therefore also legally unproblematic) use of these products. German building authorities recognised the *need* for additional information – and even *provided* it (only the UK provided information for users at a comparable level of detail – the other two countries left the interpretation costs mostly to downstream actors). However, two aspects were making this approach more problematic: One, the strong involvement of authorities in setting requirements for other actors which was left to the professional expertise of private actors in the other three Member States. Two: since other professional actors (in particular federations of manufacturers) followed the approach of linking CE marking more or less directly with the German *Ü-Zeichen*,[427] both approaches were com-

427 Guidance provided by federations of manufacturers (e.g., their websites) was indicating what type of information is needed for CE marking and what format to use to apply it on products. In addition, references were made to the *Ü-Zeichen* to improve the market acceptance for these products.

ing so close together that several actors (outside Germany) considered that acceptance on the German market was *de facto* only achievable by using both approaches together. (binding nature of *Ü-Zeichen*)

- Another simple but practical approach was mentioned by a representative of a Notified Body: *Training* of market surveillance authorities *on practical examples*. This exercise has not only linked two of the main actors in the field of the CPD together, referring to past or existing *practical* questions has also helped both actors to understand their relative needs. However, since market surveillance was still only *re*active and not active in most countries, this training and exchange of experience could only reach a small number of experts and had only limited impact on the quality of products being placed on the market and used in construction.
- Providing information effectively depends also on the realistic assumption about potential target groups and how much information is required. Here several public and private actors in the UK, the Austrian OIB and the Polish ITB were addressing a wider audience and therefore were also giving a wide range of information and links to other sites or actors. This was in fact a difficult task, keeping in mind that CE marking was only providing *some* information but not necessarily *everything* that was needed for selecting a product. However, since architects, contractors and do-it-yourself enthusiasts *were* playing a role in controlling products used on construction sites (also due to the often-mentioned lack of market surveillance) – and even taking a legal responsibility – information for these groups was important to allow them to fulfil this task.
- Industry federations (in particular in Germany) had been very active in providing not only general information on new requirements but also *guidance on how this should be used at a practical level* in publications, websites and presentations in conferences. Examples given facilitated the "translation" of a European standard into correct product declaration.
- Communication depends also on active participation in the information flow in both directions. Here Germany (via the BMVBS and the DIBt) and the UK (via the BRE) established relatively stable networks that were recognised and actively used by different actors. It could have been an advantage to both countries that they had been Member States when the CPD was adopted and that they had been involved in all implementation steps. The long period could also have helped a large number of actors become aware of CE marking (an awareness that seemed to be well-developed in both

countries despite the different emphasis given to CE marking) and growing accustomed to the information network available.

- While the "newer" Member States, Austria and Poland, experienced less active participation by national downstream actors, both countries nevertheless used their accession to the EU and the introduction of the CPD to adapt their systems in several cases to a more transnational scheme than *just "re-translating"* requirements set at EU level back to national parameters and values. At least at the national level have been significant changes compared to the "older" Member States (the "construction site" level shows more national and regional "characteristics").
- Also the wide network of market surveillance inspectors in Poland should be mentioned. Establishing and maintaining a system as in Poland was time- and cost-intensive. However, one of the main gaps in the other national schemes was the focus on manufacturers (and the manufacturing process) more or less directly under the "control" of authorities (national or EU certification systems) while little data was available on the products actually bought and installed in buildings and construction works. It is not very realistic to assume that any national market can be so closely monitored that all products entering the country (or even produced in a country) will be sufficiently evaluated and certified without the pressure of an active and effective market surveillance system in place[428].
- One expert in standardisation referred to a CEN TC which for a long time focused purely on developing a technical standard for a specific product (including the intended use and its installation). Only after most of the standard has been finalised, were the "additional" aspects of the CPD assessed and introduced into the standard. What seem logical highlights nevertheless CEN's task of providing *technical* expertise and *technical* documents. The risk for all actors at EU level was to introduce political or economic aspects outside the scope of a specific task, creating the problems mentioned above.

In general, most of these pragmatic but successful approaches have one thing in common: Individuals have realised and *accepted* that even their own systems include several "information gaps" (in particular lack of empirical data) which

428 Keeping the sometimes complex certification systems at national level in mind, one can also assume that non-compliance might not (always) be intentionally, but might happen because of lack of clear information or misinterpretations.

were "filled" with expectations that most actors would follow established norms. Not being forced to defend a specific national or sectoral approach (because its limitations were known) additional ideas and combinations of the CPD approach and instruments with national ones were more readily developed and accepted – in several cases improving both the EU and the national scheme. In these cases the "trust" in national schemes had partly been widened to "trust" into transnational/EU schemes too. The risks were known but accepted as in the national ones.

Last but not least: At the beginning of this study, it was said that the CPD brings the worst and the best out of the actors involved. One of the best is the individual interest and involvement beyond institutionalised roles and expectations. This goes for all four Member States in this study which have also kept a dialogue with other EU actors – in particular the construction unit – outside official meetings, asking questions, trying to find solutions when a common agreement seemed unlikely, and participating in the different working groups (expert groups) dealing with specific aspects within the framework of the CPD. Not every attempt was successful, but the willingness to try was shown by all four countries. Also private actors have spent significant time not only presenting and defending the positions of their federations or specific members, but also learning about and understanding the position of other actors (not only the construction unit as the main reference point). Of course, this praise does not apply to every individual, institution or organisation. Nevertheless, all the problems mentioned in interviews could have been worse had not several actors added more to the communication and interaction process at EU *and* on national level.

The relevance of this critical assessment of national (or EU) *images* of complete and successful schemes should not be underestimated. In particular when compared to the strong "path dependency" that some actors (including the Commission) were sometimes showing. The approach of putting too much trust into one (national) scheme includes the risk of fighting for solutions that have been successful in a purely national environment but could not provide the same answers and protection in a transnational (or even globalised) world. In particular the strong focus on controlling the (national) manufacturing process while largely ignoring the distribution and installation phase of construction products (market surveillance) was supporting specific approaches in national schemes, but also creating the same weakness that the CPD was criticised for: the focus on *products* at the cost of *buildings and civil engineering works*. It is surprising (and here the introduction of the CPD into national market systems could be seen as another chance to evaluate existing schemes), that despite the assumption raised by several national actors that more and more products were imported into national markets, and a certain distrust in actors of other countries (in the EU and outside)[429], market surveillance was in most countries not considered an important instrument to ensure the safety of the final users of buildings and civil engineering works – at least not important enough to invest in a more active national scheme. Keeping in mind the changing market conditions, previously (assumed) successful solutions were becoming less and less practical, the assumption that *even more of the same* (setting more and more requirements for manufactures and certification bodies only) had to be done to solve the problem indicated a lack of adaptability by national actors[430].

But also the attempt of the Commission to put even stronger binding instruments in place to remove existing different interpretations and implementations by proposing the use of a *Regulation* for construction products includes the risk of a negative "path dependency": It keeps the emphasis on opening markets for products but rarely closes the gap between products (placing on a market) and buildings and civil engineering works or reducing the scope to a smaller range of products. In both cases, the trust in one's own approach is clearly visible, acknowledging its weaknesses and accepting its limitations (and using them for the best outcome) is less obvious.

---

429 Mentioned in several interviews but also to be found in publications stressing the higher performance of actors in one's own country.

430 While just four Member States cannot be considered as representative of all EU Member States, it should be noted that actors in the "older" two Member States were more often referring to familiar (national) schemes, their advantages and their problems with the CPD approach. Cooperation with actors from other Member States – to improve common understanding and to increase the synergy effect of cooperation – was theoretically welcomed but less often put into practice. The two "newer" Member States (and here maybe Austria is the better example because the "stability" of its national framework in the last decades is very similar to the situation of the UK and Germany) clearly actively asked for and used the experience of "older" Member States before joining the EU. They had less "freedom" in "setting the rules" but could in several cases avoid costs of developing their own national approach "from scratch".

4.5 Good news and bad news for Eurosceptics …

Looking at the CPD there is fortunately good and bad news for everybody: The Eurosceptics could relax when it comes to the "power" of the European Commission and European actors (including "industry lobbyists"). Despite the *de jure* power of the Commission and the Commission services as regulators and "agenda setters", their dependency on input and cooperation from national authorities and other national actors and the partial lack of transparency of the different levels, institutions and organisations to each other could – and actually *has* – "neutralised" initiatives at EU level to a significant extent the moment it reaches the practical national implementation level.

The main problems seem to be the relative isolation of all three levels in the communication system:[431]

- All three of them were working with different but *specific* regulatory tools (the CPD, building codes, individual contracts) which were linked together "on paper", but had limited practical influence for actors at other levels.
- Since the added value of CE marking was difficult to explain within these three different environments, information provided for downstream users was only partly seen as relevant by them, which also significantly reduced the chance for upstream actors to get practical feedback.
- There were only few individuals acting as interface between these different levels, in institutionalised networks with rare contacts and not necessarily sufficiently linked to all issues that concerned building performance and construction product performance. This negatively affected the quality and quantity of data moved to upstream and downstream users.
- Most of these individuals were not actively involved in the implementation and use of CE marking. In their positions and reactions they could hardly fall back on their own experience but had to rely on input from other actors. This put these individuals in a less powerful position when trying to "enforce" decisions made at upstream level on downstream actors.

431 Which would put the CPD approach close to Cohen's "garbage can" model: problematic preferences (inconsistent/ill defined); unclear technology – processes are not understood by its members; fluid participation – participants vary in time – efforts are devoted to different domains (see: Richardson: Policy-making in the EU 2006).

- Empirical data was generally a very rare resource. To a large extent each level depended on mutual trust to compensate for "structural holes" in the system.[432]
- National actors remained in a strong position as distributors and interpreters ("expert opinion") of information from and to other levels. Their work significantly influenced the quantity of data as well as its perception by upstream and downstream actors.
- Since national actors (in particular national and regional authorities) were rarely working in information networks with actors in other Member States, "mutual understanding" could hardly be developed which left most actors in a Member State only with the existing national scheme as reference (and in the worst case resulted in the need to "translate" nearly everything back into these schemes – "barriers to knowledge").
- Depending on the stability of existing networks of interaction and trust established in local, regional or national schemes, additional requirements or instruments might have to prove their usefulness before having a chance of replacing established paths. As the acceptance and use of CE marking and other national marks has shown, the heavy "battles" about specific performance characteristics and assumed needs of downstream actors at EU and national level had limited impact at a practical level.

These problems identified within the framework of the CPD also highlights a general problem when addressing issues at EU level and developing solutions at this level – a problem that could not only have been found in national systems too, it was actually *caused* to a large extent by flaws in national systems: The focus on *what* should be achieved often neglected the question of *how* it should be achieved. While the (public and private) administrative structure might have existed (or could have been developed by creating a new organisation), knowledge about the actual abilities (e.g., technical expertise) and resources (e.g., manpower, networks or technical instruments) of downstream actors rarely existed. This was even more dangerous when shifting the actual work several levels downstream. The actors at these level had mostly not been able to follow developments at levels far away from their practical responsibilities and needs

432 There is one combination of "lack of data" and "mutual trust", which was sometimes seen in the interviews of this study: The *trust in having data available* if one would just make the effort and search for it. In particular "expert opinions" were more often considered as being a summary of existing empirical data than assumptions based on selective experience.

and were partly overwhelmed by either very complex requirements or not fulfilling their actual needs. In addition, the ongoing developments on "lean management" in the public and private sector included the risk that more responsibilities would be shifted to downstream authorities and users while they could no longer be efficiently implemented.

4.6 … and Europhiles

The limits of EU initiatives and laws on national, regional and local systems might be the bad news for Europhiles, showing that there is still a long way before they can "compete" with established systems at downstream levels. Also the lack of participation of downstream actors and the lack of information provided to upstream actors could give the impression that the implementation of the CPD was extremely flawed. However, despite the complex environment of the construction sector and the political and administrative environment changing several times (with each new accession to the EC/EU), it was never the approach (having one set of technical requirements, standards and test methods in all Member States of the EU) that was criticised by the interviewees but the (unnecessary) complexity of it. The problem highlighted was the duplication of work and overlap of national and EU approaches due to different positions of different actors at EU and national level and the lack of practical input, rather than having one common approach. More practically, the example of the CPD has shown that

- While the CPD was obviously one of the most difficult directives in its interpretation and implementation, it was also obvious that most problems did not in general result from *active opposition*. "Playing by the rules" (the *homo sociologicus* approach) was relatively well accepted and used by actors. This cooperative behaviour was supported by networks (in particular networks with a strong technical focus) which remained relatively stable and allowed for better understanding of information and facilitated its exchange between these actors. In fact, being part of and contributing to these networks was mentioned by a large number of individuals as one of the most positive developments and experiences within the framework of the CPD.

- The "historical institutionalism" (see: "After the dust has settled") – like "re-translating" requirements into existing national schemes or not using CE marking in the communication with downstream actors – cannot be seen just as "resistance" to changes (and avoidance of conflicts between actors at this level) but also as an attempt of actors to maintain the (presumed) efficiency and effectiveness of the existing system and therefore, providing necessary delays to "soften" the impact for actors who have fewer resources to remain "up to date" on all developments and still not risking deviance from new requirements. This positive assumption of the abilities of downstream actors is not limited to authorities and federations at national level, but covers also the abilities of actors at the construction site level to develop practical solutions that not necessarily need explicit and detailed guidance from upstream actors.
- The different levels (EU, national, "construction site") were also "filters" for selecting relevant information and requirements that have to be incorporated and others that were not absolutely essential. This might not put the best light on regulatory goals and their implementation. But considering the huge number of SMEs and micro-enterprises in this sector on one hand and the also huge number of regulations and other requirements that these enterprises have to be aware of and have to incorporate in their work, this "filter" function has also been essential in compensating for exaggerated expectations at EU level about the added value of CE marking and therefore, keeping these enterprises relatively operational (avoiding an "overkill" of information). In particular, since the CPD and its CE marking should be instruments for manufacturers and market surveillance authorities, and other actors need not be very familiar with CE marking.
- On the other hand, introducing an external (EU) system has motivated national actors to evaluate the existing national scheme (e.g., "expert opinions"; general, but not *verified* trust). The "threat from the outside" has helped to question the efficiency and adaptability of existing national approaches and (since this could be also a "threat" to existing structures of influence for some national, regional and local actors) could facilitate in getting more active participation from national actors than in an evaluation exercise. In the case of the two "newer" Member States the need to adapt to external systems because of the envisaged accession to the EC/EU had created systems that were more compatible with the requirements of the CPD than the "older" Member States Germany and the UK.

- Also the fact that individuals acting as interfaces between different levels might not always be directly involved in the use of CE marking has sometimes allowed these actors to be more balanced in their views and positions at national and EU level. They did not have to defend their "own" position or current practice and could therefore also work on more pragmatic solutions with other actors at EU level. This did not lead to representatives "going native" in "Brussels" but allowed for the development of a, sometimes only weak, but nevertheless *better* understanding of other positions and a better combination of interests at both levels.
- The CPD approach is profiting from the "time factor": The longer regulations on construction products and CE marking remained in place, more and more actors became aware of (relatively) new requirements for product assessment and certification. In cases where neither the quality of the harmonised European standards have been challenged by national actors nor the practical implementation has caused significant problems, CE marking *has de facto* became a (familiar) part of the (national) system. Since all actors have to deal with different technical, regulatory or "market" requirements in all systems, it seems safe to assume that CE marking too will be seen as a familiar and a (more or less) useful instrument in the national and/or European market.

4.7 Research on European Directives – "Gaps" and future fields of research?

This study went beyond most research work on the implementation of European laws and the interaction (and cooperation) between actors at EU and national level. The discussion of the "power" of "the EU" or "the Commission" often addressed by politicians, journalists, the public, but also researchers in political and administrative sciences becomes less impressive when national actors (elites, veto players) were introduced into the system. In fact, European actors depend so heavily on information provided by downstream actors, that more research in the phase *before* EU legislation has been accepted by the European Parliament and the European Council and *after* its adoption by national parliaments would help to get a more realistic picture of the influence of national actors on developments at EU level and *vice versa*. In particular national authorities and organisations closely linked to EU institutions and organisations have so far not got the attention of researchers that they deserve. Compared to industry federations (the "lobbyists") their strong role as advisors of national authorities and interpreters of information and guidance developed at EU level for national, regional and local authorities, makes them not only important actors in national environments, but puts them also on a relatively equal position vis-à-vis the Commission services on specific (technical and scientific) issues. Since European directives are in general moving to a more technical and detailed level the role of experts is becoming more relevant than purely "political" representation of MS and Industry interests.

Like most previous studies, this research work too has focused on only *one* specific law – the Construction Products Directive. But comments from downstream actors (mostly far away from the (institutionalised) political and administrative "struggles" between EU and Member State authorities, but sometimes from actors even working in "Brussels") have highlighted another problem that has so far rarely caught the attention of researchers: The "competition" between different policies and laws created by the Commission itself. Looking at it from the view of actors outside the Commission services, some activities (not only in the construction sector) do not seem to be coordinated and guidance on how they were thought to fit into a common concept is even rarer. But downstream users hardly have the choice to focus their attention and resources just on *one* policy or law. As the example "CPD" has shown, one EU directive could be partly "neutralised" by other EU policies and laws, if they were seen as more relevant for downstream actors (more "added value"). Architects and contractors (and to some extend even manufacturers), being more interested and active in "sustainability" issues, energy efficiency and other combinations of design, installation and choice of products, have mostly "ignored" the CPD. I would argue that the ability (or the lack of it) to present a coherent approach significantly influences downstream actors in their decisions to allocate (enough) resources for specific policies or regulations. However, if, when, how and how much the Commission services might unintentionally "neutralise" themselves has not been looked into when assessing compliance of Member States and national actors with European directives and policies.

Another field that has so far produced only few studies is the practical interaction and cooperation by national actors at *national* and *local* level. This was mostly left to a legalistic approach and the discussion on the distribution of power and responsibilities laid down in national constitutions and national laws.

But the practical implementation of national or regional laws – and therefore: the compliance or deviance by downstream actors – got little attention. Also research on how effective downstream actors (including local and regional authorities) could act vis-à-vis upstream actors and could participate or at least influence the decision finding process is rare or non-existent. This is even more problematic considering that actors trying to define their positions at EU level can hardly use scientific data but have to depend more on "practical experience", "expert knowledge" and (isolated) examples. This gap influences the interaction in both directions – hardly providing realistic assessments of positions, potentials and limits of national actors to actors at EU level on one hand, and having difficulties in assuming relatively correctly if and how decisions made at EU level could be implemented in a national environment. As this study has shown, the assumptions of potential problems might introduce highly complex scenarios at EU level which have relatively minimal impact on the actions of downstream users – or in the worst case: create resistance against too complex guidance or approaches that are not considered as helpful for downstream actors. It also (negatively) affects potential synergy effects that a comparison of "EU approaches" with existing national schemes could provide. Also information on approaches in other Member States and experience gained in these countries could hardly be effectively used if the knowledge on the national scheme is vague or based basically on assumptions. As shown in this study, even approaches developed at national level (like national marks) might not show the results envisaged if knowledge about the interaction between different actors, their actual legal, organisational and technical or cultural environment has not been sufficiently known and therefore only partly correctly used in the planning and implementation phase.

Therefore, this attempt of getting a first impression of how an EU directive is actually affecting the assumed target groups not only highlights the gap between the *intentions* at EU level and the *practical implementation*, it could also be used to question and reassess national approaches and their actual impact. However, this study has also shown some limits to this approach: Reaching the actual "end user" might be difficult as well as time- and labour-intensive – and still it might provide only a glimpse of the perceptions and actions of these "end users", which brings it close to the above criticised "practical experience" and "expert knowledge". However, since (EU or national) laws are supposed to produce specific results, putting more emphasis on getting scientific data on the actual impact on downstream levels cannot be avoided. Leaving this field rather "underdeveloped" would not only risk that unintended developments could be detected, but also risk that one cannot learn from these "mistakes" when creating legislation in the same (or other) policy fields. Even worse: corrections (amendments) to existing legislative tools could be based on wrong assumptions and could intensify the problem instead of providing solutions. Otherwise, the discussions on whether European directives are implemented on time, are delayed or wrongly implemented (depending on the point of view) might not be extremely relevant if these directives (and their national implementations) are intentionally or unintentionally "neutralised" by downstream actors.

Finally: Moving further downstream in the implementation chain to the (intended) "end users" would also help to identify the most important question: Is a specific law necessary and does the practical impact justify the efforts to develop and maintain its implementation tools? Here again, economic, political, social and administrative sciences could help by assessing if and where feedback mechanisms for policies and laws exist at EU and national level and how useful and effective they have been. If the often-praised and promised "lean administration" at EU and national level should be more than a vague goal, the evaluation of laws and their implementation do not stop after they have passed a (national or regional) parliament but at the intended target group. A more practical follow-up (e.g., evaluation *if* new products were available *because of* CE marking; evaluating the experience of manufacturers or contractors entering new markets for the first time) would increase transparency and would help upstream actors to make decisions that would be seen by downstream actors as more helpful and therefore, better accepted. This approach has been recommended for *EU* actors, but it seems also that *national* systems could profit from a more systematic approach than *Cohen's* "garbage model".

4.8 "Here is my brilliant plan! You work out the details!"

During the Second World War an engineer entered Winston Churchill's office and announced "Prime Minister, I have the perfect solution to neutralise the threat of the German submarines in the English Channel: We close the Channel on both ends, pump out the water, and then we only have to collect the submarines lying helpless on the ground." "Interesting idea" replied Churchill, "and how could that be done?" "Prime Minister" came the reply "I had already the idea. The practical implementation is your job."

The easiest way of writing recommendations would be to suggest additional experts being seconded to each and every level. I would not be wrong and I even would not have been the first one in a long line of consultants, individual researchers, individual civil servants or institutes who had considered more manpower as one of the most essential changes to overcome existing difficulties. On the other hand: the demand for more civil servants, lobbyists or consultants would always be the "first casualty" when proposals have to be evaluated with existing and available resources – and quite rightfully! As this study has shown, efficiency or useful approaches are not necessarily linked to the number of people working on them, but on how much thought was given to the approach, quality and quantity of data received and used, and the target groups to be addressed. Anyway, with the current resources available to EU and national actors, major changes seem rather unlikely. Also, assuming that more resources (at *any* level) would be easily available seems to be more wishful thinking than a realistic expectation.

Also dramatic changes in the regulatory framework at national level and between the EU level and Member State level are extremely unlikely to be introduced. The "gap" between requirements for *buildings* and the requirements for *products* will remain, and any concepts of creating a more harmonised approach for building laws and building codes are not very likely to be considered by EU and national actors within the next few years. The focus has to remain on the scope and framework of the Construction *Products* Directive rather than a (potentially) more complementary approach.

Therefore, I will try to develop a "*potential* pragmatic solution scenario", which will select a number of problems identified in the previous chapters and propose solutions that could be put into practice by various actors with relatively few adjustments or additional resources needed. It is not the "lowest common denominator" I am aiming for, but reasonable first steps which should allow most actors to "get on board" and to move slowly in the direction of a "best of world scenario" – which might never be achieved, but as *Immanuel Kant* pointed out, we should make at least the effort to reach the highest goal.

This "pragmatic scenario" is based on my own findings, as well as on several ideas and suggestions raised during the interviews for this study. Also existing literature offers recommendations for EU-national cooperation (mostly however leaving out the other downstream levels). I am not claiming that the following suggestions will solve *all* problems or that they will all be successful. On the other hand: one will only know after they have been tried.

The suggestion should:

- Improve clarity of the goals, target groups and instruments to be used;
- Increase understanding of the positions and possibilities and limits of other actors;
- Improve communication channels between actors involved at different levels;
- Improve sharing resources while supporting the role as constructive monitoring and alerting system;
- Reducing complexity by focusing only on relevant information at each level;
- … and by succeeding at least with some of these points: facilitating the creation of trust in the European approach (wherever useful);

Another pragmatic limitation should be introduced at this point: While the following suggestions are based on comments from all levels of the information chain, and these suggestions should improve the usefulness of CE marking, the actual suggestions are focused on *actors at EU level*. On one hand, because I do not want to pretend that the interviews I had with several individuals working at different (national) levels have made me an expert in the field of CE marking in four Member States or that solutions useful for these four countries might easily be used by the other 23. This study has shown that a lack of data on the actual needs of downstream users could result in focusing on relatively irrelevant issues and reducing the actual value of the work at EU level. Without an in-depth assessment of the actual needs of downstream users, any recommendations here might create the same confusion and in the end counter-productive results as have already been created by several EU and national approaches. On the other hand, because downstream actors have shown that they could to an extent neutralise upstream initiatives if they did not feel confident with them. The "overload" with documents experienced by downstream users but not being provided with practical guidance has resulted in the reduction of information to the absolute minimum ("you *have* to have CE marking"), but not "pushing" for a more conscious use of CE marking by distributors, architects or contractors. Since CE marking is often seen as insufficient when choosing construction products, its nature as *complementary* information should be accepted and the focus should be more on insuring that the information provided with CE marking is reliable (if this information is needed) than trying to significantly influence day-to-day practice. One should also not forget that trust in established networks at national and regional level (based on specific legal, technical and economic requirements) could hardly be replaced by well-intended but still untried instruments created at a level, where most downstream users have no real influence or possibilities to create networks of trust themselves.

To make *requirements* seen as useful, actors at EU level (including Member State representatives in the SCC) have to "prove" to downstream actors that the *information* they are developing and distributing is helpful and is based on the actual needs of downstream actors. In other words: improving *acceptance* of the work at EU level and therefore improving *compliance* at national and regional level is linked to the abilities of (EU and national) actors at EU level to create trust in the quality of the result of their work, not necessarily in the increased number of requirements or guidance documents. Therefore, the first steps to improve the system have to be made by the EU-based and national-based actors working at EU level.

As a first step, one should define **what the CPD** (or the future CRP) ***could* and *could not* actually achieve** (improving clarity):

- The CPD is a *market* instrument providing a harmonised reporting format for the assessment of product performance and (in general) reliable performance values – but since it limits itself to (not even in all Member States) *regulated* requirements and does not cover *all technical data relevant* for planners and contractors, it is therefore also not the most essential information tool for most downstream users. As the interviews have shown, information about CE marking moved down from the EU level to national and (to a lesser extent) regional authorities and federations, but was not used further downstream by architects, civil engineers and construction companies (only following the "letter of the law").
  ► Therefore, the CPD has **only three actual target groups** for whom it is providing an added value by providing harmonised test methods and reporting formats: **manufacturers, certification bodies and market surveillance authorities, and any approach shall focus on these groups**. Before any extension to other target groups is envisaged, a clear assessment of the needs of these groups has to be undertaken as well as a clear concept on how the CPD approach could actually provide added value has to be developed. In this case also a limited scope (e.g., only a selected number of products – see below) could help to focus on specific practical needs.

- Since the scope of the CPD is relatively narrow compared to the tasks, interests, potentials and limits of most actors in the field of construction, it cannot codify the behavior of these actors. In fact, other policy fields have been of more interest for downstream actors – in particular in the field of energy performance and "sustainability" – but it remains unclear how the CPD fits into the whole set of EU initiatives and laws.
  ► EU policies and laws are often "competing" with each other for the awareness, resources and compliance of downstream actors. In several cases these policies and regulations seem (at *least* in the eyes of downstream users) to be more or less isolated activities within the EU administration and only superficially coordinated at EU level. Downstream users are therefore not only forced to monitor all developments at EU level, they are also forced to combine these initiatives without sufficient support or explanations from EU actors (in particular the European Commission). By shifting this task to downstream actors, the European Commission is to a certain extent losing one of the positive aspects of its role as "agenda setter" and is seen more as "producer of requirements" in a "subtle negative way". To regain a positive steering role and to increase awareness, acceptance and efficient implementation of its initiatives, the **Commission services should provide a clear and transparent overview of *all* its activities in the field of construction, how they are connected and how these combined activities are improving the overall performance of the sector**. **This would also include setting priorities**, allowing downstream actors to plan ahead and distribute resources more efficiently.
- While all actors highlight the need for protecting consumers against flawed products, only few cases per Member State are brought to the attention of these authorities every year. This small number could result from: a lack of efficient market surveillance in most Member States; an actual small number of flawed products in EU MS; or a large number of products installed without proper quality control. This leaves a gap between actual risks and constant "gold-plating" at EU level.
  ► Guidance to the above mentioned three target groups should focus on products that have been identified as problematic by private actors and market surveillance authorities. This would allow for a more practical focus and more precise guidance instead of trying to cover all possibilities in more and more complex documents. (However, this also requires a more in-depth

analysis[433] of products on the market and their use in buildings and civil engineering works.)

- In addition, downstream actors like architects and contractors are interacting with manufacturers or distributors via specific contracts with the performance and information on their correct installation either defined or declared by at least one actor and accepted by both of them. Therefore, the actual interaction between these actors is not (significantly) affected by CE marking or any other national mark.
  ► **Instruments to reduce the complexity** of data and requirements will remain essential tools for downstream users. These instruments, selected by past experience and supported by systems of familiar norms and trust in these norms, are operational at a level that **can hardly be affected by the CPD approach**.
- In previous discussions at EU and national levels the availability and quality of harmonised European product standards were the most important issues. Therefore the **main focus was on manufacturers** and all actors supporting them or controlling the quality of products to the end of the production line. Since active **market surveillance was de facto missing** in most Member States (and private actors have indicated different reasons why they could not or did not want to rely too much on existing schemes), the actual protection of the users of buildings and civil engineering works could only partly be guaranteed by authorities and depended more on expertise and professional selection of products by downstream actors and controllers.
  ► All **actors at EU (and national) level** have to accept that **their influence on the quality of buildings** via standards, CE marking or other marks **is limited**, particularly if the product is not "followed" from the production line to its final installation. In most cases **potential problems and risks** that could occur **on the construction side cannot and should not be solved "purely" via product standards or other technical guidance**. They might only increase the complexity of approaches developed at EU (and national) level (thicker and more complex documents) without providing practical solutions for downstream actors.

433 The wide scope of the CPD has so far affected all studies on the CPD (including *this* study): It was always only possible to cover a small number of products. At the same time, the differences in materials used, the complexity of the final product and the intended uses made any comparison and assumptions on the whole sector extremely difficult and the results only under very specific settings (framework and questions of the study) relatively representative.

The second step is a closer look at the **framework provided for the implementation of the CPD** (improving clarity and optimising communication channels between the Commission and other actors):

- None of the public or private actors have enough resources and manpower to monitor all developments in the fields of politics (all national and EU policies and laws), technical specification (CEN, EOTA), certification (Notified Bodies) or market interests (manufacturers, planners, contractors). This task is even more difficult considering the wide range of products (and all their potential uses) covered. Therefore, practically all actors are working with the "fire brigade" concept – reacting and giving guidance when they are aware of problems.

  ▶ In its report to the European Parliament the Commission itself has been thinking aloud about splitting the scope into several product families to be more efficient. However, the new proposal for a Construction Products Regulation did not change the scope of products. But this would not necessarily deny the construction unit, the SCC or other actors the possibility to **focus their resources on monitoring and guiding a small and clearly defined group of products "from cradle (the mandate) to gate (the final technical specification)" and its practical use and acceptance.**[434] Instead of products coming irregularly into the focus of actors at EU and national level, being briefly discussed and (hopefully) guidance provided, before they drop out of awareness again, all actors could (and shall) follow the ongoing work and the results of their own decisions and guidance for this small group of products. Remaining in contact and dialogue with all actors relevant on specific aspects could help to **understand the complexity of the task at hand, the possibilities and limits of each actor and to learn how to improve the quality of the input provided**. With growing knowledge about these activities, national actors at EU level could also increase their competence not only as an interface between EU and national level,

---

434 This selection could be based on two different approaches: The less resource-consuming approach would be an inventory done by the construction unit and MS authorities to identify products with transnational distribution and where problems on entering markets have been reported. The second approach would require a more scientific collection of information and data (e.g., outsourced research work), but would necessarily depend as well on the identification by national actors as for the first approach.

but also by providing more detailed knowledge and potential influence on mechanisms at EU level.

- The SCC broadly fulfils its monitoring and decision making tasks. Beyond that, it can be considered to be a *re*active body within the framework of the CPD with limited ambition to be in a more initiating role or to use the potential of the SCC to be a platform for more exchange of information or coordination of national interests and activities. The official character of the SCC makes it difficult for national representatives and other actors to bypass the "representation role" they have to fulfill vis-à-vis other actors in the SCC – but also their downstream actors, monitoring their activities at EU level. Raising questions, asking about experiences in other Member States or presenting and discussing new developments or achievements in their country or sector was also not mentioned in the official role of the SCC. Member State representatives and other actors in observer roles in the SCC have a **huge amount of information on developments and achievements in construction** that is interesting – and relevant – to other actors too.[435]

  ► Many activities at national or sectoral level might not be directly related to construction products or regulatory "barriers to trade",[436] but they could provide ideas in general, or even solutions that can be used for construction products issues too ("collective learning process"). Again, additional information could not only help all actors at EU level (and increase the importance of representatives in the SCC as creators and distributors of information upstream and downstream) it could also help to identify common interests and activities and reducing the search and coordination costs for national actors. This approach would to a large extent follow the scheme that representatives of federations have developed to "share" their limited resources while increasing their abilities to provide (sector specific) information to their members (on time). By getting information on experience in other Member States, the costs for finding (national) solutions could be reduced (e.g., more options "available" and less "guesswork" because *practical* results can be seen and evaluated).

---

435 This includes information on „unwritten rules" on national or regional level which are essential to the established system of trust between actors but are difficult to see or to understand by actors from different professions or nationalities.

436 However, informing members of recent or planned notification of national laws would also increase the transparency and predictability of actors in other Member States.

► None of these exchanges has to take place within the framework of an SCC meeting. But like the Preparatory Group as an additional instrument for the SCC, an additional day before or after a SCC meeting could be used for **a more informal – but also *more informative* – meeting of all actors** (“open method of coordination”)[437]. The purpose should be an open exchange without the pressure of delivering (binding) decisions in these meetings. By including individual experts in specific fields (e.g., tendering authorities, chairmen or experts from CEN TCs or EOTA members, specific Notified Bodies, market surveillance inspectors, building inspectors) **more practical expertise** could be added while putting less pressure on the official representatives of the SCC to “know it all” (or at least to represent it sufficiently in all relevant aspects). Selecting specific topics/questions/ developments for each of these meetings would allow all actors to prepare themselves and to coordinate their presentations and input in advance.

In a way, these meetings would be complementary to (not instead of) bilateral meetings. Member States and other actors would still have the possibilities to address specific problems to the construction unit. But in particular for Member States and actors with few resources to initiate special meetings in Brussels, this informal forum of actors could help them to get more feedback and also to provide input without making binding decisions or imposing tasks to downstream actors.

Last but not least: The **“interactive social character”** of this open exchange of views should facilitate more **“professional trust”** between actors[438]. In the “best of world scenarios” this would not just lead to more trust between actors, it could also lead to more interest and an ***active* pursuit of finding common strategies and solutions** instead of waiting for and reacting to proposals developed by the construction unit. Since most of the (national) “founding fathers” of the CPD have retired or left the SCC, more and more members of the SCC have not been involved in “developing” the CPD but only in the “administration” of it. Being more actively involved in *problem solving* activities could prove that active participation is not only needed and appreciated, it could also increase the commitment

437 See also: Bulmer: Theorizing Europeanization, in: Graziano/Vink (eds): Europeanization 2008 p. 52.

438 Bonchek/Howard: “The Power to Convene”; in: Heckscher/Adler (eds): The Firm as a Collaborative Community 2007 p. 524f.

of new actors. This could be achieved by having not *one* actor (the construction unit) in identifying specific issues, collecting information and coordinating input ("agenda setting"), but sharing these tasks with *several* actors in this informal forum. The above mentioned "cradle to gate" exercise could be split and one (or several) actors would cover one specific product group each.

The third step will put more emphasis on **instruments in place and suggestions how to improve them** (improving clarity and optimising communication channels between the Commission and other actors and avoiding unnecessary complexity)[439]:

- The implementation of the CPD can be described as a *pure top-down approach*. Upstream actors (and here in particular authorities – starting with the construction unit – while federations usually have an interest in providing information to their membership) have made few attempts to find out who, how and if downstream actors – except their immediate contacts at the next level – could actually fulfill their tasks of collecting, interpreting and distributing information. In addition, for external interested actors: While downstream actors are in most cases providing links to upstream actors on their websites and publications (up to the European Commission), actors "on top" rarely give the visitors to their sites links to the implementing actors (authorities).

  ► The still-visible lack of knowledge, years after the transformation of the CPD (or other directives) not only makes it difficult for actors in the Commission services to get contact details on actors outside their specific field of experience. In particular, interested external actors can hardly rely on information on institutions or organisations that are actually implementing European or national law. **The construction unit and national authorities should coordinate their efforts to provide a clear line of links to direct actors to the next relevant contact for their interest.** An overview presented on a public website could also allow more transparency (in addition, it forces upstream actors to evaluate if they have actually reached all relevant downstream actors).

  ► Linked to the previous suggestion but also important at the start of implementing a directive is a **clear overview of all actors involved**. Again,

439 See: Falkner et al : Complying with Europe p. 355ff.

it should not only improve transparency for actors who are not familiar with national- or sector-specific structures and responsibilities, it also allows identifying if and which actors might be missing, as well as identifying paths that should be extended or reduced. The overview (which should be accessible by all actors – including the public) should include

- inter-institutional cooperation;
- consultation;
- notification and control;
- communication with other actors;
- reporting;
- sanctioning of deviance;

with clear definitions of the tasks within the administrative process and its political and operational responsibilities.[440] This could also introduce an aspect so far relatively neglected: **Assessing the *real* impact of the CPD**, its national implementations and CE marking at MS level. By clearly identifying parameters that should change when using the CPD approach and CE marking, either (relatively) regular monitoring or at least more precise evaluations done in specific studies should provide a level playing field for collecting and interpreting data from MS and identifying potentials and weaknesses of the CPD approach.

Identifying most actors at all levels (in particular national and regional authorities) would not only increase the transparency of national systems in general, it would also allow a fast selection of experts for specific questions. By addressing these experts at an early stage would shift the burden of the individuals acting as interfaces to seek, interpret and present information to leave specific questions for the experts in a specific field (following the example of the expert groups under the CPD framework but using a more flexible approach to deal faster with specific questions but also to be more "end user" oriented – see also below).

Also, private actors and the public could profit from a more transparent description of all national schemes: In particular when interested in the situation in another Member State, it could facilitate finding the right contacts in administrations (and – if this system is taken over by federations) in the private sector. However, since this overview would not be very detailed it would just be a starting point for anybody who wants to get

440 Allio/Fandel: Making Europe work 2006 p. 24ff.

deeper into a national system, but it could remove the first barrier (including the language barrier)[441] of finding the "starting point".

- While different documents have been developed at European level (e.g., Interpretative Documents, Guidance Papers) and national level, in several cases interviewees reported that it was not always clear if they would have only an advisory function or provide binding instructions and for whom they would be binding. Even more problematic was the perceived inconsistency of activities at EU level (e.g., policies, directives, mandates) or – in case of the CPD – the inconsistency of documents developed by the construction unit and the SCC which reduced significantly their usefulness as references in decision-finding processes of downstream actors.
  ▶ In particular, due to regular changes of Commission officials, **consistency in the position of the construction unit** is essential. There should be a regular screening of documents that have been made available by the unit giving guidance or clarifications. Their position within the system and their content (or position expressed) has to be confirmed or – if necessary – amended. More time-consuming would be an additional step of ensuring the quality of these documents: During the screening process, actors who are using these documents (or are *not* using them because of perceived problems with them) should be invited to provide feedback. To reduce the workload of this re-assessment, abstracts could provide an overview (and helping readers to decide if a specific document would hold relevant information for them) which in most cases might not change at all. These (easily accessible) abstracts might in several cases satisfy the first needs of a larger number of actors and should help to focus on fewer detailed questions.

A similar problem appears when it comes to the transparency of national regulatory approaches. Member States in general have no problem in following the "Notification Directive" and send their intended new regulations to the Commission for distribution and comments from all Member States. However, in most cases the notifying authorities at national level are not the same as the ones developing or implementing them. Selecting the

441 Like for most recommendations in this chapter, translating information that might be relevant for a larger audience should not be forgotten. However, knowing the stressed resources of all actors in this field (including the Commission services) I will not press this point too much or try to provide detailed suggestions.

right actors to be notified poses in some cases a serious problem for the Commission services and even national authorities might not be aware of all activities at national level touching their own field of responsibility. This can (and has) affected the content and therefore the quality of mandates given to CEN and the feedback provided to CEN TCs, EOTA members and Notified Bodies on relevant national regulations.

▶ Despite all official obligations and instruments in place, this part will remain a weak point in the information flow for the Commission services and national administrations. However, providing information on the latest national developments by each delegation in the SCC could help to identify gaps in knowledge or provide an opportunity to clarify open questions.

- Assuming that the goal of the CPD and the use of CE marking are clearly defined, all downstream actors identified, responsibilities clearly defined and information on regulatory requirements and an unambiguous and transparent guidance developed, the risk of different interpretation remains at all levels. The small number of actors at EU and national level would make it seem that a common understanding and a common approach would not be extremely difficult to achieve. But reality has shown that most knowledge had to be developed *individually*. This was partly due to the need for specific adaptations of the framework and guidance provided by the CPD for national or sectoral environments. One attempt to decrease the risk of different interpretations was the development of Guidance Papers which were discussed and approved in the SCC. However, these documents addressed only few specific issues and were *de facto* only directed to specification writers and Notified Bodies. Their complexity and usefulness as information and guidance tools for other users was also rather limited. It is interesting that while several specific technical documents (Guidance Papers) were developed, the construction unit and the SCC have never developed one common document explaining the CPD and the role of CE marking in a user-friendly way to other relevant actors.

▶ Somewhat belatedly, but most likely not too late, a short and simple "introduction document" about the CPD and CE marking and abstracts for the most relevant documents developed by the SCC (or maybe the "informal forum"?) could provide "core" information for all actors affected by the CPD and CE marking. To allow actors to quickly identify if and how they might be affected (and to raise their interest), a step-by-step approach should guide the reader from the general concept and expected advantages for each user group to a more detailed description and practical examples. This should also lower the "psychological barrier" to thick documents and allows the reader to leave when they consider their interest and questions satisfied. Nevertheless, these documents should only provide *common* format and information that all actors in the SCC could agree on. It should still leave room for national and sectoral actors (e.g., federations) to provide more practical guidance (e.g., how to use it specifically within the national or technical environment). Comparing these modules at a later stage could also help to learn from "best practice" and to identify mis-interpretations – or even gaps or practical problems that were not obvious at an earlier stage.

► A trickier aspect of providing relevant information is the question of the accessibility of standards (since they are part of a regulatory scheme of obligatory certification). While providing European standards for free would be extremely optimistic (regulators have shifted some of their work to national and EU standardisation bodies, but have also shifted the costs for developing standards to private actors – but there is no indication that the costs of developing technical standards will be taken over by national or EU authorities).

► Most likely *too* late for the CPD approach in several Member States, would be training for all parties involved.[442] However, for the new Member States this could be an useful complementary activity to ensure a common approach while lightening the burden of implementing the CPD and providing information at a practical level. But also interviewees from "older" Member States have raised the issue that information was asked for – not only from national actors but also from the construction unit, but for most members it has to be relatively easily available – indicating that conferences have to take place at national level ("You will not get anybody travelling to Brussels"). Using the "introduction document", a small number of trainers of European and national actors could come together, agreeing on the main priorities and being provided with feedback from other actors who have experience in explaining the CPD and CE marking over recent years (e.g., questions asked, potential problems or problems encountered, misunderstandings, "tricks" to facilitate understanding). These trainers will also have to provide feedback to their peers on their experience. This exercise could

442 See also: Allio/Fandel: Making Europe work 2006 p. 24ff.

also provide feedback and insight for the "old hands" who have been active in this field for a long time (in "old" and "new" Member States and could improve the knowledge and performance of all actors involved in the information chain.

- At the time this study was written, the "dominance" of generalists and co-ordinators as creators, interpreters and providers of information within the Commission, MS authorities and federations had resulted in a long information chain before the practical users were actually reached (exceeding significantly the "six degrees of separation" which, for an information chain that provides a relatively-sufficient information flow, is considered acceptable). This long way forces actors at EU level to "cover all potential scenarios" in their assumptions and guidance provided (e.g., GP, European standards, ETAGs) which would not facilitate the implementation at a downstream level but would even provoke (passive) resistance against what is considered to be unnecessarily-complex guidance and requirements.

  ► The lack of resources of actors in the private sector will hardly change to more experts available (and considering the economic crisis in 2009 one can also assume that active participation will further decrease because companies and organisations cannot spare manpower on activities which will not show immediate results). However, as mentioned before, national authorities are one of the most relevant market actors in construction. Authorities responsible for tendering, building or maintaining buildings and civil engineering works are close to the "construction site" level and therefore ideal to cover both practical technical aspects (and solutions) and regulatory requirements (and being – in general – familiar with the administrative structure of public authorities in their field of expertise). This pool of knowledge should be more often used by establishing a network of experts across national borders that could provide replies on an *ad hoc* basis. There is no essential need for establishing special groups that have to *meet* at EU level on a regular basis. It should be more a network to exchange information and discuss problems directly between experts in a specific field – which could avoid specific questions having to be discussed at EU level in the SCC (or its Preparatory Group), because solutions have been found at expert level, or could make national positions less diverse when discussing them at EU level.

- Last but not least: Raising awareness and complying with agreements also depends on **efficient and visible enforcement of rules and agreements**, not only to ensure that interpretations of these rules and agreements are done in a responsible and careful way (ensuring that compliant actors are defended against deviant behaviour – free-riders) but also to provide all actors with reliable and stable positions. Since the system consists of only few individuals – who in several cases have been provided with significant freedom to act on behalf of the interest of their institutions or organisations – changes of individuals in the system (e.g., in the construction unit) could lead to more significant changes in positions than in systems more tightly embedded in institutionalised structures (see above). Changing interpretations might provide flexibility in changing environments, but it is also highly confusing to actors who do not have the resources to follow all developments on a regular basis. In addition, specific positions provide guidance, but many actors need a guarantee in relation to if and how binding these positions will be.

  ► While this is introducing a more confrontational approach ("enforcing" could also include infringement procedures and decisions by the European Court of Justice), the intention is *not* to prove somebody *wrong* in a specific position or interpretation but **to provide clear, precise and reliable references** for all actors. This is not only relevant for deciding between positions taken by the construction unit vis-à-vis a specific national approach (and to clearly indicate which side has to change its position or has to introduce changes in its practical approach – Highly visible decisions should also help to facilitate changes in approaches vis-à-vis other veto players), but also helps actors from other Member States to interact with the construction unit, other Member States or other national actors.

  ► "Enforcement" includes effective **market surveillance systems** in place. I am not contradicting myself by suggesting a complex and expensive additional tool into the system, because the Commission services are already working on stronger obligations for Member States to install such systems. In fact, it is a reminder that current national schemes have hardly sufficiently covered the issue of ensuring the *installation* of "safe products" in buildings and civil engineering works. The "blind spot" of most national schemes has only been (relatively) successful because of self-monitoring and a rather conservative selection of products based on "reputation" ("brand names") and past experience. With more actors (architects and contractors) crossing national borders within the EU, reliance on comparable performance of products becomes more and more important. Also systems of holding products in stock or buying them on demand might change (and have partly changed) during the last decades, which would also affect the abilities of contractors to get known products or to move to similar but less-known products (including imports from outside the EU)[443]. None of these developments is sufficiently covered in the existing "cradle-to-gate" concepts of product control by national authorities, which makes it even more important to provide enough support to maintain trust in products available in (national) markets.

I have mentioned before that I was trying to provide suggestions that would not demand significant changes in manpower and other resources. However, none of the above mentioned suggestions would work *without* any re-allocation of resources or, in some cases, even increasing resources. This would be now the perfect opportunity to consider them as not feasible, and I am the last to claim that it is easy to set new priorities for allocating resources or to get more support within an organisation or institution. On the other hand, in my suggestions I am also trying to focus existing resources and by combining them I am carefully optimistic that the additional burden could be relatively small. By recognising the limits of the CPD, CE marking and of national assumptions and approaches, actors at EU and national level might be less reluctant to ignore the "worst case scenario" (which might not be very realistic) and work with "practical scenarios" which would make their reactions and guidance not only more practical but would increase their relevance to the needs of downstream users.

Another problem is outside the influence of the CPD – and often outside the influence of the representatives of Member States in the SCC: Since the CPD is a *reactive* tool to other EU and national legislation, the need for more work and more interpretation at EU level increases with every additional (national) approach, leading back, in most cases, to more interpretation work at national level – including the Member States that have introduced these new regulations in the first place. Fortunately, as we have seen, this "worst case scenario" of a vicious circle of more and more guidance and regulatory corrections at EU and national level is partly ignored at downstream levels. Having isolated levels

443 This is not judging the quality of products coming from non-Member States but highlighting the problems for contractors to easily get sufficient information on product performance values or additional support and advice for their correct use.

might reduce negative impacts of problems created at other levels, but it is also neutralising any synergy effect that the split of tasks and responsibilities should have created in the first place. Following the principle that "less is sometimes more", in particular upstream actors should have enough trust in the (professional) competence of actors at other levels. This trust will definitely not always be justified (and might even be misused) but considering the implementation of the CPD and CE marking over the last 20 years – while in most cases *lacking any effective market surveillance system at national, regional or local level* – the quality of buildings and civil engineering works was less guaranteed by discussions on quality of harmonised European standards, CE marking or national marks than by the selection of useful construction products by downstream users and the manufacturers providing them. A more careful assessment of if and when interventions would be effective and useful might also reduce the workload and the confusion at all levels.

On the other hand: I might be completely wrong. The optimistic view might collide with more skeptical positions which might later be proven by empirical data. But even if (nearly) everybody agrees with my view and considers my recommendations worth trying, the practical implementation might still be too difficult or not produce visible results. In this case – not so much as sociologist but as good civil servant – I will fall back on a more bureaucratic approach – and leave the final proposal to a master of administrative management:

> It is clear that the committees agree that your new policy is really excellent, and in view of some of the doubts being expressed, may I propose that I recall that after careful consideration the considered view of the committee was that while they considered that the proposal met with broad approval in principle, that some of the principles were especially fundamental in principle, and some of the considerations so complex and finely balanced in practice, that in principle, it was proposed that the sensible and prudent practice would be to submit the proposal for more detailed consideration, laying stress on the essential continuity of the new proposal of existing principles and the principle of the principal arguments which the proposal proposes and propounds for their approval – in principle.
> (Sir Humphrey in: Yes Prime Minister: The Ministerial Broadcast)

5 Bibliography

Abkommen über das Deutsche Institut für Bautechnik und Satzung des Deutschen Instituts für Bautechnik; Berlin 1. Juli 2004.

Ackermann, Rolf: Pfadabhängigkeit, Institutionen und Regelreform; Mohr Siebeck, Tübingen 2001.

Adler, Paul S./Heckscher, Charles: Towards Collaborative Community; in: Heckscher/ Adler (eds): The Firm as a Collaborative Community 2007.

Allen, David: The United Kingdom: A *Europeanized* Government in a *non-Europeanized* Polity; in: Bulmer/Lesquesne (eds): The Member States of the European Union, Oxford 2005.

Allio, Lorenzo/Fandel, Marie-Hélène: Making Europe work: improving the transposition, implementation and enforcement of EU legislation; EPC working paper no 25, 2006.

Anderson, Jeffrey J.: Germany and Europe: Centrality in the EU; in: Bulmer/Lesquesne (eds): The Member States of the European Union, Oxford 2005.

Bach, Maurizio (Hrsg.): Die Europäisierung nationaler Gesellschaften; Kölner Zeitschrift für Soziologie und Sozialpsychologie Sonderheft 40/2000; Westdeutscher Verlag, Wiesbaden 2000.

Barnett, Michael/ Finnemore, Martha: Rules for the World – International Organizations in Global Politics; Cornell University Press, Ithaka/London 2004.

Bauer, Patricia/Voelzkow, Helmut (Hrsg.): Die Europäische Union – Marionette oder Regisseur? Verlag für Sozialwissenschaften, Wiesbaden 2004.

Beck, Ulrich: Risikogesellschaft – Auf den Weg in eine andere Moderne; edition suhrkamp, Frankfurt/Main 1986.

Beck, Ulrich/Giddens, Anthony/Lash, Scott: Reflexive Modernisierung – Eine Kontroverse; edition suhrkamp, Frankfurt/Main 1996.

Becker, Markus C./Knudsen, Thornbjorn: The role of routines in reducing pervasive uncertainty; Journal of Business Research 58 (2005).

Bekke, Hans A.G.M./van der Meer, Frits (eds): Civil Service Systems in Western Europe; Edward Elgar Publishing Ltd, Cheltenham/Northampton 2000.

Bekke, Hans A.G.M./van der Meer, Frits: Civil Service Systems in Western Europe: An Introduction; in: Bekke/van der 'Meer (eds): Civil Service Systems in Western Europe 2000.

Bellier, Irene: The Commission as an Actor: An Anthropologist's View, in: Wallace/ Young (eds.): Participation and policy-making in the European Union, 1997.

Benz, Arthur: Entflechtung als Folge von Verflechtung – Theoretische Überlegungen wur Entwicklung des europäischen Mehrebenensystems, in: Grande/Jachtenfuchs (Hrsg.): Wie problemlösungsfähig ist die EU? 2000.

Berger, Peter/Luckmann, Thomas: The Social Construction of Reality – A Treatise in the Sociology of Knowledge; Penguin Books, London/New York/Victoria/Toronto/ Auckland 1991.

Berglund, Sara/Gange, Ieva/van Waarden, Frans: Mass production of law. Routinization in the transposition of European directives: a sociological- institutional account; Journal of European Public Policy 13:5 2006.

Bergrström Carl-Fredrik/Héritier, Adrienne: Constolling the implementation powers of the Commission (comitology0, in: Héritier: Explaining Institutional Change in Europe 2007.

Bergström, Carl Fredrik: Comitology – Delegation of Powers in the Europea Union and the Committee System; Oxford University Press, Oxford 2005.

Beyers, Jan/Trondal, Jarle: How Nation-States "Hit" Europe – Ambiguity and Representation in the European Union; European Integration online Papers Vol. 7 no 5, 2003.

Bonchek, Mark/Howard, Robert: "The Power to Convene": Creating Collaborative Community with Strategic Customers; in: Heckscher/Adler (eds): The Firm as a Collaborative Community 2007.

Börzel, Tanja A.: Eurpeanization: How the European Union interacts with its Member States; in: Bulmer/Lesquesne (eds): The Member States of the European Union 2005.

Börzel, Tanja A./Hofmann, Tobias/Sprungk, Carina: Einhaltung von Recht jenseits des Nationalstaats – Zur Implementierung marktkorrigierender Regelungen in der EU; in: Zeitschrift für Internationale Beziehungen 2/2003, Nomos Verlagsgesellschaft, Baden-Baden.

Börzel, Tanja A./Hofmann, Tobias/Sprungk, Carina: Why Do States not Obey the Law? Lessons from the European Union (Paper for EUSA conference) 2003 http://aei.pitt.edu/6473/01/001328_1.PDF.

Börzel, Tanja A.: States and Regions in the European Union – Institutional Adaptation in Germany and Spain; Cambridge University Press, Cambridge 2002.

Börzel, Tanja A.: Pace-Setting, Foot-Dragging, and Fence-Sitting, Member State Responses to Europeanization; Queen´s Papers on Europeanisation No 4/2001.

Börzel, Tanja A.: Organizing Babylon – On the different conceptions of policy networks, Public Administration Vol 76 Blackwell Publishers Oxford/Malden 1998 http://www.ceses.cuni.cz/CESES-136-version1-1C_gov_networks_babylon_borzel.pdf.

Bretherton, Charlotte/Vogler, John: The European Union as a Global Actor, Routledge, London/New York 2006.

Bücker, Andreas/Schlacke, Sabine: Die Entstehung einer „politischen Verwaltung“ durch EG-Ausschüsse – Rechtstatsachen und Rechtsentwicklungen; in: Joerges/Falke (Hsrg.): Das Ausschusswesen in der Europäischen Union, 2000.

Bulmer, Simon: Theorizing Europeanization, in: Graziano/Vink (eds): Europeanization 2008.

Bulmer/Lequesne: The EU and its Member States: An Overview; in: Bulmer/Lesquesne (eds): The Member States of the European Union 2005.

Bulmer, Simon/Lesquesne, Christian (eds): The Member States of the European Union; Oxford University Press, Oxford 2005.

Bulmer, Simon/Lequesne, Christian: New Perspectives on EU-Member State Relationships; questions des recherche no 4 2002 http://www.ceri-sciencespo.com/publica/question/qdr4.pdf.

Bundesamt für Bauwesen und Raumordnung: Studie über die Verwendungsregelungen CE gekennzeichneter Bauprodukte in den Mitgliedstaaten der EU als Grundlage für Deutschland für Verhandlungen bei der Revision der Bauproduktenrichtlinie; Bonn 2008.

Burson-Marsteller: The Definitive Guide to Lobbying the European Institutions – Based on a survey of the European Parliament, the Council and the European Commission; BKSH 2005 http://www.euractiv.com/29/images/The%20Definitive%20Guide%20to%20Lobbying%20the%20European%20Institutions%20(Spring%202005)_tcm29-140977.pdf.

Bussjäger, Peter: Homogenität und Differenz – Zur Theorie der Aufgabenverteilung zwischen Bund und Ländern in Österreich, Institut für Föderalismus Bd 100, Braunmüller Universitäts-Verlagsbuchhandlung, Wien 2006.

Consortium of European Building Control (CEBC): Building Control Systems in Europe; Building Control Report Issue 2, June 2006.

Chemillier, Pierre: Comprendre et maîtriser la directive »Produits de construction«; AFNOR, 2002.

Coleman, James S.: Foundations of Social Theory ; Belkam Press of Havard University Press, Cambridge/London 1994.

Commissariat général au Développement durable : La construction en Europe en 2004, 2005, 2007.

Commission of the European Communities: Commission Report on the Construction Products Directive; Brussels 15.5.1996 ; COM(96) 202 final.

Communication from the Commission to the Council, the European Parliament, the European Economic and Social Committee and the Committee of the Regions: “Internal Market Strategy – Priorities 2003-2006”, COM(2003) 238 final.

Council Directive 89/106/EEC on the approximation of laws, regulations and administrative provisions of the Member States relating to construction products (89/106/EEC) (OJ L 40, 11.2.1989, p.12) http://europa.eu.int/comm/enterprise/construction/internal/cpd/cpd_en.htm.

Dachs, Herbert/Gerlich, Peter/Gottweis, Herbert/Horner, Franz/Kramer, Helmut/Lauber, Volkmar/Müller, Wolfgang C./Tàlos, Emmerich (Hrsg.): Handbuch des Politischen Systems Österreichs, Manzsche Verlags- und Universitätsbuchhandlung, Wien 1991.

Dagger, Steffen/Kambeck, Michael (Hrsg): Politikberatung und Lobbying in Brüssel; Verlag für Sozialwissenschaften; Wiesbaden 2007.

Dahrendorf, Ralf: Homo Sociologicus; Westdeutscher Verlag, Opladen 1977.

Deakin, Simon/Wilkinson, Frank: Contract Law and the Economics of Interorganizational Trust; in: Lane/Bachmann (eds): Trust within and between Organizations 1998.

Demortain, David: La légitimation par les normes: experts transnationaux; Commission européenne et la régulation des aliments nouveaux; in: Sociologie du Travail 50 (2008).

Denters, Bas/Rose, Lawrence E. (eds.): Comparing Local Governance – Trends and Developments; Palgrave Macmillan, Hampshire/New York 2005.

Derlien, Hans-Ulrich: Germany; in: Kassim/Menon/Peters (eds): The National Co-ordination of EU Policy – The domestic level 2003.

Desselas, Stéphane: Un lobbying professionnel à visage découvert – Enquête sur l'influence des Français à Bruxelles; Éditions du Palio 2007.

Diekmann, Andreas/Voss, Thomas: Soziale Normen und Reziprozität, in: Diekmann/Eichner/Schmidt/Voss (Hrsg.): Rational Choice 2008.

Diekmann, Andreas/Eichner, Klaus/Schmidt, Peter/Voss, Thomas (Hrsg.): Rational Choice: Theoretische Analysen und empirische Resultate; Verlag für Sozialwissenschaften, Wiesbaden 2008.

Dimitrova, Antoaneta/Rhinard, Mark: The power of norms in the transposition of EU directives; European Integration online Papers Vol 9 no 16, 2005 http://eiop.or.at/eiop/texte/2005-01a.htm.

Directive of the European Parliament and the Council laying down a procedure for the provision of information in the field of technical standards and provisions (98/34/EC) http://ec.europa.eu/enterprise/tris/98_34_ec/index_en.pdf.

Eberwijn, Jan: How do contractors cope with the purchasing, approval and installation of products? http://eurocer-building.cstb.fr/doc/library/L06%20Contactors%20and%20certification.pdf.

EFTA: Certification and Marks in Europe; Consumer Research Associates Ltd: UK 2008.

Egeberg, Morten: The Organisational Dimension of Integration in the EU (and Elsewhere) ARENA Working Papers 2000/10 E:\political sciences\The Organisational Dimension of Integration in the EU (and Elsewhere).htm.

Egeberg, Morten: Transcending Intergovernmentalism? Identity and role perceptions of national officials in EU decision-making. Journal of European Public Policy 6:3, 1999.

Eglström, Ole/Jönsson, Christer (eds.): European Union Negotiations – Processes, Networks and Institutions; Routledge, London/New York 2005.

Eisenstadt, Shmuel: Vertrauen, kollektive Identität und Demokratie; in: Hartmann/Offe (Hsrg.): Vertrauen, 2001.

Eising, Rainer: Die Europäisierung deutscher Interessensgruppen – Passen die Institutionen und reichen die Kapazitäten? in: Eising/Kohler-Koch (Hrsg.): Interessenpolitik in Europa; 2005.

Eising, Rainer/Kohler-Koch, Beate (Hrsg.): Interessenpolitik im europäischen Mehrebenensystem, in: Eising/Kohler-Koch (Hrsg.): Interessenpolitik in Europa; 2005.

Eising, Rainer/Kohler-Koch, Beate (Hrsg.): Interessenpolitik in Europa; Nomos Verlag, Baden-Baden 2005.

Endreß, Martin: Vertrauen und Vertrautheit – Phänomenologisch-anthropologische Grundlegung; in: Hartmann/Offe (Hsrg.): Vertrauen, 2001.

Eppink, Derk-Jan: Life of a European Mandarin – Inside the Commission; Lannoo Publishers, 2007.

EUROCER-BUILDING: EB Position Paper: The use of Voluntary Product Certification in construction in European countries, January 2005.

European Commission/Bureau of European Policy Advisers: Workshop on Construction Services, Unpublished summary report April 2007.

European Commission: Thirteenth Annual Report on Monitoring the Application of Community Law (1995) COM (96) 600 final http://eur-lex.europa.eu/LexUriServ/LexUriServ.do?uri=CELEX:51996DC0600:EN:HTML.

European Parliament/Policy Department – Economic and Scientific Policy: Study on Safety and Liability Issues Relating to Construction Products; Brussels 2007.

Faber, Anne: Europäische Integration und politikwissenschaftliche Theoriebildung – Neofunktionalismus und Intergouvernementalismus in der Analyse; Verlag für Sozialwissenschaften, Wiesbaden 2005.

Falke, Josef: Komitologie – Entwicklung, Rechtsgrundlagen und erste empirische Annäherung, in: Joerges/Falke (Hsrg.): Das Ausschusswesen in der Europäischen Union, 2000.

Falkner, Gerda/ Treib, Oliver/Hartlapp, Miriam/Leiber, Simone: Complying with Europe – EU Harmonisation and Soft Law in the Member States; Cambridge University Press, Cambridge 2005.

Falkner, Gerda/Laffan, Birgid: The Europeanization of Austria and Ireland: Small can be Difficult? in: Bulmer/Lesquesne (eds): The Member States of the European Union, Oxford 2005.

Falkner, Gerda/Hartlapp, Miriam/Leiber, Simone/Treib, Oliver: Transforming Social Policy in Europe? The EC's Parental Leave Directive and Misfit in the 15 Member States; Max Planck Institute for the Study of Societies Working Paper 02/11 2002.

Falkner, Gerda: The Europeanisation of Austria: Misfit, Adaptation and Controversies; European Integration online Papers Vol 5 no 13, 2001.

Falkner, Gerda/Müller, Wolfgang C./Eder Martina/Hiller, Karin/Steiner, Gerhard/Trattnigg, Rita: The Impact of EU Membership on Policy Networks in Austria – Creeping change beneath the surface; Journal of European Public Policy 6(3) 1999.

Falkner, Gerda/Müller Wolfgang C. (Hsrg.): Österreich im europäischen Mehrebenensystem – Konsequenzen der EU-Mitgliedschaft für Politiknetzwerke und Entscheidungsprozesse; Schriftenreihe des Zentrums für angewandte Politikforschung Bd. 17, Signum Verlag, Wien 1998.

Feldman, Martha S.: A performative perspective on stability and change in organizational routines; Industrial and Corporate Change Vol 12 2003.

Feldman, Martha S.: Organizational routines as sources of connections and understandings; Journal of Management Studies 39:3 2002.

Friedrich, Dawid: Partizipatives Regieren in der EU – Die EU zwischen Laissez-faire und geregelter Partizipation zivilgesellschaftlicher Akteure; Zeitschrift für Internationale Beziehungen 2/2008, Nomos VerlagsgesmbH & Co KG, Baden-Baden 2008.

Fry, Geoffrey K.: The British Civil Service System; in: Bekke/van der Meer (eds): Civil Service Systems in Western Europe 2000.

Gabriel, Oscar W./Eisenmann, Susanne: Germany: a new type of local government? in: Denters/Rose (eds.): Comparing Local Governance 2005.

Gehring, Thomas: Die Bedeutung spezialisierter Entscheidungsprozesse für die Problemlösungsfähigkeit der Europäischen Union, in: Grande/Jachtenfuchs (Hrsg.): Wie problemlösungsfähig ist die EU? Baden-Baden 2000.

Gehring, Thomas: Die Europäische Union als komplexe internationale Organisation – Wie durch Kommunkikation und Entscheidung soziale Ordnung entsteht, Nomos Verlagsgesellschaft, Baden-Baden 2002.

Genschel, Philipp: Die Grenzen der Problemlösungsfähigkeit der EU, in: Grande/Jachtenfuchs (Hrsg.): Wie problemlösungsfähig ist die EU? 2000.

George, Stephen: Supranational Actor and Domestic Politics – Integration Theory in the Light of the Single European Act and Maastricht, in: Nugent (ed): The European Union Vol. 1, 1997.

Geuijen, Karin/'T Hart, Paul /Princen, Sebastian/Yesilkagit, Kutsal: The New Eurocrats – National Civil Servants in EU Policy-Making; Amsterdam University Press, Amsterdam 2008.

Gimpel, Jean: The Medieval Machine – The Industrial Revolution of the Middle Ages; Penguin Books, New York/London/Victoria/Ontario/Auckland 1976.

Glencross, Andrew: Post-Nationalism and the Problem of Supranational Political Representation: Legitimising the EU without the Nation-State; European University Institute Working Papers SPS 2008/01.

Goergen, Pascal: Lobbying in Brussels – A practical guide to the European Union for cities, regions, networks and enterprises; D&P Service, 2006.

Goetz, Klaus K.: The New Member States and the EU: Responding to Europe; in: Bulmer/Lesquesne (eds): The Member States of the European Union, Oxford 2005.

Goetz, Klaus K.: Making sense of post-communist central administration: moderniszation, Europeaniszation or Latinization? Journal of European Public Policy 8:6 2001 http://pdfserve.informaworld.com/Pdf/AddCoversheet?xml=/mnt/pdfserve/pdfserve/73112-731364960-713774428.xml.

Goetz, Hans K.: The Development and Current Features of the German Civil Service System, in: Bekke/van der Meer (eds): Civil Service Systems in Western Europe 2000.

Goffman, Erving: The Presentation of Self in Everyday Life; Pengiun Books, London 1990.

Grabbe Heather: How does Europeanisation affect CEE governance? Conditionality, diffusion and diversity; Journal of European Public Policy 8:4 2001 http://www.cer.org.uk/pdf/grabbe_jepp_2001.pdf.

Grande, Edgar/Jachtenfuchs, Markus (Hrsg.): Wie problemlösungsfähig ist die EU? Regieren im europäischen Mehrebenensystem; Nomos Verlagsgesellschaft, Baden-Baden 2000.

Grande, Edgar: Multi-Level Governance: Institutionelle Besonderheiten und Funktionsbedingungen des europäischen Mehrebenensystems, in: Grande/Jachtenfuchs (Hrsg.): Wie problemlösungsfähig ist die EU? Baden-Baden 2000.

Graziano, Paolo/Vink, Maarten P. (eds): Europeanization – New Research Agendas; Palgrave MacMillan, Hampshire/New York 2008.

Greenwood, Justin: Interest Representation in the European Union; Palgrave Macmillan, Hampshire/New York 2007.

Gretschmann, Klaus: Kommst Du mit der Lösung oder bist Du Teil des Problems? Politikberatung in und für Europa, in: Dagger/Kambeck (hrsg): Politikberatung und Lobbying in Brüssel 2007.

Goffman, Erving: Interaktionsrituale – Über Verhalten in direkter Kommunikation; Suhrkamp Verlag, Frankfurt/Main 1971.

Guide to the implementation of directives based on the New Approach and the Global Approach, European Commission 2000.

Haas, Peter M.: Compliance with EU directives: insights from international relations and comparative politics; Journal of European Public Policy 5:1 1998 http://www.informaworld.com/smpp/content~content=a778385115~db=all~order=page.

Hägermann, Dieter: Technik im frühen Mittelalter zwischen 500 und 1000, in: Propyläen Technikgeschichte Bd.1, Berlin 1997.

Hanrieder, Tine: Moralische Argumente in den Internationalen Beziehungen – Grenzen einer verständigungstheortischen „Erklärung“ moralischer Debatten; Zeitschrift für

Internationale Beziehungen 2/2008, Nomos VerlagsgesmbH & Co KG, Baden-Baden 2008.

Hardy, Cynthia/Phillips, Nelson/Lawrence, Tom: Distinguishing Trust and Power in Interorganizational Relations: Forms and Facades of Trust; in: Lane/Bachmann (eds): Trust within and between Organizations 1998.

Hartlapp, Miriam/Falkner, Gerda: Inkonsistent, inconsequent und intransparent? Zur supranationalen Kontrolle der Umsetzun der EU-Sozialpolitik in den Mitgliedstaaten, in: Bauer/Voelzkow (Hrsg.): Die Europäische Union – Marionette oder Regisseur? 2004.

Hartmann, Martin/Offe, Klaus (Hsrg.): Vertrauen – Die Grundlage des sozialen Zusammenlebens; Campus Verlag, Frankfurt/New York 2001.

Hartmann, Michael: Der Mythos von den Leistungseliten – Spitzenkarrieren und soziale Herkunft in Wirtschaft, Politik, Justiz und Wissenschaft; Campus Verlag, Frankfurt/New York 2002.

Haverland, Markus/Romejin, Marleen: Do Member States make European policies work? Analysing the EU transposition deficit; European Formum Public Administration Vol 85, No 3, Blackwell Publishing Ltd., Oxford 2007.

Heckscher, Charles/Adler, Paul S. (eds): The Firm as a Collaborative Community – Reconstructing Trust in the Knowledge Economy; Oxford University Press, Oxford 2007.

Heinisch, Richard: Austria: Confronting Controversy, in: Ziff/Pirro (eds.): The European Union and Member States, 2001.

Héritier, Adrienne: Explaining Institutional Change in Europe; Oxford University Press, Oxford 2007.

Herrmann, Richard K./Risse, Thomas/Brewer, Marilynn B. (eds): Transnational Identities – Becoming European in the EU; Rowman and Littlefield Publishers, Landam/Boulder/New York/Toronto/Oxford 2004.

Hooghe, Liesbet: The European Commission and the Integration of Europe – Images of Governance; Cambridge University Press, Cambridge 2001.

Hooghe, Liesbet/Marks, Gary: Multi-Level Governance and European Integration; Rowman & Littlefield Publishers Inc., Lanham/Boulder/New York/Toronto/Oxford 2001.

Horn van Nispen, Marie-Louise ten: 400.000 Jahre Technikgeschichte – Von der Steinzeit bis zum Informationszeitalter; Primus Verlag, Darmstadt 1999.

IMSAD: Insaat Malzemeleri Sektöründe AB'ye Uyum – Harmonization to EU in Building Materials Sector; Kesisim Yayincilik ve Tasarim Hizmetleri A.S., Istambul 2009.

Ismayer, Wolfgang (hrsg): Die politischen Systeme Westeuropas; Verlag für Sozialwissenschaften, Wiesbaden 2006.

Jeffery, Charlie (eds.): The Regional Dimension of the European Union – Towards a Third Level in Europe? Frank Cass, London/Portland (Org) 1997.

Jeffery, Charlie: Farewell the Third Level? The German Länder and the European Policy Process; in: Jeffery (eds): The Regional Dimension of the European Union 1997.

Jeffery, Charlie: Regional Information Offices in Brussels and Multi-Level Governance in the EU: A UK-German Comparison; in: Jeffery (eds): The Regional Dimension of the European Union 1997.

Joerges, Christian/Falke, Josef (Hrsg.): Das Ausschusswesen der Europäischen Union – Praxis der Risikoregulierung im Binnenmarkt und ihre rechtliche Verfassung, Nomos Verlagsgesellschaft, Baden-Baden 2000.

Joerges, Christian: Die Europäische „Komitologie“: Kafkaeske Bürokratie oder Beispiel „deliberativen Regierens“ im Binnenmarkt, in: Joerges/Falke (Hsrg.): Das Ausschusswesen in der Europäischen Union, 2000.

John, Peter: Europeanization in a Centralized State: Multi-Level Governance in the UK; in: Jeffery (eds): The Regional Dimension of the European Union 1997.

Jordan, Andrew: The Europeanization of National Government and Policy: A Departmental Perspective; B.J.Pol.S. 33 Cambridge University Press 2003.

Kassim, Hussein/Menon, Anand/Peters, B. Guy (eds): The National Co-ordination of EU Policy; Oxford Scholarship Online 2004 http://www.oxfordscholarship.com/oso/public/content/politicalscience/9780199248056/toc.html.

Kassim, Hussein: Representing the United Kingdom in Brussels: The Fine Art of Positive Co-ordination; in: Kassim/Menon/Peters (eds): The National Co-ordination of EU Policy 2004.

Kassim, Hussein/Menon, Anand/Peters, B. Guy (eds): The National Co-ordination of EU Policy – The domestic level; Oxford Scholarship Online 2003 http://www.oxfordscholarship.com/oso/public/content/politicalscience/9780198296645/toc.html.

Kassim, Hussein: The United Kingdom; in: Kassim/Menon/Peters (eds): The National Co-ordination of EU Policy – The domestic level 2003.

Kaeding, Michael: Lost in Translation or Full Steam Ahead: The Transposition of EU Transport Directives across Member States; European Union Politics 2008; 9;115 http://eup.sagepub.com/cgi/reprint/9/1/115.pdf.

Kaeding, Michael: Better regulation in the European Union: Lost in Translation or Full Steam Ahead: The Transposition of EU Transport Directives across Member States; Leiden University Press, Leiden 2007.

Keading, Michael/Hooghe, Lisbet: Bypassing the nation-state? Regions and the EU policy process, in: Richardson (ed): European Union 2006.

Kleinfeld, Ralf/Zimmer, Annette/Willems, Ulrich (Hrsg.): Lobbying – Strukturen. Akteure. Strategien. Verlag für Sozialwissenschaften; Wiesbaden 2007.

Knill, Christoph: Implementation, in: Richardson (ed): European Union 2006.

Knill, Christoph: The Europeanisation of National Administrations – Patterns of Institutional Change and Persistence; Cambridge University Press, Cambridge 2001.

Knorr Cetina,Karin: Sozialität mit Objekten – Soziale Beziehungen in post-traditionalen Wissensgesellschaften; in: Tänzler/Knoblauch/Soeffner (Hrsg.): Zur Kritik der Wissensgesellschaft 2006.

Kohler-Koch, Beate (ed): Linking EU and National Governance; Oxford University Press, Oxford 2003.

Kohler-Koch, Beate/Eising, Rainer (eds): The Transformation of Governance in the European Union; Routledge, London/New York 2002.

Kohler-Koch, Beate: European Networks and Ideas: Changing National Policies? European Integration online Papers 6:6 2002 http://www.eiop.or.at/eiop/pdf/2002-006.pdf.

Kopp-Malek, Tanja/Koch, Martin/Lindenthal, Alexandra: Die Europäische Kommission als lernende Organisation? Die Umsetzung des umweltpolitischen Integrationsprinzips in ausgewählten Generaldirektionen der Europäischen Kommission; Verlag für Sozialwissenschaften, Wiesbaden 2009.

Korsten, Arno/de Goede, Peter (red.): Bouwen aan vertrouwen in het openbaar bestuur – diagnoses en remedies; Elsevier Overheid, ’s-Gravenhage 2006.

Laffan, Brigid: Core Executives; in: Graziano/Vink (eds): Europeanization 2008.

Laffan, Brigid: The European Union and Its Institutions as „Identity Builders“, in: Herrmann/Risse/Brewer (eds): Transnational Identities 2004.

Lahusen, Christian: Kommerzielle Beratungsfirmen in der Europäischen Uniioin, in: Eising/Kohler-Koch (Hrsg.): Interessenpolitik in Europa; 2005.

Lane, Christel/Bachmann, Reinhard (eds): Trust within and between Organizations – Conceptual Issues and Empirical Apllications; Oxford University Press, Oxford 1998.

Lane, Christel: Theories and Issues in the Study of Trust; in: Lane/Bachmann (eds): Trust within and between Organizations 1998.

Lang, Jochen: Policy Implementation in a Multi-Level System: The Dynamics of Domestic Response; in: Kohler-Koch (ed): Linking EU and National Governance 2003.

Lankowski, Carl: Germany: A major player, in: Ziff/Pirro (eds.): The European Union and Member States, 2001.

Laylock, Paul J./Graham, Susan/Fewings, Peter: The effective implementation of the Construction Products Directive (CPD): an update; Building Research and Information Volume 23 number 2n 1995.

Leitfaden für die Umsetzung der nach dem neuen Konzept und dem Gesamtkonzept verfassten Richtlinien, Europäische Kommission, Luxembourg 2000.

Lesmeister, Christiane: Informelle politische Kommunikationskultur – Hinter den Kulissen politisch-medialer Kommunikation; Verlag für Sozialwissenschaften, Wiesbaden 2008.

Lillrank, Paul: The Quality of Standard, Routine and Nonroutine Processes; Organization Studies, SAGE Publications, London/Thousand Oaks/New Delhi 2003.

Lindenberg, Siegwart: Social norms: What happens when they become more abstract? in: Dickmann/Eichner/Schmidt/Voss (Hrsg.): Rational Choice 2008.

Ludwig, Karl-Heinz: Technik im Hohen Mittelalter zwischen 1000 und 1350/1400, in: Propyläen Technikgeschichte Bd.2, Berlin 1997.

Luhmann, Niklas: Vertrautheit, Zuversicht, Vertrauen, Probleme und Alternativen; in: Hartmann/Offe (Hsrg.): Vertrauen, 2001.

Luther, Kurt Richard: Bund – Länder Beziehungen: Formal- und Realverfassung, in: Dachs/Gerlich/Gottweis/Horner/Kramer/Lauber/Müller/Talos (Hrsg.): Handbuch des Politischen Systems Österreichs, Wien 1991.

Mahoney, Christine: Brussels versus the Beltway – Advocacy in the United States and the European Union. Georgetown University Press; Washington D.C.; 2008.

Mastenbroek, Ellen: The Politics of Compliance – Explaining the transposition of EC directives in the Netherlands; Ponsen & Looijen, Wageningen 2007.

Mastenbroek, Ellen: EU compliance: Still a „black hole“? Journal of European Public Policy 12:6 2005 http://dx.doi.org/10.1080/1350160500270869.

Matláry, Janne Haaland: The Role of the Commission: A Theoretical Discussion, in: Nugent (ed): At the Heart of the Union, 2000.

Matschi, Andreas: "Rules of the game" for the European market in the context of the CE marking – Implementable examples; ift Rosenheim – International Rosenheimer Windows and Facade Conference 2005.

Matthiesen, Ulf: Raum und Wissen – Wissensmilieus und KnowledgeSpaces als Inkubatoren für zukunftsfähige stadtregionale Entwicklungsdynamiken? in: Tänzler/Knoblauch/Soeffner (Hrsg.): Zur Kritik der Wissensgesellschaft 2006.

Maurer, Andreas: The German Case: A Key Moderator in a Competitive Multi-Level Environment; in: Kassim/Menon/Peters (eds): The National Co-ordination of EU Policy 2004.

Maurer, Andreas/Wessels, Wolfgang: Germany; in: Kassim/Menon/Peters (eds): The National Co-ordination of EU Policy – The domestic level 2003.

Mayer, Heinz: Verfassung im Spannungsfeld politischer Interessen; Studienverlag, Innsbruck/Wien/Bozen 2005.

Mazey, Sonja/Richardson, Jeremy: Interest groups and EU policy-making – Organisations, logic and venue shopping, in: Richardson (ed): European Union 2006.

Mazey, Sonja/Richardson, Jeremy: EU policy-making – A garbage can or an anticipatory and consensual policy style? in: Mény/Muller/Quermonne (eds.): Adjusting to Europe 1996.

Meijer, F.M./Visscher, H.J./Sheridan L.: Building regulations in Europe – Part I: A comparison of technical requirements in eight European countries, Housing and Policy Studies no 24, Delft University Press, Delft 2002.

Meijer, F.M./Visscher, H.J./Sheridan L.: Building regulations in Europe – Part II: A comparison of the systems of building control in eight European countries, Housing and Policy Studies no 23, Delft University Press, Delft 2003.

Mény, Yves/Muller, Pierre/Quermonne, Jean-Louis (eds.): Adjusting to Europe – The Impact of the European Union on national institutions and policies: Routledge, New York 1996.

Moog, Pierre-Emmanuel: Les Groupes de Réflexion et d'Influence en Europe; L'Expansion Paris 2008.

Morass, Michael: Austria: The Case of a Federal Newcomer in European Union Politics; in: Jeffery (eds): The Regional Dimension of the European Union 1997.

Müller, Wolfgang C.: Ministerial Government at the European level: The Case of Austria; in: Kassim/Menon/Peters (eds): The National Co-ordination of EU Policy 2004.

Müller, Wolfgang C.: Austria; in: Kassim/Menon/Peters (eds): The National Co-ordination of EU Policy – The domestic level 2003.

Musterbauordnung (German MBO): http://www.bauministerkonferenz.de/?rid=991&n=3 DAO3DFO.

Nugent, Neill: The European Commission; Palgrave MacMillan Press Ltd, Hampshire 2001.

Nugent, Neill (ed): At the Heart of the Union – Studies of the European Commission; Palgrave MacMillan Press Ltd, Hampshire 2000.

Nugent, Neill (ed): The European Union – Volume 1; Dartmouth, Aldershot/Brodefield/Singapore/Sydney, 1997.

Nugent, Neill (ed): The European Union – Volume 2; Dartmouth, Aldershot/Brodefield/Singapore/Sydney, 1997.

Offe, Claus: Wie können wir unseren Mitbürgern vertrauen? in: Hartmann/Offe (Hsrg.): Vertrauen, 2001.

Olsen, Johan P.: Eropeanization – a fashionable term, but is it useful? ARENA Working Papers 01/2 2002 http://www.arena.uio.no/publications/working-papers2002/papers/wp02_2.htm.

Ortmann, Günther: Als Ob – Fiktionen und Organisationen; Verlag für Sozialwissenschaften, Wiesbaden 2004.

Ortmann, Günther/Sydow, Jörg/Türk, Klaus (Hrsg): Theorien der Organisation – Die Rückkehr der Gesellschaft; Westdeutscher Verlag, Opladen 1997.

Ottnad, Adrian/Hefele, Peter: Die Zukunft der Bauwirtschaft in Deutschland – Umfeld, Probleme, Perspektiven; Olzog Verlag, München 2002.

Parsons, Talcot: Aktor, Situation und normative Muster – Ein Essay zur Theorie sozialen Handelns; Suhrkamp Verlag, Frankfurt/Main 1994.

Parsons, Talcott: On Institutions and Social Evolution; The University of Chicago Press, Chicago/London 1982.

Pentland, Brian T./ Rueter, Henry H.: Organizational Routines as Grammars of Action; Administrative Science Quaterly 39 (1994).

Peters, B. Guy: The Commission and Implementation in the European Union: Is There an Implementation Deficit and Why? in: Nugent (ed): At the Heart of the Union, 2000.

Peters, B. Guy: Agenda-setting in the European Community, in: Nugent (ed): The European Union Vo. 2, 1997.

Peterson, John: "Policy Networks"; Political Science Series, Vienna 2003 http://aei.pitt.edu/764/01/pw_90.pdf.

Pfetsch, Frank R.: Die Europäische Union – Eine Einführung; UTB für Wissenschaft/ Wilhelm Fink Verlag, München 1997.

Pinney, Adam A./Rein, Stephen J.: The Construction Products Directive – A practical guide to implementation and CE marking. AuthorHouse, Bloomington:Central Milton Keynes, 2007.

Pollack, Mark A.: The Engines of European Integration – Delegation, Agency, and Agenda Setting in the EU; Oxford University Press, Oxford 2003.

Pollack, Mark A.: The Commission as Agent, in: Nugent (ed): At the Heart of the Union, 2000.

PRC report: Study to evaluate the Internal Market and competitiveness effects of Council Directive 89/106/EC (Construction Products Directive, CPD) Bodegraven 2007 http://ec.europa.eu/enterprise/construction/cpdrevision/cpd_revision_intro_en.htm.

Proces, Michel: The architects and the certification http://eurocer-building.cstb.fr/doc/library/L05%20Architects%20and%20certification.pdf.

Propyläen Technikgeschichte; Propyläen Verlag, Berlin 1997.

Puntscher Riekmann, Sonja: Die Meister und ihr Instrument – Institutionenkonflikte und Legitimitätsprobleme in der Europäischen Union; in: Bach, Maurizio (Hrsg.): Die Europäisierung nationaler Gesellschaften 2000.

Rasmussen, Jorgen: Britain: Aloof and Sceptical, in: Ziff/Pirro (eds.): The European Union and Member States, 2001.

Richardson, Jeremy (ed.): European Union – Power and policy-making, Routledge; London/New York, 2006.

Richardson, Jeremy: Policy-making in the EU: interests, ideas and garbage cans of primeval soup, in: Richardson (ed.): European Union 2006.

Roose, Jochen: Die Europäisierung von Umweltorganisationen – Die Umweltbewegung auf dem langen Weg nach Brüssel, Westdeutscher Verlag, Wiesbaden 2003.

Säckl, Martin: 20 Jahre EU-Lobbying als Dienstleistung, in: Dagger/Kambeck (hrsg): Politikberatung und Lobbying in Brüssel 2007.

Sauron, Jean-Luc/Lanceron, Virginie: L'administration nationale et l'Europe – Acteurs nationaux et decisions communautaires; La documentation Française, Paris 2008.

Schaller, Christian: Verbände und Sozialpartnerschaft, in: Dachs/ Gerlich/ Gottweis/ Horner/Kramer/Lauber/Müller/Tàlos (Hrsg.): Handbuch des Politischen Systems Österreichs 1991.

Scharpf, Fritz W.: What Have We Learned? – Problem-Solving Capacity of the Multilevel European Polity; MPIfG Working Paper 2001 E:\political sciences\MPIfG Working Paper 01-4, Fritz W_ Scharpf Problem-Solving Capacity of the Multilevel European Polity.mht.

Scharpf, Fritz W.: Föderatle Politikverflechtung: Was muss man ertragen – was kann man ändern? MPIfG Working Paper April 1999 http://www.mpi-fg-koeln.mpg.de/pu/workpap/wp99-3/wp99-3.html.

Scharpf, Fritz W.: Games Real Actors Play – Actor-Centered Institutionalism in Policy Research; Westview Press, Oxford 1997.

Scharpf, Firtz W.: The joint-decision trap: Lessons form German Federalism and European integration, in: Nugent (ed): The European Union Vol. 2, 1997.

Scharpf, Fritw W. (ed.): Games in Hierarchies and Networks – Analytical and Empirical Approaches to the Study of Governance Institutions, Campus Verlag, Frankfurt/Main 1993.

Schendelen, Rinus van: Machiavelli in Brussels – The art of lobbying the EU; Amsterdam University Press, Amsterdam 2007.

Schimank, Uwe: Teilsystemische Autonomie und politische Gesellschaftssteuerung – Beiträge wur akteurzentrierten Differenzierungstheorie 2; Verlag für Sozialwissenschaften, Wiesbaden 2006.

Schimank, Uwe: Rationalitätsfiktionen in der Entscheidungsgesellschaft, in: Tänzler/Knoblauch/Soeffner (Hrsg.): Zur Kritik der Wissensgesellschaft 2006.

Schmidt, Vivien A.: Procedural Democracy in the EU: The Europeanization of National and Sectoral Policymaking Processes; 2006 http://people.bu.edu/vschmidt/documents/jeppeusa06dfinal.pdf.

Schmidt, Vivien A.: National Patterns of Governance under Siege – The Impact of European Integration; in: Kohler-Koch/Eising (eds): The Transformation of Governance in the European Union; 2002.

Schmidtchen, Volker: Technik vom Übergang vom Mittelalter zur Neuzeit zwischen 1350 und 1600, in: Propyläen Technikgeschichte Bd.2, Berlin 1997.

Schmitz, Thomas: Integration in der Supranationalen Union – Das europäische Organisationsmodell einer prozesshaften geo-regionalen Integration und seine rechtlichen und staatstheoretischen Implikationen; Nomos Verlagesgesellschaft , Baden-Baden 2001.

Schneider, Helmuth: Die Gaben des Prometheus – Technik im Antiken Mittelmeerraum zwischen 750 v.Chr. und 500 n.Chr., in: Propyläen Technikgeschichte Bd.1, Berlin 1997.

Scholz, Thomas: Lobbyismus aus der Sicht der Europäischen Kommission – Tugend oder notwendiges Übel? in: Dagger/Kambeck (hrsg): Politikberatung und Lobbying in Brüssel 2007.

Simmel, Georg: Soziologie – Untersuchungen über die Formen der Vergesellschaftung; Suhrkamp Verlag, Frankfurt/Main 1992.

Steger, Friedrich Michael (Hsrg.): Baustelle Bundesstaat – Perspektiven der Weiterentwicklung des politischen System Österreich; Braunmüller Universität Verlagsbuchhandlung, Wien 2007.

Stehr, Nico: Die Zerbrechlichkeit moderner Gesellschaften – Die Stagnation der Macht und die Chancen des Individuums; Velbrück Wissenschaft, Weilerswist 2000.

Stein, Hans H.: Vorfeldbeobachtung und Einflussnahme bei der europäischen Rechtsetzung: Politikberatung durch die Vertretung des Landes Nordrhein-Westfalen bei der Europäischen Union, in: Dagger/Kambeck (hrsg): Politikberatung und Lobbying in Brüssel 2007.

Steunenberg, Bernard/Voermans, Wim: The transposition of EC directives – A Comparative Study of Instruments, Techniques and Processes in Six Member States; Leiden University/ WODC/Ministry of Justice, Wolf Legal Publishers, Nijmegen 2006.

Steunenberg, Bernard: Turning Swift Policy-making into Deadlock and Delay: National Policy Coordination and the Transposition of EU Directives; European Union Politics 7;293 2006 http://eup.sagepub.com/cgi/content/abstract/7/3/293.

Steunenberg, Bernard/Rhinard, Mark: Hare or Turtle? Member states catching up with the transposition of EU directives (unpublished document) 2006 http://www.public administration.leidenuniv.nl/content_docs/steunenberg/hare_or_turtle_explaining_ transposition_v6.pdf.

Stevens, Anne/Stevens, Handley: Brussels Bureaucrats? The Administration of the European Union, Palgrave, Hampshire/New York 2001.

Strohmeier, Rudolf W.: Die Europäische Kommission im Gefüge von Politikberatung und Lobbying, in: Dagger/Kambeck (hrsg): Politikberatung und Lobbying in Brüssel 2007.

Strübing, Jörg: Grounded Theory – Zur sozialtheoretischen und epistemologischen Fundierung des Verfahrens der empirisch begründeten Theoriebildung; Verlag für Sozialwissenschaften, Wiesbaden 2004.

Strulik, Torsten: Nichtwissen und Vertrauen in der Wissensökonomie; Campus Verlag, Frankfurt/New York 2004.

Suvarierol, Semin/van den Berg, Caspar: Bridge builders or bridgeheads in Brussels? The world of seconded national experts; in: Geuijen/'THart/Princen/Yesilkagit: The New Eurocrats 2008.

Sverdrup, Ulf: Compliance and conflict resolution in the European Union; paper presented at ARENA seminar September 2002; http://www.arena.uio.no/events/papers/ SverdrupARENAseminar.pdf.

Swianiewicz, Pawel: Poland: a time of transition, in: Denters/Rose (eds.): Comparing Local Governance 2005.

Sydow, Jörg: Unterstanding the Constitution of Interorganizational Trust; in: Lane/Bachmann (eds): Trust within and between Organizations 1998.

Tallberg, Jonas: Leadership and Negotiation in the European Union; Cambridge University Press, Cambridge 2006.

Tallberg, Jonas/Jönsson, Christer: Compliance bargaining, in: Elgström/Jönsson (eds.): European Union Negotiations 2005.

Tallberg, Jonas: Paths to Compliance: Enforcement, Management, and the European Union; International Organisation 56 (3) 2002.

Tàlos, Emmerich/Falkner, Gerda (Hrsg.): EU-Mitglied Österreich – Gegenwart und Perspektiven: Eine Zwischenbilanz; Manzsche Verlags- und Universitätsbuchhandlung, Wien 1996.

Tàlos, Emmerich/Karlhofer, Ferdinand: Austrokorporatismus und EU, in: Tàlos/Falkner (Hrsg.): EU-Mitglied Österreich 1996.

Tänzler, Dirk/Knoblauch, Hubert/Soeffner, Hans-Georg (Hrsg.): Zur Kritik der Wissensgesellschaft.; UVK Verlagesgesellschaft mbH, Konstanz 2006.

Tricker, Ray/Algar, Rozz: Building Regulations in Brief; Butterworth-Heinemann, Oxford 2007.

Torres, Francisco: How Efficient is Joint Decision-Making in the EU? Environmental Policies and the Co-Decision Procedure; European Governance 2003, http://www.springerlink.com/content/u3670rr60786m744/fulltext.pdf.

Toshkov, Dimiter D.: Between Politics and Administration: Compliance with EU law in Central and Eastern Europe; Dissertation Leiden University 2009.

Trondal, Jarle: Beyond the EU membership-non-membership dichotomy? Supranational identities among national EU decision-makers; Journal of European Public Policy 9:3, 2002.

Trondal, Jarle/Veggeland, Frode: Access, Voice and loyalty: the representation of domestic civil servants in EU committees; Journal of European Public Policy 10:1, 2003.

UEPC Position on CE marking, November 1997.

Versluis, Esther: Explaining Variations in Implementation of EU Directives; European Integration online Papers Vol 8 no 19, 2004 http://eiop.or.at/eiop/texte/2004-019a.htm.

von Bogdandy, Armin: Links between national and Supra-national Institutions: A Legal View of a New Communicative Universe; in:Kohler-Koch (ed): Linking EU and National Governance 2003.

Wallace, Helen: Exercising Power and Influence in the European Union: The Roles of Member States; in: Bulmer/Lesquesne (eds): The Member States of the European Union, Oxford 2005.

Wallace, Helen/Young, Alasdair R.: The Kaleidoscope of European Policy-Making: Shifting Patterns of Participation and Influence, in: Wallace/Young (eds.): Participation and policy-making in the European Union, 1997.

Wallace, Helen/Young, Alasdair R. (eds.): Participation and policy-making in the European Union, Clarendon Press, Oxford 1997.

Wallace, Helen: Relations between the European Union and the British administration, in: Mény/Muller/Quermonne (eds.): Adjusting to Europe 1996.

Watzlawick, Paul: Anleitung zum Unglücklichsein/Vom Schlechten des Guten; Piper Verlag, München/Zürich 2007.

Weber, Iris: Umweltpolitische Steuerung in der Europäischen Union: Das Beispiel der Wasserrahmenrichtlinie, in: Bauer/Voelzkow (Hrsg.): Die Europäische Union – Marionette oder Regisseur? 2004.

Weber, Max: Die protestantische Ethik I; Gütersloher Verlags-Haus, Gütersloh 2000.

Weber, Max: Wirtschaft und Gesellschaft; J.C.B. Mohr (Paul Siebeck), Tübingen 1972.

Wehling, Peter: Im Schatten des Wissens? Perspektiven der Soziologie des Nichtwissens; UVK VerlagsgesmbH, Konstanz 2006.

Wessels, Wolfgang/Rometsch, Dietrich: German administrative interaction and the European Union – The fusion of public policies, in: Mény/Muller/Quermonne (eds.): Adjusting to Europe 1996.

Wilson, David: The United Kingdom: an increasingly differentiated polity? in: Denters/Rose (eds.): Comparing Local Governance 2005.

Wolf, Dieter: Deliberativer Supranationalismus und unterschiedliche Umsetzungsleistung: Ein Vergleich der Normung bei der Maschinen- und Bauproduktenrichtlinie; in: Joerges/Falke (Hsrg.): Das Ausschusswesen in der Europäischen Union, 2000.

Wynands, Robert: Quality in buildings with quality marked products, http://eurocer-building.cstb.fr/doc/library/L09%20Quality%20in%20buildings.pdf.

Ziff, Eleanor E./ Pirro, Ellen B. (eds.): The European Union and the Member States – Cooperation, Coordination and Compromise; Lynne Rienner Publishers, Boulder/London 2001.

Ziller, Jacques: Europäische Implementierungsforschung im 21. Jahrhundert; European University Institute, LAW no 2006/42.

Zürn, Michael/Wolf, Dieter: Europarecht und internationale Regime: Zu den Merkmalen von Recht jenseits des Nationalstaates, in: Grande/Jachtenfuchs (Hrsg.): Wie problemlösungsfähig ist die EU? Baden-Baden 2000.

www.ingramcontent.com/pod-product-compliance
Lightning Source LLC
Chambersburg PA
CBHW051150180926
51611CB00001B/9
9783531177878